Advance Praise for the Book

"This book brings together much of ....scholarship on whiteness. With original insights, often with humor, always with a sense of importance of their work to American democracy, these writers show how public intellectuals can help create a fresh perception of the racial issues .....l not just to 'them' but to all of 'us.' For such reasons, this Reader is not just an academic text, but a significant contribution to reformulating the central racial concerns that have plagued America since the advent of Europeans upon these shores."

—Paul Lauter
A. K. & G. M. Smith Professor of Literature
and American Studies, Trinity College

"Whether they are analyzing Rush Limbaugh's raised eyebrows, film noir, or Janis Joplin's blues, the contributors to *Whiteness* offer insights that are fresh, often provocative and always stimulating; their essays suggest some of the diverse ways in which we might approach the racial matrix of American culture. A valuable contribution to cultural studies."

—Shelley Fisher Fishkin
Professor of American Studies
University of Texas

WHITENESS

A CRITICAL READER

Edited by **Mike Hill**

NEW YORK UNIVERSITY PRESS

New York and London

NEW YORK UNIVERSITY PRESS
New York and London

Chapter 2 © by *New Left Review.* Reprinted with kind permission,
from *New Left Review* (213/1995).

Chapter 6 © 1997 by Eric Lott.

Chapter 8 From *Hard Country, High Cuture, and Postmodernism,*
by Barbara Ching, to be published by Oxford University Press, Inc.,
in 1998, by arrangement with the publisher. All rights reserved.

Chapter 13 © 1995 The Johns Hopkins University Press. Reprinted
with kind permission, from Kate Davy, "Outing Whiteness:
A Feminist/Lesbian Project," *Theatre Journal* 47: 189–205.

Library of Congress Cataloging-in-Publication Data
Whiteness : a critical reader / edited by Mike Hill.
p.   cm.
Includes index.
ISBN 0-8147-3544-4 (clothbound : acid-free paper).—ISBN
0-8147-3545-2 (paperbound : acid-free paper)
1. Whites—United States.   2. Race awareness—United States.
3. United States—Race relations.   4. Whites in literature.
I. Hill, Mike, 1964-   .
E184.A1W398   1997
305.8′00973—dc21   97-4575
CIP

New York University Press books are printed on acid-free paper,
and their binding materials are chosen for strength and durability.

Manufactured in the United States of America
10   9   8   7   6   5   4   3   2

Contents

Acknowledgments

An array of people in addition to all those between its covers helped make this book happen. First, my thanks go to Jeffrey Williams for allowing a special issue of *the minnesota review* (Spring 1997) to serve as the springboard for this idea. Rachel Gabara and Raymond McDaniel helped with sundry editorial tasks, including indexing and proofreading the book. Ross Chambers, Eric Lott, Fred Pfeil, Niko Pfund, Bob Vorlicky, and Carina Yerrasi discussed with me in casual conversation various matters, to the volume's great benefit. Thank you, finally, Dean Paula Hooper-Mayhew, my chair David Linton, my colleagues in English John and Prill Costello, and my students at Marymount Manhattan College for continued material and moral support.

1

Introduction: Vipers in Shangri-la Whiteness, Writing, and Other Ordinary Terrors

Mike Hill

On West Shangri-la road, a quiet street where children pedal bicycles past ornamental cactuses and yellow desert blooms, the two men living at number 6748 led a suburban life that was, well, different.

James Brooke, "Volatile Mix in Viper Militia"

Their Shangri-la would be populated with nice professional people.

Doris Lessing, *In Pursuit of English*

I urge each one of us here to reach down into that place of knowledge inside of herself and touch that terror and loathing of any difference that lives there. See whose face it wears.　　Audre Lorde, "The Master's Tools Will Never Dismantle the Master's House"

WHAT DOES WHITENESS WANT?

The unlikely transposition of these epigrams tells a complex story and seems to go to the heart of the white problem in the United States. The first quotation refers to the arrest of "team viper." The "vipers" were those "fairly typical [i.e., white] Phoenix suburbanites who played guerrilla games in their spare time"[1] and who, as either part of the fun or to blow up government buildings (there was circumstantial evidence for the latter), stockpiled a ton of ammonium nitrate. That amount is about half of what exploded in Oklahoma City at the alleged hand of Timothy McVeigh, that other antifederalist "face of terror," a blond-haired, blue-eyed white man—and soon to be the "all-American defendant."[2] I join the phrases "face of terror" and "all-American defendant," which are from the mainstream media, to suggest a certain redundancy in the latter term.

It certainly is part of the popular white register that to be an "American" is to be in various proportions both terrified and terrifying, oscillating between

1

muted "defense" and panicked aggression. The WASP (white Anglo-Saxon Protestant) militant next door is surely one of our most salient contemporary political icons. It could be the "terror" in Arizona or Oklahoma—or the "terror" in Jordan, Montana, and at Ruby Ridge, Idaho; the neo-Luddite "terror" arriving in the mail from the Unabomber's quiet shack; or the "terror" "out west" where, to the cheers of onlookers, Dick Carter took his flag-draped Caterpillar and chased down a Fed on the Fourth of July—but to speak of the "terror" I have in mind is to speak of a distinctly "white terror."[3]

Such a terror is at least twofold, exponentially the more terrifying for being split and compounded in that way. First, it is a terror manifest when (and now let's toss in the bombing in Atlanta during the 1996 Summer Olympics) the utterly "undistinguished" make news.[4] In other words, "white terror" is distinct in that we suddenly realize that it was always right here. Second, "white terror" is terrifying because the struggle to remain "undistinguished"—the struggle to be ordinary, to be as passive as omnipresent, as invisible as dominant, to be an essential feature of everyday life and yet unaccountable—is something white folk are finding less and less winnable.

Thus the "vipers in Shangri-la" is a phrase that signals an identification problem or, more precisely, a problem with identification's having gone wrong. Frantz Fanon labeled this the "ontogenic" crisis of whiteness. Such a thing is inherent, he suggests, in snapping the "seal" of self-perceived (white) neutrality.[5] The character Defense in the film *Falling Down* (a white and male ur-text) asks, with characteristic insularity in multicultural Los Angeles, "How did I become the enemy here"?[6] It is a question of "ontogenic" reversal that is as old as the white race itself, which is to say, a few hundred years old at best.[7] For the last five or six of those few hundred years—roughly from about 1990 to the present—a large body of writing on the topic of whiteness has emerged to make exactly this point.[8] Whiteness is a distinct and relatively recent historical fiction. As such, we should be able to address both its invisibility and impermanence.[9] Let's call the writing that establishes such a premise, a "first wave" of white critique.

In the context of the newly emergent whiteness studies, the point of my second and third epigrams should be clear. The ironies at work in Lessing's phrase "nice professional people" and Lorde's "challenge" to "touch terror" are one and the same. Irony designates the discursive ground of the "terrifyingly" ordinary, the ground on which Davidians and Derridians meet.[10]

Indeed, even though the writing, talking, and reporting on the topic of whiteness promise certain resolutions concerning what Studs Turkel terms "the American obsession,"[11] they also create many problems. Our newfound attention to the quintessentially unremarkable is itself a remarkable phenomenon. Substitute "ivory tower" for "Shangri-la" and "academic" for "professional" in Lessing's "Their *Shangri-la* would be populated with nice *professional* people," and you will see what I mean. The fast and loose accumulation of white writing as so much cutting-edge critical ethnography (or more broadly, "ethnic studies") is where whiteness struggles once again in the shadows of the "terrifyingly ordinary," this time in the form of identity politics made safe for the silent majority.[12]

Some might say that the critical rush to whiteness is leading to the bigger question of whether the political force of white writing can be separated from its political symptoms. This is an important reason for considering the current and future functions of white writing. In any case, even in the superficial sense of the way that knowledge on the topic has been accumulated, what whiteness wants seems to depend resolutely on what knowledge does.

One need go no further than the surface of this knowledge to distinguish white desire. The basis of race studies is, after all, a matter of skin. White desire is like the complaint of populism, which both targets the isolation of our corporate ruling class and too often reveals the bad race and sex politics still evident in working-class resistance. That is, the presence of whiteness alas within our critical reach creates a certain inevitable awkwardness of distance. Whiteness becomes something we both claim (single out for critique) and avoid (in claiming whiteness for critique, what else can we be, if we happen to be identifiably white?). The epistemological stickiness and ontological wiggling immanent in whiteness is precisely the conflict that a book like this one is designed to address.

Let's call this conflict the threshold of a "second wave" of work on whiteness. To articulate critically the power and banality of race privilege and to discover deep down (and, of course, on the surface) a "face of terror" not unlike what one sees all around is what today marks the limit of what whiteness wants. James Baldwin writes about "the sunlit prison of the American dream."[13] To the extent that white folk can escape such a place in ways other than using ammonium nitrate, what whiteness wants—what is at the end of white desire—is something that whiteness cannot have and still be white.[14]

In this sense, the desire for white critique may be nearly impossible. It is a desire that makes modernity's sturdiest juggernauts (e.g., liberal pluralism, majority rule, laissez-faire economics)[15] tremble, and it thus may produce a certain modernist nostalgia at both extremes of the political spectrum. Nonetheless, the desire to consider whiteness critically—and with an eye on that form of multinational corporate capitalism whose increasing brutality will in the end forget the white privilege that created it—can at least be the starting point for this book.

I do not intend to summarize the following chapters in the manner of a traditional introduction, nor will I contemplate their perfect adherence to my hypothesis about whiteness or suggest they are perfectly coherent with one another. Rather, I shall introduce the conditions that contextualize this book. There are important relationships to point out between the latest wave of white critique and preceding movements in cultural criticism, namely, the late 1970s–early 1980s feminism, postcolonial studies, and materialist theory. It is the good fortune of white men educated in the recent institutional presence of race and gender studies to be able to begin working in that context.

OTHER PEOPLE'S MODERNISMS: THE FEMINIST CHARGES OF WHITE CRITIQUE

> I haven't the faintest notion what possible revolutionary role white hetero-sexual men could fulfill; since they are the very embodiment of reaction-ary-vested-interest-power.   Robin Morgan, *Sisterhood Is Powerful*

> I don't know how to work upon my skin from within.
>   Roland Barthes, *Camera Lucida*

> "Jurra! Jurra! Walybala nyaangga" (Stop, stop. There's a whitefella here). It took me a few seconds to realize that the person being referred to as "white fella" was me, a black woman.
>   Myrna Tonkinson, "Thinking in Color"

Robin Morgan may be right. That the rigid historical peculiarities of "white-ness" and "masculinity" as they currently exist could remain intact on the other side of a more equitable future seems impracticable. By extension, and following Barthes, in the sense that otherness has agency that is not merely the simple inversion of identity's opposite, change seems to demand another ver-sion of the words "I don't know" and "my self" (or "my skin"). A still more dramatic way to put this is that political change seems to require less a positive articulation of identity as the more perfect completion of itself than the kind of identificatory mistakes made when unlikely categories of people manage to cohere: "Stop! Stop! There's a 'white fella' here." Could this mistake have been made in the reverse? What political strategies emerge in the no man's land that mediates racial distinction? Why not a politics of mistake as a politics of association?

Almost a generation ago, white feminism struggled with questions like this. The initial charge went as follows:

> White feminists tended to romanticize the black female experience rather than discuss the negative impact of that oppression. . . . When the women's movement was at its peak and white women were rejecting the role of breeder, burden bearer, sex object, black women were celebrated for their unique devotion to the task of mothering. . . . It was further assumed that identifying oneself as oppressed freed one from being an oppressor.[16]

This quotation suggests a premise for the critical examination of whiteness: distinctions of oppression are both portable and prolific. White feminists in the early 1980s heard the charge that there were margins other than (and marginal to) those on which white women were located. That is, marginality is relational (but not relative or arbitrary). Marginality exceeds its twin (the center) and is therefore accountable from the perspective of neither margins nor centers, in any static sense of those terms. To think otherwise is to entertain a sort of secondary narcissism that keeps the center—if inadvertently and with good intentions—in place. And no doubt such a tendency to join political struggle and self-recovery can be found in what has been called "our culture of complaint."[17]

In the first instance, then, the importance of 1980s feminism to white critique is that it nudged to the fore the unavoidable complexity of margins and their relationship to selfhood. It made problematic both myopic claims to oppression and liberal notions of "commonality," in which "common" precedes and contains unforeseen collectivities and alternative allegiances that might otherwise emerge at the price of (white) self-definition.[18]

Consider another set of charges related to the first:

> They [white women at the peak of the women's movement] did not want the issue of racism raised because they did not want to deflect attention away from their projection of white woman as "good," i.e. non racist victim, and the white man as "bad," i.e. racist oppressor. . . . [They] saw feminism solely as a way to demand entrance into the white male power structure.[19]

Thus, added to the notion of portable margins is the idea that oppositionality itself may sometimes function in order to maintain the status quo. When identities are sealed, valued, or derided absolutely, change lapses into becoming a game of ontological leapfrog, in which "I" want what my oppressor has and, in so wanting, reproduce him as myself. The implications are dramatic, especially in regard to issues of multiculturalism. In an age of Benetton economics, where broader and deeper labor pools are competing worldwide for lower wages and less security, shortsighted notions of group identity and competition can easily be used on behalf of corporate greed.[20]

Another way to cast the problem is in liberalism's terms of the autonomous individual.[21] Although since the Enlightenment the West has conceived of the individual as an entity in itself—categorically either one or another, oppressed or oppressing, marked or unmarked, different or the same, for power or against it, but never any of these alternatively or in combination—one discovers today a more nettlesome prospect. The distinctions between myself and my opposites are not (in fact, never were) fixed absolutely. One is oneself only and ultimately as another's "other." Consensus and community are thus less the origins of political affiliation than the effect of political events. Feminism's struggle in regard to race is similar in that it, too, calls for radically new sets of associations, new categories of belonging that are identifiable from the perspective of neither the center nor what it designates its margin: "There are other ties and visions that bind, prior allegiances and priorities that supersede [the] invitations to coalesce on their [white] terms," writes Toni Cade Bambara.[22]

The term *bind* also functions as a form of "allegiance" and complicates the absolute freedom to define what one protests and who one is. Indeed, these complications are where white critique might rightly begin.

A second moment in feminism, as in the passages from bell hooks, tries to think beyond "liberal white feminist equality," in which equality means "equality with our white brothers . . . , [i.e.] our own first hand participation with racial dominance."[23] In 1981 Marilyn Frye addressed the charge by women of color that white feminists regard gender oppression as an overdetermined experience (marked incommensurably by race and class). She also pointed out that engaging in white critique is a double bind made up of both racist features and their contradiction:

> It seemed like doing nothing would be racist and whatever we did would be racist just because we [white women] did it. . . . Am I a racist if I decide to do nothing? If I decide to refuse to work with other white women on our racism? My deciding, deciding to do anything, is poison to her [a feminist of color]. Is this what she knows? . . . It becomes clearer why no decision I make here can fail to be an exercise of race privilege. . . . What is this "being white" that gets me into so much trouble after so many years of seeming to me to be so benign?[24]

If I could choose a single passage to sum up the current state of the new whiteness studies, it is this. Consider the traditional placement of men over women, white over black, upper class over lower class, and heterosexual over homosexual, with the second terms being neither necessarily commensurate nor generically aligned under an all-purpose category of "oppressed." Nobody likes to think so, but one could, for example, be black, rich, and sexist, a working-class racist, or a feminist with classist or racist dispositions.[25] The relationship between margins and center—to make the point yet again—is a mutable arrangement. Difference crosses the ontological tracks with astonishing regularity (how else could one distinguish whiteness?), and there apparently is no going back. But from that relatively moderate premise, we must show how whiteness once critically marked by race privilege thus proceeds. Does it proceed exactly as itself (i.e., as its former neutrality), as an ideal other (i.e., its fixed inversion), or as some amalgamation of both?

In the same essay on the double bind of white antiracism, Frye calls for "disaffiliation," "disloyalty," and "treacherousness" to the "material benefits and ego supports" of whiteness. But what is important here, and easily missed, is that she is calling for white critique without assuming that doing so will totally free her from those "ego supports" she wants removed. In other words, Frye's form of race trading does not emerge as a simple decision to become distinct or invisible as she wishes and according to current classifications.[26]

Particularly striking about Frye's statements is that the "disaffiliation" she speaks of is also a move toward identifying herself as white and, therefore, "in trouble." Rather than shoring up white hegemony, Frye's encounter with race "trouble" submits whiteness to a labeling process on someone else's terms. Her desires reveal both a radical ambition and a rare humility. Frye struggles not to posit a naive distinction of otherness as the mere opposite of whatever white identity is. Rather, the intimacy by which otherness addresses her comes from a certain plurality that adds to race matters the mediating presence of gender and class and does so without collapsing one category into the ideal opposite of the other. With this complication, then, a "disaffiliation" with whiteness avoids what I called earlier a secondary narcissism based on simple inversion or benevolent margin poaching. The engendering of whiteness gestures instead toward a kind of critical exchange among and between incommensurable forms of otherness that also, but not directly or binaristically, shore up white race privilege. Thus white critique with a feminist slant is neither transparently schematic (choosing between a white/not white combination is here a gen-dered move) nor overly volunteeristic (that choice brings about the specific ontogeneric misfire of being another within a privileged category formerly one's own). It might indeed be said as a feminist lesson that "disaffiliation" from the white race, its categorical disintegration, is perhaps a form of gendered interrogation already in progress.[27]

If we begin with the premise (recalling Albert Murray) that being white enables us "to avoid circumstances that would require confrontation with [our] own contradictions,"[28] we can see that white recollection and cancellation can occur only simultaneously. Contemporary white critique may thus find its latest use in a kind of identificatory entropy, a concurrent process of naming and deferring in which whiteness is traced to an alternative that is neither white nor simply its ideal opposite. In short, white critique is learning to ask, as Frye does, "what is this 'whiteness'?" and also to take seriously, as a beginning for truly alternative forms of recognition, the Barthesian reply, put simply, "I don't know."

If my account of two limited episodes in feminism sounds idiosyncratic, I hope it nonetheless identifies the unavoidable "trouble" spots for the latest wave of white critique. That the margins are portable and power is proximate to what whiteness wants (namely, to resist what whiteness knows it is) are two feminist charges indispensable to critical writing on whiteness. However we account for the allo-identity politics in our midst, once whiteness enters the game, race exceeds the "identities" that we might have thought preceded politics and survived it. If we are talking about the real (i.e., "material") changes that everybody seems to agree are far too long in coming, this seems like race "trouble" entirely worth having.

OUR "PROXIMATE SELVES": WHITE CRITIQUE AND THE CLASS(IFICATION) STRUGGLE

We need to structure our economic system so that it cannot fall prey to the instability of capitalism.   William L. Pierce, neofascist homepage

The present can no longer be simply envisaged as a break or a bonding with the past and the future, no longer a synchronic presence: our proximate self-presence, our public image, comes to be revealed for its discontinuities, its inequalities, its minorities.

Homi Bhabha, *The Location of Culture*

Sometimes you wish you were black, don't you? Once in awhile, a little bit? I like the black way a lot. Like that Mothers of Invention song, "I'm Not White." There's a whole lot of times I wish I could say, "I'm not white." When that Spanish man was yelling, "You whites are all no good," I couldn't say, "Right."   Joan Keres, "1968"

Real change would be easy if we could simply rely on the facts. According to the U.S. Bureau of Labor Statistics, the average weekly earnings of rank-and-file workers fell 18 percent between 1973 and 1995, whereas corporate bosses increased their salaries by 19 percent between 1979 and 1989 (66 percent after tax breaks). By 1994, the 1986 tax reform alone transferred more than $200 billion to about 150,000 individuals or families who already had annual incomes of more than $500,000.[29] According to the U.S. Bureau of the Census, between 1975 and 1990 the percentage of low-wage workers grew by 142 percent, from 17 to 42 percent of the total workforce. The percentage of real income gains going to wage earners in 1993, compared with that between 1981 and 1989, fell from 52 to 38 percent.[30] The Brookings Institution reports that in 1994, the incomes of the poorest fifth of U.S. workers declined by 4 percent (the incomes of the bottom 53 percent also fell) but the incomes of the richest 5 percent of the population increased by 40 percent.[31] The Luxembourg Income Study confirms this trend. The United States is now among the worst offenders (just behind Ireland and Switzerland) regarding the unequal distribution of wealth. Indeed, the top 5 percent of the U.S. population controls three times the wealth of the other 95 percent and owns 62 percent of all assets, whereas the bottom 90 percent owes 65 percent of the debt.[32]

More facts: the *U.S. Statistical Abstracts* reports that in 1993, 24.5 million whites, 10.6 million blacks, and 6.7 million Latinos were living in poverty. That comes to about 40 million people living in poverty (or 14 percent of the total U.S. population).[33] According to a Kaiser Foundation/Harvard University survey, 58 percent of whites think that the "average African American is as well off or better than the average white in terms of jobs," and 41 percent of whites think that this is so in terms of income. But in fact, black unemployment is twice that of whites, and on the whole, blacks' incomes are 40 percent lower than whites' incomes.[34] What should we make of such persistent delusions about class? Would it be too easy to name class as the root problem of whiteness?

The earlier quotation by William Pierce calls for what effectively is the overthrow of corporate capitalism. William Pierce, the author of the infamous *Turner Diaries,* is one of our most popular and insidious white supremacists.[35] Surely, a fair number of displaced workers in California found themselves caught up in the Manichean delirium of state-sponsored scapegoating, supporting, by racial default, Propositions 182 (denying civil services for illegal workers) and 189 (or "Operation Hold the Line," which increases the police force to 5,000 members along the state's border with Mexico). The demise of affirmative action at the University of California seems only to confirm the repeated manifestations of white fright.[36] My twofold point is simply to highlight what labor historians already know: First, class consciousness does not necessarily a race traitor make, and second, race trading itself can range from the progressive to the downright patronizing, as in "wanting to be black," "sometimes, a little bit."[37]

Indeed, no hard rules automatically line up good race and class (and gender) politics on the same side. This was the hard lesson of incommensurable oppressions that the 1980s feminism recalls. If we begin from such a premise, from the understanding that the margins are portable and power is in close proximity to the desire for critique, how should we approach the pressing "factual" matter of growing material inequity as relevant (arguably central) to the study of whiteness?

Perhaps we can do this most effectively by joining the (to some) painfully obvious matters of class inequity to the somewhat hazier question of classificatory procedures. We might go as far as to consider the "classification struggle" itself as essential to a materialist-inspired postwhite analytic. Call this either a harbinger or an effect of the "new internationalism," or call it—more dramatically still—the location of "culture in the realm of the beyond."[38] The "beyond" here, at least in my reading of Homi Bhabha (and of Fanon and Levinas, from whom Bhabha so eloquently draws), is not a transcendent but a performative "beyond," a place beyond as much as between the classificatory strictures of (white) identity and its "proximate selves." This is not as far from the materialist enterprise as it might sound.

To cite Bhabha at length, the "in between"

> provide[s] the terrain for elaborating strategies of selfhood—singular or communal—that initiate new signs of identity, and innovative sites of collaboration, and contestation, in the act of defining the idea of society itself. . . . (pp. 1–2) Political empowerment, and the enlargement of the multi-culturalist cause, comes from posing questions of solidarity and community from the interstitial perspective. (p. 3)

Insofar as white critique attends to the "facts" and is a materialist enterprise, white critique operates as an "interstitial" practice. To put it another way, whiteness necessarily finds itself up against the "certain uncertainty" of "third person consciousness."[39] The "facts" and a lot of other things seem to have created that condition.

In a similar way, white critique is involved with the simultaneous recognition and misrecognition of whiteness. Therefore, associational rights between formerly distinct groups become available and in ways that majority rules cannot dictate in advance.[40] What emerges "interstitially," then, is not a form of class "solidarity" writ as the liberal consensus of fully conscious individuals.

On the contrary, "interstitial" as materialist work locates multiple features of identity (race being but one) between what is coherent only given the status quo. White critique that confronts the status quo seeks to replace majoritarian with "mass minority" discourse, "minority" in the sense that the associational rights that white critique might engage are not a priori conceived by white players, and "mass" in the sense that those associations are produced on the order, from the onset, of multiple forms of oppression that combine to dismantle the fragile fiction of white solidarity.

This is the meaning of Fanon's "collective unconscious," the articulation of which initiates the negation of whiteness by itself. Borrowing from Fanon, white critique should "grasp its narcissism with both hands," cancel itself as a majority force, and, after fragmenting its own suffocating veneer, surrender anything left to new classifications.[41]

Conceptually, this is not very far from the charges of feminism I described in reference to Marilyn Frye. In less glamorous days, to conjoin questions of property (class) and properties (classification) might have simply been called "mass struggle." But it is also a struggle over the status of oneself. It is, of course, a materialist boilerplate that the social processes in which mass struggle has a part produces self-consciousness, and not the other way around.[42]

A more difficult proposition is that mass struggle also permits—indeed depends on—fractures in the consciousness it creates. In other words, materialist as classificatory work seeks both ontogenic rifts and their renegotiations. It attempts to link the desires of ideologically "interpellated" individuals to some radical exterior that might change both who individuals suppose they are and, more important, might change the formal distinctions of the groups to which individuals suppose they belong. We should leave aside the long-running debate over whether the social processes are scientifically distinguishable as either real or rhetorical.[43] I would rather simply state that the generic struggles attendant to "class" mark an intersection of radical feminism, postcolonial race studies, and materialist theory, in which worthwhile political goals for white critique just might emerge.

All this discussion of "ontogenic rifts" and the "classification struggle" is, of course, academic longhand for what already is starting to be the case in the "real world." In California, for example, the Latino population has risen by 70 percent, the Asian population by 127 percent, and in the next decade, whites will become the state's new minority.[44] The "portability of margins" could not be more graphically apparent. But after whiteness—that is, in the wake of demographic movements that will eventually lead to the de facto abolition of the white race—whether the 1.7 million poor folk who will cross north into California this year in search of work are able to see the benefits of white "disaffiliation" is a question central to the "classification struggle" I have tried to describe. Whether race, class, and gender slip past one another once again or collide and hold on long enough to see truly innovative exchanges is a question in which the value of white critique hangs entirely in the balance.

AFTER WHITENESS: FROM WHITE "DISAFFILIATION" TO THE "HYDRA-HEADED MULTI"?

There is no Marx left to fight; so forth we go in knightly array against the vague and Hydra-headed Multi. Both sides are trapped by mutual obsession in an otherwise empty side-trench of an extinct Cold War.
Robert Hughes, *The Culture of Complaint*

The Negro knocks down the system and breaks the treaties. Will the white man rise in resistance? No, he will adjust to the situation. This fact . . . explains why many books dealing with racial problems become best sellers.
Frantz Fanon, *Black Skin, White Masks*

Anytime Fidel is ready to leave Cuba, the Benetton Jet will be there to take him away.
Oliveiro Toscani, CEO of Benetton

Is anyone actually fooled by the political efficacy of the new whiteness studies? Rather than some sort of fractured "mirror with a progressive infrastructure," is this newfound attention to whiteness not instead simply about missing a "multi-culti" jet ride to glory down the "length of the chromosome corridor,"[45] now that Marxism allegedly no longer exists? Baldwin declared in 1955 that "this world is white no longer, and it will never be white again." Is the new whiteness studies just an attempt to "lactify" ethnic difference and stay relevant in these lean, mean times of liquid cultural capital? Whiteness is already, "in all but actual fact, obsolete."[46] Why speak of it at all?

These are good questions for a book like this one. But they, perhaps by necessity, are not resolved in the following twenty chapters. This book shares the insistence of keeping the feet of an academic Great White Hype as close as possible to the political fires raging outside.[47] Whence those fires come and what they burn depends on where each chapter locates our white problem. The topics range widely across disciplines and content, although most (there are a few obvious and worthwhile exceptions) deal explicitly with whiteness and contemporary "mass" culture in the United States.[48]

The first section of the book, White Politics, addresses whiteness as related to the stuff of glossy magazines, what might best be called "current events":

militias, hate radio, the Clarence Thomas confirmation, and (the first exception) postapartheid South Africa. The second section, White Culture, examines white popular artifact, such as film noir, contemporary Hollywood movies, hard country music, white girl grunge music, doo-wop, and media representations of "white trash." The third section, White Bodies, explores whiteness as a libidinal force. The topics addressed here are the relationship between desire and comparability, lesbian performance art, male autoperformance, and immigration in the context of the white racial imagination. The final section, White Minds, examines whiteness as a problem inherent in the production of knowledge itself, as found in the subjects of whiteness and the Enlightenment (the second exception), the pedagogy of whiteness, constructions of whiteness in humanities scholarship in general, and the institution of "literature" as white high culture (the third exception). At the end of this section, and as this book's parting shot, is a short manifesto from the folks at the *Race Traitor* collective.[49]

But what about the success or failure of white critique? Perhaps failure is mixed with the critical articulation of white historical success, no matter how successful that critical articulation may be. Race critics have been looking for the backhanded ruse of white solidarity for a relatively short time. On the other hand, white critique is stumbling along well enough, and frankly, the target of our work is still among us. So I cannot know absolutely whether the exigencies of whiteness will ultimately help initiate new associational rights in the context of an expanding and increasingly ruthless economic system. I cannot know whether white critique will prove politically worthwhile, whether in the end it will be a friendlier ghost than before or will display the same stealth narcissism that feminists of color labeled a white problem in the late 1970s. I claim a modest optimism for "the new international" on the chance that uncertainty about a more equitable future is implicit in the potential for its arrival. In any case, I hope that the struggles concerning whiteness described in (and ultimately, performed by) this book will contribute to what will probably be a difficult moment of reckoning all around.

NOTES

1. Patricia King, "Vipers in the 'Burbs,' " *Newsweek,* July 15, 1996, p. 21. On the militia movement generally, see Gary Wills, "The New Revolutionaries," *New York Review of Books,* August 10, 1995, pp. 50–54. See also Kenneth S. Stern, *A Force upon the Plain: The American Militia Movement and the Politics of Hate* (New York: Simon & Schuster, 1995).

2. See James Booke, "All-American Defendant: Lawyer Works to Soften Image of Bombing Suspect," *New York Times,* June 2, 1996, p. B14.

3. A separate but related issue is the burnings of black churches (seventy-one in the last three years alone). In an article on this topic, *Newsweek* refers to something called "honky-tonk terrorism" and notes that the 1990s have seen the worst years of white terror since the 1950s. See Jon Meacham and Vern E. Smith, "Southern Discomfort: Why Honky-tonk Terrorists Are Roiling the South," *Newsweek,* June 24, 1996, pp. 32–34.

4. "Undistinguished" is the way the FBI tried initially to describe the Atlanta bombing suspect.

5. See Frantz Fanon, *Black Skin, White Masks,* trans. Charles Markmann (New York: Grove Press, 1962), pp. 10–11. Fanon speaks provocatively of a "zone of non being" as "an utterly naked declivity where authentic upheaval can be born" (p. 8).

6. On *Falling Down,* see Fred Pfeil, "Chips off the Old Block," in his *White Guys: Essays in Postmodern Domination* (London: Verso, 1995), pp. 233–62.

7. See the seminal books by Theodore W. Allen, *The Invention of the White Race,* vol. 1 (London: Verso, 1994); and David Roediger, *The Wages of Whiteness* (London: Verso, 1991). Also see Eric Lott, *Love and Theft: Blackface Minstrelsy and the American Working Class* (Oxford: Oxford University Press, 1993). For early allusions to the split condition of racially marked individuals, see Fanon: "Self-division is the direct result of colonialist subjugation," *Black Skin, White Masks,* p. 17.

8. Both the *Chronicle of Higher Education* and *Lingua Franca* have carried articles making official the emergence of the new whiteness studies. See Liz McMillen, "Lifting the Veil from Whiteness: Growing Body of Scholarship Challenges a Racial 'Norm,' " *Chronicle of Higher Education,* September 8, 1995, p. A23; and David W. Stowe, "Uncolored People," *Lingua Franca,* September–October 1996, pp. 68–77. Scholarly journals that have had special issues or sections on whiteness include the *American Quarterly, Lusatania, the minnesota review, Socialist Review,* and *Transition.* Among more mainstream magazines covering whiteness, see the *Village Voice, Voice Literary Supplement, Newsweek, Time,* and the *New Republic.* For an encyclopedic review of the growing body of scholarly white writing, see Shelly Fisher Fishkin "Interrogating 'Whiteness,' Complicating 'Blackness': Remapping American Culture," *American Quarterly,* September 1995, pp. 428–66.

9. A locus classicus for addressing white invisibility is Richard Dyer's "White," *Screen* 29 (1988): 45–64. See also Jane Gaines, "White Privilege and the Right to Look," *Screen* 29 (1988): 13–27.

10. On state-sponsored "white terror," see Judith Butler, "Engendered/Endangering: Schematic Racism and White Paranoia," in Robert Gooding-Williams, ed., *Reading Rodney King/Reading Urban Uprising* (New York: Routledge, 1993), pp. 15–22; and Henry A. Giroux, "White Panic," *Z Magazine,* March 1995, pp. 12–14.

11. Studs Turkel, *Race: How Blacks and Whites Think and Feel About the American Obsession* (New York: New Press, 1992).

12. For a dubious example of white ethnic pride, see (the other) Michael Hill, *Cracker Culture: Celtic Ways in the Old South* (Tuscaloosa: University of Alabama Press, 1989). In 1995 in Tuscaloosa, Hill founded the Southern League, which, as far as I can tell, is a thin cover for a mildly rehabilitated southern nationalism. See also Joseph A. Ryan, ed., *White Ethnics: Life in Working-Class America* (New York: Prentice-Hall, 1973).

13. James Baldwin, *Notes of a Native Son* (Boston: Beacon Press, 1983), p. 19. See also Mike Davis, *Prisoner of the American Dream* (London: Verso, 1991). Davis's book is a tour de force chronicle of white working-class racism from the 1850s to the 1920s. In challenging the "majoritarian fallacy," Davis suggests that race is "the real weak link in the domestic base of imperialism" (p. 314). He also refers, as does Jacques Derrida in the field of semiotics, to the dawn of a "new internationalism." See Derrida, *Specters of Marx* (New York: Routledge, 1994), p. 314.

14. Race trading is by no means my idea. As I shall describe later, Marilyn Frye explored its possibilities in the early 1980s. Recall James Baldwin's well-known statement: "As long as you think you are white, there is no hope for you" (*The Price of a Ticket,* 1985). Of late, see the *Race Traitor* journal and activist collective. For an anthology of *Race Traitor* writing, see Noel Ignatiev and John Garvey, eds., *Race Traitor* (New York: Routledge, 1996). See also David Roediger, *Towards the Abolition of Whiteness* (London: Verso, 1994); and Mab Segrest, *Memoirs of a Race Traitor* (Boston: South End Press, 1994).

15. The relationship between whiteness and civil society in a juridical sense is being directly challenged in legal studies as "critical race theory" (CRT). See Kimberlé Crenshaw, Neil Gotanda, Gary Peller, and Kendall Thomas, eds., *Critical Race Theory: The Key Writings That Shaped the Movement* (New York: New Press, 1995). For a handy summary of the emergence and current status of CRT, see Lisa MacFarquhar, "The Color of the Law," *Lingua Franca,* July–August 1996, pp. 40–47; and Gary Minda, *Postmodern Legal Movements: Law and Jurisprudence at Century's End* (New York: New York University Press, 1995). For an analysis of racial marking and modernity with a more philosophical approach, see David Theo Goldberg, *Racist Culture: Philosophy and the Politics of Meaning* (Oxford: Blackwell, 1993). In the Marxist tradition, see Etienne Balibar and Immanuel Wallerstein, *Race, Nation, Class: Ambiguous Identities* (London: Verso, 1991).

16. bell hooks, *Ain't I a Woman?* (Boston: South End Press, 1981), pp. 6, 9. hooks is one of many radical feminists of color who around 1981 were making similar charges. In the contemporary study of whiteness, hooks is often cited as having made the call for white folk to examine themselves. See bell hooks, "Representations of Whiteness in the Black Imagination," in her *Killing Rage: Ending Racism* (New York: Holt, 1995), pp. 31–50; and similarly, Toni Morrison, *Playing in the Dark: Literature and the White Imagination* (New York: Vintage Books, 1992); and Hazel Carby, "The Politics of Difference," *Ms.,* September 1990, pp. 84–85. For further feminist white critique, see Elizabeth Abel, "Black Writing, White Reading: Race and the Politics of Feminist Interpretation," *Critical Inquiry* 19 (1993): 470–98; and Ruth Frankenberg, *The Social Construction of Whiteness: White Women, Race Matters* (Minneapolis: University of Minnesota Press, 1993).

17. On alterity as a function of "racial recovery," see David Aaron Gresson III, *The Recovery of Race in America* (Minneapolis: University of Minnesota Press, 1995). The phrase "culture of complaint" is from Robert Hughes's multicultural-back-lash book *Culture of Complaint: The Fraying of America* (Oxford: Oxford University Press, 1993).

18. hooks critiques white "commonality" in *ain't i a woman,* p. 144.

19. Ibid., p. 150.

20. The capitalist ruses of multiculturalism are critiqued by Crystal Bartolovich in

"The Work of Cultural Studies in the Age of Transnational Production," *the minnesota review* 47 (1996): 117–46. See also Henry A. Giroux, "Consuming Social Change: The 'United Colors of Benetton,' " *Cultural Critique* 26 (1993–94): 5–32. See, generally, David Theo Goldberg, ed., *Multiculturalism: A Critical Reader* (Oxford: Blackwell, 1994).

21. Liberal notions of ethnicity as more complete forms of individuality still limit official discussions of multiculturalism. For example, see Michael Walzer, "Multiculturalism and Individualism," *Dissent* (Spring 1994): 185–91.

22. Toni Cade Bambara, foreword to Chérie Moraga and Gloria Anzaldúa, eds., *This Bridge Called My Back: Writings of Radical Women of Color* (Watertown, MA: Persephone Press, 1981), p. iv.

23. Marilyn Frye, "On Being White: Thinking Toward a Feminist Understanding of Race and Race Supremacy," in her *The Politics of Reality: Essays in Feminist Theory* (Trumansburg, NY: Crossing Press, 1983), pp. 110–27.

24. Ibid., pp. 112–13.

25. Ross Chambers draws on the term "mixed doubles" from genre theory to point out the vexed relationship between subordinant or "examinable" identities and their comparatibility (see Chapter 12 in this book). See also Anne Freadman and Amanda Macdonald, *What Is This Thing Called Genre* (Mount Nebo, Qld: Boombana, 1992).

26. Frye's struggle seems to be a serious response to Baldwin's pessimism regarding white benevolence, what he calls the "jewel of [white] naiveté." This is not an overt form of racism but the maintenance of a structural one in which whiteness retreats by way of liberal benevolence to a kind of inoffensive and politically anesthetized acceptance of "diversity." See Baldwin, *Notes of a Native Son*, p. 166. There is also an association here between Frye's antiracist work *within* racism and Derrick Bell's "racial realism." Both seem to reject the "equality ideology" inherent in liberal white benevolence. See Bell's "Racial Realism," in Crenshaw et al., eds., *Critical Race Theory*, pp. 302–12. See also Derrick Bell, *Faces at the Bottom of the Well: The Permanence of Racism* (New York: Basic Books, 1992).

27. I have written further about the idea of multiple alterities in "What Was Race? Memories, Categories, Change," *Postmodern Culture* (January 1997).

28. Albert Murray, "White Norms, Black Deviation," in Joyce A. Ladner, ed., *The Death of White Sociology* (New York: Vintage Books, 1973), p. 112.

29. See Donald Barlett and James B. Steele, *America: Who Really Pays the Taxes* (New York: Simon & Schuster, 1994), p. 17. Cited in Joel Kivel, *Uprooting Racism: How White People Can Work for Racial Justice* (Philadelphia: New Society Publishers, 1996).

30. These and the preceding statistics are taken from Simon Head, "The New, Ruthless Economy," *New York Review of Books,* February 29, 1996, pp. 47–52. See also Sheldon Danziger and Peter Gottschaulk, *America Unequal* (Cambridge, MA: Harvard University Press, 1995).

31. See Jason DeParle, "Class Is No Longer a Four-Letter Word," *New York Times Magazine,* March 17, 1996, pp. 40–43.

32. See Doug Henwood, "America: Still World Capital of Inequality," *Left Business Observer,* January 22, 1996, pp. 4–5.

33. See Tom Wicker, "Deserting Democracy: Why African Americans and the Poor Should Make Common Cause in Their Own Party," *The Nation,* June 17, 1996,

pp. 11–16. See also Jennifer L. Hochchild, *Facing up to the American Dream: Race, Class, and the Soul of the Nation* (Princeton, NJ: Princeton University Press, 1996).

34. *Washington Post,* October 8, 1995. Cited in *The Left Business Observer,* November 4, 1995, p. 1.

35. The *Turner Diaries* has sold more than 200,000 copies by direct mail and has been purchased by an eager editor (the same one who released *The Anarchist Cookbook*) who intends to do an initial print run of another 70,000.

36. For a provocative analysis of the July 20, 1995, U.S. Supreme Court decision to uphold the *Bakke* case against affirmative action, see "Race and Representation," a special issue of *representations 55* (Summer 1996).

37. See Roediger, *The Wages of Whiteness*; and Noel Ignatiev, *How the Irish Became White* (New York: Routledge, 1996).

38. Homi Bhabha, *The Location of Culture* (New York: Routledge, 1994), p. 5.

39. Fanon, *Black Skin, White Masks,* pp. 110–11.

40. The idea of racial identity in flux has been introduced elsewhere as "racial formation theory." See Michael Omi and Howard Winant, *Racial Formation Theory in the United States: From the 1960s to the 1980s* (New York: Routledge, 1986); and Howard Winant, *Racial Conditions: Politics, Theory, Comparisons* (Minneapolis: University of Minnesota Press, 1994).

41. I want to distinguish this two-handed grabbing of narcissism from softer versions of self-help, as evident in the "sensitivity training" of displaced whites. For examples of this, see Judith H. Katz, *White Awareness: A Handbook for Anti-Racism Training* (Norman: University of Oklahoma Press, 1978); Joan Steinau Lester, *The Future of White Men and Other Diversity Dilemmas* (Berkeley, CA: Conari Press, 1994); and Kivel, *Uprooting Racism.*

42. The exact, well-known, quotation from Marx is as follows: "It is not the consciousness of men that determines their being, but, on the contrary, their social being that determines their consciousness." From *A Contribution to the Critique of Political Economy* [1859], in Robert C. Tucker, ed., *The Marx–Engels Reader,* 2nd ed. (New York: Norton, 1978), p. 5.

43. I discuss competing materialisms in "Towards a 'Materialist' Rhetoric," in Michael Bernard-Donals, ed., *Rhetoric in an Anti-Foundationalism World* (New Haven, CT: Yale University Press, 1997).

44. In 1990, whites made up 57 percent of the total population of California and, of Los Angeles, 38 percent. See Richard Walker, "California's Collision with Race and Class," *representations* 55 (Summer 1996): 163–78; and Dale Maharidge, *The Coming White Minority in California* (New York: Random House, 1996).

45. Fanon, *Black Skin, White Masks,* pp. 185, 52.

46. Baldwin, *Notes of a Native Son,* pp. 146, xxxv.

47. In fact, they are raging in academe as well, as evident in the current de-funding of higher education. On the relationship between knowledge and class inside the academy, see my "Cultural Studies by Default," in Amitava Kumar, ed., *Class Issues* (New York: New York University Press, 1997), pp. 245–71.

48. Interestingly enough, white-on-white ambivalence (if not white critique) is already widely available in mass culture. Consider popular music. The white rock group Cowboy Junkies released the blues tribute album *Whites off Earth Now* in 1990. The

Beastie Boys live album is called *White Trash*. Both Social Distortion and Marilyn Manson identify "white trash" features in their latest albums. Rage Against the Machine has songs on the album *Evil Empire* about "the white wall," which rhymes "cannon" with "Fanon." And there was the short-lived FOX sit-com called *The Show,* which depicted a white writer for an all-black comedy hour struggling with and against his whiteness, as well as films like *Great White Hype, White Man's Burden,* and *Celtic Pride.* For a less optimistic view of white racial encodings in contemporary youth and media culture, see Henry A. Giroux, "White Panic and the Racial Coding of Violence," in his *Fugitive Cultures: Race, Violence, and Youth* (New York: Routledge, 1996), pp. 25–55.

49. The address for *Race Traitor* is P.O. Box 603, Cambridge MA, 02140-0005.

WHITE POLITICS

2

Sympathy for the Devils: Notes on Some White Guys in the Ridiculous Class War

Fred Pfeil

It seems like another era, though it was less than five years ago, when I was sitting in the Men's Wisdom Council, grunting "Ho" with the guys and studying their hodgepodge, Shake-and-Bake "traditions" for a book I was writing on changing conceptions of white straight men. But now, just as my little political ethnography of the men's movement has come out, that silly dufus weeping around the campfire with the Native American speaking, stick in hand, has morphed into the image of the militiaman holding his assault weapon across his chest, the denim cutoffs and raw cotton shirts exchanged for camouflage fatigues, those formerly damp and sensitive eyes transformed into opaque chips glinting out an implacable and vicious rage. For most of what passes for the leftist and/or feminist progressive community these days, white men are assumed to be on a rampage against both women and nonwhite minorities, who for the past three decades have been clamoring for the power

Adapted from *New Left Review* 213 (1995).

and rights they deserve. According to this view, white men are racist, sexist *fleurs du mal,* self-defined by their lust for power over women and nonwhites. The *Washington Post*'s Juan Williams had it right when he said the April 19 bombing at Oklahoma City was committed by "white men in their natural state."

It seems to me, though, that such a broad-brush portrait of American white men or, for that matter, of any gender and/or racially coded group, is bound to occlude more than it reveals—and that the differences between the guys around these two types of campfire count at least as much as their similarities. The men's movement and the militias can be seen as differential responses to a general cultural and political situation, characterized by both a widespread confusion as to what men—including and perhaps especially white men—are supposed to be, mean, and do and a related uncertainty about what this country—as a polity but even more as what Benedict Anderson terms an "imagined community"—is supposed to be, including whether it even works as a country any more. Yet another such response, as cynical as it is sentimental and as successful as it is imaginary on both counts, is the box-office blowout *Forrest Gump.* But the differences between the two responses speak above all to the chasm separating one group of white guys from the other: the subjective and objective, felt-from-within and known-from-without fault line of class.

I know a fair bit about what both sides of that gap look and feel like, having crossed over from one side of it to the other when such passages were more possible than they are now, but remaining, despite that journey, something of a partial exile in both. I come from exactly the kind of part-industrial, part-agrarian small town and white working-class culture in which the militia movement is now flourishing. While I was home for a few weeks in the summer of 1995, I spent a fair amount of time visiting some of the men and one of the women with whom I went to school and have kept in touch since I went away to college and afterward, in the years in which they had their kids and brought them up while working in the plant or on their declining farms or off in the woods. But as a college-educated, post-1960s baby boomer guy, outside and beyond Port Allegany, I've lived a long time now along the left edge of what was once the counterculture but has now been upscaled and remarketed as a spectrum of "alternative" or "New Age" lifestyles and milieux.

In this chapter, I would like to sketch out both these habitats as they appear to the white guys in them—that is, to those with one foot in alternative culture and with the other usually somewhere along the professional–managerial slopes of the postindustrial divide and also as they appear to the other white guys in the hollows back around home. Maybe the place to start is with the accusation leveled at both groups and, indeed, at white men as a group: that racism and misogyny are at the core of both movements and groups and at the base of the white man's soul.

I recall a moment at the Day for Men retreat with Robert Bly and Michael Meade that I attended with some five hundred other, mostly white, men early in 1991, when someone stood up and challenged Bly to justify the absence of other men with more melanin. Bly's telling response was to insist that even though it was indeed important for men of other racial and ethnic backgrounds to recover and defend their own traditions, there was a genuine need for white men to do the work of getting back in touch with their own traditions and wisdom. Yet the myths, folktales, and homilies that filled out the day were, like the drumming itself, as likely to be drawn from Native American or African culture as to come from the North Woods.

Likewise, in all the time I spent hanging around the Wisdom Councils and neighborhood groups, I never heard a single word of overt feminist bashing. On the contrary, the main line on feminism was that now that women were recovering their own strengths and truths, it was time for men to do the same. Also in relation to feminism, it was the same with the appropriations of tales and rituals from nonwhite and non-Western cultures, with both the formats of many of these meetings and the new/old masculinities that they celebrated and espoused. Stripped of their rituals, many circles of men look and sound a lot like male versions of the consciousness-raising groups that launched second-wave feminism a few decades back. Beneath the "wild man" alibi, the wisdom "recovered" by the guys of Bly—the wisdom of nurturance and playfulness, of emotional expressivity and deep connectedness to the earth—sounds a lot like what used to be foisted off on women and denied to real he-men.

Of course, it's possible to claim that these assertions and silences are simply deep cover for impulses that remain misogynist and racist at the root. But if we consider them at face value and ask where they come from, a more accurate and interesting picture of these men's world and worldview starts to emerge. Above all, what seems salient about the latter is the assumption that women, African Americans, Native Americans, and other nonwhite or nonmale persons are self-enclosed communities of people whose identities are first and foremost cultural rather than political and historical. Each group is understood to be its own tribe, with its own organically held traditions, rituals, and essential knowledge passed down from one generation to the next. Such pridefully organicized and exclusive definitions of various racialized and gendered groupings on U.S. terrain are hardly the invention of white men. Increasingly, despite the tendencies toward repressive orthodoxy and, consequently, fissiparousness that lie coiled within them, they constitute the common sense not only of alternative culture but also of those women and racial "minorities" who, in and beyond that culture, used to be thought of in the post–New Left 1970s as the core constituencies of the American Left. And all that white men—white men in the men's movement, that is—are doing is doing it now for themselves as well.

Only, as we've already seen, they're not. Not *by* themselves, at any rate; not without a lot of covert help from the other tribes. In fact, what all those largely elided or unacknowledged appropriations from the wisdom traditions of the other tribes suggests is the fundamental fear among these relatively upscale post-1960s boomers that white men as a whole are without traditions and are bereft of wisdom. A few years back, Kathryn Robinson of the alternative newspaper *Seattle Weekly* asked various members of her own hip, alternative circle of friends to find as many good qualities as they could for men and women, respectively. What she found was that her male and female friends had no problems coming up with female virtues, from the traditional caring and sharing ones to the newer ones of autonomy, sisterhood, and empowerment. But the only one anybody mentioned in regard to men was—from a couple of the women, no less—that they sometimes were pretty good providers.

Being the person who makes the best deal in the dull and morally dirty marketplace of mainstream economic life is not apt to win a man many points in alternative cultural circles—not to mention in his own deep masculine soul. And being white is, of course, another problem. The consensus on white culture that my friend Mary Smith-Nolan found among the New Age Native American spiritualists she was studying and writing about holds today across a wide spectrum of alternative progressive and/or New Age cultural habitats. Smith-Nolan's "neo-natives"—most of them white and female, by the way—identified white culture with the "outside (urban) world," "mainstream society," "scientific, rational society," and "patriarchy" and agreed that it was "materialistic," "greedy," "obsessed with the self," "false," "removed from nature," "entrapped by a linear view of time," "controlled," and "violent"; whereas "Native Culture" (or African or African American culture, Balinese culture, or "womyn's" culture) embodies all the good opposites of these evils.

The problem for many if not most of those in the men's movement is that they themselves agree with this indictment—as, for that matter, I do myself in some respects. As Afro-American thinkers like Albert Murray and James Baldwin argued for years and as contemporary historians like David Roediger and Alexander Saxton have documented, becoming "white" in this society usually means trading in whatever ethnic culture one brought to this country at the immigration doorway, cashing in such traditions of communitarianism and contact with nature as that culture provided in exchange for industrial work discipline, the soul-less pleasures of Populuxe consumer culture, and the right to hold one's own clean, well-regulated self superior to any dirty nigger, injun, or spic.

But I also sympathize with men who do not want to be this kind of repressed and oppressive white person anymore yet find the exits blocked. Blocked, that is, not only by familial and economic structures that reward men who hustle a professional identity and paycheck and penalize those who don't, but also, and just as much, by the tribalist assumption that more and more nonacademic feminists and racial spokespersons subscribed to in the 1980s and early 1990s as moral consolation for their increasing political and economic powerlessness (call it "Women's Ways of Knowing" or "It's a black thing—you wouldn't understand"). It is no wonder that a bunch of graying post-1960s boomers—living under a cloud of perpetual suspicion in an alternative culture whose politics and interior-decorating styles are based on this assumption—cobbled together a tribal identity from the spare parts of other groups defined by their virtuous Otherness from the natural evil of white Guy-dom and constructed a white men's "movement" with nowhere to go.

All this has virtually no connection to what I hear from those other white men, the militia-friendly, working-class ones back home—although in these conversations as well, much to my surprise, I heard not a peep about women, blacks, or even general assistance programs. My one encounter with a member of the Patriot movement took place around a campfire around which almost all the other men in fatigues and with semiautomatics looked distinctly black, even though they claimed, with at least some justice, to be Native Americans, members of the near- (some would say long-) extinct tribe of the Golden Hill Paugussetts of eastern Connecticut.

I was there as part of an ad hoc delegation of local Quakers invited by the tribe's legal council to help keep the peace in the armed standoff between those who, despite the strikingly visible evidence of their interminglings with African Americans over the years, were insisting on their tribal rights to sell untaxed tobacco products to one and all, and the state of Connecticut, which insisted that the tribe had no such rights. Bill (as I'll call him) had driven up and plunked himself down, with his beat-up car and banged-up computer and fax, to lend his hand and publicity skills to the cause of these black Native Americans against the evil, totalitarian state—the same one, he was fond of insisting, that had taken out Koresh and the Davidians the previous spring.

I, too, have read up on militia-style groups like the Aryan Nation, Christian Identity, and the other creepy ultraright racist organizations. I know that neo-

Nazi hatemongers like Tom Metzger have plowed and sown the fertile soil of working-class white male *ressentiment* across the land, and I agree that Timothy McVeigh is seriously messed up. But Bill's support for these Afro–Native Americans and the absence of racist and sexist talk from the racist sexist guys I grew up with when they're talking about why they support militias makes me suspect the blanket contention that the militia movement and its white men all run on the high-octane leaded of misogyny and racial bigotry.

Rather, it seems to me that *ressentiment* emanates from a psychosocial infrastructure that has rotted away and collapsed. In places like the area around Lockport, New York, where Timothy McVeigh came from, or my hometown of Port Allegany, Pennsylvania, this infrastructure rested on an old, unwritten social contract. Under its terms, if you were a regular working-class white male, you were expected to resign yourself to a lifetime of economic and political subalternity and self-repression in exchange for a small clutch of real and symbolic benefits. You learned to execute the often unsafe and always mind-numbing routinized labor set out for you to do at one of the small plants that support these towns. (As one of the older men told me when I worked in one, without a hint of irony, "The first ten years are the hardest.") You take the fairly cruddy pay that the company union, if there is one, and the management have arranged for you and live in one of the old frame or clapboard houses or buy a trailer and fix it up. You learn not to expect to be called on or recognized for much but, rather, to be shortchanged for most of what you do and not to expect that things will get much better for yourself or your kids.

All this is what you might call the downside of the deal, though I forgot to mention that up through the end of the Vietnam war, it usually included a stint in the military, too, with its own lessons in taking your place and doing what you're told. What did you get in return? The "wages of whiteness" just described, to which we might add the right to feel yourself superior to all those shiftless folks and families sucking on the welfare tit. And as a grim corollary to those wages, I would also list the dubious satisfaction you were able to get from keeping your economic and emotional expectations low enough to meet.

A friend of mine, another working-class boomer kid turned academic, told me a story about a conversation she had with her father while he was weeding the vegetable garden in the backyard of the house where she'd grown up. Ruth was telling him about the problems she was having in her current love relationship and, for a long time, was getting no apparent response. Finally her father straightened up from the row of plants he'd been tending and looked up to where she was standing. "Do you know how much happiness I wanted out of life?" he asked and held his hard, soiled hand up between them, with its thumb and forefinger almost touching. "This much," he answered himself, "and I got it." And then, he bent back down again.

This was the basic lesson: Keep your head down and do what you're told, we were warned by the bosses who owned and ran the plants, and we'll take care of you when you need it and stay out of your business when you don't. I grew up in Port Allegany, whose economy depends on two glass plants. Pitt Corning had its headquarters in Pittsburgh but still had a lot of middle-class managerial personnel on site; Pierce Glass was owned by the Hergers, a family whose place in the community was not unlike the Cartwright family's at the Ponderosa. Every summer, for example, at the Pierce picnic, while the men drank beer and whiskey, ate fresh cherrystones brought in on chunks of salted ice in wooden kegs, and played poker, craps, and pool, old man Herger would show up at the community pool where the women and children were hanging out and toss change out of a big cloth sack into the water for us kids to dive in and grab.

Likewise with politics itself. While I was growing up in Port Allegany, the guy who ran it all was the registrar of wills, Merle Dickinson. If you wanted a job on the roads or anything else from the state, you'd better be a Republican and go through him. The larger point, though, is that in work and politics alike, if you were a man and played your weak hand right, you got not only your smidgen of actual, material gravy but also the less tangible yet no less important taste treat of imagining yourself—and, in turn, being imagined—to be part of a continuum of power with the big boys, the Hergers and the Dickinsons, just like sergeants and lieutenants in the military, in a spectrum that stretched up through your do-nothing congressman to the president of the United States and out to the country as a whole. And just as the big guys got to run things in their own domains, so you did in your own little kingdom. Most obviously, of course, you got to be the big dog at home with your wife and family, but you also got to use your property as you liked, have the lousy, underfunded school system you wanted, own as many guns of whatever kind or manufacture you wanted, and blast away in or chop down as much of the woods as you saw fit.

That was the deal, and I'm not saying it was in any sense a good one—only that it was for a long, long time in many parts of the country, particularly those outside the major cities and their suburbs, the take-it-or-leave-it one most white guys got. What has been happening for quite a while now and in quite a few places is that the deal itself seems to have taken off. In Port Allegany, unlike a lot of other towns, the plants are still running, and the Republican vote is still solid as well. But Pittsburgh Corning pulled out most of its management team a long time ago, and the Hergers sold Pierce Glass twenty years back. Since then it has been Indian Head, Ball-Incon, and now—I think—just plain Ball. At any rate, it's part of a conglomerate, which as far as I or anyone in town knows is probably multinational like the rest of them, with headquarters who knows where, and a top brass as anonymous as the winds of fate. Moreover, as Richard Harwood tells us, only 20 million households have stayed ahead of inflation since the 1970s, and 78 million households fell behind. Like most working folks across the country, people in Port saw their real incomes decline steadily through the 1980s and 1990s as both inflation and their personal income and property taxes ate away at wages that stayed flat.

At the same time and despite the local Republican Party's ongoing lock on the region, a lot of people have come to sense and resent the presence of the federal government in their backyards and their business. Federal regulations were part of the reason that the town hospital had to shut down a few years ago and are part of the reason that the town probably will have to have a bond issue and maybe a property tax increase to fund some costly repairs and reconstruction on the local high school. Then there were all those needlessly expensive, federally mandated specifications on the bridge on lower Mill and those bags of stones that had to be brought in and walled up behind chicken wire to shore up the hillsides and riverbanks on the south side of town, even though there'd never been a problem with slides or erosion before, plus those new HUD apartment and housing units for low-income and old people which, especially the low-income ones, started out looking about twice as nice as what you could afford when you were just starting out but now already look like hell. Plus now they're telling you what you can and can't do with your so-called wetland, what you can and can't cut on your woods, and even what guns you can't have and what loads you can't shoot any more. And there doesn't seem to be a thing that you, or the ghost of Mr. Herger or Merle Dickinson, can do it about it, either.

A few weeks ago when I was back home talking to folks, I heard a number of litanies like this one, from men and women alike. The same men and women almost invariably segued from such local complaints to the ATF's assaults on Randy Weaver and the Waco compound in 1992 and 1993. Yet they also wanted to make sure that I knew both how appalled they were by the Oklahoma City bombing and how pissed off they were to be lumped in with white supremacist organizations and other hate groups as racist wackos whose beliefs are off the charts.

So—to choose just one example—the first thing my old buddy Dave (as

I'll call him) had to tell me over our cheeseburgers and drafts when I saw him a few weeks ago was that as soon as he heard the news that a bunch of white guys were responsible for the April 19 bombing, he got out his assault rifle and the fifteen hundred rounds he had to go with it and put up the whole works for sale. "Ashamed" and "unclean" were, I think, the words he actually used. Like most of the other people I talked to, he wanted me to know that he wasn't in the local Bucktail Militia himself, although he had a fair amount of sympathy with their views. On the one hand, he himself had no particular opinion on what the Founding Fathers had in mind when they wrote the Second Amendment or whether the state or federal government had jurisdiction over such matters. Besides, he said, he recognized that it was not a good thing for kids in cities to have access to Tec-9s and MAC-10s. It was different here, where everybody grows up with guns and learns what they're supposed to be used for and how to use them right, but the government can't seem to see or care about that difference.

Dave was convinced that the government's long-term aim was to disarm the population completely; just look at the way they went after Randy Wheeler in Idaho and the Davidians in Waco; look at the way they and their friends in the media were going after the NRA now. Plus you've got to pay more and more in property taxes every year, even as they're telling you more and more what you can and can't do with your land. Then he launched into a long, hazy story he thought he'd read somewhere in one of his woodsman's or sportsman's magazines, about a guy who took the government to court because they said he couldn't build a house on his own land, because some small piece of that land would no longer serve as habitat for some endangered species of mouse or something, if the house were built and if global warming occurred. Although my tactic was basically to let Dave's monologue roll out unimpeded, I did break in here to ask whether the government had ever tried to take away or constrain his rights over the land at Card Creek Hollow, where his family's farm used to be. He thought about that for a second and said no but that he *felt* as though they could any day. And he declared that even though all he had left was his rifles, which he knew would be no match if and when the government showed up to take away what was his, he'd take down at least a few of them with him when he went.

All this I got in more or less the same form in which I've recounted it, with very little solicitation on my part, and all of it was more or less what I expected. What drives the militia movement in my part of the country—and, I suspect, in most others as well—is neither garden-variety racism nor sexism in any direct sense but antifederalism. But that antifederalism is itself neither a pure nor a simple thing. On the one hand, it rests on a legitimate perception by the people who hold it in Port A that the same powers are behind both the media and the federal government and that those powers don't give a damn about people like themselves. Yet on the other hand, those same people seem incapable of understanding that the most powerful and most indifferent players and interests behind the scenes are those of corporate capitalism itself—perhaps because it is too large and abstract for comprehension, perhaps because of the ongoing strength of those old affiliations and identifications that working people in my town still feel with business, including those tough-love local/transnational plants they must continue to love and hate and need.

So too with the widespread sense of increasing powerlessness that comes in a combination of paranoia about and contempt for a government conceived to be, like the Simpson defense team's portrait of the LAPD, viciously totalitarian and ridiculously incompetent in equal measure. After all, the Clinton administration's greatest successes to date have been helping construct, through NAFTA and GATT, a new world system for corporate capital's needs and demands. Even though some militia spokesmen do explicitly mention GATT and NAFTA in their bill of particulars against the government, such charges typically take second place to wild extrapolations from the admittedly brutal excesses of the ATF's assaults on Randy Wheeler and the Branch Davidians to black helicopters watching us from the skies and shadow New World government organizations preparing to seize all our guns and take control.

Finally, I believe that there is something to do with gender and race at the source of all these misperceptions and half-truths, however much it may differ from active racism and sexism. It is these men's bafflement, grief, and rage at the breakdown and/or removal of a profoundly undemocratic patriarchal and neofeudal hierarchy into which they once believed they fit organically, with their own zones of autonomy and deserved privilege, no matter how small. No one attends to or speaks for us, they are saying (for in truth, they have never spoken for themselves), and we do not have control over our lives. All this was crowded onto the bumper sticker for the Republican candidate for the Senate who upset the incumbent Democrat in the 1994 off-year elections: Protect Freedom/Vote Santorum.

Far from being one and the same, then, these two movements and their white male constituencies are more like—pardon the expression—dialectical obverses of each other, in terms of both what they want and what they avoid. The men's movement is trying to break through the repressions that white men in industrial society have internalized, the rigidities and body armor and emotional numbness, but they rarely look at the external social conditions and structures that pressure them to deform themselves in this way and much less at the comparatively privileged positions that allow white men like themselves a partial exemption from the rules.

Militiamen, however, have no such slack, nor would they be quick to take it if it were offered. They're the ones who know what's right, who get things done, who see their mission of protecting and restoring the republic as an extended and exalted version of protecting their property and providing for their wife and kids. For them, the enemy must be external—indeed, for some of them, even the federal government is too close to home, and it's the UN or the Zionist conspiracy that's at fault. Above all, as with the working-class Germans that Wilhelm Reich studied sixty years ago or Adorno's "little man" of fascism, what must never be questioned are the inner terms of the deal such men have already cut with power, the one that offers them a limited, localized, and at least partly fantasized taste of the juice the Big Boys who really rule us give them in exchange for clamping down on their desires and submitting to their subordination not only without complaint but with a perverse pride.

If neither group deserves the collective victim/hero status that each claims for itself, neither quite deserves the blanket condemnation they've received. At least, the white guys I know in and around the militia movement are as sad as they are scary, and the other guys in the men's movement as simpatico as they are silly. Although both groups are struggling in their own scary and/or silly ways to figure out what it means to be a white male today, neither group's struggle need be reduced to just another racist sexist plot. Obviously, before the men in the militia movement could join any genuinely progressive movement, they would have to give up their old deference to political and economic power and the sense of privileged rights and autonomy that it got them; in effect, they would have to refuse to accept what little is left of their "wages of white maleness." Likewise, for the more upscale New Agers in the men's movement to live up to their desire—as one local spokesman I talked to put it, to be men "for something; for equality, for feelings" and against a business culture inimical to both—they would have to join with those both spiritually and materially alienated from its code of hyperrationalized and repressive selfishness and to work with them to construct an alternative and oppositional culture in both the public and the private spheres.

For those upscale men's movements to become movements and for militiamen to stop being chumps for the Right, both must muster the strength and wisdom to call their foremost enemy by its correct name, corporate capitalism, the enclave of those (largely) white men who really own the field and call the shots. But it is hard to imagine either group's ever overcoming its internal resistances to taking this plunge in the absence of any encouragement or invitations to do so from outside their ranks, from other communities suffering as much and, in most cases, more than these men are. Does what's left of the Left and feminism and the struggle against racism really want at least some white males not to be sexist white supremacists? If so, it is for those of us who oppose the white men who run this country and much of the world to help these other white men to realize that they should oppose them and their rule as well—and indeed, that in part they already do.

Could such efforts bear fruit? I don't know, but I think I know what will happen if progressives keep lumping together and writing off all white men as being welcomed by reactionaries as an inherently racist sexist tribe. The old homeless black man I was walking with up to the state capitol to protest the newest proposed cuts in general assistance and aid to the state's shelter facilities put it just right: "You know what's gonna happen if this shit keeps up?" he said. "There's gonna be class war—and it's gonna be *ridiculous*." Until we—all the rest of us, disaffected white males included—get the names and the sides right, that's what we'll get: ridiculous, obfuscated, unrecognized class war.

POSTSCRIPT, JUNE 1996

In the year since I wrote this piece, a lot of polluted water has passed under the bridge. Yet despite all the white spite over the Simpson verdict, despite the Montana Freemen taken gently under custody in such marked contrast to, say, the firebombing of the MOVE folks in Philadelphia, I shakily persist in advocating the course of political action I sketched out last June.

In lieu of any comprehensive update or revision of this piece, what I would like to offer here instead is a clarification of what *shakily* means in the preceding sentence and use one isolated and now virtually forgotten bit of news to do so. The bit of news is the brief spurt of popularity and votes for Pat Buchanan in his run for the Republican nomination for president of the United States and, more specifically, the debate that ensued on the Left about the significance and political potential of the anticorporate, anti-NAFTA, antimultinational rhetoric he mixed into his usual racist, homophobic, jingoist, and misogynist diatribe.

For leftist analysts of the Buchanan phenomenon, the key question was, first, how much the white working-class votes he got in Iowa and New Hampshire had to do with this addition of a pinch of economic populism to the basic recipe and, second, whether the appeal of that rhetoric would or could under different circumstances retain its power to move voters if separated from the bigotry and chauvinism of the rest of Buchanan's message. These are, in electoral form, the questions I tried to raise in "Sympathy for the Devils," so I was glad to see them aired in the pages of the leftist press—that is, until Buchanan ran out of steam, at which point they seemed to melt away like the winter's snow.

Before that spring melt, though, two articles appeared side by side in the April issue of *The Progressive,* whose diametrically opposed views of the potential of economic populism as a galvanizing force in American political life today still seem relevant. In "Ebony and Ivory Fascists," Adolph Reed Jr. claims that this potential has virtually disappeared, that "what we want to interpret as economic populism could just as easily be resonance with a *Herrenvolk* democracy—a political assertion of white, male, nativist entitlement as the only truly legitimate citzenship—that has a long history in American politics."[1] But in "Buchanan Fodder," John Nichols, backed by quotations from Ralph Nader, Jim Hightower, and Ronnie Dugger, contends that "progressives" can and must "enter that court [i.e., of economic populism], grab hold of the economic message, cleanse it of Buchanan's bigotries, and use it to advance positive social change."[2]

Reed's argument rubs hard against the grain of my own and eloquently evokes the long and bitter history of white working-class bigotry in defense of its pessimistic conclusion. "The fascist ideas" in Buchanan's rhetoric, he points out, "are not peripheral to the more radical-sounding stuff; if anything it's the reverse. Many people are fundamentally committed to that fascist vision. We'll never win them over, no matter what their place in the system of production."[3] And indeed, given the white working-class town I come from, I know something firsthand about how deeply that awful history is inscribed in the minds and enshrined in the hearts of those I grew up with and still hang around with, as well as how difficult and incessant my struggle has been to unlearn and expel it from my own mind and heart.

Thus, the "shakiness" of my stand in these pages: but why and how can I continue to hold out for a renewed and newly inclusive economic populism? My replies here, given the exigencies of time and space and my own befuddlement, must be brief and sketchy; more scandalously still, they run straight from the theoretically abstruse to the shamelessly anecdotal, skidding right across all the properly materialist stops along the way.

First, theoretically I believe in the possibility and potential of a clarified and inclusive economic populism for white men among others, because I believe in the possibility and necessity of what Gramsci speaks of as the long, grinding labor of *counter-hegemony* and Althusser, Stuart Hall, and Laclau/Mouffe speak of as *disarticulation*—albeit not as a mere twist of rhetoric but as the hard, slow political work of building organizations, parties, and constituencies; work, that is, that takes into account the shadows cast by historical divisions of race and gender in its efforts to create new and different citizens and communities, in order to redeem the time that is now. Second, anecdotally, on the level of local knowledge and individual experience, from the Jackson Rainbow Coalition campaigns in 1984 and 1988 to a union's organizing drive this past spring among the largely nonwhite food service workers at the college where I teach, I saw firsthand how principled, inclusive coalitions can be built across race and gender divides and go on to win at least partial victories. Third, and finally, despite all the historical odds against us and despite all the power and justice in Reed's argument, if we want to construct a majority for progressive change in this country's social and economic structures, we must bring a substantial number of white men, especially including white working-class men, along with us—and if we don't want to do that, those of us still willing to think of ourselves as the Left in this country will be condemned not to act but merely to act out.

NOTES

1. Adolph Reed Jr., "Ebony and Ivory Fascists," *The Progressive* 60 (April 1996): 20.
2. John Nichols, "Buchanan Fodder," *The Progressive* 60 (April 1996): 25.
3. Reed, "Ebony and Ivory Fascists," 22.

White Looks: Hairy Apes, True Stories, and Limbaugh's Laughs

David R. Roediger

The chauvinism and touchiness that begin this otherwise modest and even-tempered chapter derive from my having grown up along that part of the Mississippi River that divides Missouri from Illinois. It is easy to be chauvinistic about that stretch of the river, the lone portion of the Mississippi to divide slavery from freedom. Along the river and its banks, from Hannibal to East St. Louis and from St. Louis to Cairo, great artists and great art have long been created. To an unrivaled extent, that art has challenged the lie of white supremacy, both implicitly in its celebration of black beauty and creativity and explicitly in its probing of the relationship between race and freedom. Geniuses such as Miles Davis, Chuck Berry, Scott Joplin, Katherine Dunham, Redd Foxx, Tina Turner, Quincy Troupe, Josephine Baker, Maya Angelou, Ntozake Shange, and Mark Twain have drawn on experiences along the river to chart, move, explode, and ignore the color line. Even T. S. Eliot, the writer most

Adapted from *the minnesota review* 47 (Spring 1997): 41–52.

eager to lose the region's accents, carried with him much of the river's race lore and popular culture.

As a setting for works of genius, the river separating Missouri from Illinois is equally impressive. Huck Finn learns the differences between slavery and freedom drifting down the river and discovers that it is not worthwhile to be white. Twain sets *Pudd'nhead Wilson,* with its fierce ridiculing of biological racism, in a town between St. Louis and Cairo. Sterling Brown's "Tornado Blues," with its wonderful meditations on race and tragedy, unfolds in St. Louis. Herman Melville's *The Confidence Man,* on one level a remarkable exploration of whiteness as a performance, unfolds on a steamboat bound from St. Louis south.[1]

The churlishness follows from the chauvinism. These days I seldom get through a month without hearing or reading—often the source is someone on the Left—that "whatever his politics," Rush Limbaugh is a "genius." His "genius" sometimes is said to lie in comedy, sometimes in understanding media, sometimes in knowing how to speak to the American people, and often in all three. I (always managing to smile cordially when such nonsense is trumpeted about William F. Buckley's "seriousness" and "intellect") rage when the adulation comes Limbaugh's way. The reason lies largely in Limbaugh's hometown of Cape Girardeau, Missouri, and in his roots in the local elite of that southern Missouri River city. He is my age, and because I grew up in cities north and south of the Cape, his type is familiar to me. It was this long-standing distaste for his class and his kind that made me bristle when Limbaugh was praised until I began watching his television show. Then I realized how thoroughly his "genius" rests on an unreflective and banal performance of whiteness, whose elements were as familiar to me as Limbaugh's sneer.

This chapter pairs the analysis of one piece of cultural work on race written partly by Twain with one written by Limbaugh. The juxtaposition underlines not only the difference between genius and banality but also the reality that banality can carry much more social power than genius can in regard to white consciousness. More broadly, this chapter uses the material from Twain and Limbaugh, as well as from Eugene O'Neill, to call for a theorizing of racial formation that takes into account both what I call the "white look" and the imperialist gaze. My conclusion examines questions of method that emerge from the pairing of Twain's "white look" with Limbaugh's and O'Neill's, suggesting how we might examine historically why certain white looks work and others do not.

"LOOKING IT" AT THEM

Eugene O'Neill's fabulous 1922 play *The Hairy Ape* contains a striking line with great potential to challenge and enrich a materialist analysis of race. The play's drama hinges on the demise of Yank, a coal handler in the stokehold of an oceangoing ship. In the early scenes, Yank personifies all-American manhood, rejecting any and all hints that his work enslaves him, disdaining the hard scrubbing after shifts that other workers view as necessary to avoid acquiring the complexion of a "piebald nigger" and loudly enjoining others on the gang to ravage the "hungry," dark, and female furnace. But Yank's bravado cannot survive his obsession over a brief encounter with the steel heiress/social worker Mildred Douglas.

Preternaturally white and paler still in the presence of heat and "bored by her own anemia," Douglas goes below, convinced she can find life, or at least diversion, there. She finds Yank and faints at the combination of his dirt, his ferocity, his power, and his "gorilla face." Yank's mates explain to him that Douglas had to come to look at "'er slaves," to survey "the bloody animals below," to take in an exhibition of "bleedin' monkeys in a menagerie."[2]

Since Yank is the focus of her gaze and her terror, he is most susceptible to the fear of being seen as "a queerer kind of baboon than ever you'd find in darkest Africy." Lost in anxious reflection, Yank becomes both nonwhite and inhuman. Declaring himself the enemy of the "white-faced skinny tarts and de boobs that marry 'em," Yank wildly spirals downward. He comes to agree that he is a "hairy ape" and ends his life entering the gorilla cage at a New York City zoo. He wants to join the gorilla's "gang" who, instead, savages him. But the play's most revealing line reveals that Douglas probably never called Yank an ape. Instead, responding to Yank's panicked questioning about exactly what she said, the Irish character Paddy tellingly remarks, "She looked it at you if she didn't say the word itself."[3]

The idea that whiteness and nonwhiteness can be "looked at" others sits uneasily in a play saturated with references to the concrete realities of class, work, and power. To see these structural matters as counterpoised to the subjectivity of a look is wrong, however. As the best of the substantial recent scholarship on "imperialists gazes" has demonstrated, looks both frame and capture relations of power. They at once express racism and privilege, valorizing tropes that grow out of and alter how classes within the imperialist powers see both the colonized and one another. Not merely the symptom of imperial exploitation, the imperialist gaze is a shared social activity of imperialist domination and consciousness. According to Mary Louise Pratt, for example, the gaze therefore can be a perfect site to study the relation of domination.[4]

Indeed, in many ways, the recent writing on the imperialist gaze and imperialist culture illuminates the process by which O'Neill makes plausible the transition from native-born American worker to ape. Douglas displays the desire to categorize and classify that is characteristic of imperialist gazers, to "investigate everything" in London's slum as she has done in New York. The commanding position of surveying from above, which is typical of imperialist gazes, appears in Douglas's obsession with going below and, negatively, in her collapse when she looks at the workers from their level. Her search for ersatz reciprocity with those she watches also typifies the ways in which imperialism "looks."

Most important, the coal handlers who insist that Yank (and they) are looked at like zoo animals are right. The zoos, world's fairs, and natural history museums gathered the world's, but especially Africa's and Asia's, animals, and sometimes humans, classifying and displaying them, creating hierarchies and spectacles. As Donna Haraway observes, the display of monkeys and apes offer opportunities to teach lessons of race and hierarchy. Indeed, Anne McClintock posits "simian imperialism" as an important link between scientific and popular racism.[5]

The idea that an American-born white worker could be looked into non-whiteness becomes far more plausible in light of the history of New York City's Bronx Zoo, which in the early twentieth century housed a human with its monkeys and apes in the hugely publicized exhibition of him, an African, Ota Benga. When he was released after protests and his own rebellion, his controllers attempted to transform Benga into a factory worker. Cornelia Sears's penetrating work on the display of "man-like apes" and "ape-like men" in proximity demonstrates that the animality of humans received emphasis alongside the humanity of the primates.

The Bronx Zoo's director, William Temple Hornaday, constructed in his writings a hierarchy of animals from large brained to small brained, paralleling imperialist taxonomies. Hornaday postulated that both Ota Benga and other big-brained mammals were "workers" in his zoo. His remarkable "The Wild Animal's Bill of Rights" held that "superior" animals had "no more inherent right to live a life of lazy and luxurious ease . . . than a man or woman has to live without work." Real life almost outdistanced O'Neill's art in the case of the Bronx Zoo. In 1924, a blue-eyed young Scottish American proposed that Hornaday confine him in the ape house, to be displayed with the "Orang-outang and the Chimpanzee."[6]

But the imperialist gaze and imperialist culture take us only so far in understanding Mildred Douglas's ability to "look" Yank out of the ranks of white humanity. Rooted in the heritage of slavery as much as in the expansion of empire and in U.S. peculiarities as much as in global realities, Douglas's ability to do in Yank rested as much on a "white look" as on an imperialist gaze.[7] Yank is every inch an American, so much so that at one point he can scarcely recall his own name, having for so long identified with his nickname.

O'Neill's play unfolds amidst the early 1920s race baiting of Southern and Eastern European immigrants, which culminated in the race-based immigration restriction legislation of 1924. References to Italian "ginees" (guineas) and "wops" dot the text, alongside slurs on Irish American workers ("paddies" and "micks") who earlier faced questions about their whiteness. The references to workers as "slaves," though not peculiar to the United States, carried particular resonances in Yank's nation, the only one to begin industrializing with a huge slave labor force.

Most broadly, the drama in *The Hairy Ape* turns critically on a vicious parody of the blackface tradition of theatrical performance—a tradition that in the United States focuses on black–white issues rather than on imperialism.[8] Minstrelsy and vaudeville blackface made comedy out of the ability of white performers and their audiences to find fraternity based on the ease with which blackening could be put on and taken off. O'Neill fashioned tragedy out of a proletarian blackface in which "rivulets of sooty sweat" could hardly be scrubbed out and ultimately helped kill Yank.[9] The audience was disinvited to participate in those happy white looks, at the stage and at one another, which made minstrelsy such a powerful glue in white consciousness. Instead, Mildred Douglas's white look was divisive—and sad, dead, and deadly. Mark Twain's take on the white look is even more withering than O'Neill's, and Rush Limbaugh's performance of the white look banally reprises the minstrel tradition. Taken together, these gazes go far toward defining the problems and possibilities of understanding the white look.

ANOTHER LOOK

In 1874, the ex-Confederate soldier Mark Twain sent a pair of sketches to William Dean Howells, editor of the prestigious *Atlantic Monthly*. Twain, trying hard to escape being typed merely as a regional humorist, had high hopes for one of the two stories. The other he titled "A True Story" and made more modest claims for it. Inviting Howells to pay for it "as lightly as you choose," he explained that it was not his creation. Rather, he had merely "set down" the story of an "old colored woman," altering it only by choosing to "begin at the beginning." The ex-abolitionist Howells, cool to the story Twain favored, settled enthusiastically on "True Story."[10] Thus came a major breakthrough in Twain's career—and the publication of one of his most enduring short stories—even though he professed not to have written the story at all. Instead he presented—as the subtitle put it, "Word for Word as I Heard It"—a marvelous critique of white looking, an "autoethnography" fashioned by an ex-slave.[11]

"True Story" begins with a paragraph of stage setting. The narrator, with other whites, gazes down from a farmhouse porch at Aunt Rachel, a "mighty" sixty-year-old black servant sitting on the steps "respectfully below our level." Drawn from Twain's residence in New York State, at the outset the tale features "peal after peal" of laughter, rather than dialogue, from Aunt Rachel. Unlike James Fenimore Cooper, who earlier in the century reacted to blacks laughing in New York "in a way that seemed to set their very hearts rattling in their ribs" with a combination of fascination and unease, Twain's narration is utterly at ease.

Her work done, Rachel is "under fire" from the white family, but the narrator sees her being "chafed without mercy and . . . enjoying it." Her pleasure is natural, its being "no more trouble for her to laugh than it is for a bird to sing." Rachel's performance can be just what the narrator wants it to be. His language echoes fantasies in which white men look down on black women as sexual objects—Rachel would "sit with her face in her hands and shake with throes of enjoyment which she could no longer get breath enough to express"—but his gaze is apparently innocent. "Aunt Rachel," he asks, "how is it that you've lived sixty years and never had any trouble?"[12]

Then the story turns true. Rachel "stops quaking," is silent, and finally asks the narrator, "Misto C—, is you in 'arnest?" The narrator, "sobered," trusts in his white looks: "Why, you *can't* have had any trouble. I've never heard you sigh, and never seen your eye when there wasn't a laugh in it." Facing the narrator directly, Rachel tells him about a life full of trouble, of slavery from the viewpoint of someone who has "ben one of 'em my own se'f." Rising as she speaks, she soon "towers above" the white listeners. She describes the slave sales that tore her from her husband and seven children, describing how she was beaten for her tears during the sales and how she attempted to resist losing her "little Henry," her last child sold, by using her chains to beat those taking him. She spins out a wonderfully impossible tale of how, years later during the Civil War, fate and faith reunite her with Henry. Her closing words are withering examples of the "vigorous eloquence" with which Twain credited Mary Ann Cord, the former slave said to have related the story: "Oh, no,

Misto C——, I haven't had no trouble. An' no joy." White looks saw nothing in this view.[13]

"True Story" explicitly turns on gazes, but it does not grow out of the dynamics of imperialism, rather, out of race and slavery. Twain explodes the logic of the white look but not that of the imperialist gaze. That he may have had private, career-connected reasons for doing so, that what he "heard" was not an untainted truth, and that Twain somehow ended up with the byline for a black woman's story all are of interest. But so too is the remarkable set of circumstances that made possible such a critique of whiteness.

The fact that such major literary figures as Howells and Twain, from the North and the semi-South, could validate this critique of the viewpoint of whiteness is remarkable. Two decades earlier, when Herman Melville made a parallel effort to equate whiteness and blindness in *Benito Cereno*, his marvelous novella about a slave revolt, the reception had been largely uncomprehending. But in 1874, a decade after slaves freed themselves and four years after they achieved full citizenship and suffrage, whites could not look at black subjects in anything like this fixed manner. The behavior of many supposedly privileged and loyal ex-house slaves who, like Aunt Rachel, supported the Union Army during the war and moved away from the plantation after it, made into a reality the possibility that African Americans "are not what they seem."[14] For a time, the leading ex-abolitionist and the leading ex-Rebel cultural figures in the nation could agree that white looks are white lies and could write about an ex-slave's self-representation, a view that was also a searing commentary on whiteness.

RUSH TO WHITENESS

Rush Limbaugh likewise hands over his medium to a black speaker, but with a far different look and intent from Twain's. He regularly replays videos of excerpts of speeches by prominent African Americans. But Limbaugh chooses the replays for their bombast and grandiloquence for a point or two that he might later challenge, and especially for their stammers, mispronunciations, or grammatical shakiness. During the clip, Limbaugh appears in a small box in a lower corner of the screen as well as live before an overwhelmingly white studio audience. He wordlessly and continually comments on the speech and on the very idea of black expertise with a panoply of rolled eyes, raised brows, nods, snickers, and chortles. At the clip's end, the camera surveys the studio audience's satisfaction with Rush's performance and Rush's satisfaction with himself. In millions of homes, bars, college "Rush Clubs," and Limbaugh rooms of discount steakhouses, the chain is continued. White viewers can look at themselves, looking at the studio audience, looking at Rush, looking at Lani Guinier, or at Kweisi—Rush says Queasy—Mfume.

Deep connections between Limbaugh's white looks and the history of imperialist gazes determined that Dr. Joycelyn Elders would be the favorite object of his split-screen attention. Indeed, so treasured were the former surgeon general's appearances that when she was removed from office, Limbaugh and his listeners were nearly inconsolable. That she was an African American woman with medical expertise made Elder an appropriate choice for ridicule. Her scientific jargon, her frequent slips, and the pseudoarmy uniform of her office played perfectly into the right-wing populist delight in deflating liberal intellectual pretensions that run through much of Limbaugh's lampooning of what he calls "the Left," black or white.

But beyond all that, Limbaugh brought together through Elders familiar elements of the long history of the imperialist display of nonwhite female bodies. Like the promoters of the Hottentot Venus, like P. T. Barnum, and like *National Geographic,* he offered to the white male gaze the combination of sexual suggestion, images of black female bodies, and scientific expertise. The wonderful (for Limbaugh) twist in this instance was that the black woman provided the talk about sex and science on which Limbaugh could sit in judgment. Indeed, Elders's final undoing, which resulted from her open discussion of masturbation, put virtually the whole complex of images and actions surrounding the *National Geographic* into a house of mirrors.[15]

The dynamics of Limbaugh's clowning, leering gambit, however, differ enough from what we know about the workings of the imperialist gaze to suggest again the need to scrutinize and historicize the white look as a distinct subject. Limbaugh's look clashes dramatically with one much-emphasized attribute of the imperialist gaze—its production of the illusion of an absence of the European male viewer, an absence one critic characterized as the "real meaning of the Orientalist project." Limbaugh is not only present as he looks but is never more active on the show than when watching others speak. Moreover, Limbaugh does not occupy the vantage point of the imperial "master of all I survey." He is instead boxed in, dwarfed, low, and *still* in power. That power hinges in critical ways on a sense of reciprocity within the look, as theorists of the imperialist gaze would put it. But Rush-on-TV seeks none of the reciprocity with nonwhite subjects that Pratt so ably discusses in *Imperial Eyes.* He instead cultivates the reciprocity of white entertainer, white studio audience, and white viewers to endow his look with awful power. There is no risk for

Limbaugh, as Homi Bhabha argues that there is for imperialist gazers, of the "threatened return of the look" by the nonwhite subject.[16]

This white reciprocity rests in large part on Limbaugh's ability to reprise the role of the straight man/interlocutor in countless blackface entertainments. He registers the initial interest and growing exasperation with the supposed crudities and excesses of black speech, appearance, and behavior. To be reminded of this resonance is apposite in that it evokes the white audience's ritualized watching of blackface comedians and of one another that by the 1830s had already made the production of white looks an important commodity on the minstrel stage.

Anne McClintock offers a wonderful argument, centered mainly on the British Empire, that at imperialism's peak, the "commodity racism" attaching imperial conquest to advertised images of domestic products replaced scientific racism. But in the United States, minstrelsy, the massive commodification of black labor, and the more generalized connections of "whiteness" and "property" all made the commodity and consciousness of race connect far earlier and, especially through minstrelsy, influenced subsequent imperialist gazes. The most ubiquitous symbol of commodity racism in the United States, Aunt Jemima, was directly inspired by minstrel performance.[17] The hundreds of millions of white looks at her image on boxes helped allay the anxieties raised by the possibility that the Aunt Rachels were not what they looked to be. The hundreds of millions of white looks at a chortling Rush in boxes on the screen likewise reestablish control over the meaning and direction of laughter across the color line.

THE WORKINGS OF WHITENESS

Rush Limbaugh's white look has ratings. If his producers wish, they can obtain figures on just how many viewers decide to tune out and go to sleep as he gapes and guffaws at tapes of "The Reh-vaarh-oond Jock-soon," as he pronounces it. They can find out how many are moved to stay tuned. Sophomoric and repetitive to the point of ritual, Limbaugh's antics are infinitely more popular than any of the brilliant critiques of whiteness—from slaves' folktales, to Twain, to Melville, to James Baldwin, and to Toni Morrison. This hard fact creates dilemmas in our theoretical and historical approaches to the understanding of white looks.

One temptation is to assume that because a minstrel-derived white look like Limbaugh's still carries so much power, it represents the "white look"—

singular and virtually transhistorical. This misstates the case, as do analyses that posit a singular imperialist gaze. However much one look might work better than others, white looks also come in multiple forms, carrying differing class and gender dynamics. The task is to investigate why some looks come to undergird a mass sense of whiteness and others do not. Mildred Douglas's "looking it" at Yank clearly qualifies as a white look and, like all white looks, centers on inclusion and exclusion. But however convincing O'Neill is in showing that a white look could work to make Yank nonwhite at a particular early 1920s juncture, its extreme identification of whiteness with great wealth made race too narrowly and purely a stand-in for class to compete with the populist, "y'all come" whiteness typified by Limbaugh's look. (Indeed, in many shows Limbaugh first delivers his populist performances of whiteness and then goes on to defend explicitly great differences of wealth as a positive good.)

In understanding why and how white looks work, it is necessary to emphasize that such looks are historical. As such, they draw on long patterns of seeing, such as those of the minstrel tradition, but they also change over time. The ability of "A True Story"'s white look to be shared by Twain, Howells, and at least some readers in the era of emancipation was clearly greater than it would have been in the period of reconsolidated white supremacy and diminishing opportunities for the black self-activity of the early twentieth century, for example. Even Limbaugh's look responds to its historical context in ways that make it far more than just minstrelsy plus electrification. For all its glee, it remains very much a post–black freedom movement look. Its utter silence — its boxed-in protection against any dialogue with the Other — fits snugly into a situation described by Michael Omi and Howard Winant, who argue that the recent rightward political motion on race has not been able to find easily an openly racist voice. The capture of the moral high ground by the civil rights movement's rhetoric of equality has proved to be quite durable.[18] Even initiatives against racial equality have adopted the rhetoric of equal treatment and pressed white claims to status as victims, from the anti–affirmative action campaigns to Limbaugh's own recent protests that black folks can get away with saying *nigger* but whites cannot.

In this soil has grown among the white Right a feeling of being silenced. Limbaugh frequently describes his own "rightness" and "excellence" as resting on his saying what his listeners already believe. But he equally shares and embodies silent white looks. Limbaugh's jowls and blankness of expression perfectly suit him to be a put-upon white man at a time when many of his watchers see their whiteness as a weight rather than a privilege. But at the same time, silence itself has become far more freighted with meaning. Thus, when the successful 1991 Mississippi gubernatorial candidate Kirk Fordice closed his dramatic antiwelfare campaign advertisement, it was with silence and a still photograph of a black woman and her baby. Fordice trusted that white viewers would fill in the gaps.[19] Limbaugh is seldom without words but is perhaps never more dangerous than when he is. The performance enables Limbaugh to walk the border between the unspoken and the (until recently) unspeakable. He both participates in the refurbishment of an openly racist discourse à la *The Bell Curve* and its mainstream press attention and retains the possibility of defending his performance not only as a joke and a neutral attack on liberals but also on the grounds that he didn't say a word.

But if this powerful, banal, silent onlooking fills new functions at the end of the twentieth century, it also should remind us of the need to consider the white look in the much longer run. From slave sales and whippings, to highly publicized and massively attended lynchings, to the world's fair displays of confined nonwhites, to Rush Limbaugh, white consciousness was formed not only out of terror but also out of the mutual, self-recognizing and changing witness of terror, out of white looks at the oppression of others and the privileges of one another.

NOTES

1. Michael North, "The Dialect in/of Modernism: Pound and Eliot's Racial Masquerade," *American Literary History* 4 (Spring 1992): 56–76; Sterling Brown, *Southern Road* (Boston: Beacon Press, 1974), pp. 70–72; Carolyn Karcher, *Shadow over the Promised Land* (Baton Rouge: Louisiana State University Press, 1980), pp. 256–57.

2. Eugene O'Neill, *The Hairy Ape, Anna Christie, The First Man* (New York: Boni and Liveright, 1923), pp. 37–38, 19, 33, 39.

3. Ibid., pp. 44, 84, 42.

4. George Robertson, Melina Mash, Lisa Tickner, Jon Bird, Barry Curtis, and Tim Putnam, eds., *Travelers' Tales: Narratives of Home and Displacement* (London: Routledge, 1994); Linda Nochlin, "The Imaginary Orient," in her *The Politics of Vision* (London: Routledge, 1991); Homi Bhahba, "The Other Question: The Stereotype of Colonial Discourse," *Screen* 24 (1983): 16–36; Catherine Lutz and Jane L. Collins, *Reading National Geographic* (Chicago: University of Chicago Press, 1993); Mary Louise Pratt, *Imperial Eyes: Travel Writing and Transculturation* (London: Routledge, 1992).

5. O'Neill, *Hairy Ape,* p. 21; Donna Haraway, *Primate Visions: Gender, Race and Nature in the World of Modern Science* (New York: Routledge, 1989); Anne McClintock, "Soft-Soaping Empire: Commodity Racism and Imperial Advertising," in Robertson et al., eds., *Travelers' Tales,* p. 139; Stephen Jay Gould, *The Mismeasure of Man* (New York: Norton, 1981), pp. 113–45.

6. Phillips Verner Bradford and Harvey Blume, *Ota: The Pygmy in the Zoo* (New York: St. Martin's Press, 1992), pp. 176, 227–28; Robert Rydell, *All the World's a Fair:*

Visions of Empire at American International Exhibitions (Chicago: University of Chicago Press, 1984); Cornelia Sears, "Man-like Apes and Ape-like Men," paper delivered at the annual meeting of the Organization of American Historians, Washington, DC, 1995.

7. See bell hooks, "Representations of Whiteness," in her *Black Looks: Race and Representations* (London: Turnaround, 1992), pp. 165–78; Richard Dyer, "White," *Screen* 29 (1988): 44–65.

8. Eric Lott, *Love and Theft: Blackface Minstrelsy and the American Working Class* (New York: Oxford University Press, 1993); Alexander Saxton, "Blackface Minstrelsy and Jacksonian Ideology," *American Quarterly* 27 (1975): 3–28.

9. O'Neill, *Hairy Ape,* pp. 30–31.

10. Shelley Fisher Fishkin, *Was Huck Black? Mark Twain and African-American Voices* (New York: Oxford University Press, 1993), pp. 96–99.

11. Pratt, *Imperial Eyes,* pp. 7–9.

12. Twain, "A True Story," in Charles Neider, ed., *The Complete Stories of Mark Twain* (Garden City, NY: Doubleday, 1957), pp. 94–95; James Fenimore Cooper, *Satanshoe* (Albany: State University of New York Press, 1990 [1845]), pp. 70, 69–86.

13. Twain, "True Story," pp. 95, 96, 98; Fishkin, *Was Huck Black?* pp. 8, 7–9, 31–33, 36–38, 99.

14. Karcher, *Shadow over the Promised Land,* pp. 2, 13; Robin D. G. Kelley, " 'We Are Not What We Seem': Rethinking Black Working-Class Opposition in the Jim Crow South," *Journal of American History* 80 (June 1993): 75–112; Leon F. Litwack, *Been in the Storm So Long; The Aftermath of Slavery* (New York: Knopf, 1979), esp. pp. 105–7, 136–38, 155–57; Elsa Barkley Brown, "Negotiating and Transforming the Public Sphere: African-American Political Life in the Transition from Slavery to Freedom," *Public Culture* 7 (1994): 107–46.

15. Coco Fusco, *English Is Broken Here* (New York: New Press, 1995), pp. 37–63; Lutz and Collins, *Reading National Geographic*; Bluford Adams, *Barnumizing Popular Culture* (forthcoming).

16. Giselda Pollock, "Territories of Desire," in Robertson et al., eds., *Travelers' Tales,* p. 77.

17. Anne McClintock, *Imperial Leather: Race, Gender and Sexual Conquest* (New York: Routledge, 1995), pp. 31–36, 207–31; Cheryl Harris, "Whiteness as Property," *Harvard Law Review* 106 (June 1993): 1707–91; Maurice Manring, "Aunt Jemima Explained: The Old South, the Absent Mistress, and the Slave in a Box" (master's thesis, University of Missouri, 1993).

18. Michael Omi and Howard Winant, *Racial Formation in the United States* (New York: Routledge, 1994), pp. 140–42.

19. See David R. Roediger, *Towards the Abolition of Whiteness* (London: Verso, 1994), pp. 6–8. See also Rachel DuPlessis, " 'Hoo, Hoo, Hoo': Some Episodes in the Construction of Modern Whiteness," *American Literature* 67 (December 1995): 671, for the acute observation that the "free white gaze upon blacks is part of the power of whiteness."

The Whitest I: On Reading the Hill–Thomas Transcripts

Michael E. Staub

> We can now stop deluding ourselves about how far we have come on race and gender issues. — Anita Faye Hill, "Marriage and Patronage in the Empowerment and Disempowerment of African American Women"

In *The Alchemy of Race and Rights* (1991), her remarkable book about her experiences as a law professor, Patricia J. Williams tells the story of a first-year law student who arrives in her office in tears. The student is upset about a criminal-law exam in which the problem was to "identify the elements of murder" in an updated version of Shakespeare's *Othello*. According to the exam problem, Othello is an "African leader" who has been "deceived by the wiles of a more sophisticated European" and so is driven to kill "young white Desdemona" in "a fit of sexual rage." When the student argues to an administrator that the exam is racist, she is told that she is "an activist" and "should be more concerned about learning the law and less about the package in which it comes." When Williams speaks to the criminal-law professor on behalf of this student, he tells her that this exam problem "was merely his attempt to respect the minority and feminist quest to bring issues of race, class, and gender more directly into the curriculum." For Williams, this perspective represents "a deep misunderstanding of the struggle, a misunderstanding that threatens to turn the quest for empowering experiential narrative into permission for the most blatant expressions of cynical stereotypification." Williams writes:

> The problem presents a defendant who is black, militaristic, unsophisticated, insecure, jealous, and sexually enraged. It reduces the facts to the very same racist generalizations and stereotypes this nation has used to subjugate black people since the first slave was brought from Africa. Moreover, it places an enormous burden on black students in particular who must assume, for the sake of answering these questions, these things about themselves—this is the trauma of gratuitous generalization. The frame places blacks in the position of speaking against ourselves. It forces us to accept as "truth" constructions that go to the heart of who we are.[1]

I begin with Williams's experiential tale about race, sexuality, and gender relations because of how it reads against that highly charged televised American history that followed it in time: the Clarence Thomas confirmation hearings and the allegations of sexual harassment from law professor Anita Faye Hill[2] (another tale in which Shakespeare's *Othello* played a rhetorical role, a point to which I will return later).

When the Senate hearings of October 11–13, 1991, ended and Thomas had been (narrowly) confirmed to the U.S. Supreme Court, much of Williams's phrasing proved prophetic. It echoed, for example, in the words of Rosemary Bray, who eloquently agonized in the wake of the hearings about how African American women had so often been "asked in a thousand ways, large and small, to take sides against ourselves, postponing a confrontation in one arena to address an equally urgent task in another."[3] And it also resonated when in "a national effort to bring the voice of African American women before the American public,"[4] "African American Women in Defense of Ourselves," a full-page statement signed by 1,603 African American women, appeared in the *New York Times* as well as seven African American newspapers across the United States.[5]

Since November 1991 much has been written about the ways in which Thomas exploited his own purported "experiential narrative" and turned a horribly distorted rendition of African American history—especially the history of lynching—to cynical personal advantage. What Robert Gooding-Williams once so astutely observed with regard to the Rodney King beating and the Simi Valley verdict—that they "implicated so much of what is repugnant, though ordinary, in postmodern and post–Civil Rights America"—applies also to the Hill–Thomas hearings.[6]

The hearings and accompanying discussions intersected with ongoing and unresolved problems in this nation's racial, gender, and class relations and its partisan politics and political life more generally. All these issues were addressed in both academic and more popular venues. Important academic contributions, for example, can be found in Toni Morrison's *Race-ing Justice, En-gendering Power*; the special issues of *Black Scholar* and the *Southern California Law Review*; an excellent piece by Nancy Fraser in *Critical Inquiry*; *Race, Gender, and Power in America,* a collection edited by Hill herself together with Emma Coleman Jordan; and a collection, *African American Women Speak Out,* edited by Geneva Smitherman and composed solely of contributions by African American women. Although neglected by the media at the time, the voices of black women are finally getting a hearing.

Like the earlier Morrison anthology, the two most recent books make black women's voices central in both their authorship and their subjects. Both rectify—with brilliance and passion—the hearings' and the media's outrageous neglect of the history of the sexual abuse and malicious stereotyping of black women.[7] Both point to the paradoxical but effective way that race and gender were pitted against each other in the course of the hearings and accompanying discussions and how Hill was de-racialized and put in the "gender corner" while Thomas was put in the "race section of the arena," even as Hill was also subjected to grotesque racial stereotyping.[8] Both call for attention to the complicated "intersectionalities" (critical race theorist Kimberlé Crenshaw's term) of race and gender. And both also raise the painful issue of tensions over sex and gender within the black community.

But in all this crucial attention to the complexities of African American lives, the issue of whiteness—and the particularities of the white senators' (mis)management of the hearings—has gone out of focus. Certainly no one would argue that a lesson of the Hill–Thomas controversy is how the underrepresented voices of white men need to be brought before the American public. There they were—front and center—interrogating, with gross impunity, both Thomas and Hill about intimate sexual matters. Yet—in odd but significant ways—the hearings did find politically powerful white men speaking against (and among) themselves, with serious consequences for many aspects of American society. It might not be an overstatement to say that the Hill–Thomas hearings were one of the more influential moments in the contemporary history of American whiteness.

I suggest that looking at how whiteness functioned in the Hill–Thomas hearings helps illuminate a number of broader developments, among them the tensions within contemporary American whiteness, the changing shape of American racism, and the consolidation of a sophisticated and highly successful right-wing assault on both leftism and liberalism. Among many other things, the Hill–Thomas hearings were a benchmark tragic moment within the broader 1980s–1990s dismantling and rewriting of the progressive legacy of the 1960s (and earlier and later efforts for civil rights)—what Williams calls "the struggle." It was the phenomenon of what Williams termed that "deep misunderstanding of the struggle" that preoccupied me in my investigation of how whiteness functioned in the Hill–Thomas hearings.

After all the analyses, what I still find amazing is that the obfuscations and wholesale rewritings of (both historical and contemporaneous) reality generated by Thomas and his Republican sponsors triumphed. That triumph is surely a testimony to the depth and persistence of both racism and sexism (and their interconnections) in this country, as both the Smitherman and Hill/Jordan books indicate. It is also a testimony to the extraordinarily complicated—and still inadequately understood—changes taking place in both of these forms of prejudice. There is a need to explain not only how Thomas fooled the senators (if in fact they were fooled)[9] but also how the senators together with Thomas fooled large parts of the public.

Different theories for Thomas's and the Republicans' success have been devised. In the Hill/Jordan collection, Adele Logan Alexander points out that given the ferociousness of the lies about black womanhood (as indiscriminately sexual, emotionally infantile, unintelligent, and lacking in veracity and virtue) that are so pervasive and persistent in this country, it was almost impossible for the all-male, all-white Senate committee to respond differently than they did to Hill's allegations. That is, she believes that given the power of these stereotypes, the results of the hearings were almost a foregone conclusion.[10]

Charles J. Ogletree Jr. offers a powerful complementary explanation, documenting in detail how the "procedural flaws in the concept and execution of the hearings" (the way it turned into a trial of Hill, because there was no way for her counsel to "raise objections" and no fairly applied rules of evidence) made their results practically inevitable.[11] Judith Resnik reminds her readers of, and also offers compelling evidence for, the Senate's sexism and the extraordinary recentness (and superficiality) of any concern for women's rights. Smitherman's collection pays more attention to the impact of the hearings on the African American public (implicitly revealing how polls' reports of black public opinion affected white public opinion as well). Smitherman herself offers important insights into Thomas's relatively greater success in using traditional African American linguistic strategies to reach past the white senators to major segments of the black TV audience. Linda F. Williams analyzes the current crisis in black leadership, and a number of contributors explore the painful legacies of racism and sexism that caused many African American women, in particular, to turn against Hill.

When I watched the hearings in October 1991, it seemed obvious to me that another major reason for the travesty of justice that occurred that weekend had to do with the fact that all the Democrats seemed hamstrung by their own whiteness while the Republicans were able to make their whiteness work for them. Despite the plethora of publications that the hearings provoked, how whiteness functioned in these pieces has received almost no direct attention. Numerous essays both at the time and since noted that the Senate Judiciary Committee was all-male and all-white, and many refer to "white male power and privilege" or "white male political hegemony" and even occasionally to the dynamics of "white guilt," but none offers a sustained analysis of how white identities operated in the hearings.

This chapter, therefore, is my response to reading the published transcripts of the hearings, with a special focus on the Judiciary Committee's whiteness. When I read through the transcripts in search of written evidence of what I had sensed while watching the hearings on TV, whiteness operated in quite elusive and, at times, truly bizarre ways. In general, I tried to understand how the different senators' whiteness structured their approach to Hill's allegations, to Thomas's denials and countercharges, and to the testimony of witnesses on both sides.

I approached this project with the following questions:

Who among the fourteen senators laid claim to his own white identity, who tried to erase it, and how?

Which senators made race an issue, and which ones tried to erase race as an issue?

How were the pro-Thomas forces able to misappropriate so successfully the history of lynching (and all its attendant meanings), so that nobody involved with the hearings could correct them?[12] Indeed, how is it that they, the senators, could presume to educate the American public about the long-standing "intersectionalities" of race and sexuality in this country, specifically in regard to black manhood?

Furthermore, how were the pro-Thomas forces able to get away with being so blatantly racist toward Anita Hill and then succeed in styling themselves as antiracist? And finally, how were the Republicans able to present the Republican Party as the champion of African American rights while linking the Democratic Party with white racism (thereby turning inside out the conventional wisdom about which party has stood for what, at least since the civil rights movement)?

These questions cannot be answered without considering the changing shape of American racism. Although there recently has been a proliferation of books and essays examining white identities and, more generally, the construct of whiteness, whiteness scholarship is only beginning to come to terms with the complexities of the recent shifts, increasingly encapsulated in the term the *new cultural racism*. Cultural studies scholars and, above all, critical race theory legal scholars have done the most to explore the new developments.[13] They are analyzing new cultural racist phenomena such as the consideration of multiculturalism's celebration of diversity in order to legitimize "white pride"[14] or, in an interesting contrast, the use of calls for legal color blindness in order to stress "whites' victimization"—most evident today in the backlash against affirmative action.[15] They also are analyzing the way that the new cultural racists rely on coded cultural references that, though seemingly race neutral, nonetheless contain raced messages (such as disdainful references to "welfare queens" or "the inner city").[16]

The insights generated by these scholars help make sense of several inadequately understood aspects of the Hill–Thomas hearings. At least three features of the new cultural racism emerge as relevant when trying to elucidate how whiteness worked during the hearings. One is that the new cultural racism takes its strength from its contradictory applications. Another is that it relies on an inversion or misappropriation of antiracist conventions. (Particularly important here is the new level of aggressive sophistication on the Right, for which middle-of-the-road liberals' self-presentation as "objective" and "fair" is no match.) The third feature is that racial references are also being strategically deployed in intrawhite ideological conflicts.

Eve Kosofsky Sedgwick points out in her discussions of contemporary sexual politics that conservatives have been able to use successfully for their own strategic ends not only "knowledge" (in the Foucauldian sense) but also "ignorance."[17] This insight could well be applied also to racial politics. One important racial strategy the pro-Thomas senators used was situating their own whiteness as vastly distant and "different" from Thomas's blackness.

This technique allowed Senator Orrin Hatch, in particular, to position himself as ignorant (and thus innocent) of Thomas's "authentic" inside knowledge and experience of blackness. During the Saturday, October 12, session of the hearings, when Thomas stated that Hill's allegations were "playing into a stereotype," Hatch remarked, "What an interesting concept that you have just raised."[18] Although (as his prepared comments confirm), Hatch was not caught off guard, the senator acted as if he were a racial know-nothing: "When you talk in terms of stereotypes, what are you saying here? I mean I want to understand this. . . . You said some of this language is stereotype language? What does that mean, I don't understand" (pp. 201–2).[19] Such a line of "questioning" subsequently allowed Hatch to linger on each of Hill's allegations in lurid detail and then consult with Thomas as to whether or not it represented "a black stereotype" (pp. 202–3).

In one stroke, then, Hatch portrayed Hill as a traitor to her race and himself as the concerned antiracist. No doubt, too, Hatch's role playing invited white viewers to see in his racial innocence a version of their own. Other pro-Thomas senators soon joined in the white innocence/ignorance act. Dennis DeConcini, for example, the only pro-Thomas Democrat, speculated that this was all about "uppity blacks being different or something" (p. 407). Republican Charles Grassley, in a related vein, wanted to know why some blacks felt that Thomas "doesn't even speak our language": "What is meant by that? I honestly don't know" (p. 379).

Hatch's rhetorical maneuver, in short, quickly gained adherents and so structured much of what followed during the hearings. The result was to set up Thomas as the expert on anything relating to blackness, establishing his rendition of his own life as unchallengeable by any white man. It was, in sum, a preemptive strike against those senators resistant to Thomas's confirmation. Indeed, when his questioning time was up, Hatch was no longer puzzled. "The burden of proof," he announced with sudden authority, "is on those who use statements that are stereotypical statements" (p. 214). Moreover, Hatch had earlier used a related technique to silence Democratic Senator Howell Heflin: "He [Thomas] has personal knowledge of this [lynching]" (p. 161).[20]

But significantly, the Republicans' strategies were contradictory. For example, at other points, there was no gulf between black and white worlds, with the pro-Thomas senators recurrently citing how well known and familiar Thomas was to them. Hatch, for instance, repeatedly remarked to Thomas that "I have known you almost 11 years" (p. 184). And Alan Simpson announced, "I have known you for several years, and I have known Ginny [Virginia Thomas] before I knew you" (p. 253). Thomas, Simpson effused, was "a man of joy . . . and laughter and a great friend to be around" (p. 301).[21]

This approach was supplemented most strikingly by another variety of white validation, best exemplified by Strom Thurmond, formerly famous for his virulent racism and antimiscegenation efforts.[22] Thurmond hardly participated in the hearings at all, but he did intervene once to stress how "clean" a man Thomas was (p. 414).

That such pro-Thomas rhetoric passed as antiracism was disturbing enough, but even worse was the blatant effort to demonize Anita Hill. She was cast as a hapless puppet of white feminism, a scorned and deluded woman with a perverse imagination, an egomaniac, a martyr for civil rights, or (according to Arlen Specter) a black woman with "a possible concern" that Thomas preferred "dating" women "of a lighter complexion" (p. 264).[23] In short, Hill became both "whitened," in contrast to Thomas (whose black masculinity was made to stand in for blackness in general), and a contradictory bundle of nearly every ugly stereotype about black womanhood that the pro-Thomas senators could conjure up.[24]

At the same time, Specter (Hill's main questioner) also used coded references to race by implicitly contrasting his own whiteness (represented as rational, precise, highly literate, and empirically grounded) with Hill's blackness, which he not too subtly linked to a hyperbolic African American oral tradition—a set of racist mental associations well analyzed by such scholars as Richard Dyer and Henry Louis Gates Jr.[25] "Why not make notes?" Specter asked Hill, adding that "the notes would have been something which would have been done by an experienced lawyer" (p. 79). In his later remarks, Specter repeatedly referred to "the expanded nature of the charges" and "those expanded charges" made by Hill. He emphasized that Hill had "substantially enlarged a testimony" against Thomas, something that "because I wrote this down, it is difficult for me to understand" (p. 134). Specter's coded references to race turned Hill into a teller of tall tales; her variant narratives were always different; she never got her story straight. The senator, meanwhile, mastered the written record, cross-checking references as a law clerk would, and, finally, using his "findings" to conclude that Hill had committed "flat-out perjury" (p. 230).

At the other end of the senators' table sat the Democrats who, largely as a consequence of Thomas's explosive accusations, scrambled to erase their own whiteness. The Democrats most sympathetic to Hill, Ted Kennedy and Herbert Kohl, actually insisted that the hearings were not about race. In his single most dramatic statement, Kennedy announced, "I hope we are not going to hear a lot more about racism as we consider this nominee. The fact is that these points of sexual harassment are made by an Afro-American against an Afro-American. The issue isn't discrimination and racism. It is about sexual harassment" (p. 308). Kohl made nearly identical remarks, asking pro-Thomas witnesses J. C. Alvarez and Phyllis Berry on Sunday: "How do we wind up saying this is a

racist conspiracy" when "I mean aren't we all here and hasn't a Senate committee convened to hold this hearing, because of a charge leveled at an African-
American man by an African-American woman?" (p. 424). Their goal in
pointing out that the charges against Thomas had been brought by a black and
not a white woman was meant, however, less to educate the American public
about the ways in which the Republicans were misusing the lynching metaphor
and opportunistically invoking racism in general—since neither directly challenged their abuse of the metaphor or the Republicans' decidedly uneven
application of "antiracism"—than to absolve themselves of the charge that they
were members of a "high-tech" lynching party.

The larger number of Democrats who continually avowed their own objec-
tivity and impartiality also tried to downplay their own whiteness. Chairman
Joseph Biden was the classic example. Oddly, awkwardly, and even paradoxically teetering between obsequious fawning and efforts at male bonding, Biden
strove to direct attention away from race by focusing on a shared masculinity
with the African American men he questioned—and yet he also indulged in
white fantasies about black manhood. With Clarence Thomas, for example,
Biden tried rather unsuccessfully to talk football:

> Let's say that you and I are sitting and watching a football game and you watch
> some 280-pound tackle blow away a 158-pound flankerback. You and I might
> describe that in a way, sitting with one another and both having played football,
> that we would not describe in the same way if there were five women sitting in
> the room. (p. 222)

When Thomas categorically asserted that "I would describe it the same way,"
Biden summarily dropped his line of questioning—as his flankerback suddenly
lost a lot of weight: "Well, that's interesting. Maybe that is because you were
closer to the 280-pound lineman and I was closer to the 130-pound flankerback [Laughter]" (p. 222). Likewise, in Biden's equally fruitless effort to
defuse John Doggett's charge that Hill was "unstable" and "had fantasized
about my being interested in her romantically" (p. 554), the senator flattered
Doggett as a "virile person" and deprecated himself: "Maybe I am just accustomed to being, turned down more than you were, when I was younger" (p.
556).

Biden stumbled even more conspicuously into an inadvertent reinforcement
of precisely the kind of racist stereotypes the Republicans had been high-
lighting so effectively when he tried the male-bonding maneuver with Hill's
former boyfriend John Carr:

THE CHAIRMAN: Was she [Hill] someone who yielded to intellectual or any other kind of pressure?

MR. CARR: I would not call her malleable. I don't recall strenuous intellectual debate with her.

THE CHAIRMAN: I guess that wasn't what you had in mind [Laughter.] I don't mean that in a bad way. I wasn't trying to be facetious. . . . I should drop this. [Laughter.]

SENATOR HATCH: Yes, you should drop that. (p. 328)

But Biden's most unfortunate encounter with his own whiteness came in a conversation with Professor Nancy Fitch. Biden seemed to hope that Fitch would help him clarify the historical record about African American woman-hood. Biden appealed to Fitch's authority "as a black historian" and asked whether "to immediately question the veracity of a black woman [like Hill] . . . doesn't that just as neatly fit into a stereotypical treatment of black women who dare speak up? That's my question" (p. 426). Fitch, however, pointed out that the problem of stereotyping black women "comes first from their experiences with white men in this country." Biden rushed to reassure her: "I agree with that—":

MS. FITCH: Yes.

THE CHAIRMAN [continuing]: I agree with that, with white men.

MS. FITCH [continuing]: Yes, and of course, it can be extended to any other men.

THE CHAIRMAN: I understand, okay, thank you for clarifying that. (p. 426)

Brought up short by his own whiteness, Biden's actually quite relevant questions about the stereotyping of black women were abruptly abandoned—and never returned to.

Most striking is the contrast between the Democrats' insecurity and the Republicans' confidence in regard to acknowledging their own white identities. One instance made the Republican confidence especially clear. On Saturday afternoon, not long before Thomas's day-long testimony ended, Alan Simpson of Wyoming announced that "I do love Shakespeare, and Shakespeare would love this" (p. 255). Having just referred to his long-standing friendship with Virginia Thomas (who sat right behind her husband), Simpson added:

This is all Shakespeare. This is about love and hate, and cheating and distrust, and kindness and disgust, and avarice and jealousy and envy, all those things that make that remarkable bard read today. But boy, I will tell you, one came to my head, and I just went and got it out of the back of the book. Othello, read Othello,

and don't ever forget this line . . . Who steals my purse, steals trash. Tis something, nothing. Twas mine, tis his, and has been slave to thousands. But he that
filches from me my good name, robs me of that which not enriches him, and
makes me poor indeed. (p. 255)

Simpson was presumably linking Thomas to Othello because both were
black men who had been asked to explain their innermost romantic feelings to
an all-white Senate. And certainly, too, Simpson was linking Hill to Iago: a
trusted associate who became a betrayer by deliberately playing on a black
man's sexual anxiety and racial alienation.[26] Moments later, Thomas himself
echoed Simpson quoting Shakespeare:

I have already lost. I have lost my name . . . I have lost everything in this process.
I am here not to be confirmed; I am here to get my name back. All I have to
gain from this process is to salvage a little bit of my integrity and a little bit of my
name. Nothing more. (p. 258)

What really happened here? Simpson was actually quoting Iago, the deceit-
ful white man, and not the innocent black Othello; Iago spoke those words, in
a clever sort of con game, in order to gain Othello's trust.[27] Marjorie Garber
interprets Simpson's choice of source as an unwitting revelation of his own
hypocrisy. She sees his deployment of Shakespeare as indicative of a broader
phenomenon of "quoting Shakespeare out of context" in the way she notes
that many public figures do: as an "apparently apolitical gesture," a middlebrow
Bartlett's Quotations way to authorize and lend moral weight to one's own
position and to assert its transhistorical truth value.[28] But (in view of the larger
patterns of pro-Thomas strategy) another reading of this moment is possible—
one that starts from the assumption that Simpson was really quite alert to the
racial and sexual themes structuring *Othello*.

In the tradition of blackface minstrelsy and the Amos 'n' Andy radio shows,
white men adopted black personae for humorous or dramatic effect. Now—
by pretending to blacken up while he played a white role—and particularly by
getting Thomas to restate (and thereby lend black "authenticity" to) Iago's
words, Simpson simultaneously built on and inverted blackface conventions.
Conveniently—and significantly—this maneuver also allowed Simpson to
bring into focus the white woman (Desdemona in the play/Virginia on the
TV screen) who, in white mythology, often provided the pretext for a lynching
(and whose existence Kennedy and Kohl sought so strenuously to deny),
thereby once again reinforcing the most effective metaphor of the entire
weekend.[29] Simpson's citation of one of literary history's most famous white

deceivers may well have constituted a moment of remarkable self-reflexivity. The fact that Simpson did it—and got away with it, despite the Democratic staffers responsible for checking into literary references—suggests a great deal about the pro-Thomas position's supreme arrogance.

As the various strategies used by the pro-Thomas senators suggest, the key to the Right's new politics of race is the confusion of categories: the mixing and matching of old and new forms of racism and (perhaps most crucial here) the appropriation of progressive strategies for conservative ends. Perhaps unlike Patricia Williams, who suggests that the criminal-law professor who "updated" *Othello* engaged in "a deep misunderstanding of the struggle," I believe that the practitioners of the new cultural racism rely too much on a deep understanding of both the struggle and what is currently at stake. Over the years since the 1960s, many progressive scholars and activists have called for critical interrogations of a race-neutral stance and the validation of minority subject-positions, for attention to the burdens and legacies of history, and for white self-referentiality.

One of the many tragedies of the Hill–Thomas hearings was the revelation that the Right has learned more from the Left than the liberal middle has. Rarely has the poverty of self-styled neutralism been so apparent. Anita Hill had no advocates. What we saw was a bunch of white men running for cover— while other white men chased them.

NOTES

For their supportive comments on earlier drafts of this essay, many thanks to Dagmar Herzog, Mike Hill, Victor Jew, Eric Lott, David Roediger, and Geneva Smitherman.

1. Patricia J. Williams, *The Alchemy of Race and Rights* (Cambridge, MA: Harvard University Press, 1991), pp. 81–83.

2. For Williams's most recent reflections on the Hill–Thomas controversy, see the essay "Clarence X" in her *The Rooster's Egg* (Cambridge, MA: Harvard University Press, 1995), pp. 121–36.

3. Rosemary Bray, "Taking Sides Against Ourselves," *New York Times Magazine,* November 17, 1991, p. 56.

4. Geneva Smitherman, introduction to Geneva Smitherman, ed., *African American Women Speak out on Anita Hill–Clarence Thomas* (Detroit: Wayne State University Press, 1995), p. 10.

5. "African American Women in Defense of Ourselves," *New York Times,* November 17, 1991, p. 19.

6. Robert Gooding-Williams, "Introduction: On Being Stuck," in Robert Gooding-Williams, ed., *Reading Rodney King/Reading Urban Uprising* (New York: Routledge, 1993), p. 11.

7. Particularly important here are the essays by Elsa Barkley Brown, "Imagining Lynching: African American Women, Communities of Struggle, and Collective Memory," pp. 100–24; and Darlene Clark Hine, "For Pleasure, Profit, and Power: The Sexual Exploitation of Black Women," pp. 168–77, both in *African American Women Speak Out*; and by Adele Logan Alexander, " 'She's No Lady, She's a Nigger': Abuses, Stereotypes, and Realities from the Middle Passage to Capitol (and Anita) Hill," pp. 3–25; A. Leon Higginbotham Jr., "The Hill–Thomas Hearings—What Took Place and What Happened: White Male Domination, Black Male Domination, and the Denigration of Black Women," pp. 26–36; and Emma Coleman Jordan, "The Power of False Racial Memory and the Metaphor of Lynching," pp. 37–55, all in Anita Faye Hill and Emma Coleman Jordan, eds., *Race, Gender, and Power in America: The Legacy of the Hill–Thomas Hearings* (New York: Oxford University Press, 1995).

8. Linda Susan Beard, "Of Metaphors and Meaning: Language, Ways of Knowing, Memory Holes, and a Political Recall," in Smitherman, ed., *African American Women Speak Out,* p. 185. A pertinent insight into the ways that Thomas, as both an honorary white man and a black man, obtained immunity from answering charges—while Hill was forced to acquire the negative characteristics associated with both white and black women—is provided by Jordan, "The Power of False Racial Memory," esp. p. 38.

9. Compare on this point Judith Resnik, "From the Senate Judiciary Committee to the Country Courthouse: The Relevance of Gender, Race, and Ethnicity to Adjudication," in Hill and Jordan, eds., *Race, Gender, and Power in America,* p. 107.

10. Alexander, " 'She's No Lady, She's a Nigger,' " esp. pp. 5, 16–17, 19.

11. Charles J. Ogletree Jr., "The People vs. Anita Hill: A Case for Client-Centered Advocacy," in Hill and Jordan, eds., *Race, Gender, and Power in America,* p. 142.

12. Note that the "lynching" concept was publicly introduced not by Thomas but by a white Republican, Senator John C. Danforth, Thomas's chief sponsor in the Senate, who brought it up in a news conference before the hearings even began. See Tom Wicker, "Blaming Anita Hill," *New York Times* (national ed.), October 10, 1991, p. A17. The "lynching" idea achieved a kind of apotheosis in a commentary by Peggy Noonan about Judge Thomas: "Regular Americans *do* think he's being lynched, not because he's a black man—they saw Robert Bork swinging from the same tree—but because he is a conservative." Noonan, "A Bum Ride," *New York Times,* October 15, 1991, p. A15.

13. Compare Kimberlé Crenshaw, Neil Gotanda, Gary Peller, and Kendall Thomas, eds., *Critical Race Theory* (New York: New Press, 1995).

14. See the analysis by Henry A. Giroux, "Living Dangerously: Identity Politics and the New Cultural Racism: Towards a Critical Pedagogy of Representation," *Cultural Studies* 7 (January 1993): 1–27.

15. Two especially good examples of critical race theory legal scholars' analyses of these misappropriations are provided by Thomas Ross, "Innocence and Affirmative Action," *Vanderbilt Law Review* 43 (March 1990): 297–316; and Patricia Williams, "The Obliging Shell: An Informal Essay on Formal Equal Opportunity," *Michigan Law Review* 87 (August 1989): 2128–51. Notable court decisions that illustrate the tendency to use

"color blindness" for whites' benefit include *Richmond v. Croson* (1989) and *Reno v. Shaw* (1993). In recent years, such examples have seemed to proliferate. Note the debate surrounding the Clinton administration's decision to bring suit against Illinois State University "over a program to train janitors that excluded white males." See Neil Lewis, "U.S. Sues College over Training That Bars White Men as Janitors," *New York Times,* March 4, 1995, p. A1. Also note the "bitter conflict surrounding university affirmative action policies" at both the University of California and the University of Texas. See Peter Applebourne, "Two Decisions Reflect Bitter Conflict Surrounding University Affirmative Action Policies," *New York Times,* March 22, 1996, p. A12.

16. See especially Patricia J. Williams, "Lani, We Hardly Knew Ye," *Village Voice,* June 15, 1993, pp. 25–28; Howard Winant, "Difference and Inequality: Postmodern Racial Politics in the United States," in Malcolm Cross and Michael Keith, eds., *Racism, the City, and the State* (New York: Routledge, 1993), pp. 108–27; and Michael Omi and Howard Winant, "The Los Angeles 'Race Riot' and Contemporary U.S. Politics," in Gooding-Williams, ed., *Reading Rodney King,* pp. 97–114.

17. See Eve Kosofsky Sedgwick, *Epistemology of the Closet* (Berkeley and Los Angeles: University of California Press, 1990), pp. 4–8.

18. *Hearings Before the Committee on the Judiciary United States Senate One Hundred Second Congress First Session on the Nomination of Clarence Thomas to Be Associate Justice of the Supreme Court of the United States, October 11, 12, and 13, 1991: Part 4 of 4 Parts* (Washington, DC: U.S. Government Printing Office, 1993), p. 201. All further quotations from the hearings are from this volume. The transcripts have also been published in Anita Miller, ed., *The Complete Transcripts of the Clarence Thomas–Anita Hill Hearings: October 11, 12, 13, 1991* (Chicago: Academy Chicago Publishers, 1994).

19. Hatch went on like this: "Well, I saw—I didn't understand the television program, there were two black men—I may have it wrong, but as I recall—there were two black men talking about this matter and one of them said, she is trying to demonize us. I didn't understand it at the time. Do you understand it?" (p. 202). Despite the ritual incantations of his own ignorance, however, Hatch was actually well prepared, for in the midst of his questioning of Thomas, he introduced "an interesting case that I found" from 1988 in which precisely the stereotype Thomas had just been "educating" him about (an elongated black penis—"Long Dong Silver") played a crucial role (pp. 203–4). (Hatch's goal in this moment was to imply that Hill had drawn her allegations against Thomas not from her own experience with him but, rather, from the University of Oklahoma law library).

20. This particular technique was elaborated even further in John C. Danforth, *Resurrection: The Confirmation of Clarence Thomas* (New York: Viking Press, 1994), pp. 10–11.

21. Simpson was referring to a statement by Senator John Danforth, who had said that Thomas "is his own person. That is my first point. Second, he laughs. [Laughter] To some, this may seem a trivial matter. . . . I concede that there is something weird about Clarence Thomas. It's his laugh. It is the loudest laugh I have ever heard. It comes from deep inside, and it shakes his body." Quoted in Toni Morrison, "Introduction: Friday on the Potomac," in Toni Morrison, ed., *Race-ing Justice, En-gendering Power: Essays on Anita Hill, Clarence Thomas, and the Construction of Social Reality* (New York: Pantheon, 1992), p. xii. As Morrison notes: "Weird? Not at all. Neither the laugh

nor Danforth's reference to it. Every black person who heard those words understood. . . . For whites who require it, [laughter] is the gesture of accommodation and obedience needed to open discussion with a black person and certainly to continue it" (p. xiii).

22. In 1991, Thurmond justified his "new" racial position by stating that black people "had developed and developed and come up and we've got to acknowledge people when they deserve to be acknowledged, and the black people deserve to be acknowledged." Quoted in Nadine Cohodas, *Strom Thurmond and the Politics of Southern Change* (New York: Simon & Schuster, 1993), p. 497.

23. See also David Brock's speculation that Hill "knowingly [made] a false charge of sexual harassment against Clarence Thomas" because she "may have been suffering from some kind of love–hate complex" due to an "obsessive, even perverse, desire for male attention." For Brock, "the real Anita Hill"—to cite the title of his best-selling book—"may be a bit nutty, and a bit slutty." David Brock, "The Real Anita Hill," *American Spectator* 25 (March 1992): 25, 27. Also see a *New York Times* review that labels Brock's position "carefully reasoned and powerful in its logic." Christopher Lehmann-Haupt, "Assembling a Case Against Anita Hill," *New York Times,* April 26, 1993, p. B2. For invaluable criticism of Brock's "theory," see Jane Mayer and Jill Abramson, "The Surreal Anita Hill," *New Yorker,* May 24, 1993, pp. ˙90–96; and Deirdre English, "Un-Telling the Story," *The Nation,* June 28, 1993, pp. 910–15. In "Jane and Jill and Anita Hill," *American Spectator,* August 1993, pp. 24–30, Brock responds to his critics. These debates continue in Jane Mayer and Jill Abramson, *Strange Justice: The Selling of Clarence Thomas* (Boston: Houghton Mifflin, 1994); and Danforth, *Resurrection.*

24. For especially incisive analyses of the "whitening" and "blackening" of Hill and the senators' mobilization of black female stereotypes, see Nancy Fraser, "Sex, Lies, and the Public Sphere: Some Reflections on the Confirmation of Clarence Thomas," *Critical Inquiry* 18 (Spring 1992): 595–612; Wahneema Lubiano, "Black Ladies, Welfare Queens, and State Minstrels: Ideological War by Narrative Means," in Morrison, ed., *Race-ing Justice, En-gendering Power,* pp. 323–63; Kimberlé Crenshaw, "Race, Gender, and Sexual Harassment," *Southern California Law Review* 65 (March 1992): 1467–76; Nell Irvin Painter, "Who Was Lynched?" *The Nation,* November 11, 1991, p. 577; and Charles R. Lawrence III, "Cringing at Myths of Black Sexuality," in Robert Chrisman and Robert L. Allen, eds., *Court of Appeal: The Black Community Speaks out on the Racial and Sexual Politics of Clarence Thomas vs. Anita Hill* [the essays from *Black Scholar*] (New York: Ballantine Books, 1992), pp. 136–38.

25. For example, see Richard Dyer, "White," *Screen* 29 (1988): 44–49; and Henry Louis Gates Jr., "Writing 'Race' and the Difference It Makes," in Henry Louis Gates Jr., ed., *"Race," Writing and Difference* (Chicago: University of Chicago Press, 1986), pp. 1–20.

26. Compare Stephen Greenblatt's discussion of *Othello* in his *Renaissance Self-Fashioning: From More to Shakespeare* (Chicago: University of Chicago Press, 1980), esp. pp. 233–54.

27. See *Othello* 3.3.154–60.

28. Marjorie Garber, "Character Assassination: Shakespeare, Anita Hill, and *JFK,*" in Marjorie Garber, Janne Matlock, and Rebecca Walkowitz, eds., *Media Spectacles* (New York: Routledge, 1993), pp. 25, 31, 26. For a fuller exposition of Garber's

argument on popular appropriations of Shakespeare, see her *Shakespeare's Ghost Writers: Literature as Uncanny Causality* (New York: Methuen, 1987).

29. For one of the best and most subtle analyses of the many ways in which the lynching metaphor worked, see Jordan, "The Power of False Racial Memory." For additional insight into the visual impact of Virginia Thomas's presence, see Anna Deavere Smith, "The Most Riveting Television: The Hill–Thomas Hearings and Popular Culture," in Hill and Jordan, eds., *Race, Gender, and Power in America,* pp. 264–65.

5

Bulletproof Settlers: The Politics of Offense in the New South Africa

Grant Farred

You wanna keep me down keep me down, Revolution,
against this racist institution.
The white man shall sleep forever with one eye open.

Me'shell NdegeOcello, *Plantation Lullabies*

[T]o overcome racism in one's personal experience or in collective experience is not simply a matter of abandoning prejudice or opening one's eyes to reality with the possible help of science; it has to do with changing one's mode of thinking, something much more difficult.

Etienne Balibar, *Masses, Classes, Ideas*

THE CULTURE OF WHITE CONFIDENCE

Richard Rive's *"Buckingham Palace," District Six,* a moving account of apartheid-engineered deracination in 1960s Cape Town, concludes with an injunction rare and prescient in its historical force. Published in 1986, Rive's novel issues a call to arms unusual in its ability to echo with a disturbing urgency and unexpected resonance in the new South Africa. Surveying the devastation of District Six, a vibrant community located on the fringes of downtown Cape Town, Rive's protagonist is defiant in his challenge to his fellow black South Africans: "We must never forget."[1] District Six, a mainly colored neighborhood that was also home to Indians, whites and blacks, was among the many racially mixed areas systematically razed by apartheid's bulldozers. Sophiatown in Johannesburg and Marabastad in Pretoria were among the other prominent communities to suffer this same fate.

Against the backdrop of the Afrikaner regime's innumerable injustices over some forty years, why would *Buckingham Palace*'s injunction bear so much

63

weight? Surely the legacy of apartheid is too recent to be forgotten by the newly enfranchised black community. Who needs to be reminded that the National Party government's rule was marked by violent repressions; the devastation of black communities such as District Six, Sophiatown, and Marabastad; and brutal incarcerations? At first glance it seems incomprehensible that black South Africans' struggle to remember this history is today an inordinately onerous task. It was only in 1990 that political prisoners such as Nelson Mandela were released and the black liberation movements were unbanned.

In the current climate of racial conciliation, however, the battle to retain the memories of oppression is not such an inconceivable struggle. Black South Africans are located at a crucial historical juncture representing the potentialities and vulnerabilities of the early postcolonial or postrevolutionary moment. (Neither of these conditions, individually or collectively, fully or accurately, describes black South Africans' current position, but they are the most historically analogous.) The moment at which a majority assumes political authority after a sustained period of oppression is beset with challenges, possibilities, and uncertainties. The newly empowered have to negotiate the history (histories) of the past, the demands of the present, and the anticipations for the future. The founding moment of the new society is one in which all these historical forces coincide, overlap, blur, jostle, and overwrite one another. It is the conjuncture at which the production of national memory presents itself as a predicament. Charged with the responsibility of creating a postindependence culture, the historically oppressed must engage the demands of their location: the convergence of forgetting and remembering.

Which memories of subjugation should be retained? Which moments of struggle should be enshrined and celebrated in the new society? Which have to be discarded? Which memories will inhibit or aid the process of postapartheid nation building? Confronted with a situation in which blacks are constitutionally enfranchised but still significantly impoverished, undereducated (both by dint of apartheid ideology), and, most important, dependent on white capital, the new African National Congress (ANC) government decided on political accommodation. By adopting a policy of national reconciliation, the ANC implicitly requires that its black citizenry forget (presumably by absolving their white counterparts) or only selectively recall instances of the apartheid state's repression and exploitation. Self-induced historical amnesia, always an essential part of the post-independence/apartheid political imaginary, is a central feature of the new South African culture.

This is not to say that the ANC's privileging of racial reconciliation over ethnic and racial differences is historically inexplicable. There are sound economic, political, and strategic reasons for pursuing this course. Economically, this policy makes sense because South Africa's wealth is controlled by whites, whom the new black-dominated government does not want to antagonize; they are still, it is tacitly acknowledged, the ruling class. Politically, the ANC has a long history of nonracial campaigning, and it can now use this tradition strategically in the project of reconciliation. Moreover, how can they produce a sense of national identity without a strong rhetorical appeal to postapartheid unity? The past, overdetermined as it is by racism, numerous injustices, and deeply ingrained ethnic divisions, is unusable unless it is refashioned as a discerning political tool. The apartheid past must become an ideological tool that is used sparingly, and occasionally expediently, in the new era of nonracial electoral campaigns. There are, however, potentially serious historical consequences for embracing this approach. A diminution of the past's significance may estrange large and important sectors of the black community. Already there are constituencies for whom the new government's narrative of reconciliation is an alien, even ironic, prospect.

Most prominent in the ranks of the disaffected is the black nationalist–inspired Pan African Congress (PAC). For the PAC, the exploitation of black workers by white-controlled industry and the violences inflicted on blacks by the apartheid regime is still an all too vivid and historically immediate experience. Animating this discontent is the pressing reality that black subjugation continues to be the dominant experience of a community nominally enfranchised but still economically disempowered. It is on this volatile terrain, in the interregnum between reconciliation and disaffection, that ideological tensions regarding class and race abound. This is the theater in which the potentially explosive incommensurability between the articulations of reconciliation and the dominant black experience of poverty is being staged. The dynamic of this idiosyncratic interregnum—a condition that concurrently provides the space in which the major conflicts of the new society can be conducted and facilitates the production of a postapartheid culture (with its attendant problematic of white confidence)—is the ideological space that this chapter explores. This is a crucial political terrain because it is here that the national culture is ostensibly replacing color as an ideological hegemony. All the while, however, the real hegemony, white property, remains in place. This space is also significant in that it is the context in which the struggle among postapartheid nationalism, the liberal state, and Marxism is being waged.

The culture of white confidence functions well in the bourgeois state, with its emphasis on constitutional "equality" and "rights" and its de-emphasis on class, because it privileges a liberal discourse that does not attend to the issue of material redistribution. As Etienne Balibar points out in his work *Masses, Classes, Ideas,* the omission of class as a political category in the enterprise of nation building is not incidental. Furthermore, Balibar argues in his essay "Racism as Universalism" that class presents the single most important threat to this project. Nation building is a "process that necessarily combines the creation of the nation-state *and* production of a social entity in which national solidarities, or rather dependencies, regularly prevail over other social group-ings, above all those which have to deal with class conflicts."[2] Because apartheid was a racist ideology constructed out of a specific "national solidarity," critiques of class in the South African context have always had to take account of the ways in which it was reconfigured, complicated, and distorted by race.

As this chapter demonstrates, the relations among the postapartheid nation, race, and class are nowhere more complex or entangled than in the black nation-alist slogan "One Settler, One Bullet." In the past few years, this chant has been transformed into a political formulation that has been adept at, if not always ar-ticulate about, conforming a Marxist understanding of class to its race-based ide-ology. Although the slogan is firmly grounded in the discourse of black national-ism, this chapter discusses those postapartheid moments when class becomes the primary category of political critique, by both substituting for and incorporating race. The project of (re)constructing the postapartheid state is sometimes so un-certain and has no prospect of material change for black workers that the slogan's Marxist underbelly is revealed, rendering class the dominant ideological mode. South Africa is a society in which the black working class and its unemployed and unemployable cohorts continue to bear the brunt of apartheid's historic in-equities, and this scenario promises to be the experience for generations to come. Whites, on the other hand, now enjoy the benefits of those disparities in its post-apartheid formation, albeit in the increasingly gated, if relatively safe, suburban neighborhoods they have always occupied.

"One Settler, One Bullet" is a densely layered engagement with the limita-tions and potentialities of postapartheid nationalism, a historical condition burdened (and sometimes overdetermined) by the legacy of racial separatism. The slogan raises fundamental questions about whiteness in South African society from a vantage point in the postapartheid social formation that is politically marginal (because it is presumed to be a PAC-identified, minority party) but ideologically pivotal (because of its appeal to a youthful constituency that exceeds conventional party affiliations). "One Settler, One Bullet" stands as a commentary on the history of white dominance, an interrogation of the consequences of white control in apartheid and postapartheid society, and a skeptical viewing of the postapartheid guises that white authority assumes.

It remains an open question whether the conflicts of the interregnum will prove combustible, but it is certain that these tensions will be exacerbated in the new democratic dispensation. Black South Africans are beginning to identify some of the consequences of a settlement in which historic white entitlement has, up to now, been ineffectively challenged in the discourse of reconciliation. The narrative of postapartheid, nonracial South African unity does not require any form of sacrifice from whites beyond rhetorical accommodation and psychic adjustment.

More disturbing, however, is the recognition that white South Africa will not need to make any material concessions so long as Nelson Mandela's government makes no concerted effort to reallocate land or redistribute wealth or mineral resources.[3] Unless white South Africans are compelled to accept their culpability—a condition containing the possibility of reparation to the nation's black citizenry—there is no reason to expect that the previously dominant group will behave in a fashion dissimilar from its past. Only a keen sense of historical accountability will inhibit the repetition (or continuation) of hegemonic behavior.[4] Since none of these checks is in place, it is not surprising that the white community has shown a tendency toward domination.

Postapartheid white South Africa has displayed a confidence rare among previously oppressive or colonizing constituencies; this community has an authoritative sense of its place in the new society. White South Africa has demonstrated a self-assuredness modulated just slightly by the new democratic political arrangement. The demise of apartheid has universalized the franchise and installed a black government, but whites' continuing experience of entitlement has made them a separate, privileged entity. They represent, in Balibar's terms, the *"ideal nation* inside the nation."[5] White South Africa's claim to its status as an "ideal" meta-nation derives from a confidence grounded in economic, military, and political authority. There is a direct correlation among the whites' control of the country's wealth, their de facto authority in the armed forces (most of the higher-ranking officers are white, even though the defense minister is black), their political and ideological accommodation by the ANC government, and their unexpectedly high level of self-assurance.

"ONE SETTLER, ONE BULLET"

While white confidence is proving to be a contagious condition, erupting in both likely and unlikely places and in predictable and unexpected forms, black South Africans are crafting their own responses. Some black constituencies tolerate the continued white hegemony for the sake of national unity; some are wary and watchful; and some are openly cynical. Undoubtedly, however, the most challenging, engaging, and disruptive of these black ripostes is contained in the slogan "One Settler, One Bullet."[6] In a South African political climate that is carefully nurturing reconciliation, this is a particularly incendiary phrase. Moreover, what is revealing about this slogan is how amorphous it is in terms of its political affiliations and also in the origins of its recent rise to prominence. Not surprisingly, many black and white South Africans automatically attribute this slogan to the PAC. In the long view, this understanding of the phrase is historically accurate. But such a myopic account does not consider ideological developments in contemporary black South Africa, which explain the reentry of this combustible term into the nation's political vocabulary. The term's reemergence and efficacy can be grasped by engaging the specificities of the current political conjuncture.

Despite its long(er) history in the black community, "One Settler, One Bullet" received national attention in South Africa only in April 1993. Before this, the phrase was used only by small pockets of black leftists and had limited currency in the larger black community itself. The slogan achieved widespread prominence when the ANC and South African Communist Party leader, Chris Hani, was assassinated.[7] Although he was a high-ranking member of the ANC's executive committee, Hani was identified differently by black youth in the townships. There he was regarded as an idiosyncratic member of the ANC leadership elite, the rare postapartheid politician who understood the extent of the township youth's anger. To the young township cadres, he represented an embryonic—some might prefer latent—black nationalist constrained by his more conciliatory colleagues on the national executive. At a press conference in Cape Town a few days after Hani's death, the ANC's secretary for the Western Cape, Peter Mokaba (flanked on stage by the estranged Mrs. Winnie Mandela), promised "death to the Boers." Despite its restricted use, the slogan "One Settler, One Bullet" lent itself easily to this occasion, and Mokaba—who would have encountered it in his exchanges with his youthful constituents—quickly appropriated it. More to the point, the maxim followed logically and rapidly from that April 1993 declaration of race war—no matter how fanciful, justified, or vengeful Mokaba's project was considered to be.

Identifying the phrase's ANC roots serves a dual purpose: it draws attention to (and accentuates) the fissures in the ruling party, and just as important, it undermines the ideological foundation of Nelson Mandela's avowedly nonracial government. Uncovering the slogan's dependence on the ANC for its extensive dissemination speaks directly to the issue of ANC hegemony and unmoors the phrase from its PAC identification. In its PAC-only phase, "One Settler,

One Bullet" functioned as the marker and repository of South African black nationalism—a code word for racism, in contradistinction, of course, to the ANC's pristinely nonracial image. In its current ANC-inflected incarnation, however, the phrase is a much more inflammable political expression, one that renders extremely precarious the project of national reconciliation. As it is now constituted, "One Settler, One Bullet" stands as a combative expression indexing the ambivalences in South Africa. The black community is divided, and the black majority government and its white partners in the government of national unity have split, with the National Party of F. W. de Klerk assuming the role of the official opposition.[8] Despite Mr. de Klerk's assurances, it is clear that the political harmony of the initial postapartheid moment is being replaced by ideological and racial antagonisms, even as the rhetoric of nonracial national unity finds ready articulation in the pronouncements by Mandela and his officials.

In this context, "One Settler, One Bullet" is proving to be a resilient slogan, an expression of historic political anger and black ideological ambition that must be addressed. Its salience is such that it will not be easily liquidated. As racially divided as South African society was (and continues to be), it is a sociopolitical arrangement remarkable in its inability to produce a black nationalist movement. Steve Biko's fledgling Black Consciousness organization of the late 1960s and early 1970s is the lone (and brief) exception. Because the phrase has achieved such tremendous currency so quickly, we should examine its ideological effects. Does it unsettle both black and white South African psyches? Does it create different anxieties for the two sides of the racial divide? What does it suggest about the prospects for nonracial national unity? Does it demand a particular kind of racial vigilance from white South Africans?

One of the most interesting and provocative, though by no means representative, responses to the "One Settler, One Bullet" problem was offered by white South African novelist J. M. Coetzee. An internationally acclaimed author who, among his many honors, won a Booker Prize, Coetzee presented a paper entitled "Offending and Being Offended" in April 1995 at Yale University. The lecture was delivered in his capacity as the Henry Luce Visiting Scholar at the school's Whitney Humanities Center.[9] Coetzee's paper was a contemplation on censorship in South Africa, with one of its central contentions being Coetzee's engagement with the slogan "One Settler, One Bullet." His grappling with the phrase continues in more politically explicit tones in the opening chapter of his new book *Giving Offense: Essays on Censorship*; in fact, the first few pages are dedicated to this issue. In his Yale talk, though not in *Giving Offense,* Coetzee maintained that as a white South African intellectual he could not take offense at this political maxim, and he did not deny that the slogan had a political currency. As he put it in his book: "One of the war-chants of the Pan-Africanist Congress struck a particularly sensitive nerve: 'ONE SETTLER, ONE BULLET.' Whites pointed to the threat to their lives contained in the word 'bullet'; but it was 'settler,' I believe, that evoked a deeper perturbation."[10] Nor did he doubt that the slogan had found articulation in combustible exchanges between the police and black protesters. But Coetzee did argue in his presentation that it lacked any efficacy, ideological, political, or otherwise.

In view of the maxim's nationalist imperatives, Coetzee's position is remark-able—we might even say shocking. "One Settler, One Bullet" is a slogan aimed specifically at him and members of his race, yet it did not affront the novelist in any way. We are compelled to ask Coetzee: Why was he not offended? By not taking offense, was he rejecting the Manichean structures (and strictures) of his society? Was he trying to create a place for historically enfranchised South Africans that was outside the white/black binary? Was he attempting to exceed or possibly even eliminate whiteness as a category of historical privilege and oppression? However, even if the novelist was not personally affronted because he refused the designation of "settler," surely he could not locate himself outside the binaries of a postapartheid paradigm while the structural inequalities of apartheid persisted. Was it not the legacy of apartheid that continued to divide the society along clear racial lines? To what did he attribute his sense of security, physical and psychic? How did he think black South Africans intended their slogan to be received by their white counterparts? And finally, how did Coetzee come to inhabit such a unique space, a political terrain, in which he could offend without being offended?

The overriding insight that emerges from this litany is simple. By taking no offense, Coetzee was giving considerable offense to the black community. Not to take offense is not to take seriously this form of postapartheid black resis-tance. More disconcertingly, it is to imply that there can be no black resistance beyond the achievement of the postapartheid state. There are few black South African intellectuals, whether or not they subscribe to the ideology of the slogan, who could dismiss the importance of this phrase so authoritatively. (A range of white intellectuals on the left and the right of the political spectrum replied very differently to the maxim's public enunciation.)

Black South Africans have been schooled more insistently than most subju-gated communities in the practice of being offended as a matter of course. Apartheid was, to be sure, deeply rooted in the politics of offense. It was a complicated politics, operating in ambivalent and yet reciprocal ways. The

Nationalist Party regime systematically violated the humanity of black South Africans. Conversely, the white government took offense at any form of opposition by the disenfranchised communities. The regime considered black resistance an affront to its rule, a disputation of its right to govern. Blacks, in their turn, invested the very act of resisting with a challenge to apartheid's ideological undergirding. To amend Frantz Fanon slightly, we might say that in South Africa, the disenfranchised disputed the notion that the "black man has no ontological right to resistance in the eyes of the white man."[11] Through their protests, demonstrations, and strikes, the disenfranchised registered the ways in which they were affronted by the brutalities of apartheid.

Apartheid South Africa was a social arrangement overdetermined by race. There is no clearer marker of the power differential in this society than the different approaches to the giving and taking of offense. By virtue of being a member of the dominant group in their society, whites have the privilege of choosing what, how, and when they will respond to occurrences around them. Dominance gives whites a powerful luxury: choice, or the right to intervene or ignore events as they choose, the power to attribute significance, ignominy, or even notoriety to the actions of black South Africans; the authority to read themselves into or to extricate themselves from black public transcripts—the power to take offense or not take offense, as they determine. The positions or actions of the dominated black majority can be read or represented in any fashion by the white minority. Blacks, on the other hand, are severely restricted in their choice of response. As members of the subservient group, they found that their sociopolitical location largely determined the appropriate form, manner, and time in which they could respond. Even when the subjugated community engaged in acts of sly civility or transgressed the dominant transcript, it was still acting within a predetermined paradigm—a document founded on and expressive of their disenfranchisement. Coetzee's rendering of "One Settler, One Bullet" reflects apartheid's historical privilege: the tendency toward misreading, misrepresenting, or selectively emptying out an oppositional ideology. To coin a phrase, one that borrows from Homi Bhabha's notion of "sly civility," Coetzee's reading marks an instance of sly hegemony.

From their particular vantage point, white South Africans have been able to rid the slogan of its ideological import by disregarding the political urgency inscribed in its enunciation. By stripping the slogan of an impulse that was as much antiapartheid as it was anticolonial, they have been able to reduce the maxim to an empty linguistic signifier (a signifier, moreover, without a material referent). The ideological impact of "One Settler, One Bullet"—which is nothing less than a rhetorical call for the abolition of whiteness in South

Africa—is too resounding an appeal to be discounted. As chanted by black youth at political rallies, during exchanges with the police, and in confrontations with their white compatriots, the slogan reverberates with the intensity of black nationalism. "One Settler, One Bullet" is a highly public articulation aimed specifically at disrupting the psyches of white South Africans. The phrase is overwritten by the specter of the violence committed against white colonial regimes in other African countries—the antisettler campaigns conducted by the Mau Mau in Kenya spring immediately to mind in this regard. In South Africa, "One Settler, One Bullet" implicitly threatens the same kind of violence, if not necessarily the possibility of genocide.

To name white South Africans "settlers" is to mark them as aliens when they present themselves as unproblematic nationals. By designating white South Africans as settlers, their black counterparts are invalidating more than three centuries of white residency in the subcontinent. All white occupancy, which started with the Dutch settlements in 1652, is contained under the rubric of colonial expansion. Because this project was so indelibly marked by the plunder, exploitation, and oppression of the indigenous peoples, to be a white South African is to be contaminated by this experience.

White South Africans are singularly disqualified as nonnatives ad infinitum by their past. They have perpetually rendered themselves as "foreign," "othered" by their history of invasion and illegitimate control of the indigenous peoples and their resources. "One Settler, One Bullet" is an interrogation and invalidation of the authenticity of whites' identities as South Africans. The slogan is a pointed reminder that the white community's origins are non-African. It is, in its more astute and historically critical moments, an indictment of the consequences of imperialism. The phrase "One Settler, One Bullet" is a strategic disenfranchisement of white South Africans. Because the slogan threatens the elimination of whites, it is considerably more unsettling than the apartheid laws that made blacks into noncitizens but never disputed their right of traditional residence. To call white people "settlers" is to deny their right to lay claim to any kind of South African-ness. Not even the white regime was capable of such an assault on the black community's national identity, since it never explicitly challenged blacks' historical rootedness. Apartheid disenfranchisement was a direct (and less layered) process, relying as it did on the colonialist principle of racial hierarchy.

White South Africa's confidence has thus far been able to withstand this new ideological onslaught from voluble and angry sectors of the black community. This resilience can be comprehended in large measure by understanding whites' own history of violence. White South Africans have the privilege of not being offended by so vituperative a slogan because they have little or no collective memory of violence being done to them. Although the white community has as a matter of course meted out punishment to protesting black teenagers and striking black workers, it has no similar precedent of retribution being inflicted on white youths or workers. White South Africans have always been immunized from black violence. The army and/or the police has always protected them from acts of insurrection, in the course of which these repressive forces committed atrocities against the black community—a practice carried out in the faraway townships, usually outside the purview of whites. The specter of black-on-white violence in South Africa is without a substantial precedent. The rare instances such as the 1976 Soweto uprising, the insurrections of the mid-1980s, and the attacks on white motorists by black gunmen in cities such as Johannesburg are relatively recent.

The slogan "One Settler, One Bullet" establishes a historical precedent that could prove crucial if the (origins and) threats of black violence are to be publicly engaged or treated with any political seriousness. Me'shell Ndege Ocello's lyrics capture the spirit of foreboding at the core of the slogan: "The white man shall sleep forever with one eye open." White South Africans are being systematically un-settled by these attacks on their bodies and their psyches. Traditionally enfranchised South Africans have to develop a new vigilance—sleeping with "one eye open"—because their sense of place in their society is endangered in real, ideological, and metaphorical terms. The prescience of the message is in the music, or the chanting, of the slogan. South Africa, for centuries the province of white dominance, now presents itself as an "unhomely" space, a country rapidly becoming inhospitable to, if not uninhabitable by, its white occupants. The "unhomeliness" derives not, as in the case of Bhabha's reading of Toni Morrison and Nadine Gordimer, from the "estranging sense of the relocation of the home"[12] but from postapartheid South Africa's inability to provide physical and mental sanctuary for a community accustomed to such protections by virtue of its race.

A MARXIST CONUNDRUM FOR A NASCENT BLACK NATIONALISM

It could be argued with historical accuracy and theoretical conviction that South Africa is a society that never had a revolution, an unusual postcolonial state in which the transition to black rule was relatively smooth, if not altogether peaceful. South Africa is a sociopolitical entity that does not lend itself easily to the anticolonial model. The reverberations of the phrase "One Settler,

One Bullet" are therefore somewhat inapplicable, even if they do not ring entirely hollow. This contention, however, in no way offsets the depth of black anger underwriting the articulation of the slogan. Not quite historically appropriate but made to fit the demands of the postapartheid context, "One Settler, One Bullet" has nonetheless served as a fairly accurate harbinger of antiwhite sentiment, if not always antiwhite violence.

As emotionally stirring and politically empowering a call to arms as this slogan may be for black South Africans, its inadequacies are such that it does not hold out much promise of a solution for the predicament of the black working class—the constituency for whom the slogan ostensibly holds the greatest promise. The antisettler rhetoric does not account for the extent to which white South Africans have made themselves a part of the country's fabric for the last 350 years or so.

Their integration into the subcontinent is expressed most clearly by the fact that Afrikaans-speaking white South Africans took the name "Afrikaners," the Afrikaans term for white Africans. The "alien-ness" of whites thus must be explained in terms not derived from the anticolonialist settler paradigm. In South Africa, white settlement has been more permanent and more psychically entrenched. Here, identification with the colonized country has for centuries replaced any affinity with the European motherland. That is, repatriation is not a solution and has not been for hundreds of years. Despite the slogan's obvious ideological limitations, "One Settler, One Bullet" continues to mobilize people in the black (and colored and Indian, though to a lesser extent) communities because it functions at a level other than a strictly nationalist one. This other way in which it operates is, of course, the economic one.

The South African context is ideologically fascinating because it reveals the difficulties of reconciling Marxism and nationalism in a black politics of resistance. The paradoxes and possibilities endemic to linking these two modes of thinking are played out in an intriguing fashion. "One Settler, One Bullet" addresses indirectly the ways in which black South Africans identify in Marxism an analysis of their material condition. The maxim provides an explanation for the disproportionate white wealth because apartheid was both a racist and an exploitative practice.

Paradoxically, it is in the pejorative description of whites as "settlers" that black South Africans implicitly acknowledge the authority and resources of the enfranchised community. "Settlers," after all, have traditionally exercised great power in the societies they have colonized. It is in the very contradiction that we have uncovered at the heart of the slogan that it is most compelling: the recognition of black subjugation inspires the commitment to reverse that condition, by force if necessary. Embattled as the black working class is, exposed to enemies traditional and new, the maxim offers a different set of historical possibilities. Inscribed in it is a nationalist vision in which black political enfranchisement will be continuous, not disjunctive, with black economic empowerment.

Propelled by this vision, "One Settler, One Bullet" is a strident attack on the ANC government's inability (or refusal) to redistribute the country's land and wealth. Reductively put, to be an antiwhite settler is simultaneously to deny the apartheid rulers any property rights and to claim that property for the black community. This particular brand of black nationalism—or "African nationalism" as it is sometimes called—depends on its underutilized class critique to redress this situation. In order to restore the country's wealth to its indigenous citizens, the settlers must be removed. The ways in which that wealth will be redistributed and the economy reorganized are not specified, but this unspoken assumption nevertheless holds the promise of greater economic opportunities. Such opportunities include substantially increased black employment, the return of the resources to the country's black inhabitants, and improved living conditions for black citizens, all of which rely on the general presumption that the economy will be controlled by blacks.

Because of the idiosyncrasies and vagaries of a context in which race and class overwrite and reinforce each other, black nationalism brings to the foreground the class divisions in the black South African community. Black nationalism draws attention to the ideological tensions and structural inequities of postapartheid life for a specific purpose: to highlight the material and political differences in order to separate the black working class from the black middle class. The former is composed of the working poor and unemployed and unemployable blacks, and the latter is an employed, potentially prosperous constituency that is being given the opportunity to parallel the accomplishments of its white counterparts. These differences present the black working class with a predicament. At the point where the nationalist rubric breaks down, class intercedes by mapping out and accounting for different, but no less telling, national(ist) divisions. Because of the nationalist tendency, the black working class is prevented from making common (economic) cause with white workers or unemployed coloreds or Indians.

Marxism and nationalism can cohabit for only so long, after which they become mutually constraining. This is not to argue that one or the other has to take precedence. Nor is it to suggest that Marxism has to subsume nationalism or that nationalism has to override Marxist discourse. Class affiliation does not have to be privileged over racial identification, or vice versa. Rather, in recognizing the complexities of the South African situation in which race and class have a contingent and unpredictable rapport, it is to propose that these two philosophies negotiate a supportive, if not symbiotic, relationship. Ideally, of course, each would take precedence as the historical moment demands. Failing that, Marxism and nationalism need to take account of the categorical imperatives of each ideology. The context in which they are operating dictates that they structure themselves carefully in relation to each other—they must determine how they complement one another and identify the conjunctures where they overlap and where they conflict. If these philosophical negotiations are not conducted, Marxism and nationalism could easily cancel each other out, reducing themselves to contesting ideologies (which, to some extent, they are) instead of functioning as supplementary political programs.

These are some of the historical complexities, nuances, economic pressures, ideological contradictions, and hesitancies at the core of the phrase "One Settler, One Bullet." Above all, the slogan (and its multiple resonances) is a call for white South African accountability. Unlike their black counterparts, whites have already begun the process of selectively forgetting the ravages caused by their racist rule. "One Settler, One Bullet" is an urgent reminder that there should be political consequences for the act of white forgetting. White South Africa must acknowledge the effects of its forgetting so publicly; they should be reminded of how much offense they have given and continue to give and how much arrogance underlies the absence of their memory. Their forgetting is disrespectful to black South Africa's past and present struggles. White amnesia is tantamount to invalidating the black struggles of Langa and Sharpeville in 1960, Soweto 1976, and the insurrections of Eastern Cape and the Vaal Triangle in the mid-1980s.

Black South Africans find themselves in the unenviable position of having to conduct a new and rare historical struggle: the battle to not be offended anymore, the campaign to attack a white confidence that is rapidly becoming a white smugness, an arrogance that is historically offensive. White South Africans must be compelled to engage, as Balibar would have it, the most difficult of tasks: they must change their "mode of thinking," rethink their place in the postapartheid society. The newly enfranchised, though not empowered, are charged with the responsibility of transforming the culture of white confidence into a culture of postapartheid civic accountability. White arrogance is tolerable only insofar as blacks are prepared to endorse the continuation of apartheid's practices, inequities, and injustices under a new regime. This is a daunting political undertaking, a struggle begun with few resources, the most potent of which may be a vivid memory of black history and the commitment to keeping it alive. White South Africans should be confronted with that history. Richard Rive's dictum must be applied to the constituency that most offended him: white South Africans must not be allowed to forget. The consequences of white amnesia are unacceptable to all black South Africans, in particular, the black working class. They have neither the means nor the will to forget.

NOTES

I would like to thank Amitava Kumar, my "comrade," for his careful reading of this chapter. Laced as always with humor, his comments were helpful. I am indebted to David Attwell for his thoughtful and challenging observations. Mike Hill was generous in his support and astute in his criticism. Finally, I am grateful to Cynthia Young for her comments. The chapter benefited considerably from her suggestions.

1. Richard Rive, *"Buckingham Palace," District Six* (Cape Town: David Philip Publishers, 1986), p. 198.

2. Etienne Balibar, *Masses, Classes, Ideas: Studies on Politics and Philosophy Before and After Marx,* trans. James Swenson (New York: Routledge, 1994), p. 202 (italics in original).

3. It is even more disturbing to learn of the inefficacies of the ANC's land redistribution plans. The ANC announced that within the next several years, it would require white farmers to make available for purchase 30 percent of their land to the black tenants in their employ. Then it was discovered that white farmers, unwilling to give up any property (even when they would be compensated at market prices), had devised a simple strategy to counter the government's injunction: they were firing these black tenants rather than allow them to own neighboring land.

4. Among the more worrisome aspects of the new South Africa is the way in which whites who have committed political crimes against blacks have been able to secure indemnity. At its first national conference after the 1990 unbanning of the liberation movements, the PAC opposed a measure that would have (and in fact did) free several white police officers and personnel in the security forces from criminal charges. In the first few months of 1996 there were signs indicating the reversal of this trend.

5. Balibar, *Masses, Classes, Ideas,* p. 194 (italics in original).

6. This slogan has taken on many permutations, although it has maintained the dominant form of "One Settler, One Bullet." For instance, it was modulated into "One Settler, One Air Ticket"; at other moments, however, it adopted an aggressively anti-ANC stance and became "One Slovo, One Bullet," "Slovo" being a reference to the late white ANC and Communist Party leader Joe Slovo. Sometimes the phrase was extended into "One Settler, One Bullet, Every Settler Deserves a Bullet." This last form is usually encountered at political rallies or the trials of black youths—such as the murder trial of U.S. scholar Amy Biehl, where the slogan punctuated the judge's pronouncements.

7. The Hani assassination undoubtedly gave the slogan unprecedented exposure, although the phrase had been steadily gaining media coverage for some time before that. The phrase had repeatedly come into the public eye because of attacks by the

APLA (Azanian People's Liberation Army, the armed wing of the black nationalist movement AZAPO—the Azanian People's Organisation) on white citizens—mainly in the Johannesburg area. In 1992 the APLA claimed responsibility for an attack on a white church in Kenilworth, a Cape Town suburb.

8. De Klerk, the second vice president in the government of national unity, announced the withdrawal of his party from the Mandela cabinet in May 1996. De Klerk said that the decision demonstrated the maturity of democracy in the new South Africa.

9. Coetzee's talk is part of a new book of essays entitled *Giving Offense*. I was unable to obtain a copy of the presentation, from either the author or the Whitney Humanities Center. This piece constitutes the response of one black South African intellectual who attended that event and engaged J. M. Coetzee in the course of it. I want to make clear that I am taking issue here with the Yale speech and not the opening chapter ("Taking Offense") of the book, in which Coetzee's position is different from his earlier pronouncements. In fact, I agree with some of his articulations in "Taking Offense," especially his reading of the changing public transcript, the colonialist history of the term, and the issue of naming.

10. J. M. Coetzee, *Giving Offense: Essays on Censorship* (Chicago: University of Chicago Press, 1996), p. 1.

11. Frantz Fanon, *Black Skins, White Masks,* trans. Charles Lam Markham (New York: Grove Press, 1967), p. 110.

12. Homi Bhabha, "The World and the Home," *Social Text* 10 (1992): 141–53.

WHITE CULTURE

The Whiteness of Film Noir

Eric Lott

In the final moments of Edward Dmytryk's *Murder, My Sweet* (1944), the police offer private detective Philip Marlowe (Dick Powell) the priceless jade necklace that he has at last recovered for his wealthy client. The chief object of mercenary desire in the film and therefore a figure for the corruption and deceit of its dramatis personae, the necklace also suggests an Oriental(ist) languor whose fruits could now be Marlowe's. Marlowe declines: "No thanks," he says, "it's wrong for my complexion." We are led to understand "complexion" first in the moral sense; Marlowe has beaten the forces of greed and graft that threaten to swamp him no less than the roués, quacks, idle rich, and petty mobsters by whom he is surrounded. In another sense, though, Marlowe remains true to a racial physiognomy, that of whiteness, which indexes his pristine soul.

Film noir—"black film," as French critics first dubbed it in 1946—has long fascinated observers with its interest in darkened frames and darkened lives. But

Adapted from *American Literary History* 9, no. 3 (fall 1997), by permission of the author and Oxford University Press.

the specifically racial means of film noir's obsession with the dark side of 1940s American life has been ignored. Perhaps this should come as no surprise: raced metaphors in popular life are as indispensable and invisible as the colored bodies who give rise to and move in the shadows of those usages. Yet not to call attention to film noir's insistent thematizing of spiritual and cinematic darkness by way of bodies beyond the pale is to persist in a commonsense exploitation enacted by films (from roughly the early 1940s to the middle 1950s) stressing the predicaments of whites and accepted by the subsequent history of commentary on them.

In this chapter, I enlarge the frame of recent work by Toni Morrison, Kenneth Warren, and others concerning the ways in which racial tropes and the presence of African Americans have shaped the sense and structure of American cultural products that seem to have nothing to do with race.[1] The informing presence in the American imaginary of racial difference, which amounts to little less than cultural articulation, has created a cinematic mode known to traffic in black hearts and minds. At a moment when bold new forms of black, Latino, and Asian activism and visibility are confronting resurgent white revanchism and vigilantism, film noir's relentless cinematography of chiaroscuro and moral focus on the rotten souls of white folks, I argue, invoke the racial dimension of this play of light against dark.

Criticism of film noir since the 1940s has addressed its various uses of otherness. In the French criticism that brought "film noir" into our vocabulary, that otherness is chiefly moral or psychosocial—a preponderance of crime, violence, obsession, and guilt—the "dark" side of the white Western self.[2] Nicholas Ray's *In a Lonely Place* (1950), for instance, associates its protagonist Dixon Steele (Humphrey Bogart) with all of these, although his actual culpability is left in some doubt.

The burst of critical activity on film noir in the United States in the late 1960s and early 1970s, which brought the form firmly into the orbit of American critical allure, took for granted this emphasis and began to expand on its innovative stylistic expressions.[3] Paul Schrader went so far as to claim that film noir was characterized primarily by its concentration on visual style. First noting the hardened sociopolitical mood of the 1970s that precipitated an embrace of noir's thematic affinities (p. 8), Schrader observes the 1940s films' peculiar cinematic attack made on their own political moment: film noir

> tried to make America accept a moral vision of life based on style. . . . Film noir attacked and interpreted its sociological conditions, and, by the close of the noir period, created a new artistic world which went beyond a simple sociological

reflection, a nightmarish world of American mannerism which was by far more a creation than a reflection. (p. 13)

In Schrader's account, the stylistic recurrence in film noir of night scenes, shadows, oppressively composed frames, odd angles of light, actors dwarfed by overly prominent surroundings, complex chronologies, and the like (p. 11) is itself a negation of the corrupt society responsible for producing this corrosive cinematic response. Given a social prod, in other words, film noir has come back with style. Although its world is bleak, stylistically it is (as Richard Poirier once called American literature) a world elsewhere; we confront it in forms that transcend its perils. What Schrader calls film noir's "shades of black" are in fact strategies of artistic othering meant to surmount the cynicism, meaning-lessness, and psychosis that they portray.

If the blackness of style is seen here as a kind of clear-eyed, panicky refuge— which only extends earlier critics' celebration of film noir's bringing the dark to light in what Mike Davis calls its "Marxist cinema manqué"[4]—many recent critics have, instead, seen the frightening "other" side of American life in film noir as relying on the villainous and villainized women it portrays.

Ann Kaplan's collection *Women in Film Noir* first established the way in which faithless, ruthless women exemplify and perform the dark deeds that signify the underside of the self that upstanding men must refuse in the interest of self-preservation.[5] Female power is these women's apparent crime, and film noir typically requires them to renounce, compromise, or destroy that power. But noir men like Walter Neff (Fred MacMurray) in Billy Wilder's *Double Indemnity* (1944) often fall prey to them, thereby succumbing to the "darkness" that film noir associates with feminine wiles.

The feminist critique of noir is the most far-reaching account of the self's partitioning (into good/masculine and evil/feminine) in these American films, and without it our understanding of noir would be impoverished. This chapter follows in its tracks, and since the processes of identification and disavowal that I explore usually involve overlapping gender and racial feelings, feminist work on noir has already begun to ask the sorts of questions whose answers require a racial component. My purpose is to ask why no one has yet challenged the association in these films of the self's and society's darkness with a racial dimension and why that dimension in the form of black appearances on film has seemed merely marginal, local, and insubstantial. Even Joan Copjec's collection *Shades of Noir,* which places noir in more specific urban and political topographies, does not question the racial unconscious of noir, found even in its title.[6] The opening pages of Manthia Diawara's contribution to the Copjec anthology—on the way that noirs by current black directors use the film's classic codes for their own purposes—have a clear sense of the racial metaphors of noir's "shades," but otherwise the book does not undertake this sort of analysis.[7]

Diawara observes the interanimation of noir's stylistic, moral, and implicitly racial concerns: A "film is noir if it puts into play light and dark in order to exhibit a people who become 'black' because of their 'shady' moral behaviour" (p. 262). The slippage in Diawara's own exact epigram—"black" racially or morally?—hints at the ease with which racial tropes are both literalized and dissipated. Or rather, since the racial and moral senses here are metaphorical, it shows us how elusive yet coherent is the metaphorical character of racial definition. Such slippages indicate the ready use-value and real centrality of racial tropes despite their origin in the margins of white texts and lives.

Here the figurations of race work in the same way that important features of the psychosymbolic domain do. As Peter Stallybrass and Allon White write, the "most powerful symbolic repertoires" of bourgeois societies are situated at their "borders, margins and edges, rather than at the accepted centres"; they reprocess, displace and condense, and perform the labor of the signifier on the social formation's boundary-defining events, materials, and relationships and thrust them to the center of its socially symbolic narrative acts; there are no simple correspondences or one-to-one relations here.[8] Indeed, the apparent marginality of racial Others in the postwar U.S. social formation (whatever their centrality to its labor and culture) might encourage us to dismiss any seemingly racial associations in film noir as merely coincidental tricks of demography or ruses of metaphor when in fact such metaphorical ruses and the presence of black, Asian, or Mexican bodies confirm the central symbolic significance of color in the black-and-white world of many noirs, which revolve on a racial axis that displays great force at more key moments in more films than can easily be written off as exceptions.

Whether it is the racialized dramas of interiority in such films as Wilder's *Double Indemnity,* Delmar Daves's *Dark Passage* (1947), George Cukor's *A Double Life* (1948), Orson Welles's *The Lady from Shanghai* (1948), Max Ophuls's *The Reckless Moment* (1949), or Ray's *In a Lonely Place;* the Asian or Mexican urban landscapes and underworlds of Dmytryk's *Murder, My Sweet, The Lady from Shanghai, The Reckless Moment,* or Welles's *Touch of Evil* (1958) (the self-conscious end point of noir and its racial tropes, as we shall see); the hysterically racialized family romances of Michael Curtiz's *Mildred Pierce* (1945), Charles Vidor's *Gilda* (1946), *The Reckless Moment,* Otto Preminger's *Angel Face* (1953), Fritz Lang's *The Big Heat* (1953), and others; or any of a number of minor reliances and major subtexts, the troping of white darkness in noir has a racial source that is all the more insistent for seeming off to the side. Film noir is replete with characters of color who populate and signify the shadows of white American life in the 1940s. Noir may have pioneered Hollywood's merciless exposure of white pathology, but by relying on race to convey that pathology, it in effect erected a cordon sanitaire around the circle of corruption it sought to penetrate. Film noir rescues with racial idioms the whites whose moral and social boundaries seem in doubt. "Black film" is the refuge of whiteness.

"No visible scars—till a while ago, that is": Walter Neff's account of himself at the start of *Double Indemnity* refers us not only to the gunshot wound administered by femme fatale Phyllis Dietrichson (Barbara Stanwyck) but again to the "complexion" of a man so scarred by his own deceit, violence, and cunning and so immersed in blackened cinematic compositions that his darkness threatens to manifest itself on his very skin. In a stylish conceptual move, Neff's shoulder wound bleeds through his suit jacket little by little throughout his voice-over flashback so that the stain, which of course appears black onscreen, grows larger with Neff's deepening involvement in passion and crime. Alone after hours in the darkened Pacific All-Risk Insurance Company office building tended almost wholly by black janitors and custodians, Neff now inhabits the racial space that *Double Indemnity* constantly links with his dark deeds.

From the beginning, Neff's adulterous partnership with Phyllis Dietrichson takes the form of a passage out of whiteness. Phyllis lives in a "California Spanish house" built, Neff surmises, in the mid-1920s, a moment of racial exoticism and primitivism appropriate to Phyllis's designs. When Neff first sees her, she has been sunbathing, and this relatively new white interest in fashionable self-othering—together with the redoubtable signifier of Phyllis's anklet or "slave bracelet"—makes even more necessary her cosmetic masquerade to get her "face on straight."

Already the open visage of Los Angeles is consigned to the realm of mere appearances and masks, which hide the unwhite portents of no good. This diagnosis is clinched by the cut from this scene to the office of Pacific All-Risk's claims manager Barton Keyes (E. G. Robinson), who is in the process of sniffing out Greek American Sam Garlopis's fraudulent insurance claim (he's torched his own truck—a foretaste of the "blacker" attempts at fraud to come). Garlopis's Greekness suggests his potential for moral lapse as his duplicity defines his excessive ethnicity; showing him the door, Keyes gives Garlopis a mock naturalization lesson in how to turn the handle and open it. Moral rot is quite unself-consciously aligned with nonnormative Americanness in *Double Indemnity,* giving rise to an uncontrollable profusion in the film of ethnic, national, and racial signifiers, from English soap to Chinese checkers. By the time Neff says of his voice-over confession to Keyes that he is "not trying to whitewash myself," we know exactly what he means.

Perhaps he knows the attempt would be futile. Hasn't Keyes described Neff's job of salesman—in contrast to his own managerial brainwork—as a species of lowbrow "monkey talk"? And after Neff strangles Mr. Dietrichson from the back seat of Phyllis's car, doesn't he find himself under a great (literally blackening) shadow of vulnerability, the one that hobbles on crutches into the film's opening frames? Isn't this compounded by his ultimate failure to put up a convincing "impersonation" (as Keyes calls it) of Dietrichson's Stanford-educated whiteness in faking his accident? When Dietrichson's daughter Lola—herself a paragon of whiteness carrying on a dangerous, proscribed relationship with Nino Zachetti, whom Lola meets clandestinely at the superbly patriotic (and parodic) corner of Vermont and Franklin Streets—begins to suspect Phyllis and her own erstwhile paramour (ethnicity will out) of plotting her father's (not to mention her mother's) death, Neff takes her, by now unsurprisingly, to a Mexican restaurant to literally seduce her into silence. Such a figural crossing of the border perfectly conveys *Double Indemnity's* sense of the iniquity to which Neff has sunk. Neff himself is now a moral resident of Phyllis's Spanish house.

There is no greater index of this fate than Neff's two alibis for Dietrichson's murder. The first is the black garage attendant, Charlie, whom Neff visits in the parking garage to establish his whereabouts before exiting (by the service stairs Charlie himself presumably uses) to execute his plot. The second is the Westwood Jew, Lou Schwartz, whose name derives from the Yiddish word for *black* and whose status as another of the film's resident Others helps secure Neff's uncriminal whiteness while suggesting his moral fall.

What interests me about Neff's alibis is that they reveal the way in which white selfhood exploits boundary-defining nonwhites even as they register the dark depths of Neff's spiritual condition. The character and color of his excuses indicate his moral otherness, his guilt. The same is true at the end, when a black janitor calls Keyes over to the insurance company to finger Neff in his office—the black presence here an embodiment of the outer darkness to which Neff has traveled and perhaps the visible sign of his guilt returning mid-confession to indict him. It is no accident that at the end Neff tries to escape across the Mexican border.[9]

Film noir is a cinematic mode defined by its border crossings. In it people fall from (g)race into the deep shadows that the new film technologies had made possible. With the help of technical innovations such as the Norwood exposure meter (which for the first time could take a weighted average of light from all directions rather than a single direction), faster film stock, photoflood bulbs that permitted better location filming, antireflective lens coatings, and the like, film noir found a world in the dark.[10]

The moral and visual passage into "shadiness"—conjoining states of psychological and social definition with the actual look of white skin on screen—has, almost by definition, a racial analogue in the American context. Racial borders are invoked and implicated in social and representational borders, analogizing easily with and even providing a conceptual framework for Americans gone afoul of actual and cinematic laws. Hollywood's lighting conventions demonstrate this multiplex drama of transgression.

Richard Dyer suggests that the lighting of white big-screen icons (such as Lillian Gish) gave their ethical purity a racially particular form. Associations of worth and whiteness are by now so naturalized as to pass beneath conscious notice, and Hollywood has always exploited them. Commenting on the racial import of the brightly lit star, Dyer writes: "She is more visible, she is aesthetically and morally superior, she looks on from a position of knowledge, of enlightenment—in short, if she is so much lit, she also appears to be the source of light."[11]

Translucence in film—the people on screen literally have light shining through them—is aligned with spiritual hygiene, provided the people on screen are white. And it certainly helps if they are men, too, given the always available equation of radiant femininity (Rita Hayworth in *Gilda* [1946]), or at least a blonde wig (Barbara Stanwyck in *Double Indemnity*), with the entrapments of desire. But with the advent of noir, even the women were mostly cast into blackness, living, like the men, in shadows that suggested their racial fall from Hollywood's lighting conventions no less than they mimicked the moral transgressions on-screen. Notably, the exception to this rule in *Double Indemnity* is the innocent Lola, whose glowing white face at one moment evidently enchants Walter Neff in his condition of moral disrepair. More typically, the intensely shadowy scenes featuring Phyllis and Walter that plot and punctuate the film, from the drinks Walter makes in the gloom of his kitchen, to their postmurder kiss in a shadow that bisects their heads, to their final meeting in the near-total darkness of Phyllis's house, confirm their departure from social as well as stylistic norms.

Noir's crossings from light to dark, the indulgence of actions and visual codes ordinarily renounced in white bourgeois culture and thereby raced in the white imaginary, throw its protagonists into the predicament of abjection. Noir characters threaten to lose themselves in qualities that formerly marked all that the self was not and that now unsettle its stable definition. Antisocial acts of lawlessness and passion, deceit and recklessness, signify the state that according to Julia Kristeva, makes borders irrelevant, repression inoperative, and the ego an Other.[12]

Stable demarcation (moral, visual, racial) replaced by fluidity, straying, "going all the way to the end of the line" (as *Double Indemnity* has it), noir's abject selves meet the world without boundaries—no mere moral failing, since it involves disturbances around the disavowal of the mother in the formation of (principally masculine) gender definition and of the racial Other in the formation of white self-identity. The two converge in the opening shadow of Walter on crutches: his wounded manhood the result of Phyllis's duping control and finally the bullet she puts in his shoulder; his "blackening" the outcome of actions he is willing to perform for thrills, passion, and cold hard cash. Thus Neff observes about his abject state after the murder that his "nerves were pulling me to pieces." Likewise, Phyllis's "black" widow role in several respects represents the film's worst white male nightmare: the former nurse of Dietrichson's first wife—an occupation resembling other service occupations in the picture, from the black office custodians to Charlie the garage attendant to the "colored woman" Walter says cleans his apartment—mothering her charge badly enough to "accidentally on purpose" kill her before becoming Lola's evil stepmother and Dietrichson's scheming wife. It must indeed be said that Phyllis is so typical of 1940s Hollywood women that her boundary loss, endangering poor Walter's own, is hard to perceive as abjection. Yet the illicit pleasures, fantasies of omnipotence, and thoroughgoing "rottenness" she inspires are those attributes most imagined to have a black as well as a female source.

As Slavoj Zizek notes, the formation of selfhood in white Western societies requires the remanding of the unspeakable powers of enjoyment—pleasure is, by definition, illicit and rotten—which are imagined to be the special privilege or province of racial Others and whose experience or return, therefore, threatens the white self girded by specifically racial negations.[13] *Double Indemnity's* attempted escape from the iron cage of respectable morality that is the prime benefit and lure of whiteness reckons the racial component of its disrespectable pleasures. By villainizing the desires that drive the narrative and utilizing racial norms coded in moral terminologies and visual devices, it preserves the idea of whiteness that its own characters do not uphold.

Why, other than the pathological social formation of white interiority, might this contradiction have been present in films of the 1940s? As many historians have observed, the decade's civil rights activism presaged the better-remembered struggles of the 1960s. A. Philip Randolph's massive March on Washington movement against discrimination in the wartime defense plants, begun in 1940, motivated President Franklin Roosevelt to issue an executive order outlawing discriminatory hiring practices by defense contractors and to establish the (ineffectual) Fair Employment Practices Committee. In 1941 black Ford workers at the River Rouge, Michigan, plant threw their weight behind the United Auto Workers, forcing the company for the first time to sign a union contract. The ranks of the NAACP began to grow in tandem with rising black political and economic desires—more than half a million blacks migrated out of the South between the beginning of defense hiring and the end of the war—and in 1943 the Congress of Racial Equality was founded. The "double V" campaign endorsed by many black newspapers and civil rights organizations signified the cry for a double victory over racism at home as well as fascism abroad.

Hollywood itself felt the heat in 1942 when its major studio heads met with the NAACP's Walter White and agreed to reshape black movie roles in accord with the new times; this was the period of *Cabin in the Sky, Stormy Weather, The Negro Soldier, Crash Dive, Sahara,* and *Bataan* (all 1943). Lest we underestimate the white hostility toward this surge of activity, we should note, for instance, that at the same moment, black noir writer Chester Himes was race-baited from the studios (Jack Warner proclaimed, "I don't want no niggers on this lot") and spent the war years working in defense plants, writing in *If He Hollers Let Him Go* (1945) and *The Lonely Crusade* (1947) about what he later termed the "mental corrosion of race prejudice in Los Angeles."[14]

In the long hot summer of 1943, such militant disgust with unbending American racism took to the streets. Urban insurrections erupted in Harlem, Detroit, and twenty-five other U.S. cities. These were often labeled "zoot-suit riots" because the black and Mexican youths so attired (in defiance, it might be added, of the War Production Board's rationing of cloth) were convenient targets of attack for the white servicemen and police whose violence often sparked such street combat. Pathologizing accounts of zoot subcultures were embraced as a means of defining the civilized self, as in Kenneth Clark's 1945 study of what he called the "zoot effect in personality" (published in the *Journal of Abnormal Psychology*). Writers from Ralph Ellison to Chester Himes to C. L. R. James and others grasped the political urgency of apparently trivial squabbles over sharkskin; meanwhile, the Los Angeles City Council voted to make wearing zoot suits a misdemeanor, thereby facilitating the arrest of Mexicans and blacks.

The concurrent ordeal of the Sleepy Lagoon trial, in which seventeen pachuco zoot-suiters were convicted of and imprisoned for murder under extremely questionable legal circumstances (they were later released and the charges dismissed after the protests of the Sleepy Lagoon Defense Committee, with whom Orson Welles was allied), secured the image of the Mexican juvenile delinquent, sparked fears of internal subversion by a foreign conspiracy (the prosecution insisted on the "Oriental," pre-Columbian source of the Mexicans' "total disregard for human life"), gave rise to "Lil Abner" creator Al Capp's widely read and virulent "Zoot-Suit Yokum" comic strip in which a zoot-suit manufacturers' conspiracy is happily thwarted (perhaps inspiring a *Los Angeles Times* caricature of Japanese premier Hideki Tōjō in a zoot suit), and symbolized the beginning of the Chicano movement in America. Meanwhile, as is well known, hysteria concerning the yellow peril and the internment of Japanese Americans in California completed this picture of panicked whites in dubious battle.[15]

Noir responded to these specific social threats not by presenting them outright but by subsuming the social energy associated with them into the untoward aspects of white selves. The "dark" energy of many of these films is villainized through the associations with race that generated some of that energy in the first place.

Film noir is in this sense a sort of whiteface dream work of social anxieties with explicitly racial sources, resolved on film to the criminal undertakings of abjected whites. This may explain two otherwise random or unremarkable matters in *Double Indemnity*. The first is Nino Zachetti's portrayal as a juvenile delinquent, a UCLA dropout dallying with both Phyllis and Lola and liable at any moment to boil over with hotheaded anger (as he does when he finds that Neff has given Lola a ride to meet him downtown—Zachetti's natural setting). He might as well be wearing a zoot; what we have instead is his ethnically marked name. Zachetti may be a mask for social anxieties in the United States of 1943. The L.A. zoot-suit riots occurred in June; *Double Indemnity* started filming there in September.

The second matter is the Southern Railroad observation car, the site of Neff's and Phyllis's faking of Mr. D's death. The train, not least because of the active leadership of A. Phillip Randolph of the Brotherhood of Sleeping Car Porters, was in the popular imagination associated with its black caretakers, the redcaps, pullman porters, and cooks who serviced railroad lines across America. In 1941, Randolph had used his power to desegregate the defense plants. *Double Indemnity* follows James M. Cain's novel only in placing the train at the center of Phyllis's and Walter's plot, but the scene in which Walter mimics

Dietrichson's death prominently features several black railroad workers, both sentinels and servants of the racially marked space of the coach. Not one of these workers, interestingly, casts an identifying look at Neff's face as he boards the train. *Double Indemnity* seems to suggest again the importance of black help in marking off the white self—hence their aid in this alibi—even as the black attendants betray Walter Neff's criminality by their very presence. Neff has chosen the perfect place to evince his "black" heart.

Rarely are the raced double lives of noir protagonists made as plain as they are in George Cukor's *A Double Life* (1948). Actor Tony John (Ronald Colman), who has great difficulty leaving his stage roles in the theater, takes the part of none other than Othello. He is reluctant at first because he knows he will, as usual, get too involved in the character. But the shadowy glimpses he catches of himself in mirrors and dark plate glass (which make casual use of noir's links between dark lighting and blackness) convince him there is an Othello somewhere inside him. In fact, this may be intimated early on when Tony says that becoming ambitious as an actor meant "tearing myself apart, and putting myself together again, and again," papering over inner life and unself-conscious rages. These come out as the play's run continues. Tony falls into a romantic intrigue with a waitress, Pat Kroll (Shelley Winters), whom he chokes to death Othello-style when he becomes jealous of the affair he suspects between his former wife Brita (Signe Hasso) and the play's publicity agent. (The racial underpinnings of this crime are stressed, albeit unconsciously, when Pat, in response to Tony's raving about all the assumed nationalities he carries within him, says, "I got mixed blood too.") The publicity agent's decision to link the unsolved murder to their production of Othello presses on the substantial interpenetration in *A Double Life* of art and reality and also black rage and white crime, particularly because it is Tony's violent rage when he hears of this scheme that helps reveal his crime. Carrying the theatrical metaphor into the world, the police arrange to have a waitress disguised as Pat confront Tony, his horrified response to whom confirms his guilt. Wandering the black streets in his blackened state, Othello is exposed: Tony impales himself on a knife during his character's final speech and dies, like Othello, of the uncontrollable rage released by his alter ego.

Usually the presentation is a bit more oblique. Delmar Daves's *Dark Passage* (1947), for instance, plays cosmetic changes on *Double Life*'s conceit. Vincent Parry (Humphrey Bogart) has been wrongly imprisoned for murdering his wife and escapes from San Quentin. Although the film is interested in exonerating

Parry, it nonetheless saddles him with a complexion that he must leave behind because it is recognizable. In fact we don't see Parry/Bogart's face for more than an hour into the film because its pivot is the cosmetic surgery that results in Bogart's face and the chance at a redemptive new life. The suspicious, as-good-as-guilty "true" face is invisible to us, either not shown in the frame or (of course) heavily shadowed. The key taxi ride that leads Parry to the plastic surgeon who transforms his face is a striking instance of "blackening" as Bogart sits in a deep, localized shadow. For all intents and purposes, Parry is guilty, and moreover, his new face does nothing to keep blackmailers and conniving snitches off his back. Parry's "true" complexion only goes underground, first submerged under the white bandages that help heal his face and then under the face naturalized as Bogart's. Against the film's wishes and despite our glimpse in a newspaper photograph of Parry's old face, we can't help feeling that there is something waiting to manifest itself or continuing to cause the difficulties from which Parry has so much trouble extricating himself. When he and his newfound sweetheart Irene Jansen (Lauren Bacall) escape to Peru, we realize that this exigency was necessary and, given the locale and its racial associations in noir, fitting.

Now I shall show how three films bring out the racialized interiors of whites in extremis, which are all the more interesting for being key texts in the noir series: Max Ophuls's *The Reckless Moment* (1949), Nicholas Ray's *In a Lonely Place* (1950), and Robert Aldrich's *Kiss Me Deadly* (1955). *Kiss Me Deadly* is perhaps the most typical in its casual exploitation of racial tropes. The inner states and plot predicaments of detective Mike Hammer (Ralph Meeker) are conveyed at crucial moments through black characters and counterparts. The film opens with Nat King Cole on Hammer's car radio singing "I'd rather have the blues than what I got"—a lyric that later reappears in a low moment of Hammer's trajectory. The song portends the depths to which Hammer will be plunged, and it is amusing that he feels he has to turn it off as he approaches a police roadblock, the law beyond whose barricades he himself will cross as a man of the "jungle," in the film's phrase. Hammer's whiteness may contrast with the Greekness of his yammering friend Nick, who runs around hysterically, salivating over nice sports cars and shouting "va-va-voom" like the automobiles with which the so-called grease monkey is identified before he is murdered, by having one lowered into his chest.

Despite this intermittent differentiation that confirms Hammer's racial stature—not to mention one in which a seductive mob moll named Friday tempts

Crusoe Hammer—Hammer is figured as black at significant moments in the narrative. At a time of crisis, Hammer loses himself in, of all things, a black lounge, where a woman is singing "I'd rather have the blues than what I got" while Hammer drowns his sorrows so much that he has to be carried out of the club. What is more, the climactic scene in which Hammer fights the mobsters who have drugged and caged him in a bedroom plays out against the radio broadcast of a boxing match that we can only guess is the one involving black boxers whose venal promoter, Eddie, Hammer had earlier visited in search of information. With some wit, but with little sense of the racial stakes, Aldrich stages Hammer's big fight as a black one, occurring on the other side of the barricade to which Hammer routinely travels yet from which he can somehow always return.

In a Lonely Place is far richer and deeper in its racialized suggestiveness. The cranky, hard-drinking, and, it is rumored, disturbed and violent Hollywood screenwriter, Dixon Steele (Humphrey Bogart), invites a warm and quick-witted hatcheck girl back to his place so she can narrate to him a best-selling novel from which he is supposed to craft a script. She is apparently open to romance, but Steele sends her away in a taxi, whereupon she is murdered and Steele is presumed to be the murderer. His alibi comes in the form of Laurel Gray (Gloria Grahame), with whom he quickly becomes involved and with whose aid and comfort his writing recovers its power. His jealousy and temper, however, make her uneasy, and she begins to suspect his involvment in the murder. Likewise, Steele's volatility increases as he senses her doubts. When Laurel tries to leave on the day of their wedding, Steele finds her and nearly chokes her to death. At this moment the police call with the news that the hatcheck girl's killer has been discovered, but all that has transpired between Steele and Laurel has doomed their relationship.

Two crucial moments in this drama go straight to the heart of Steele's situation. The first occurs when Steele, upon hearing of the hatcheck girl's death, decides to send flowers but does not want to take them himself to her funeral. So he asks a black man spraying down the sidewalk in front of a department store if he will buy some white roses and deliver them. This appears not only to alleviate Steele's feelings of guilt (with white roses) but also to implicate by association the black man in a crime that Steele may sense he is perfectly capable of committing. The anonymous black figure signifies Steele's dark past relationships with women, whom, we are told, he has beaten and otherwise abused. Steele atones by sending his black double with white (and whitening) flowers.

The second such moment comes when Steele and Laurel go to a club and a black woman lounge singer (Hadda Brooks) sums up Steele's inner disturbances in her song. Or are they Laurel's? This *Casablanca*-style scene in which the black woman mediates white heterosexual desire suggests a homosocial bond equal to and opposite from that of Bogart and Sam, namely, one that involves Laurel and the unnamed singer, who may express the fears and loneliness Laurel feels in her relationship with a man she suspects is highly unstable. If guilt and the capacity for violence are figured in Steele's deal with the black man, the effects on Laurel of his violent, obsessive love are intimated in a black woman's song. I believe that Steele's love for Laurel is indeed a failed search for his own innocence; she is, after all, his alibi as well as his lover, and when she discovers his dark underside, Steele loses everything he originally sought in her. It is interesting to learn, then, that the working title of the film was *Behind This Mask*.[16]

There is also, incidentally, an odd moment of Hollywood self-consciousness in a quip by Steele's agent, Mel Lippman (Art Smith), who softens the blow in telling Steele he doesn't like the latter's filmscript by saying: "But then I'm the one who told Selznick to drop *Gone with the Wind!*" Here the Jew references his good racial taste—no plantation tradition for Lippman—while acknowledging what Michael Rogin has read as the Jewish role in black exploitation on-screen, from *The Jazz Singer* (1927) to *Gone with the Wind* (1939).[17] In also equating Steele's script with *Gone with the Wind,* Lippman unconsciously highlights the racial usages in which we have seen Steele engage.

The Reckless Moment departs in an important sense from these films because it uses a black figure to present the forbidden aspects of a white woman's life and thus complicates its implicit racial exploitation. The film tells the story of well-positioned Lucia Harper (Joan Bennett) who, in the absence of her traveling husband and in an attempt to keep her daughter Bea from being implicated in the accidental death of a suitor (Bea hits him with a flashlight to stave off a sexual assault, and he pitches over a railing), hides the body she has discovered on the nearby beach. Soon, however, blackmailers inform Lucia they have love letters from Bea to the suitor, Darby, that they are sure the police would want to see. But Martin Donnelly (James Mason), one of the blackmailers, falls in love with Lucia and tries to protect her, ultimately killing his partner in blackmail and being wounded in the fight. He leaves with his partner's body before Lucia can stop him, and at this point Lucia and her black maid Sybil (Frances Williams), whom we have seen several times around the house, follow Donnelly, with Sybil at the wheel. They find him at the scene of his wrecked car, dying but not before he can confess to both of the killings and exculpate Lucia's daughter.

The role of Lucia's maid Sybil is another fine illustration of a black character occupying the margins brought on to do major thematic work. Lucia's "recklessness," her independence and incipient adulterous desire for Donnelly, as well as her self-sacrifice in the effort to protect her daughter, is figured succinctly by her maid. The black woman whose very name calls up clichéd notions of penetrating wisdom not only divines the desire for Donnelly from which Lucia shrinks and expresses it for her ("I always liked him," she says); she also stands as a black double for Lucia's descent into reckless self-sacrifice, the only role we see Sybil play in all her table setting and assiduous caretaking. Her commanding the wheel at the picture's climactic moment (Lucia curses her failure of autonomy earlier, saying, "I should've driven my car") is the fullest expression of Lucia's agency in love and trouble—completes that agency, rounds it out, and makes it plainer than is respectable for a white woman to do. The maid here is not, that is, a figure of aversive lampoon but one of sympathetic identification, and the sympathy encompasses the interracial friendship as well as the female power and mobility for which Sybil stands as much as Lucia does. For all that, however, Sybil's gifts of knowing and action, which reveal Lucia's own plot and cement white and black female solidarity, nonetheless exile the black woman from the womanhood depicted at the film's end, when white suburban law—the law-abiding harmonious family telephoning long-awaited Daddy on Christmas—has been, however ironically, restored.

What such films appear to dread is the infiltration into the white home or self of unsanctioned behaviors reminiscent of the dark figures exemplified in the 1940s and early 1950s imaginary by zoot-suiters, pachucos, and Asian conspirators. What the films apparently cannot do is completely remove these figures from the picture, though noir may stave off their most fearsome shapes or place them safely elsewhere.

Many films, *The Reckless Moment* included, imagine a dark underworld that is out of sight and (usually) downtown—thus when Lucia is scheduled to meet in a bus station with the blackmailer Donnelly, one shocking frame has their conversing faces suddenly obscured by a working-class Chinese man's face in the very close foreground, as though suggesting what is out there and what, too bad for both of them, has crept in here. Or there is the Chinatown to which Elsa Bannister (Rita Hayworth) tries to escape in the last section of Welles's *The Lady from Shanghai*, a film that, for all its interest in narrating ethnicity (from Welles's "Black Irish" O'Hara to the various national and ethnic origins of his sailor associates to the abused black maid Bessie to Arthur Bannister's "Manchester Greek" mother to Elsa's own sojourn in China), is not above playing stereotypes for a laugh. For example, during the trial scene, two

Chinese women in the courtroom speaking sotto voce in their native tongue break it off, with one saying "you ain't kiddin'!" Chinatown and Elsa's Chinese gang herald the darkness of Los Angeles's would-be El Dorado and also summon the ghastly nature of Elsa's fatal plotting, although the final scene in the Chinese funhouse asserts how easy it is for such racialized corruption to gnaw at the hearts of whites split (by the famous funhouse mirrors) into dissociated parts and, as O'Hara puts it, "chewing away at their own selves." For his part, Marlowe in Dmytryk's *Murder, My Sweet* (1944) refuses the temptations of this encroaching underworld of Asian erotic enchantments (the Asian dancer in the Coconut Beach Club at whom thug Moose Malloy takes a long look) and Asian styles of adornment (the jade necklace, Ann Grayle's subtly Orientalist makeup). But they certainly have laid claim to the gruesome crew by whom he is surrounded.

Racial Others indeed keep coming back into white lives in film noir. Untoward behavior and its seemingly inevitable racial echoes indelibly mark the white inner lives of the characters—and the films—for whom race typically exists somewhere else. This is clear from the foregoing examples, but it is on spectacular display in films anxious to narrate the fate of the white family.

Murder, My Sweet, like several important noirs, depicts with varying degrees of self-consciousness a specifically racial deviance at the center of the domestic sphere. The film opens with the appearance of a dark phantom in Marlowe's office window. Turning around, Marlowe discovers the reflection's source in (still fairly dark) Moose Malloy, who speaks with what sounds like a Mexican accent and whose suit looks suspiciously zootlike. Moose is looking for the similarly ethnically resonant Velma Valento and takes Marlowe to the bar Florians—which, because of a burned-out neon lightbulb, has appropriately become "Forins"—to find her.

This plot crosscuts the one in which Marlowe tries to recover a lost jade necklace for some wealthy clients, Mr. and Mrs. Grayle. The circle of people revolving around Mrs. Grayle is rotten in ways already suggested by their lust for jade, and a quack psychoanalyst, Amthor, delves deep into Mrs. Grayle's past and predictably finds much with which to blackmail her. As Mrs. Grayle admits, "I haven't been good, not halfway good." Finally, since, as Marlowe says, "I had to know how the jade figured," he convenes all the parties in the Grayles' beach house only to discover, in a furiously doubled racial whammy, that Mrs. Grayle is Velma Valento. And to think Marlowe nearly succumbed to her seductive come-ons! In the storm of bullets that ensues, Marlowe escapes with scorched eyes that come too close to a firing gun, this near-castrating close call externalized in the eye patches he wears during his movie-long voice-over flashback and the implicitly mixed-race predicament of the Grayle family implicated in their demise.

Mothers, wives, and lovers are typically abjected in film noir, of course, but their symbolic racialization clinches its sense of immanent familial dysfunction. Otto Preminger's *Angel Face* (1953) works an interesting twist on this scheme, since it places a bickering Japanese couple in the home they serve and whose topsy-turvy gender relations they evoke. The Japanese wife who, it is alleged, has become "too American" and so no longer obeys her husband is the counterpart of the daughter of the house, Diane Tremayne (Jean Simmons), who takes too much power into her hands and finally kills her father and stepmother by—highly significantly—tampering (like a mechanic) with their car. *Angel Face* laments a putative postwar loss of innocence; Diane's real mother was killed during the war (there goes the nuclear family); and Diane's villainized discontent, which finally ends in the auto death (in both senses) of Frank Jessup (Robert Mitchum) and herself, signifies an America mired in Orientalized triviality, female usurpation, and domestic war—for all of which the rancorous Japanese couple stands as a perfect figure. The Japanese wife has not become too American; the Americans are turning Japanese.

Michael Curtiz's *Mildred Pierce* (1945) perceives this sort of threat most compellingly. Mildred (Joan Crawford) determines to win her daughter Veda's love by providing her with all available luxuries, and when this desire is stymied by her husband Bert, she leaves him. Her departure, for which (as Pam Cook rightly argues) she is demonized, sends her into a dizzying narrative space of female autonomy and ultimate defeat and punishment.[18] Mildred takes a waitress job to provide financially, but when Veda finds out about it, she is scornful and wounding—which goads Mildred into plans to open her own restaurant. The restaurant is very successful—her former boss Ida (Eve Arden) comes to work for her, and Mildred's initial investment blossoms into a whole chain of restaurants—although the success depends on the help of Monte Beragon (Zachary Scott), a mysterious roué whom Mildred marries. Unthrifty Monte ultimately bankrupts the chain of restaurants and seduces Mildred's daughter Veda to boot. Mildred catches them together, and Monte disavows his interest in Veda, whereupon Veda kills him; Mildred attempts unsuccessfully to take the rap.

What interests me about this rise and fall of an independent woman is that her trajectory is shadowed at every step by her black maid Lottie (Butterfly McQueen), who figures the proletarian fate Mildred is driven to beat and whose disabling likeness suggests Mildred's darkest dread. Lottie is the kitchen worker that always lurks somewhere inside Mildred, less the representative of the hard labor that Mildred is willing to perform for her own interest than of the "nigger work" this labor echoes. Hence Veda's joke when she discovers her mother's waitressing: she has Lottie don Mildred's work uniform to wear about the house. The two women are versions of each other. At one key moment, their interchangeability is suggested by someone's shouting for Mildred to come into the restaurant kitchen, to which Lottie, misunderstanding, answers. Not surprisingly, then, Mildred increasingly uses Lottie for the differentiating purposes of household adornment, as a sort of failed mistress of the house who puts on ridiculous airs. Even in this device, however, one sees the parodic likeness between the women amid the instituted difference.

This ambiguity in the meaning of Lottie—all that Mildred has left behind or her hidden unfitness?—is overlaid with the resonance of the "gypsy fortune teller" (as he calls himself) Beragon. He is a strange sort of raced creature—his lineage, which he says includes Spanish and Italian blood, is made the subject of fascination and discussion—now close the family circle as Mildred's husband. His counterpart is Mildred's other daughter Kay, whose memorable little "gypsy dance" perhaps indicates her danger to the family and therefore presages her death. Beragon's racial aura is in some sense aligned with his profligacy, and it is exploited in the striking scene in which we see him kiss Veda. This kiss, which is of course a near-incestuous one, is nonetheless portrayed as its opposite—as a kind of interracial seduction, with Beragon hovering in full shadow over the virginal Veda, the metaphorics of interracial sex hardly submerged at all in the lighting of the scene.

This is an extraordinary moment, and it raises the question of just what the racial crime is here. Is it mere miscegenation, or is the racial Other living much closer to home, within it in fact, part and parcel of the incestuous act that might seem diametrically opposed to the racial threat from outside but in fact only accesses it? There is an Other in the house. Thus when Monte is killed, Mildred is not automatically restored; on the contrary, in the brilliant final scene, in which Mildred and her first husband walk out into the light of day past two washerwomen scrubbing the floor on their knees, suggests that the hard labor and its racial dimension she seems to have left behind are not in fact distant but are part of the frame.

The often-stated consensus of Orson Welles's *Touch of Evil* (1958) as film noir's epitaph makes sense also because of its superb playing with the notion of white border crossings. Welles demonstrates an awareness in *Touch of Evil* of everything I have argued about film noir's sense of the intimate proximity of racial

Others to American national identity and its hysterical (if unconscious) attempts both to use and to exile in portraits of white corruption.

In Welles's counternarrative, the law comes in the form of Mexican Mike
Vargas, whose nemesis is the bloated, criminal, white police detective Hank
Quinlan (Welles). That Vargas is played by none other than a brown-faced
Charlton Heston—or Charlton Moses, as Edward Said once called him in
reference to his part in the blockbusting film of three years earlier, *The Ten
Commandments* (1956)—wittily communicates (to use Homi Bhabha's terms)
his not-white and yet not-quite-Mexican status with which Welles teases
our perception of justice's racial tropes. Vargas's brownness curiously (and, I
think, purposely) oscillates in and out of focus as we forget and remember that
this is after all Charlton Heston, undermining the simple demarcation of
whiteness. The film in fact takes internal and external border construction as
its very theme: Vargas is married to a white woman (Janet Leigh), and at the
film's start, the two are seen crossing the Mexican border into the United
States.

Does America's designation of "us" and "them" adequately parse moral
definitions between right and wrong? the film asks us, and it mixes up the
racial clues we might use to answer the question. Quinlan's attempted framing
of Vargas and other Mexicans only cements our sense of Vargas's moral purity
and exposes the processes of projection and abjection that would pin white
criminal activities on dark bodies and deploy them as racial metaphors for
white crimes. After crossing the border, when Vargas and his wife Susan kiss
for the first time in, as Susan says, "my country," the bomb explosion that
interrupts their forbidden kiss is a self-conscious turn away from black films of
racial marking and disavowal.

NOTES

Many thanks to Nancy Loevinger for putting together the panel on film noir at the
1993 Virginia Festival of American Film that generated the first version of these
remarks, and to Phil Mariani for his extremely generous and indispensable help in
getting my ideas off the ground.

1. Toni Morrison, *Playing in the Dark: Whiteness and the Literary Imagination* (Cambridge, MA: Harvard University Press, 1992); Kenneth W. Warren, *Black and White
Strangers: Race and American Literary Realism* (Chicago: University of Chicago Press,
1993), pp. 10–11; William Boelhower, *Through a Glass Darkly: Ethnic Semiosis in American Literature* (Venice: Edizioni helvetia, 1984), p. 109.

2. Nino Frank, "Un nouveau genre 'policier': L'Adventure criminelle," *L'Écran
français* 61 (1946): 8–9, 14; Jean-Pierre Chartier, "Les Américains aussi font des films

noirs," *Revue du cinéma* 2 (1946): 66–70; Raymonde Borde and Étienne Chaumeton, *Panorama du film noir Américain* (Paris: Éditions de minuit, 1955).

3. Charles Higham and Joel Greenberg, *Hollywood in the Forties* (Cranbury, NJ: A. S. Barnes, 1968), pp. 19–36; Barbara Deming, *Running Away from Myself: A Dream Portrait of America Drawn from the Films of the Forties* (New York: Grossman, 1969); Paul Schrader, "Notes on Film Noir," *Film Comment* 8 (1972): 8–13; J. A. Place and L. S. Peterson, "Some Visual Motifs of Film Noir," *Film Comment* 10 (1974): 30–35.

4. Mike Davis, *City of Quartz: Excavating the Future in Los Angeles* (New York: Vintage Books, 1990), p. 41.

5. E. Ann Kaplan, ed., *Women in Film Noir* (London: British Film Institute, 1978).

6. Joan Copjec, ed., *Shades of Noir: A Reader* (London: Verso, 1993).

7. Manthia Diawara, "Noir by Noirs: Toward a New Realism in Black Cinema," in Copjec, ed., *Shades of Noir*, pp. 261–63.

8. Peter Stallybrass and Allon White, *The Politics and Poetics of Transgression* (London: Methuen, 1986), p. 20.

9. For useful critical remarks on this film, see Richard Schickel, *Double Indemnity* (London: British Film Institute, 1992).

10. Barry Salt, *Film Style and Technology: History and Analysis* (London: Starword, 1983), pp. 287–308; Place and Peterson, "Some Visual Motifs of Film Noir."

11. Richard Dyer, "The Color of Virtue: Lillian Gish, Whiteness, and Femininity," in Pam Cook and Philip Dodd, eds., *Women and Film: A Sight and Sound Reader* (Philadelphia: Temple University Press, 1993), p. 2.

12. Julia Kristeva, *Powers of Horror: An Essay on Abjection,* trans. Leon S. Roudiez (New York: Columbia University Press, 1982), pp. 7–10.

13. Slavoj Zizek, "Eastern Europe's Republics of Gilead," in *Tarrying with the Negative: Kant, Hegel and the Critique of Ideology* (Durham, NC: Duke University Press, 1993), pp. 200–14.

14. Jacqueline Jones, *Labor of Love, Labor of Sorrow: Black Women, Work, and the Family from Slavery to the Present* (New York: Basic Books, 1985), pp. 233–34, 236; August Meier and Elliot Rudwick, *From Plantation to Ghetto,* rev. ed. (New York: Hill & Wang, 1970), pp. 242–44, 246–48; St. Clair Drake and Horace R. Cayton, *Black Metropolis: A Study of Negro Life in a Northern City* (New York: Harcourt, Brace, 1945), pp. 89–91; Fred Stanton, ed., *Fighting Racism in World War II* (New York: Monad, 1980), pp. 75–79, 157–58; Thomas Cripps, *Slow Fade to Black: The Negro in American Film, 1900–1942* (New York: Oxford University Press, 1977), pp. 374–83; Davis, *City of Quartz,* p. 43; Chester Himes, *The Quality of Hurt* (New York: Paragon House, 1972), p. 75.

15. Drake and Cayton, *Black Metropolis,* pp. 91–94; Stanton, ed., *Fighting Racism in World War II,* pp. 254–55, 258–75, 281–86, 342–44; Kenneth Clark, "The Zoot Effect in Personality," *Journal of Abnormal Psychology* 40 (1945): 143–48; Chester Himes, "Zoot Riots Are Race Riots," in his *Black on Black: Baby Sister and Selected Writings* (Garden City, NY: Doubleday, 1973), pp. 220–25; George Breitman, " 'Zoot Suit Riots' in Los Angeles," in Stanton, ed., *Fighting Racism in World War II,* pp. 254–55; Mauricio Mazon, *The Zoot-Suit Riots: The Psychology of Symbolic Annihilation* (Austin: University of Texas Press, 1984), pp. 15–53 (quotation from p. 22); Dana Polan, *Power and Paranoia: History, Narrative, and the American Cinema, 1940–1950* (New York: Columbia University Press, 1986), pp. 1–3.

16. Alain Silver and Elizabeth Ward, ed., *Film Noir: An Encyclopedic Reference to the American Style,* rev. ed. (Woodstock, NY: Overlook Press, 1992), p. 144.

17. Michael Rogin, *Blackface, White Noise: Jewish Immigrants in the Hollywood Melting Pot* (Berkeley and Los Angeles: University of California Press, 1996).

18. Pam Cook, "Duplicity in Mildred Pierce," in Kaplan, ed., *Women in Film Noir,* pp. 68–82.

7

Basketball, Rodney King, Simi Valley

Matthew P. Brown

Arguably the most disturbing media representation of the Los Angeles riots occurred on April 30 on the *NBC Nightly News*. This was the day after the Simi Valley verdict was announced and one of the jurors from the trial was being interviewed. What became clear was that the worldview allowing the verdict also governed the reaction to the city riots. In rationalizing the trial outcome, the juror expressed sentiments about the unrest in line with the psychology that transformed the excessive use of batons on the head of a U.S. citizen into Rodney King's transgression.

First, the juror explained that the officers were not racially motivated in their beating because two docile blacks arrested at the same time were not harmed—a sad standard for law enforcement and a deeply colored color blindness.[1] Second, the juror asserted that the aggression of the four cops paled next to the violence of the day's events in the city. This is a painful relativism, blind to what the video tells us about the normalcy of police brutality in the Los Angeles Police Department (LAPD), more blind to what the legal system charged the juror to judge, and most blind to what inner-city African Americans experience. King's transgression and the destructive actions of South Central residents are of a piece, a black thing that suburbanites would not understand, even though the uprisings featured a rainbow of participants. To the juror, urban African Americans were "acting up," unable to behave as decently as the people of Simi Valley do.

For many people, the most pleasurable form of media representation in the spring of 1992 was their coverage of basketball. Basketball held an inordinate amount of attention, reflected not only in college and professional play-offs and in anticipation of the summer's Olympic "Dream Team" but also in the entertainment offerings of local theaters. Versions of the Los Angeles game were evident in Ron Shelton's box-office hit *White Men Can't Jump* and in the final run of Lawrence Kasdan's *Grand Canyon*. In such a realm, basketball is more than a sport; it is a cultural practice, and in contemporary America, its symbols and myths are deeply racialized. Images of basketball become a site for understanding relations between the black and white races and between the city and the suburbs. The pleasure has a politics.

The social meanings of basketball construct a way of seeing race that can help explain the worldview of the Simi Valley juror, and I shall use the game's visual semiotics in the Kasdan and Shelton films. Basketball's stereotypical association with black American males has become the matter of popular visual narrative, converted by Hollywood and Madison Avenue to countless movie tie-ins (*Blue Chips, Above the Rim, The Air up There, Celtic Pride, Sunset Park,* and *Eddie,* to name a few) and ad campaigns (from Nike's, Reebok's, and Foot Locker's various "street" aesthetic spots to the parodies of "ball in the 'hood" delivered by Pizza Hut, Dollar Rental Car, and Sprite).

The representation of black masculinity in these popular texts visually defines racial ideology, a crucial analytic category when discussing the Simi Valley verdict. It was the visual evidence of the Rodney King beating and the video's confirmation of the way of seeing that described the suburb's attitudes toward race. As Judith Butler points out, the jurors—with the help of the defense attorneys—decoded the King video, seeing in it not the brutal victimization of a citizen by representatives of the state but, rather, the bodily threat of a black man in "control" of the conflict and in need of constraint. This feat suggests that visual evidence never "speaks for itself," that structures of visibility preexist and frame the evidence. Butler construes a white paranoic way of seeing that emanates from Simi Valley, a visual field that inverted and projected the police officers' behavior onto King, locating in the black male body "the source of danger, the threat of violence."[2] Popular entertainment, the Rodney

King videotape, and the officers' trial form a visual epistemology that helps us hypothesize one mode of white suburban thinking about race.

Although studying the circulation of media images concerning basketball and popular film provides a visual ideology of race, such an approach also enables a more immediate contextualization of the cultural work done by *Grand Canyon* and *White Men Can't Jump.* Missing from the excellent criticism of the films is their location in the circuits of media representation during the spring of 1992.

For example, Thomas DiPiero links the films in his discussion of the hysteria of white masculinity, a psychoanalytic reading that theorizes the dynamics of idealized race and gender norms without situating these insights in the ideological field of contemporary U.S. race relations.[3] Hazel Carby places *Grand Canyon* in a genealogy of liberal U.S. crisis narratives traced back through Stowe's *Uncle Tom's Cabin* and Sturges's *Sullivan's Travels.* For Carby, Kasdan's didactic film intervenes in the chaos of current race relations—a prophecy borne out by the events of April 29–May 4, 1992—by exhorting its white middle-class audience to perform selfless acts of patronage, "acts that are enacted upon black bodies . . . [as means to] secure and confirm racialized national identities and, in doing so, to bring narrative coherence and cohesion to the incoherence and fragmentation of [its] own historical time."[4] Carby's abstraction here produces a theoretically sophisticated argument about *Grand Canyon,* demystifying its noxious fantasy, but it begs several questions. How are the film's themes of benevolent white liberalism reconciled with the embattled paranoia of white vision in Simi Valley, a community that is 1.5 percent nonwhite and home to both the Ronald Reagan Presidential Library and more than 24 percent of the LAPD?[5]

It is precisely this complication, however, that more fully exposes a white way of seeing, a perceptual model evidenced in the films, a visual mode that coordinates both the liberal sentiments of the films' directors and the more reactionary attitudes that resulted in the Simi Valley verdict. Judith Butler's accurate focus on the perceived threat of the black male body in the King video neglects the counterimages that fuel this stereotype. Consider again the Simi Valley juror who began this chapter and whose language leans toward a certain type of black character. The juror suggested that white suburbia likes its black men passive, happy, and ethically pure, all the better to justify their oppression when they deviate from this ideal. This idealization of black men is deeply etched in the Simi Valley field of vision as well, and the aesthetics of basketball performance—its graceful moves and bodily display—also contributes to the perceptual model. Such a way of seeing blackness is fundamental to the Shelton and Kasdan films, and a reading attentive to spectacle, style, fashion, casting, and point of view—as they inform narrative and character— can uncover the ideological function of this idealization. With attention to how vision is structured in popular representations of race, gender, and sexuality, I will trace the damaging moral and erotic myths attached to images of basketball, damage staged daily on television and in theaters during that spring of 1992.

It is an arresting montage: the glamour and style of 1990s urban basketball set to an anthem of confrontational optimism for the counterculture of the early 1970s. In the spring of 1992, Nike Shoes cannibalized the corpse of John Lennon a second time, its celebrated advertisement trading gorgeously static images of young black men with fade-away text from the lyrics of "Instant Karma." A Great Black Scorer sits on a backboard, judging the fate of errant shots; superstars Michael Jordan and Scottie Pippen stretch for a moment on playground asphalt; even white men jump, as we glimpse an especially dorky jam by a fellow in a bandanna headdress (a fashion choice caught somewhere between the hippie ethos and the inner-city gang uniform).

The Nike ad constructs two ways of seeing black masculinity that are mediated through the sport of basketball. It represents young black men as objects of a spectacle, objects of beauty and terrifying prowess on which we whites are to gaze with awe. For many whites, the grace and athleticism of basketball are hard to separate from the language of "flash" and "showtime" that is overassociated with black players and "street" hoops. This language not only denigrates the labor it takes to perfect the moves, fakes, and dunks that comprise such "flashiness"; it also insists on seeing black players as performers on display, as mere entertainers offered up for our pleasure. Indeed, the Nike ad underlines this stereotype with images of young blacks posing for a photo- graph and before a mirror. Most egregiously, the ad alludes to this history of representation—of "happy darkies," blackface minstrels, and pimps—with a cut from the gleaming smile of a young black to a billboard of one of the Lennon chorus's key words: *shine.*

The ad also uses another stereotype, referred to obliquely in the image of the Great Scorer: the stereotype of the Conscientious Negro. The "Great Scorer" is a term from Christian sports rhetoric, the idiomatic expression of certain school coaches and summer camp leaders: "When the Great Scorer comes to mark against your name,/He marks not whether you won or lost, but how you played the game." The figure seated on top of the backboard recalls this image of religious judgment. Omnipotent and indifferent, the God figure controls the game from a unique vantage point; his massive figure towers above the earthly viewer in an unreal position of power, and he administers justice with calm aplomb.

This moral power also has a history in the representation of African Americans, in which blackness is used to educate whites through figures of judgment and martyrdom. Think of Harriet Beecher Stowe's Tom, or the funeral scene at the close of Douglas Sirk's *Imitation of Life*. The images have their roots in the real suffering that African Americans have endured; Christian discourse teaches that suffering grants its victims a moral power. White investment in the moral purity of black images creates another stereotype, one that sees skin color solely as a lesson in ethics.

These two paradigms are given narrative shape in the films I am considering: protagonists act in a world in which the paradigms of blackness have both erotic and moral valences, in which racialized imagery shapes character and defines value. The opening sequences of both films establish basketball as a black spectacle while making blackness a site of moral value, following the Nike ad in this regard. These sequences also introduce us to the films' black leads and "black" aesthetic. The films' opening versions of the "street" game thus become resources for the subsequent narratives to exploit. *Grand Canyon* begins with a highly stylized depiction of a fenced-in inner-city game; title credits and a moody, somber musical sound track float over slow-motion, black-and-white photography of black men on the asphalt court, with Danny Glover the recognizable star of the group. The images—which are then contrasted with the indoor color of the L.A. Lakers "showtime," pumped by an upbeat version of the same music—cry sincerity. The editing emphasizes the fragmented body parts of the players, who wear little besides sneakers and shorts. Topless torsos and "ripped" biceps stress the immediacy of the black body, its ability, in this instance, to signify authenticity and naturalness according to Western perceptions of race.[6]

Similarly, by using black-and-white photography, Kasdan's sequence connotes documentary realism. Formally, the slow motion judges the value of any information it presents, asking the viewers to attend to its content. Here it is used to instruct them about the value of "truly seeing" the "real" black men of the inner city. Finally, the viewers' recognition of Danny Glover lends further moral purchase to the game's representation. Wearing a knee brace, Glover signals a star presence that is essentially the image of the earnest martyr. One of his most popular roles is in the *Lethal Weapon* buddy films, in which he plays the patient family man responsible for the unpredictable Mel Gibson.

White Men Can't Jump styles basketball and blackness in different terms.

Rather than *Grand Canyon*'s sincerity, the street game that opens the former film celebrates the trash talk of the court, the psychological and linguistic competition between opponents. The black players insult and brag to one another, argue over the correct score, and protest fouls as the camera moves in a dizzying circle to record and involve the community on and off the court. Particular emphasis is given to Sidney Deane (Wesley Snipes), who is his own best cheerleader but who also postpones the game momentarily to meet with his wife and child and to give them money. The players offer the requisite "mama" jokes and denigrate the speakers' bodies. The emphasis on talk could emerge from specific African American traditions like toasting and playing the dozens, forms of communication that rejoice in speakers' oral feats and the words they choose.

The white hero (Billy Hoyle, played by Woody Harrelson) repeatedly invokes a criticism of a presumed black ethic—that looking and sounding good is the ultimate behavioral value, over and above victory or material security—which is endorsed here both visually and verbally. Shelton significantly sets the first game at Venice Beach, a multicultural site in the Los Angeles area known as a place for bodies to see and be seen. The film goes on to present games in South Central neighborhoods, but the exclusive presence of African Americans on the beach court underscores how blackness is to be offered up for the gaze.

Unlike Kasdan's cool control, Shelton's aesthetic suggests that the camera is overwhelmed by the dizzying spectacle of the black players. Rather than shooting from the sidelines, the camera is often placed in the midst of the action on the court, and in some ways this creates a nonobjectifying relationship between subject and camera. At the same time, the movie's editor works doubly hard to include the sideline action, the communal investment, the spectatorial obsession with basketball's blackness. Style and spectacle—looking good at all costs, one of the film's principal definitions of blackness—shape the meaning of basketball in the narrative.

But as with Kasdan's opening, the scene refers to the moral significance of blackness, here specified as an individualized focus on Sidney/Snipes.[7] In the scene's very first minute and constituting the bulk of the first lines of this principal character, we hear Sidney/Snipes say about his opponent no fewer than five times: "It's hard work making you look so bad." This sentence is a distillation of the moral complexities that the film tries to address. The insistence in this sentence is asking us to revalue "stylishness" as it relates to Snipes's character, arguing that it is indeed hard work, that basketball's beauty and grace requires labor. The cut to Sidney/Snipes with his wife and child is likewise a point at which we are to understand his character's ethical stability, his role as a "family man" responsive to—and financially responsible for—the woman he is committed to. This responsibility is developed as the film unfolds.

These images of black basketball are themselves contextualized in terms of the two films' central white male protagonists. Because basketball is offered as a site of essential blackness, the respective narratives create means for *Grand Canyon*'s Mack (played by Kevin Kline) and Billy/Harrelson to define their place racially, establishing identification patterns for the white viewers at the narratives' beginning.[8]

Grand Canyon is a kind of "answer" film to Spike Lee's *Do the Right Thing,* a composite portrait of urban crisis told by an ensemble of actors. It begins working its titular metaphor as it cuts from the street game to the Forum crowd, where we are introduced to wealthy, front-seat spectators Davis (Steve Martin) and Kline. The script soon tells us that Kline's yuppie character is in a midlife crisis, and the film communicates this visually as well. Viewers are made to take Mack/Kline's perspective. After noticing his stiff facial discomfort, we see Mack's gaze shift from the game to the guiltily consumed images of the crowd's young women, pictured, like the earlier street game, in slow motion. Whereas Glover was an object in our view, the camera explicitly allows us to follow Kline's gaze. Although this point of identification is no doubt sensible for the imagined market of a Kasdan film, the politics of the subject position is problematic. Kline's performance style stresses the guilt of the white gaze. We are asked to compare the sincerity of the earlier images of blackness with Kline's voyeuristic character and to understand the former as a reproof of the latter. (The entire sequence functions like this, with the glitz of the Forum crowd being reproved by the honest immediacy of the street game.)

The erotic gaze is no less burdened with guilt. For Kline's character Mack and the identifying audience, the slow motion and the shift from the Laker players to young women imply that white male desire is itself mediated through attraction to the black male body. In the social construction of desire, black masculinity is a zone of mythical sexuality that is the choice of women and the envy of the inadequate straight white male. This myth of potent sexuality— which in other contexts can threaten, panic, and justify terrible violence—is coded here as another erotic option, another form of beauty open to the privileged white male viewer.

Compare this scene with the theater of the beaten black male body, wit-nessed in lynching rituals and, of course, the King videotape. The white male perpetrators of such violence are driven in part by their perceived lack in the face of such a sexual ideal, and their punishment—intended to de-sexualize the victim—reveals their own erotic investment in the black male other. As Butler notes, the sexual slurs used against King by the officers, the repeated references to his "ass" and "the image of the police standing over Rodney King with their batons" are conflicted expressions of homophobia, of "a sexual degradation which ends up miming and inverting the imagined scene of sexual violation that it appears to want and to loathe."[9]

Although the emotional subtext of the Rodney King brutalization is rage and lust, for the viewer caught in Mack/Kline's gaze, it is lust and guilt. The conflicted expression of homoeroticism drifting toward straight eroticism leads Mack not to externalized violence but to internalized punishment. His wayward desire—ambivalently and pleasurably caught between the black men and the young women in a kind of liberal *aporia*—indicates both his spectatorial access and his guilt for possessing such voyeuristic power. The story's action follows up on this characterization—Mack cheats on his wife with a younger secretary and feels bad about it. But in defining this waywardness through point-of-view shots, the film makes the black male body into a site of libidinal attachments that secures straight white masculinity in a form of privileged crisis. This waywardness is what the narrative seeks to reform in Kline's character.

What the film communicates visually in the opening sequence—the investment of blackness with moral purpose and objectified beauty—is developed narratologically in Mack's reformation, which in the movie's limited ethos means a way out of liberal guilt. How does the film relate this transformation? A crucial scene after the Lakers game has Mack/Kline's car breaking down in an abandoned Inglewood neighborhood and a young black gang threatening him until tow-truck driver Simon/Glover appears, to calm the situation.

The scene effectively typologizes blackness for the film, distinguishing between the good individual and the bad mob.[10] The narrative is then able to feel good about the representation of its other black characters, all of whom wrongly suffer. Simon's wife has left him; his daughter, attending college in Washington, D.C., is deaf; Simon's sister, nephew, and niece are victimized by a drive-by shooting; after the family moves, the nephew is wrongly suspected by police officers in Canoga Park; and Alfre Woodard plays a lonely secretary at Mack's firm, who is placed in the narrative as Simon's arranged love interest. None of this is to suggest that African Americans are not actually harassed by the police, gang violence, or patronizing whites. Rather, it is to argue that Kasdan's representation quickly silences their collective anger and protest over systemic injustice by demonizing the young gang in the film's second scene. It also claims that the individual martyrs among the black characters betray their liberal pleasure in seeing African Americans sentimentally, as nobly good as long as they are weak and needy.

These sentimental images are an extension of the stylized authenticity given to the opening rendition of the street game. They place that "black" aesthetic of sincerity and immediacy in a dramatic context that serves to assuage Mack's guilt and waywardness by answering it with the moral law, delivered by Glover's Simon. Their friendship gives Simon a Delphic role as he repeatedly utters folk platitudes and proclaims idealized social relations, which are meant to soothe Mack/Kline and the audience. Simon's first extended speech, to the gang leader, establishes his role. He tries to persuade the youth of the wrongness of the gang's position:

> The world ain't suppose to work like this. Maybe you don't know that. But this ain't the way it is supposed to be. I'm supposed to be able to do my job without asking you if I can. That dude [Mack/Kline] is supposed to be able to wait with his car without you ripping him off. Everything's supposed to be different than it is.

Soon after the showdown has been resolved, Mack and Simon discuss the state of the city's suffering. Simon explains the insignificance of the human condition in the face of natural beauty, in a speech that prefigures his deliverance of Mack and family to the Grand Canyon at the film's close:

> It took so long for that thing to get to look like that. It ain't done either. It happens right while you're sitting there watching it. It's happening right now as we sit in this ugly town. . . . When you sit on the edge of that thing . . . you realize what a joke we people are, what big heads we got thinking what we do is gonna matter all that much. . . . Those rocks were laughing at me and my worries. It's real humorous to that Grand Canyon.

This is Grand Mystification, a tourist site used to explain away more than interpersonal crisis; it renders all "petty" human problems—like gang warfare, neglected urban neighborhoods, access to guns: that is, what the film's setting and previous scene witness—insignificant before the canyon's transcendental, ahistorical space. Later in the film, Mack returns to Simon to thank him and explain Simon's salvational force in his life, but here, too, Mack is lost, wanting to repay Simon but sensing that this action is patronizing. Mack offers to fix up Simon's sister in an apartment, and Simon laughs again at Mack's insensitivity: "You're a piece of work. . . . Sometimes mucking around in people's lives is *dangerous*." The story cleverly admits and disavows the issue of patronage for the self-aware liberal audience. They discuss this problematic power-relation as

Kline asks whether he has offended Simon by offering to help his sister and whether race matters to Simon (Simon jokingly responds, "You white?"). Patronage is nevertheless endorsed as the story proceeds, with Kline helping Simon's sister move and offering him a girlfriend.[11]

The racial politics of *White Men Can't Jump* is more complicated. Thematically, the film is about hustling, dissembling, and prejudice, issues that make the story's racialized ethics anxiously present. In other words, hustling, as the film's narrative dynamic, permits racial anxieties to surface that can also be read as mere psychological warfare. Billy Hoyle is a white hustler who is on the lam with his girlfriend Gloria (Rosie Perez). He is being pursued by the Stucchi brothers, gambling operatives for whom Billy was to throw a college game in Louisiana. Billy is $7,000 in debt because he resented an opponent's calling him "honky" and so played the game honestly. But Billy's pleasure in gambling is an equally important motivation. He comes to Los Angeles to hustle games and forms a partnership with Sidney/Snipes. Their ploy will be to use Billy's race to fool black playground opponents, who presumably will not see the hustle coming.

As I suggested earlier, assumptions about the style and moral value of blackness underpin the story, and as with *Grand Canyon,* we can trace their development through the education of the film's white male protagonist. Unlike *Grand Canyon*'s Mack, who agonizes over (while securing) liberal white privilege, Billy/Harrelson is situated in a "black" milieu, the various playground games that advance the story's plot. The film's explicit lesson is that Billy needs to value a more mature responsiveness to women, and he learns it through the essential blackness posited by the film's representation of basketball and its characterization of Sidney Deane.

Just as the opening of *Grand Canyon* contrasts white privilege with black authenticity, so too racial difference can be understood relationally at the start of *White Men Can't Jump.* We are introduced to Billy Hoyle before the basketball game, and his actions relate a dumb brashness that is meant to be both appealing and in need of reform. Billy appears at Venice Beach in the morning before the human traffic arrives. Three elderly black men sing a swing version of the church hymn "Closer Walk with Thee," to which Hoyle goofily jukes. He cheers them and rudely offers $50 as a joke after he is asked for a contribution. Then when he gives them a dollar, he asks about the King and the Duck, two legends of the court about whom Holye boasts, in an emphasized close-up, that he surpasses. He then reviews the old men's performance: "Keep singing. You know, my old man was a preacher. . . . I love that shit."

Shelton has it both ways in the scene, enabling identification for the white spectator while displaying flaws in the character of Billy Hoyle. Unlike the communal vitality of the subsequent images of Venice Beach, Hoyle is pictured as the irreverent outsider, alone in the early morning, a convertibled rebel on the road, a duffel bag of worldly belongings replacing the traditional bandanna on a stick. He is a twentysomething Huck Finn, as the allusion to the "King and the Duck" indicates. His position as viewer of the doo-wop group recreates the motif of black spectacle of all these texts, and the motif is problematized more acutely in Shelton's script.

Hoyle's attitude is proudly thick to black traditions like gospel music, and his irreverence is intended to be mean and humorous. The bravado about his basketball skill is to be received as similarly unwise. Harrelson's dress, performance style, and star presence also signal the character's dumbness in the black context. Long, hemmed khaki shorts; a tie-dyed baseball cap; a T-shirt that features Tipper Gore's cautionary label for "adult" musical recordings—all these fashion choices allude to the black style of urban youth but rigorously reject it as well (there's no team logo on the cap and no bright team colors on the long shorts, nor do rap fans care for the "Parental Advisory" sign's censorship of the music's content). Harrelson's speech is usually slow and sluggish, conventionally signifying a dull mind. Finally, Billy Hoyle is also Woody Harrelson's "Woody" from the TV show *Cheers*, the country's favorite exemplar of the dumb-guy convention in the sitcom genre. The film assertively constructs the category of the "dumb white guy," a figure with whom white viewers are to identify and critique but whose validity must be acknowledged.

Although the film's story traces the limits to which we can appreciate this brash irresponsibility, we should pause to understand the way that whiteness is functioning as a cultural style in Shelton's narrative. The creation of a white style in reaction to a perceived black style is perhaps the most troubling sign of how deeply ingrained the film's assumptions about blackness are. For although Hoyle's dumbness is also a ruse in the context of the story's dramatic action— he's a hustler—the story occasionally takes a Bakke-like pride in its implicit commentary on "reverse racism." As Hoyle explains during his initial hustle, black players have preconceptions about his "geeky chump" style that make them dupes.

In the humorous, racialized debates over musical taste, Billy/Harrelson proudly carves out a space for George Jones in the black-inflected sound track, and the character later croons a country song to Gloria cowritten by Harrelson and Shelton. Hoyle is in some ways obsessed with this racial difference. He loses an entire day's payoff to prove what the film's title says he can't do. And the story is itself organized around a racial slur, the "honky" taunt of an opposing player that ruined Billy and sent him on the run. Again, these are partially understood as flaws in his character, but they also are meanings available to white viewers that comprehend whiteness as an embattled position, that parallel the beliefs of the juror who could construe Rodney King as being in "control" of his confrontation with white cops.

The answer to Billy/Harrelson's irresponsibility is Sidney/Snipes, who plays Jim to Harrelson's Huck. The thickheadedness of the "dumb white guy" is most fervently devalued on the domestic front, where Sidney provides a pointed contrast. Shelton's self-satisfied treatment of the relationship between Gloria/Perez and Billy mocks or questions Billy's insensitivity and jealousy. When Gloria agrees with Sidney's distaste for George Jones, Billy quickly becomes domineering, demanding that she throw out her chewing gum. When Sidney first mentions Billy's good fortune to be seeing Gloria, Hoyle stiffens and immediately suspects Sidney of illicit desire. Sidney recognizes this racialized envy for the phantasm it is, and the script asks us to criticize Billy here.

This critique of traditional white masculinity is undermined, however, by the characterization of Gloria. Shelton compliments himself for presenting female characters who express intelligence and sexual desire; here it is Gloria's prowess on *Jeopardy* and her repeated verbal and bodily injunctions to have sex with Billy that announce Shelton's supposedly progressive vision. Just as dubiously enlightened is Billy's "new male" education. In a postcoital bedroom scene, Gloria/Perez claims that women's demands on men are merely interpersonal. Basing her argument on a magazine article, Gloria maintains that Billy should not give her water when she is thirsty but, rather, empathize with "the concept of dry-mouthedness." Billy later wins Gloria back by singing a song that includes lyrics about his ability to sympathize with dry-mouthedness. There's a clever satire of *Cosmo* feminism in here somewhere, but the script ultimately heroizes Billy for learning a lesson about sympathy originally mocked when it came from the mouth of Gloria/Perez. His newfound sensitivity to women is riddled with "bad faithedness."

The development of Snipes's character in relation to Billy/Harrelson is perhaps the chief means by which the narrative reforms Hoyle, through bonds that are unconsciously erotic and signally moral. Although the happy ending that finds Billy and Sidney together (rather than with their respective female partners) tells us the film's principal attraction is between men, there are subtly fraught moments of sexualized play as well. When Billy first hustles Sidney, in a shooting contest after the Venice Beach game, we hear the white protagonist resort to name-calling that is suggestively gendered. Billy Hoyle is first elaborately identified by Sidney and Junior (Kadeem Hardison) as Cindy Brady, the youngest *Brady Bunch* girl from the 1970s TV show. Billy Hoyle then repeatedly becomes "Billy *Ho*"—Sidney and other black ballplayers converting his name to a slang term for prostitute (a contraction of *whore*).

This feminization of Billy—alternating between the excessive innocence of iconic white girlhood to the degradation of alienated sex work—finds its authority in the myth of the potent straight black man, who can have his way with the virgin/whore Billy. But because it is a hustle, this humiliation turns to triumph for Billy and for the identifying, potentially threatened white audience. His triumph also stimulates Sidney's interest as he longingly looks at Billy after the geeky white chump has taken his $60. Sidney's smiling desire comes manifestly from his plot to hustle games with Billy. But the rhetoric of their joking implies that a sexual exchange has taken place, and within the social construction of desire, gaining the black man's erotic attention is a coup for white masculinity. To be sure, the name-calling is intended to be a joke, but it would not be a joke without the slippage of meaning that, in this case, establishes Sidney's sexual authority and investment.

More explicitly, Sidney progressively fits the role of the Conscientious Negro. The story gradually shows Sidney in more and more roles of responsibility. After the early hustling scenes, we see him and his family trying to buy a house; we see him at a hot-dog stand that is his makeshift office, contracting a client for home remodeling work; after his home is robbed, we see him firmly committed to pulling his wife and daughter out of Crenshaw, the impoverished section of Los Angeles where they live. Moreover, Sidney adopts the role of moral guide in his exchanges with Billy. After rocky times, at an admission of his friendship with Billy, Sidney comically states, "Everyone's got a cross to bear and you are my cross." From here on, Sidney advises Billy on his love life. Sidney continually intones him to "listen to the woman."

When the King and the Duck are open for a challenge and Sidney needs the money to recoup losses from the burglary, Billy has to choose between Sidney and Gloria, and the game—which they ultimately win—takes precedence. After Gloria leaves him for good, Billy turns imploringly to Sidney for guidance, who simply says that he gave Billy advice from which Billy must make a choice. In the film's final scene, Billy presents more questions to Sidney about the incantatory advice ("If I listen to the woman, does that mean I have to agree with her?"), and Billy realizes that he needs a job, which Sidney will try to get for him.

Ultimately, the narratives and images of basketball from the spring of 1992 suggest that an ideology of bald racism cannot fully explain the beliefs of Simi

Valley suburbia. The phobic treatment of black men that reduces them to threatening figures of physical danger is complicated by white notions of ethical purity and erotic attraction. At one level, the perceived actions of Rodney King and of black men in the streets of many cities after the Simi Valley verdict seem distant from the conventions of entertainment and moral instruction traced in the Nike ad and the films. "Rioting" and "looting" conform to a tradition of arguably more destructive stereotypes: the irrational primitive, the angry, group-thinking mob.

The roles played by Glover and Snipes, along with basketball's images of beauty and grace, seem to be a healthy corrective to this tradition. But replacing one set of stereotypes for another does not address systemic racism. Rather, racial discrimination and violence are fueled by a psychology dependent on all these traditional stereotypes, and it is a psychology that motivates not only sensational hate crimes but also the country's institutional life, its hiring practices, its law enforcement, and its legal decisions. (The LAPD's actions make the last two difficult to distinguish.) When young black men defy their mythic status as passive objects, as "gifted" athletes, as moral paragons, the other, demonizing myths of gangs and gangsterism—myths the media overemphasize—are enabled and so take on added force.

The perceptual models portrayed in the films turn on notions of whiteness, on the central characters' and the implied white audience's investment in the black other. To construe the liberal sentiments of these basketball images as a white way of seeing is also to discover the overlap between Simi Valley conservatism and more moderate political positions, like the 1992 Democratic presidential campaign. Engineered by the Democratic Leadership Council, the Clinton/Gore strategy toppled the party's historic platform for black minority protest—wrecked dramatically in Clinton's denunciation of Sister Souljah before the national convention—as a means to claim the political "center." By casting Simi Valley residents as beyond-the-pale reactionaries, we blind ourselves to a racial ideology that encouraged both Bill Clinton's and Newt Gingrich's incumbency. Such a hegemony is one model for understanding these narratives, whose troubling images of race should look all of us, as Lennon chants, "right in the face."

NOTES

1. The juror remarked that "if it had truly been a racial incident, all three of them would have been beaten."

2. Judith Butler, "Endangered/Endangering: Schematic Racism and White Para-

noia," in Robert Gooding-Williams, ed., *Reading Rodney King/Reading Urban Uprising* (New York: Routledge, 1993), p. 15. Also see Robert Gooding-Williams, "Look, a Negro!" in Gooding-Williams, ed., *Reading Rodney King/Reading Urban Uprising*, pp. 164–67.

3. Thomas DiPiero, "White Men Aren't," *Camera Obscura* 30 (May 1992): 113–37.

4. Hazel Carby, "Encoding White Resentment: *Grand Canyon*—A Narrative for Our Times," in Cameron McCarthy and Warren Crichlow, eds., *Race, Identity and Representation in Education* (New York: Routledge, 1993), p. 237.

5. Marc Cooper and Greg Goldin, " 'Some People Don't Count'," *Village Voice*, May 12, 1992, pp. 28–29, 36–40.

6. Richard Dyer, *Heavenly Bodies: Film Stars and Society* (New York: St. Martin's Press, 1986), pp. 71–88, 120–24.

7. Following Dyer, Stanley Cavell, and others, I use the convention of naming the character and the star simultaneously, a rhetorical device that emphasizes the inseparability of star and role when analyzing a particular film's character. The importance of casting, celebrity, and audience taste in Hollywood film argues for the virtue of this interpretive strategy. At times, however, I use only one name, for purposes of style and clarity.

8. Richard Dyer studies the construction of whiteness in commercial film, understanding it as always relational to a narrative's positing of blackness. See his "White," *Screen* 29 (1988): 44–64.

9. Butler, "Endangered/Endangering," pp. 18, 21.

10. Carby offers a sharp reading of the aural signifiers of this scene, suggesting the siege mentality of the white middle class in urban America through a study of the confrontation between Mack's music (Warren Zevon's "Lawyers, Guns and Money") and the black youths' (NWA's "Quiet on the Set and F★★★ the Police"). See her "Encoding White Resentment," pp. 240–42.

11. Carby's focus on patronage mistakes it as an issue to which the narrative is blind. This reads the film's ideology too crudely, missing the effectiveness of the film's cultural work: the story must build in this structure of disavowal in order to convince an enlightened liberal viewership.

The Possum, the Hag, and the Rhinestone Cowboy: Hard Country Music and the Burlesque Abjection of the White Man

Barbara Ching

The hard country galaxy glows with dimly christened stars. Contrary to whatever logic that glamour possesses, these luminaries use such pejorative stage names as "Ol' Hank" (Hiram "Hank" Williams, 1923–1952), "The Hag" (ex-convict Merle Haggard, 1937–), "The Possum" (George Jones, 1931–), and "The Mysterious Rhinestone Cowboy" (ex-convict David Allan Coe, 1939–). Alvis Edgar Owens (1929–), better known as Buck Owens, changed his first name to match that of his Okie family's mule. When they decide to preserve their given names, hard country stars stick with the fence-post plain or the downright unflattering: Ernest Tubb (1914–1984), Hank Thompson (1925–), or John Anderson (1954–). Kentucky-born Dwight Yoakam (1956–) even shares his (real) last name with the hillbillies of Al Capp's comic-strip backwater Dogpatch.

From the moment they enter our consciousness, these singers strike a lowly pose, and their sad songs, whining steel guitars, and wailing fiddles set that pose to music. But their physical images hardly fulfill the tall, dark, and handsome celebrity ideal. Although these stars can project a certain sexual magnetism, most of them could also be called pale and paunchy. These flaws, though, fuel the star-making machine: George Jones and Johnny Paycheck released a duet in 1980 called "When You're Ugly Like Us,"[1] and in 1992, Waylon Jennings sang "I'm too dumb for New York City and too ugly for L.A."[2] Yet since so many people love to hear their woeful stories and their heart-wrenching voices,[3] these stars succeed at being abject failures. This paradox can be illuminated by an almost forgotten term: *burlesque,* a comic mode that can be used to undermine any cultural ideal. Most examples of burlesque contain intentional and spectacular violations of the standards of good taste and good behavior.[4] These violations can be either disgusting or hilarious, depending on your attachment to the cultural ideals in question. If your good taste justifies your social status,[5] you may not like to see the standards of sophistication torn down too often, but if you are down so low that your only hope is a new ideal, applauding the burlesque can give subversive pleasure.

Because it so happily scorns the standards of good taste and decency, the burlesque would seem the ideal mode for expressing and easing abjection. But cultural critics have yet to link the two phenomena, and country music itself has never been considered burlesque;[6] instead, observers note lavish sadness consoled by religious fervor.[7] Ethnographer Aaron Fox brilliantly analyzed the "trial by irony" to which hard country artists often submit their themes,[8] but irony seems both too mild and too artsy a term for the ludicrous lapses of taste and conduct that hard country obsessively displays.

Although many hard country stars write their own material, reverence for original genius is foreign to this performance style. In its place is a compulsion to repeat the sins and songs of musical relatives. With an imitative bent typical of what Bernstein calls "the abject hero,"[9] hard country singers eagerly display their dependence on their forbears and peers. For them, fine whines get better with time, so re-recordings, cover versions, and duets are important components of most hard country careers. Likewise, hard country songs cultivate triteness by alluding to earlier songs and singers. Along with creating a sorrowful rustic persona, these singers use the typically burlesque techniques of imitation, allusion, and collusion to call attention to the fact that they are falling short of any number of cultural imperatives.

According to Bernstein, such display also characterizes the theater of abjection:

> Abjection is a social and dialogic category, and its expression is always governed by the mapping of prior . . . cultural models. Abjection is only felt in conversa-

tion with another, with a voice whether internal or external, whose oppressive confidence arises through its articulation of the normative values of society as a whole. (p. 29)

Although Bernstein recognizes that the abject hero's dialogic confrontation with "normative values" can provoke laughter, articulating the comic potential of this confrontation is not his primary purpose. But in hard country, abjection is constantly portrayed by an absurdly unregenerate white man while women and conventionally successful men solemnly brandish "the normative values" that underscore abjection.

The success of hard country stars, since it lies in a formulaic articulation of failure, can only be given plain, disdainful, and darkly humorous names. When they perform, the stars themselves rarely manifest in their own right the "oppressive confidence" of which Bernstein speaks. Historian Peter Stearns names this confidence "American Cool," the "dominant emotional style" of our twentieth century. The stylists, Stearns notes, are the high-achieving middle class. In other words, the stable middle-class American male has set the tone for the whole society,[10] demanding an almost purely economic success with no emotional intensity allowed, especially crying. As all of you know who wince when you hear a steel guitar and a twangy nasal voice, hard country is American uncool. Its heartaches and hangovers don't fit the mold at all.[11] John Anderson's 1983 "Black Sheep," for example, describes a character who is the family outcast simply because he shows little enthusiasm for the economic pursuits and conversational gambits of his brother the doctor and his sister the banker's wife who talk only about their status symbols.[12]

Add tears and beers to the silly names and alienating economic failure and you have the unstable concoctions that result in hard country's burlesque routines. "What's Made Milwaukee Famous Has Made a Loser out of Me" cries Jerry Lee Lewis (1968),[13] and David Allan Coe, in a duet with George Jones, complains that "the only thing I can hold onto is this bottle in my hand" (1980).[14] Merle Haggard gave "The Days of Wine and Roses" a hard twist when he "kept the wine but threw away the rose" (1967).[15] Some country radio stations refused to play Webb Pierce's classic drinking song "There Stands the Glass," since programmers evidently took seriously the singer's ponderous alcoholic optimism—"there stands the glass that will hide all my tears, that will drown all my fears" (1953).[16] Plenty of songs make it clear that sorrows don't drown. Ernest Tubb explained this in 1950 with "You Don't Have to Be a Baby to Cry,"[17] and George Jones used the same metaphor in 1990: "I sleep just like a baby—I wake up every hour and cry."[18] Buck Owens, too, exposed the frequency of crying jags with a song that stresses predictability as if it were introducing a weekly television show: "it's crying time again" (1964).[19]

Perhaps this abject destruction of "American Cool" explains why hard country now seems a virtual monopoly of white males:[20] a truly effective burlesque of the American dream may have to be enacted by those who in theory should stoically enjoy the privileges of power. Hence, unlike towering Trumps and yuppies in tasteful suits, hard country stars rise and shine because of the unexpected darkness of the background they create. Similarly, in contrast to mainstream country singers who croon reassuringly about rural idylls, cloying romance, family values, and patriotism, hard country singers moan the blues of white-trash tragedy: broken homes, decrepit houses, blackout drinking, dead-end jobs, and life sentences.

In tune with their names, the themes of hard country singers violate the standards of American dreaming. Instead of striving for the good lifestyle, they portray themselves and their listeners as the "low other" of American culture. I borrow this term from Peter Stallybrass and Allon White, who contend that interlocking hierarchies of high and low are a "fundamental basis of . . . sense-making in European cultures," [21] and as the cultural historian Lawrence Levine has shown, American culture since the nineteenth century is not nearly so far removed from the old countries' cultural hierarchies as we would like to think.[22] After all, we still get the self-deprecating joke that changed the name of the central institution of country music from *WSM Barn Dance* (1925–1927) to *The Grand Ole Opry* (1927–).[23]

Since this particular form of country music is now dominated by white males, the "low otherness" of the hard country stars can be nothing other than a class distinction. Merle Haggard, for example, is very conscious of his whiteness, working it into the title of at least two of his songs: "I'm a White Boy" and "White Man Singing the Blues." Although this emphasis on skin color presumably allows Haggard to proclaim his membership in the most powerful group in class-unconscious America, in songs like "Working Man Blues" and "A Working Man Can't Get Nowhere Today," he reminds his listeners that the hard work, hard luck, and hard times that characterize hard country lives are class-based phenomena.[24] In fact, the theme of "White Man Sings the Blues" is a class solidarity that transcends race: after describing a duet sung with a black bluesman, the singer uses the chorus to comment on this harmony: "On the same side of the railroad track where people have nothing to lose/I'm . . . a white man singin' the blues."[25] Likewise, the "white boy" seeks "to find me . . . a line of work that don't take no diploma." In Haggard's eyes, the working class doesn't disappear with its traditional work. In "They're

Tearing the Labor Camps Down" (1972), he bemoans the postwar prosperity by asking, "Where's a hungry man gonna live in this town?" That hungry man can be pushed out of mainstream sight, but he is never out of Haggard's or other hard country minds.

For now, this man can only, in Freudian style, slip away; he still underpins the most pleasant American dreams. Even though it is sometimes suggested that we are living in an age that has dismantled the traditional barriers between high and low culture,[26] no analysis of postmodern culture indicates that social hierarchy itself has collapsed. Thus, when Stallybrass and White speak of a "psychological dependence upon precisely those Others which are being rigorously opposed and excluded at the social level," they could be talking about the ignorant rube who subtends the postmodern cultural archetype, the cyborgian master of "information." Rubes have always filled the role of "know nots," so this stock character can easily find work these days playing a loser stalled on the information highway.

As Andrew Ross notes, the division between the "knows" and the "know nots" is increasingly the form that class distinction takes in postindustrial America,[27] and hard country songs now play off and play down the "oppressive confidence" of the technocrat. George Jones's "High-Tech Redneck" (1993) gives the ideal a typically abject spin as he portrays a foolish rustic's unrequited love for modern gadgets. The title character's satellite dish broadcasting "13 channels of rasslin' " and NASCAR shows us only that "he's a bumpkin but he's plugged in."[28] This character's attempts to join the information age lead him deeper into redneck abjection (and perhaps debt). While reveling in this technophile's burlesque lowness, the song works by allowing Jones and his listeners to laugh at the animating lie of most American popular culture: the equation of tasteful purchasing power with power.[29] Money isn't enough to blanch this white man's neck; it is the lack of some mysterious acculturating knowledge that seems to keep permanently the "low other" redneck in his alienated place.

This is why one of the white man's places is called a honky-tonk; tonks are shacks, and we all know what honkies are.[30] Even though mainstream country songs often evoke a countrified party spot,[31] the hard country honky-tonk isn't even in the country. Hank Williams spells out the chain of events in his typically compressed style: "I left my home down on the rural route" is the beginning, but the end is a bad case of the citified "honky-tonk blues" (1949).[32] In fact, many songs complain that whatever pleasure the honky-tonk offers is fleeting if not illusory.

Hank Thompson exposed the good-time myth with an atrocious pun: "If a tear betrays your eye, if a memory slips too far, don't tell them that you're crying, just say smokey the bar" (1966).[33] Not that "they" really want to know; those who just wouldn't understand the honky-tonk thing are better off. As Davis Daniel sings, "She took off to a high-society school, but I earned my degree from ol' Honky-Tonk U."[34] As this cheerfully paced chorus becomes more specific, it uses hard country names to signify provincial ignorance and failure: "She went to William and Mary; I went to Haggard and Jones." Burlesque punning lets the woman rise above this squalor: at William and Mary she takes the "*high*" way" while the male graduate of Honky-Tonk U is following Haggard and Jones down a "dirt road" to possible stardom and certain alienation (1994).[35]

A honky-tonk is the proverbial school of hard knocks in which an abject white man literally and figuratively hits the bottom: he breaks his home (with some help from a honky-tonk angel), he wastes his paycheck, he falls off bar stools,[36] he bursts into tears. Condemned by both the conventionally successful man and the striving woman, honky-tonk alumni resort to ever more estranged metaphors to sing about their abjection. A George Jones song from 1981 even equates the honky-tonk with a life sentence: "Still doin' time in a honky-tonk prison, still doin' time where a man ain't forgiven."[37] Breaking out is rarely imagined, although it is suggested in one of the most popular songs of the 1970s, "Take This Job and Shove It" (1977).[38] In fact, the song is about the failure of such impulses. Even though the verses describe abusive supervisors, dead-end labor, and an unhappy home, the song never goes beyond venting dissatisfaction. As it turns out, losers never quit. The line introducing the final refrain tells us that the singer won't change his life of abject desperation: "I'd give the shirt right off of my back if I had the nerve to say: Take this job . . . " and so on.

George Jones specializes in such fantasy. In "I'm Gonna Burn Your Play-house Down" (ca. 1960), he threatens that he's "got an achin' in my heart and arson on my mind," although no sparks fly.[39] The opening verse of his 1989 "The King Is Gone" vividly describes the collapse into abject failure. The song opens with the simple strumming of an acoustic guitar as the singer tells us that he spent the previous night pouring Jim Beam out of an Elvis decanter into an empty Flintstones jelly jar. The scene is even more sloppily set when he evokes the kitchen where this binge takes place: he has to clear a table to find room for his little glass, and as he pulls up a chair, he also pulls up pieces of the floor. The locale is clearly a trailer park or a remote suburb where cars rot in the front yards, and the situation is deliberately ambiguous. The speaker implies that he has been unjustifiably dumped by his beloved. As his misery overtakes him, a bass and a steel guitar begin to throb, and he bathetically makes his point: "I pulled the head off Elvis, filled Fred up to his pelvis, Yabba dabba doo, the King is gone, and so are you."[40]

While the singer wallows in this 90-proof self-pity, he catalogs not so much his flaws as a mate but, rather, his failure to live up to American standards of good taste and affluence. He sings about tacky mass merchandise and childish popular entertainments, his low-status symbols. The last verse reduces to absurdity the metaphor that parallels this peon's downfall with the King's: "Then I broke Elvis's nose pouring the last drop from his toes." Even in a spectacle of self-destruction, the hard country hero cannot outdo the bloated rock star on Graceland's bathroom floor; he must make do with broken bottles on a disgraceful kitchen floor.

Since we live in a culture that defines masculine success by "making something of yourself,"[41] making a spectacle of oneself is a lot better than nothing, in hard country accounting. As Jones sang in 1992, "if they held a losers' playoff, well there'd be no contest; 'cause I've had lots of practice, and wrong's what I do best."[42] Songs like this force us to recognize that hard country is not simply about naive blunderers and unrestrained crybabies. These types would never enter, let alone win, a "losers' playoff." Self-made men can flaunt their riches, but in a burlesque universe, there also are prizes for those who pursue the prodigal pleasures of doing wrong.

Yet another Jones song, "The Grand Tour" (1974),[43] uses the spectacle motif from the start: "Step right up, come on in" proclaims the inexplicably abandoned husband turned "carnival barker"[44] who invites listeners to view the painful memories on display in every room of the house. Jones's "If Drinkin' Don't Kill Me" (1981) opens with an even more ludicrous image: as the singer pulls up to his house at dawn after an evening in a honky-tonk, he falls asleep over the steering wheel. This collapse sets off the horn, which announces to the whole block that he's home and drunk as usual.[45] Jones sings the first line of each verse in a conversational a cappella, a technique that, combined with the present-tense narration, heightens the spectacle of abjection. The chorus adds an unforgettable boast to this effect: "With the blood from my body I could start my own still." The title, repeated in the chorus, reminds us that the situation is supposed to be sad: "If drinkin' don't kill me, her memory will," and the plaintive harmonica of the accompaniment evokes some semblance of sorrow. The obtrusive steel guitar, however, wobbles as if to mock the drunken stupor that the narrator falls into at the end of the last verse.

These songs seem to mirror the tabloid cocktail of comedy and failure that characterizes stories about Jones's lurid marriage to Tammy Wynette, his extravagant addictions, his arrest record, and his lavish spending sprees and bankruptcies. According to Jones's producer Billy Sherrill, in concert Jones would close "If Drinkin' Don't Kill me" by replacing "*her* memory will" with "*Tammy's* memory will." At the same time, Jones's instability was reputed to be at least partly theatrical. He may have earned his nickname—The Possum—from his facial features, but his habit of feigning incapacitating intoxication in order to avoid unpleasant situations allowed the name to stick.[46]

The private George Jones may suffer from unnameable demons, but the more a fan knows about him, the more complicated the choice between laughter and tears becomes. As Norro Wilson, one of Jones's chief songwriters in the 1970s, says, "If people laughed at some of the things we've written, well great, 'cause we laughed, too."[47] Jones himself mentions another possible blend of emotion—anger and hilarity—as he imagines himself in yet another abject dialogue: "I really get mad about it when somebody calls me a hillbilly. . . . A lot of your so-called educated people tend to look down on other kinds of people, almost like they was peasants. Sure, we're from the country, but we went to school. I went to the seventh grade." As he concludes this complaint, Jones claims the best revenge: "Course . . . when they're talkin' like that, we're laughin' all the way to the bank."[48] More frequent, though, are Jones's public violations of masculine taboos, his breaking down, going broke, and passing out, all of which provide burlesque pleasure, whether on a disk, a stage, or a tabloid page.

The barroom standard "I Never Go Around Mirrors" delivers another strong dose of such pleasure. Merle Haggard's 1976 rendition begins with a plodding beat, a keening steel guitar, and what seems to be some scolding from a standard-bearer of American Cool: "I can't stand to see a good man go to waste, one who never combs his hair or shaves his face, a man who leans on wine . . . oh it tears me up to see a grown man cry."[49] The chorus reveals that this song, like "Wrong's What I Do Best," actually burlesques the secrets of success. The singer explains that in order to cope with his objections to abjection, he simply arranges things "so I never go around mirrors." The rest of us get to look, though.[50]

A similar twist animates Haggard's most successful and notorious song: "Okie from Muskogee" (1969, written with Roy E. Burns). This song is Haggard hitting his most compellingly discordant pitch, since he creates a persona who voices both sides of the dialogue of abjection. Much of what Haggard has said about this song suggests that it contains strong elements of satire. Nevertheless, those whose only exposure to Haggard is this song tend to see it as an anthem to redneck provincialism. Those who have always and attentively listened to Haggard, though, hear differently. In fact, the prettified acoustic picking and subdued brush percussion that accompany Haggard's calm delivery are far from rousing. "I didn't intend for "Okie" to be taken as strongly from my lips as it was," Haggard explains.[51]

In an interview, his interpretation of the song underscores the autobiographical themes that have always characterized Haggard's songwriting. He mentioned the family farm just twenty miles south of Muskogee:

> My father worked hard on his farm, was proud of it, and got called white trash once he took to the road as an Okie. . . . There were a lot of other Okies from around there, proud people whose farms and homes were foreclosed . . . and who then got treated like dirt. Listen to that line: "I'm proud to be an Okie from Muskogee." Nobody has ever said that before in a song.[52]

Haggard's father was forced to leave the farm and headed to Bakersfield three years before Merle was born. Haggard himself is thus not technically an Okie, although he has good reason for sympathizing with the displaced and estranged men he associates with the term.

Nevertheless, Okie pride in "livin' right" is also punctured in the song. In concert, I heard Haggard introduce it as a "song for mothers," in contrast to "Hungry Eyes," which he called a "song for mamas."[53] The description of the Okie's clothes smacks more of *Gentleman's Quarterly* than the sincere musings of an ordinary guy—only a fashion hack or a parodist would call "leather boots . . . *manly footwear.*" Likewise, when a high school dropout who's done solitary confinement in San Quentin writes that "football's still the roughest thing on campus, and the kids here still respect the college dean," he just might be poking fun at his fellow Okies who want so badly to ape the mild manners of the middle class. In fact, on the record, the word *college* seems to be sung with a bit of a sneer.

This skepticism is confirmed when Haggard recounts the inspirational remark that sparked the twenty-minute songwriting session that produced "Okie." He recalls that as his tour bus passed a sign that said "Muskogee, thataway, or whatever," one of his band members jokingly differentiated the musical passengers from the Oklahomans. From this contrast comes Haggard's smug first-person-plural announcement in the first line that "we don't smoke marijuana in Muskogee."[54] (Away from Muskogee it's a different matter: in his autobiography Merle openly describes what happens when he does smoke marijuana, most notably a middle-of-the-night phone call to Dolly Parton bemoaning his unrequited love for her.)[55] For the citizens of Muskogee, the equally illegal and more forcefully mind-altering white lightning is "still the biggest thrill of all." At the end of "Okie," Haggard sings this twice, underscoring the fact that these thrill-seeking Okies don't hold themselves completely in line.[56]

The "responses" to "Okie from Muskogee" seemed to overlook Haggard's abject dialogue with the "oppressive confidence" of those straight and narrow-minded Oklahomans. Thus, according to Jimmie Rogers, Jerry Jeff Walker's "Up Against the Wall, Redneck" (1973) "carried the original idea [of Haggard's song] to its illogical conclusion."[57] The thirty-four-year-old redneck of this song is also an Oklahoman. The chorus portrays him as a violent loser and honky-tonk habitué, "kickin' hippies' asses and raisin' hell." Lacking the tonal and social complexity of Haggard's song, the threatening title and third-person description of the redneck in this song clearly separate the singer from the subject, and the only insight into the "redneck" that the singer offers is crudely Freudian: this psychopathic mama's boy is "not responsible for what he's doing; his mother made him what he is."[58]

Similarly, Kinky Friedman's "Asshole from El Paso" (1973) presents a character so despicable that no one can seriously endorse his grotesque braggado-cio.[59] Although their link to "Okie from Muskogee" is clear, the "illogic" of these songs lies in their choice of epithets: although the term *redneck* certainly carries some historical and political freight, Walker's song doesn't unload it,[60] and no matter how you look at it, an asshole is just that. "Okie," however, is unmistakably a class-, race-, and history-laden name that Haggard needs in his bag of aliases. So committed is Haggard to maintaining the alienated stance of the hard country star that he walked away from a taping of the *Ed Sullivan Show* and the enormous audience it would have provided when he was asked to sing "Surrey with the Fringe on Top," a selection from Rodgers and Hammerstein's treacly *Oklahoma*.[61]

At least one "redneck" song preserves some of the complexity of "Okie": David Allen Coe's "Longhaired Redneck" (1975). Coe announces this kinship in the chorus: "They tell me I look like Merle Haggard and sound a lot like David Allen Coe" (although he mimics Haggard as he sings this line).[62] Whereas Haggard created an ambivalent character in "Okie," Coe seems to be abjectly responding to a heckler who criticizes his earrings and long hair. The burlesque twist comes when we hear what name he *wants* to be called; he's upset when the heckler accuses him of *not* being "country," and he proudly insists that "my long hair just can't cover up my redneck." He then menacingly suggests that someone warn the heckler that he (Coe) is a vicious ex-convict.[63]

What is interesting about this scenario is the blurred distinction between the countercultural "hippies" and the fierce redneck that Coe claims to be.

Both wear long hair and jewelry to reject middle-class masculinity, yet people who can't tell the difference enrage Coe. The distinguishing factor turns out to be "country": that's what rednecks are that hippies aren't. What the literal-minded heckler in this song wants to see is an ignorant hick, a straightforward Muskogee-esque performance featuring a simpleminded rube with an uncool brush cut and manly footwear. That's what he means when he says "country."

Coe, acutely aware of the status differences such a definition both requires and conceals, disrupts the heckler's vision of "country," replacing his sense of superiority with a threat.[64] The inappropriately ethereal "oohs" and "ahs" of the "girl singers" in the background reinforce the burlesque representation of country simplicity, but the rest of the song goes on to place Coe in the lineage of hard country music. In addition to resembling Haggard, Coe claims that Johnny Cash supported his release from prison and that he can sing all of Hank Williams's songs. In fact, as he goes through this roll call, he skillfully mimics all the hard country acts he follows even as he amplifies their angry, edgy humor.

Coe is thus in some ways the "hardest" and most burlesque performer of recent times. He bills himself as "The Mysterious Rhinestone Cowboy," an unflattering nickname that conjures up all the low-rent traumas and low tastes associated with hard country. "You Never Even Called Me by My Name" was his first record to receive significant airplay (1975). Written by Steve Good-man,[65] this song may seem to be a series of non sequiturs. Put in the context of hard country, though, it makes hopeful sense out of the desperate clichés of abjection. Accompanied by an ostentatiously twangy electric guitar and an overbearing steel guitar, the solemn opening lines portray the whiny fatalism of the rustic loser: "It was all that I could do to keep from crying, sometimes it seems so useless to remain." The chorus reinforces this impression, adding a vaguely delineated woman to victimize her man: "I'll hang around as long as you will let me. . . . But you don't have to call me darlin', Darlin', you never even called me by my name." In the woman's typically disdainful eyes, the singer is a nameless nobody, but as in "Longhaired Redneck," the mention of name-calling leads to a hard country roll call and impersonation routine. This time the singer claims that he doesn't need to be called Waylon Jennings, Charley Pride, or Merle Haggard.

But whatever he is called, it is the hard country performance that gives him an identity. That established, Coe breaks into a recitation while the musical twanging and wailing continue. He tells his listeners that the songwriter claimed that this composition was "the perfect country and western song." Coe explains that he wrote Goodman that a song that didn't say "anything at all about Mama, or trains, or trucks, or prison, or getting drunk" could not be considered flawless. Goodman responded to the criticism by writing a new last verse; this cliché-rich addition persuaded Coe to make a record of this now perfected song:

> I was drunk the day my Ma got out of prison
> And I went to pick her up in the rain
> But before I could get to the station in my pickup truck
> She got runned over by a damned ol' train.

Personal disasters can't get much worse or more perverse than this, but hyperbolic hokiness is what makes the song perfect. It has all the elements of burlesque abjection: the contrived comedy and stunning unoriginality make it part of an immediately recognizable tradition that allows the wretched white man to emerge from the spectacle of failure with a hard country star's inglorious name. When The Possum, or The Hag, or The Mysterious Rhinestone Cowboy deliberately sink in our estimation, they tempt us either to take up the mostly white banner of "oppressive confidence" or to wave the white flag with these winners of losers' contests. As they repeat (and perfect) what seems to many to be the same old song, hard country stars show us history repeating itself as rustic farce. But when the joking is laid aside, they also remind us that white men can and do lose that struggle, and it gets harder and harder to call it by its name.

NOTES

I want to thank Kay Easson, Lesley Ferris, Allison Graham, Kevin Hagopian, Mike Hill, and Soo Mee Kwon for their helpful advice and expertise.

1. D. Goodman and R. Schulman, Polygram International. Unless noted otherwise, the singer is also the songwriter; publishers hold the copyrights. The dates listed are the first release dates of the recorded version in question rather than the copyright or composition date. In most cases, the date of composition is unknown, and occasionally I have not been able to ascertain publishers or recording dates. As Nolan Porterfield noted, thorough discographic information for country music is still difficult to obtain. See his "Country Music Discography: Esoteric Art and Humanistic Craft," *Southern Quarterly* 22 (1984): 15–29.

2. Jennings and Basil McDay, "Too Dumb for New York City," Irving Music Inc. and Waylon Jennings Music.

3. Peter Guralnick reports that Ernest Tubb "has often insisted that part of the basis for his popularity is the very modesty of his talent, encouraging the guy in the tavern who hears an Ernest Tubb record to say, 'Heck, I can sing as good as that.'" Peter

Guralnick, *Lost Highway: Journeys & Arrivals of American Musicians* (Boston: Godine, 1979), p. 24.

4. For general discussions of the burlesque, see Gérard Genette, *Palimpsestes: La Littérature au second degré* (Paris: Seuil, 1982); and John Jump, *Burlesque* (London: Methuen, 1972).

In *Horrible Prettiness: Burlesque and American Culture* (Chapel Hill: University of North Carolina Press, 1991), p. 21, Robert Allen argues that American burlesque is "inextricably tied to . . . troubling questions about how . . . femininity should and could be represented." To the extent that "burlesque" implies a skin show, that's true. Allen's book is excellent, but in this case he is generalizing from a rather limited field.

5. Pierre Bourdieu provides the most thorough discussion of the interrelations between cultural tastes and social hierarchy. See his *Distinction: A Social Critique of the Judgment of Taste,* trans. Richard Nice (Cambridge, MA: Harvard University Press, 1984).

6. See, however, Barbara Ching, "Acting Naturally: Cultural Distinction and Critiques of Pure Country," *Arizona Quarterly* 49 (1993): 107–25. Don Cusic provides a general discussion of humor in country music in his "Comedy and Humor in Country Music," *Journal of American Culture* 16 (1993): 45–50. For discussions of the cultural manifestations of abjection, see Julia Kristeva, *Powers of Horror: An Essay on Abjection,* trans. Leon S. Roudiez (New York: Columbia University Press, 1982); and especially Michel André Bernstein, *Bitter Carnival: Ressentiment and the Abject Hero* (Princeton, NJ: Princeton University Press, 1992).

7. Most recently, see Curtis Ellison, *Country Music Culture: From Hard Times to Heaven* (Oxford: University Press of Mississippi, 1995).

8. Aaron A. Fox, "The Jukebox of History: Narratives of Loss and Desire in the Discourse of Country Music," *Popular Music* 11 (1992): 69.

9. Bernstein, *Bitter Carnival,* p. 3.

10. Peter Stearns, *American Cool: Constructing a Twentieth Century Emotional Style* (New York: New York University Press, 1994), p. 4.

11. Two recent essays view Hank Williams's success from this angle, although neither views him as part of a hard country tradition. See Kent Blaser, " 'Pictures from Life's Other Side': Hank Williams, Country Music, and Popular Culture in America," *South Atlantic Quarterly* 84 (1985): 15–26; and Richard Leppert and George Lipsitz, "Age, the Body and Experience in the Music of Hank Williams," in George H. Lewis, ed., *All That Glitters: Country Music in America* (Bowling Green, OH: Popular Press, 1993), pp. 22–37.

12. Daniel D. Darst and Robert Altman, EMI Al Gallico Music Corp., EMI Algee Music Corp., and Irving Music Inc.

13. Glenn Sutton, EMI Al Gallico Music Corp.

14. "This Bottle," publisher unknown.

15. Sony ATV Songs Tree holds the copyright on the entire Haggard catalog.

16. Written with Russ Hull and Mary Jean Shurtz, Jamie Music Publishing Co., and Unichappell Music Inc. In *Country Music USA,* rev. ed. (Austin: University of Texas Press, 1985), p. 234, Bill Malone mentions the controversy provoked by the song.

17. Bob Merrill and Terry Shand, RFD Music Publishing Co.

18. J. Chambers, L. Jenkins, and B. Sherrill, "I Sleep Just Like a Baby," Jones Country Music.

19. "Cryin' Time," Sony ATV Songs Tree.

20. The *Journal of Country Music* 14 (1992) is devoted to the history of black artists in country music. Mary Bufwack and Robert Oermann provide a good overview of women artists in *Finding Her Voice: The Saga of Women in Country Music* (New York: Crown Books, 1993).

21. Peter Stallybrass and Allon White, *The Politics and Poetics of Transgression* (Ithaca, NY: Cornell University Press, 1986), p. 3.

22. Lawrence Levine, *Highbrow/Lowbrow: The Emergence of Cultural Hierarchy in America* (Cambridge, MA: Harvard University Press, 1988).

23. Bill Malone explains that in 1927, George Hay's *WSM Barn Dance* played after NBC's *Musical Appreciation Hour* with Dr. Walter Damrosch. One night while introducing a number, Damrosch remarked that "while most artists realize that there is no place in the classics for realism, I am going to break one of my rules and present a composition . . . which depicts the onrush of a locomotive." When the WSM country music show came on the air, Hay announced that even though there was no room for realism in the classics, the following three hours would be devoted to nothing but realism. Then Hay introduced one of the show's most popular players, Deford Bailey, who played a train song, "Pan American Blues," which had been inspired by the famous southern train that ran near Bailey's home. When the performance was over, Hay said, "For the past hour we have been listening to music taken largely from grand opera, but from now on we will present "The Grand Ole Opry." Malone, *Country Music USA*, p. 75.

24. Becky Hobbs's "Mama Was a Working Man" makes note of the fact that women work too (1988, written with Mike Darwin and Donald London, Beckaroo Music, Careers BMG Music Publishing, and Track of Don Music).

25. This theme occurs throughout Haggard's career: listen to "Uncle Lem" about an ex-slave who offends a snooty ladies' garden club with his ill-kept shack (Glenn Martin, Sony/ATV Songs, 1990). Both "Go Home" (1966, written with Tommy Collins, Owens Publications) and "Irma Jackson" (ca. 1970) describe interracial romances destroyed by social pressure.

26. Andreas Huyssen, *After the Great Divide: Modernism, Mass Culture, Postmodernism* (Bloomington: Indiana University Press, 1986); and Fredric Jameson, *Postmodernism, or the Cultural Logic of Late Capitalism* (Durham, NC: Duke University Press, 1991).

27. Andrew Ross, *No Respect: Intellectuals and Popular Culture* (New York: Routledge, 1989), p. 227.

28. Byron Hill and Zack Turner, MCA Inc.

29. Listen also to Randy Travis's "Better Class of Losers," in which the singer is preparing to abandon a snooty female and her sophisticated crowd in favor of those who "don't pay their bills on home computers" (written with Alan Jackson, Sony ATV Tunes LLC and WB Music Corp., 1991).

Barbara Ehrenreich describes the increasing tendency of the affluent to use refined taste to separate their purchases from readily available mass-produced items, in *Fear of Falling: The Inner Life of the Middle Class* (New York: Pantheon, 1984), pp. 131–32.

30. Cecelia Tichi, *High Lonesome: The American Culture of Country Music* (Chapel Hill: University of North Carolina Press, 1994). Compare Nick Tosches, *Country: Living*

Legends and Dying Metaphors in America's Biggest Music, rev. ed. (New York: Scribner, 1985), pp. 26–27; and Malone, *Country Music USA,* pp. 153–55.

31. Joe Diffie's country-pop "Honky-Tonk Attitude," for example, exults that "everybody knows that's where everybody goes just to dance their blues away" (written with Lee Bogan, Songwriters Ink Music, Regular Joe Music, Modar Music, and Sony/ATV Songs Tree, 1993).

32. "Honky-Tonk Blues," Acuff Rose Music Inc., and Hiriam Music. Oddly enough, Charley Pride's unself-conscious cover version of this song was a number one hit in 1980. For the sake of authenticity, Pride went so far as to hire some of Williams's band members to play on the record. Tom Roland, *The Billboard Book of Number One Country Hits* (New York: Billboard, 1991), p. 254.

33. "Smokey the Bar," written with Penix Williams, Songs of Polygram International.

34. In other words, the man lacks what Pierre Bourdieu calls "cultural capital," the kind of credentials that determine class standing.

35. "William and Mary," George McCorkle and Rick Williamson, Sixteen Stars Music and Kicking Bird Music, Inc.

36. Dwight Yoakam's 1985 "It Won't Hurt" also wrings low comedy from drunken bragging: "It won't hurt when I fall down from this barstool; it won't hurt when I stumble in the street" (Coal Dust West Music and Warner Tamerlane Publishing Co.).

37. "Still Doin' Time," John Moffatt and Michael Heeney, publisher unknown.

38. David Allan Coe, Warner Tamerlane Publishing Co.

39. Lester Blackwell, Glad Music Co. Also listen to Jones's "Burn the Honky-Tonk Down," Wayne Kemp, Sony/ATV Songs Tree (ca. 1960).

40. Roger Ferris, Harding Park Music, Inc.

41. Richard Sennett and Jonathan Cobb, *The Hidden Injuries of Class* (New York: Random House, 1972), p. 264.

42. Dickey Lee, Mike Campbell, and Freddy Weller, "Wrong's What I Do Best," Songs of Polygram International and Young World Music, Inc. Listen also to Jones's "The World's Worst Loser," L. Reynolds, Sony/ATV Songs Tree, ca. 1966.

43. Norro Wilson, Carmol Taylor, and George Richey, EMI Al Gallico Music Corp. and EMI Algee Music Corp.

44. George Richey, one of the writers of this song, used this phrase to describe the speaker of the first line. Roland, *The Billboard Book,* p. 120.

45. Richard Beresford and Harlan Sanders, Careers BMG Music Publishing, Inc. and Warner Tamerlane Publishing Co.

46. In *George Jones: The Saga of an American Singer* (Garden City, NY: Doubleday, 1984), Bob Allen explains the nickname as resulting from the possumlike appearance of Jones's close-set eyes (p. 81). But he also catalogs many incidents of Jones's "possumlike" stupors (pp. 156, 176–77, 180, 201). Jones seems perfectly content with his nickname, and he dubs his current backup singers "The Possumettes."

47. Quoted in Roland, *The Billboard Book,* p. 130.

48. Quoted in Allen, *George Jones,* p. 180.

49. Lefty Frizzell and Sanger D. Shafer, Acuff Rose Music Inc.

50. Aaron Fox also discusses this song in "Split Subjectivity in Country Music and Honky-Tonk Discourse," in Lewis, ed., *All That Glitters,* p. 135.

51. Quoted in Roland, *The Billboard Book,* p. 35.

52. Ibid., p. 32. Melton McLaurin also argues that the positive statements such as this are "the key lines." See his "Songs of the South: The Changing Image of the South in Country Music," in Melton A. McLaurin and Richard A. Peterson, eds., *You Wrote My Life: Lyrical Themes in Country Music* (Philadelphia: Gordon and Breach, 1992), p. 25.

53. Sam's Town River Palace Arena, Tunica, Mississippi, October 1, 1994.

54. Quoted in Paul Hemphill, "Merle Haggard," in Bill Malone and Judith McCulloh, eds., *Stars of Country Music: Uncle Dave Macon to Johnny Rodriguez* (Champaign-Urbana: University of Illinois Press, 1975), p. 331.

55. Merle Haggard with Peggy Russell, *Sing Me Back Home: My Story* (New York: Simon & Schuster, 1981), p. 257.

56. The very mention of the drink echoes George Jones's first number one hit, "White Lightning" (J. P. Richardson, Glad Music, 1959). In another skillfully drunken sounding performance, Jones stresses the lawlessness of the brew that the singer's father supposedly perfected: "The T-Men, G-Men, revenuers, too, searchin' for the place where he made his brew." The last verse describes how an arrogant "city slicker" passed out after taking one sip.

57. Jimmie Rogers, *The Country Music Message: Revisited* (Fayetteville: University of Arkansas Press, 1989), p. 173.

58. Ray Wylie Hubbard, Tennessee Swamp Fox Publishing. For contrast, listen to Haggard's "Mama Tried" (1968). In this song, the singer, who "turned 21 in prison doing life without parole," claims that "I have only me to blame 'cause Mama tried."

59. Written with C. Chavin, publisher unknown.

60. Charlie Daniels's 1989 "What This World Needs (Is a Few More Rednecks)" takes on the project: "Now what most people call a redneck he ain't nothin' but a workin' man" (written with J. Gavin, C. Hayward, and T. DiGregorio, Miss Hazel Music and Music Corporation of America).

61. Hemphill, "Merle Haggard," p. 330.

62. Written with Jimmy Rabbitt, Careers BMG Music Publishing Inc., and Lotso Music.

63. Coe claims that he murdered a fellow convict who tried to rape him. Although researchers have never been able to confirm this tale, it is true that Coe spent most of his first thirty years in institutions, ranging from a reform school to the Ohio State Penitentiary.

64. Charlie Daniels's "Long Haired Country Boy" (1980) makes a similar distinction between country boys and hippies. The first verse seems to describe hippie hedonism— "People say I'm no good 'n crazy as a loon 'cause I get stoned in the morning, I get drunk in the afternoon"—but the party's over by the time the menacing chorus opens. Accompanied by a growling bass, Daniels's delivers a threat in a deadpan drawl: "I ain't askin' nobody for nothin' if I can't get it on my own. If you don't like the way I'm livin', you just leave this long haired country boy alone" (EMI Blackwood Music Inc., Kama Sutra Music Inc., and Music Corporation of America).

In interviews, Dwight Yoakam, too, has expressed hostility to those who ignore the unsettling class connotations of hard country: "I'll maybe have a fist fight with you about it," he warns. Quoted in Todd Everett, "Dwight Yoakam: Not Just Another Hat," *Journal of Country Music* 15 (1993): 13. Paul Kingsbury notes that "for Yoakam, the hardscrabble lives of people like his coal-miner grandfather, Luther Tibbs, are still inseparable from country music." "Dwight Yoakam: Honky-Tonk as Cutting Edge," *Journal of Country Music* 11 (1986): 13.

    65. EMI U Catalog, Inc.

"Story Untold": The Black Men and White Sounds of Doo-Wop

Jeffrey Melnick

When I was real little, I heard the Platters' "City Harbor Lights." I was from Lubbock; I didn't know what a harbor was. But the melody, the sound of the voice, gave me a feeling of pleasant longing that had nothing to do with anything that had yet happened to me. I wasn't old enough to have had sad love affairs.
                                                                    Jimmie Dale Gilmore

> I sing like a girl,
> and I sing like a frog.
> I'm a lonely boy.
>
>   Clarence "Frogman" Henry,
>   "Ain't Got No Home"

As popular music slowly makes its way onto the American Studies playlist, it becomes interesting to see which forms hit the top of the charts. Not surprisingly, teen-identified musical styles have a hard time breaking into heavy rotation. Those that receive serious attention—as rap and hip-hop have begun to do—often owe their privileged position to the agreeable ways they mesh with existing scholarly paradigms of cultural production (such as signifying and hybridity, in the case of rap and hip-hop).[1] But doo-wop, a popular vocal-group style of the post–World War II era, has never been comfortably incorporated into the major narratives of American musical history or African American history.[2]

Regret is the thematic heart and first musical principle of doo-wop, and it also infuses commemorations of the music. Ntozake Shange articulates this regret and connects it to doo-wop's integrated character in her poem "just as the del vikings stole my heart" (1978). Here, Shange describes a girl being abandoned by her "fairy godmother" in the wake of *Brown v. Board of Education*. The godmother reasons that the little girl has been divested of her "separate/but equal status & waz entitled/to whatever lil white girls got." [3] One of the things "lil white girls" get, the poem's title tells us, is the Del Vikings, an integrated doo-wop group whose biggest hit, "Come Go with Me," was first issued in late 1956.

The godmother grew up in a segregated culture that the poem's narrator accepts as superior to anything offered by this new world which, in the name of progress, asks her to miscegenate "her powers/integrate em." Comparing a segregated yesterday (with its authentic "blues saw dust/of a raunchy dawn") and the false promises of an integrated present, the poem explains that whatever the law says, the Del Vikings are bound to remain the exception that proves the rule: "i am separate/i am equal." Pedro Pietri pushes doo-wop even further in his poem "The Last Game of the World Series" (1973), in which he mobilizes doo-wop (and particularly the music of the doo-wop revival in the early 1960s) as testimony against false nostalgia: "yes those oldies/but goodies/remind me of you/on trial for first degree murder." [4]

A number of contemporary white artists have also contemplated the sorrows of doo-wop. The music inspires them to develop theories of popular art—at once satirical and celebratory—rooted in the delectable suffering of young men. When John Waters pays homage to the genre in his movie *Cry-Baby* (1990), he finds the perfect symbol for doo-wop in teardrops. In Waters's movie, the single tear that appears on Johnny Depp's face whenever he sings is a sign of his power.

Contemporary poet Robert Pinsky makes a similar move in his poem "Hearts" (1990), in which he connects the pain described and enacted in Lee Andrews and The Hearts' "Teardrops" (1957) with that of Romeo. The leader of the doo-wop group sings his hurt in the same "extravagant" style as Shakespeare's hero does:

> In the Italian manner, his teardrops cover
> His chamber window, says the boy, he calls them crystals,
> Inanely, and sings them to Juliet with his heart. . . . [5]

What is new in these tributes to doo-wop is the hint that the white and African American teenagers in question, separated by so much, might be drawn and give voice to similar songs of love. Mark Halliday invokes just this landscape in two of his poems—both of which construct doo-wop as a nonracialized artistic site, a separate sphere in which teenagers have developed an in-group language.[6]

In fact, many doo-wop songs encourage readings in which generational likeness trumps racial or class differences. A case in point is The Five Keys' "Ziggus" (1960). By elaborating a separatist language ("When I want a kiss I say ziggus/When she wants a hug she says zag") the group concludes that theirs is "not Greek or Latin they teach in school" but "a language all our own." The pronoun here refers to teenagers, not African Americans.[7]

In their suggestion that "standard" English is used when adults are around, The Five Keys create the mask, the key racialized figure of American popular culture. But "Ziggus"—like much of doo-wop song—insists that life behind the mask is vibrant, abundant, and complex. American popular culture has been so shaped by minstrelsy that it is hard to imagine that the props, tropes, and imagery of masking belong to a particular group. If adolescence is a time when trying on different masks is directly regulated by authority figures, it is also a time when such dramatic expressions receive broad social sanction. We should not be surprised, then, to find clowns running all through the teenage music of the time. Smokey Robinson was not the first popular composer to work the tears of a clown into a teen-identified song, nor was he even the first to mention Pagliacci. No doubt he had heard Nolan Strong—also working in Detroit—sing about that clown in his version (one of many in doo-wop) of "The Masquerade Is Over." With the help of all this clowning, doo-wop generally rendered the teenage condition as pleasantly melodramatic but not deeply traumatic.[8]

If it seems laughable to believe that tears (of lovers or of clowns) could be the solvent in which racial and class difference could at least momentarily disappear—*West Side Story* came out in the important doo-wop year of 1961—there is still a challenging question asked between the lines of Pinsky's poem: How do we come to terms with the "black" music made by Lee Andrews and The Hearts if we admit that its guiding imagery comes from the Shakespeare they learned in school? What if some African American teenagers turn out to have been a lot like some white ones, especially in their expressive practices? Doo-wop might turn out to be a good position from which to examine the current "whiteness" boom in academia. With only a few exceptions, this project has been focused on "white" people probing their whiteness through situational comparisons with black people and expressions of "blackness." But what about the young African American men of doo-wop, not sounding particularly "black" in any of the commonly described ways and learning how to emote from the original teenager—one of Shakespeare's and not one of Frankie Lymon's?

The genealogy of doo-wop is complex, but its main roots are in quartet gospel singing, popular vocal groups of the 1930s and 1940s such as the Ink Spots and the Mills Brothers, Tin Pan Alley balladry, and the urban rhythm and blues of the World War II era. Despite its multifarious racial and ethnic provenance, doo-wop's emergence onto the national scene is generally understood only in terms of "crossover"—the movement of an "authentic," previously segregated black music into a wider and whiter market. The year 1954 has become fairly well fixed in standard music histories as the year that doo-wop went national, mostly because it was when two black vocal group numbers—"Sh-Boom" by The Chords and "Gee" by The Crows—became pop hits.

One of the problems with studying doo-wop is that it never named itself as a separate genre in its own moment. Even the term itself gained popularity only in the early 1970s.[9] It is easy to recognize the general characteristics of doo-wop, even if it is rather difficult to determine whether particular groups and songs belong to it. Anthony Gribin and Matthew Schiff offer a workable definition of the music in their book *Doo Wop: The Forgotten Third of Rock 'n Roll* (1992): Doo-wop is a vocal-group style of music that rose to prominence in the 1950s, often featuring high male voice leads, a distinct bass voice, light instrumentation and a simple beat, nonsense syllables, and elementary lyrical concerns.[10]

The book by Gribin and Schiff reminds us that doo-wop was transformed into a collector's artifact more quickly, more decisively, and more zealously than perhaps any other subgenre of American music. By the early 1960s, doo-wop had become the property of collectors and anthologizers. Art Laboe's *Oldies but Goodies* albums and Irving Rose's Times Square record shop were the key contributors to the doo-wop revival of the early 1960s.[11] The music then found its key framing device in Richard Nader's 1969 rock and roll revival concert in New York City, a bill that included Sha Na Na, who also played at Woodstock. Tracking doo-wop as a form originating in urban rhythm and blues reveals that it began as a music created and consumed by African American adults, caught on with African American and then white teenagers, and finally came to rest (in eternal revival) as the special favorite of white, middle-aged ethnics.

Some scholars have attempted to read doo-wop's rise in the 1950s and its revival in the 1960s as utopian moments of interracial understanding. This is certainly one of the central arguments in Rhino Records' *Doo Wop Box,* a collection of 101 songs, only one of which—The Chantels' "Maybe"—is by an all-woman group. The box highlights such integrated groups as The Del Vikings, The Marcels, The Impalas, The Crests, The Rob Roys, and The Fascinators. Doo-wop surfaces here as a charming remnant of another time, when questions of racial oppression and privilege could be avoided, at least for the two minutes or so of a great song and the four years of high school. In this universe, Sonny Til of The Orioles is supposed to help you forget about Emmett Till of Chicago.

Doo-wop did responded to, and helped create, a confluence of audience tastes due mostly to the emergence of teenagers as a separate market group. Even so, *crossover* has become the key term for understanding doo-wop music. Steve Perry rightly observes that "cross over" suggests "sell out," and indeed, it has been almost impossible to conceptualize moments of broad acceptance of black performers by white audiences without the idea that something in the "authentic" original performance has been lost, diluted, or minstrelized. This is certainly the assumption behind W. T. Lhamon's broad description of the "crossover" hits of the 1950s as "enacting the I'm-whatever-you-need tomfoolery" of the clown. Doo-wop, especially in its nonsense lyrics and its spoken monologues (especially Vernon Green and The Medallions, left off the Rhino box) has roots in the minstrel stump speech and a close relative in the King-fish.[12]

The notion that doo-wop acted out for white audiences a devastating public abasement by African Americans must be taken as the starting point for understanding its relative neglect in academic discourse. Writing about rhythm and blues generally, Andrew Ross tries to account for its low prestige in certain "protonationalist" histories by suggesting that its status as "a ghetto music, confined to and confirming a segregated culture" makes it difficult to stitch this form into the privileged genealogies of African American music.[13] But in the case of doo-wop, the "problem" is that it moved too easily into a wider market. To tell the story of doo-wop is almost to describe it as a fall from grace: the vital music of African Americans converted into fodder for oldies radio and package shows, for novelty usages ranging from John Travolta's clowning on *Welcome Back, Kotter* to the soggy tributes of collegiate a cappella groups, from Billy Joel's earnest schlock to Paul Simon's arch middlebrow schlock.[14]

In trying to explain doo-wop's disappearance from the major narratives of African American popular music, we can look at analogies: what if jazz had

stopped evolving around 1935 and became the special domain of those responsible for the Dixieland revival of the 1940s? But doo-wop did not freeze in the
middle years of the 1950s. One problem with conceiving its history in this way
is that it forces us to understand doo-wop as springing only from doo-wop and
leading only to doo-wop nostalgia. Such a history gives us no idea of what
doo-wop owes to jump blues, say, or how it contributed to girl groups,
Motown, and the Beach Boys. There are few indications here that the vocal
dynamics of doo-wop donated much to classic soul music, as well as to the
most visionary black performers of the post-Soul age—Sly Stone, George
Clinton, and most of all, Prince.[15]

One problem with doo-wop's status as teenagers' music is that it never
developed homegrown theorists of the form—organic intellectuals—to explain to itself and to outsiders why it mattered. Try to imagine telling the story
of early jazz without Jelly Roll Morton's input, or early rock and roll without
the testimony of Sam Phillips. Think of how many of our best-known music
writers—academic and popular—have had special informants whispering in
their ears—Amiri Baraka with Archie Shepp, George Lipsitz with Johnny
Otis, Peter Guralnick with Charlie Rich and Solomon Burke. Doo-wop has
collectors instead.

To be fair, we cannot possibly explain doo-wop's neglect by blaming its most
loyal white fans for contaminating it with their whiteness. Doo-wop's whiteness (or its lack of blackness) is not so easily explained. In the modern era,
standard histories of African American music deal in a few major ways with
the appearance of recognizably "white" contributions to and stylizations in
black music. Separatists tend toward either the racist–obsessive pole (it all is
really white music) or the justifiably defensive pole (anything "white" sounding
is a perversion of authentic blackness). More integrationist approaches often
frame their discussions of whiteness in African American music by appealing to
a few popular theoretical formulations—most commonly Albert Murray's
famous description of American culture as "incontestably mulatto"—but also
anthropological concepts of hybridity and creolization and literary theories of
dialogism and polyvocality.[16] For the most part, however, these progressive
attempts to explain integration in music cannot explain how a music socially
marked as "black" (in its personnel, accompanying dances, chart classification,
and so on) could sound so "white."

We need to begin formulating schemes for understanding those kinds of
black music that do not easily fit into the familiar accounts of African American

music. This is not only an archaeological project, though it is that too: resituating musical formations that have been previously suppressed in the historical record is a worthy goal. But these projects (studying doo-wop is only one) also require that we try to explain how the sounds and performative postures of whiteness within black music have disappeared from the record of African American music in the United States. What happens to those black musical performances lacking a threshold level of recognizable "blackness"? Without backsliding into the always moralistic language of "crossover" and "sellout," can we discover new ways to discuss racially complicated artistic labors that will allow us to understand better how whiteness—and, not incidentally, age, sexuality, and masculinity—come to be constituted and received in music?

Doo-wop did not spring from an exclusively black location. The black vocal groups that populate this subgenre can claim no sacred or quasi-sacred space as their point of origin, no brush arbor, juke joint, after-hours jam session, or rent party to locate as the crucial site of blackness. How could an "authentic" black art find a congenial home—as the music of The Harptones and The Dreamers did—in a battle of the bands at the Jewish Center of Englewood, New Jersey?[17]

Doo-wop's storied home place is the street corner. Nelson George calls the image of young black teenagers "on a corner under the streetlight" one of the most romantic in popular culture. (Johnny Keys of The Magnificents demystifies all this by insisting that public bathrooms had much better acoustics).[18] In either case, doo-wop's dwelling is public, exposed, and vulnerable. Unlike those places of insurgency that gave birth to the spirituals and bebop, the starting point for doo-wop suggests little resistance to the dominant culture. Whatever mythic stature the urban street corner has gained over the years, it figured in doo-wop's dissemination mostly as a place of competitive male activity. Shirley Alston remembers that The Shirelles were "like a street-corner group, only being girls, we weren't allowed on the corner, so we'd go down to the basement of Beverly's house."[19] Alston makes it clear here that the landscape of doo-wop was first characterized by its maleness—not its racialness.

But this is a truism. What is more interesting about doo-wop is that it developed standard vocal techniques—it came, in fact, to rely on a specific interplay of gendered voices—which made it possible to enact allegedly heterosexual dramas of romantic loss and lack without the participation of women. Of course we have plenty of the usual sort of evidence about the aphrodisiac gifts of doo-wop lead singers—women falling out while listening to Sonny Til and so on.[20] But in doo-wop we are nowhere near the ecstatic bluesmen/ preachers of Charles Keil's famous formulation. The key sexual relationship postulated in doo-wop is not that between performer and (implied) audience but of one group member to another. The crucial dyad is that matching the high-end lead singer to the booming bassman, and the two or three mediating voices are the agents of this meeting.[21]

Group publicity photos often tell this story. Organized to call attention to the lead singer, the young black men in these pictures touch faces, gaze at one another, and often do the "loving lean"—back to front, back to front.[22] These photographic conventions were established by the gospel groups from which doo-wop borrowed so much, but it matters whether the group in question in the framed moment is going to spring to life singing "Marching up to Zion" or "Ten Commandments of Love."

The gender dynamics of doo-wop group singing cannot be explained by either of the major traditional academic projects that might be expected to show interest in them. On the one hand, the long and mostly ignoble attempts to chart black masculinity in America cannot possibly do justice to doo-wop's multiple subject positionings. On the other, the voluminous scholarship on postwar youth cultures rarely takes note of African American teenagers. In short, we have little useful information on what it meant to be a young African American man during the 1950s and early 1960s.

A convention of 1950s scholarship, nicely summarized by W. T. Lhamon, is that in this decade Americans stopped "producing and participating in their own lore" and instead "began buying it ready-made."[23] But with all the critical interest in the "invention" of the teenager in the 1950s, little serious attention has been paid to their consumption habits. The African American male teenager, particularly, remains a cipher, except when criminalized and/or pathologized. One thing that separates major trends in British and American cultural studies is that the British have always been more comfortable studying youth behavior. Think of two signal achievements on the American side in the 1980s, Janice Radway's *Reading the Romance* (1984) and Michael Denning's *Mechanic Accents* (1987): both pay serious attention to consumers of previously scorned forms (romance and dime novels, respectively) with the confidence that the behaviors of these adult consumers have much to tell about American culture. Denning, for instance, argues persuasively that dime novels performed the "dream-work of the social." What apposite claim might be plausibly made at this moment about doo-wop? That it performed the dream-work of the study hall? Or the boys' bathroom?

Things get more complicated when we remember that doo-wop performance valorized the body as a site of production at just the time when, historians tell us, Americans were becoming less involved with making the cultural goods they consumed. This makes it doubly fascinating to listen to what the young black men of doo-wop actually made as they tacitly insisted on the sufficiency of their voices. Doo-wop groups—from the "moony and mild" leads (Gribin and Schiff find more than forty groups with some variant of "mellow" in their name) to the comic bassmen—posit a fluid and noncoercive world of abundant gender positioning.[24] In doo-wop—as Suzanne Moore writes about Prince's song "If I Was Your Girlfriend"—masculinity "appears to be just a place on the map" and not "the centre of the world." [25]

This multiplicity bothers some critics, especially those whose normative sense of African American male voices has been shaped by those specific conventions of blues, gospel, and soul singing that place a premium on gritty realism and overt emotionality—that is, on the "natural." When trying to understand Sonny Til's artificiality, the best Charlie Gillet could do was describe his style as "accentless" (meaning "white" or at least not recognizably "black") and "almost effeminate" (i.e., gay or traditionally feminine). As many heard it, doo-wop falsetto captured young African American men pretending to be white and female.[26] The "types" in doo-wop—for example, sweet young fellows and good-natured parodists of "real" men—are not overly familiar ones. They appear as neither the "supersexual stud" nor the "fragile and exotic 'oriental' " who, as Kobena Mercer writes, characterize the popular imagery of black men.[27] The young men of doo-wop voiced "vulnerability" while hardly ever suggesting the feminized weakling who is the flip side of white racial fantasies about oversexed black men.

The arrangement of voices in doo-wop suggests a highly stylized and complex sexual universe. It is tempting to think that the gendered vocal dynamics merely replicate the compulsory heterosexuality of mainstream American culture. In this account, the lead ("almost effeminate") voice implies—often with an obvious dose of misogyny—a fragile woman who is supported by the sturdy bass. This would certainly be true for the moments when the usually hidden sexual motives of doo-wop singing were revealed as burlesque or projected as homage. In the first instance, we might point to Milton Love and Bobby Baylor of The Solitaires, who performed duets of the "The Wedding" and "The Honeymoon" on stage, with Love wearing a mop over his head to play the female role. Or on the other hand, we find Adam Jackson of The Jesters attempting (in 1958) a note-for-note copy of Arlene Smith's lead vocal on The Chantels' song "The Plea" (1957).[28]

That the young men of doo-wop often sounded "like" women has caused some consternation. One writer insists that even though doo-wop produced numerous "bird" groups (Orioles, Flamingos, Crows, Cardinals, Blue Jays, Swans, Larks, and so forth), they were "not to be confused with the English colloquialism of 'birds' for girls." But the homophobia and misogyny of this description have been challenged by a number of gay artists who have been attracted by the fluidity of roles offered by classic doo-wop. For the group The Flirtations, the singer David Lasley, and the video artist Marlon Riggs (as for filmmaker John Waters), doo-wop provided a way to explore nontraditional race/gender postures in mainstream popular culture.[29]

Doo-wop's plots cannot be reduced to a simple heterosexual scheme. First, many of the lead voices actually belonged to, or at least sounded like, children. Here the concerns of adult sexuality are sidestepped, and the vocal signification bolsters the usual adolescent lyrical stance toward romance. In The Teenagers' song "Teenage Love" (1956), for instance, Sherman Garnes's bass voice introduces Frankie Lymon's lead with a run of "nonsense" syllables that sound like "Come a laddie, say de-boom." Lymon joins in on the next line to sing "Run run run de-run de poppa to run-ton." It is easy enough to hear this as a standard sexual plot (in which the male, older, and/or more powerful lover plays "poppa") but just as easy to hear the relationship as parent to child.[30]

Even when the lead voice in doo-wop does not belong to a child, it frequently launches into falsetto, with all the affective complexities peculiar to that vocal stance. Wayne Koestenbaum explains that falsetto is a skill, a patently "false" voice, that "functions as patriarchal cultural lore." Falsetto develops from a position of power. Its context announces that the singer is male but has the ability to travel away from this established identity. Falsetto is also risky. Koestenbaum tells us that he has often heard it as "the voice of the bogeyman, voice of the unregenerate fag; voice of horror and loss and castration; floating voice, vanishing voice."[31]

The trick is to disguise the "true" voice completely in order to sustain the illusion of the vocal masquerade, and the best doo-wop singers do just this. Even when the falsetto starts the song, as with Earl Carroll's lead on The Cadillac's "Gloria" (1954), the voice seems ambient, the sound of the recording studio or the city air itself. The musical formation of these vocal groups naturalizes the falsetto. With one fixed pole at the bassman's spoof of masculinity and the other at the lead's spoof of femininity, doo-wop presents a continuum of logically related but separate gendered voices.[32] The central fact of these performances is that they are by men. Goethe loved listening to castrati for the "conscious illusion" they produced, for the "double pleasure" of listening to "persons" sing who "are not women, but only represent women."[33]

Hence the distressed tone of Marcia Vance's account of seeing a thirtieth anniversary show by The Teenagers in the early 1970s, which featured Pearl McKinnon of The Kodaks on lead vocals: "But why is a girl singing Frankie's leads?"[34]

In doo-wop, falsetto belongs to the lead voice and is in the privileged position of stating the major romantic motif. But the mock argument in The Marcels' 1963 song "I Wanna Be the Leader" makes it clear that the social status attached to the voices was variable. The lead voice—a callow youth if I ever heard one—opens the song complaining that these days everyone is "talking about Mr. Bassman." He is responding mostly to Barry Mann's 1961 hit "Who Put the Bomp?" which satirically insisted on the prestige of this singing position. But, the leader wonders, "What would Mary say if I said 'Rama Lama Ding Dong?' " (No doubt she would say, "I'm not that kind of girl.")[35] Instead, the leader wants to sing things like "our day will come."

Weaving in and out of his part comes the bassman, sounding dirty and singing a typical Marcels' nonsense tag (lots of "buns" and "boms").[36] "I Wanna Be the Leader" reveals, albeit comically, some of the complex vocal positioning in doo-wop. With the lead ("feminine") voice remaining in the rarified world of private fantasy and abstract teen romance, the bass becomes the public voice of sex. At first this seems perfectly in keeping with the sexual and gender formations asserting their dominance in postwar America. But doo-wop vocals subvert rigid role definition by emphasizing their own fraudulence. "Natural" voices are rarely privileged in doo-wop. Rather, they are bridges connecting comic "men" to frivolous "women." The teenagers of doo-wop, one could say, perform heterosexuality as a satire of their elders.

> Beware of the bearded lady. . . .
>
> Richard Thompson, "Wall of Death"

It should be clear by now that I am claiming for doo-wop a surprising expansiveness for men with regard to gender and sex roles. This fluid dynamic in doo-wop suggests a few provisional conclusions about the performers and about "race" scholarship more generally. One major reason that doo-wop singers could dodge the narrow typecasting usually plaguing African Americans in American popular culture is that they were (or "played") teenagers. If "teenage" usually appears to us as an affliction, especially as it is portrayed in the scholarship on white middle-class youth in the 1950s (as in Wini Breines's *Young, White, and Miserable*), it seems likely that expressions of teenage angst induced a feeling of "pleasant longing" in young white and African American people. It might be the false consciousness of a raceless society, but also an example of how race consciousness changes with age.

Scholars of slavery long ago noticed that in the antebellum South, African American children played, as John Blassingame puts it, "in promiscuous equality with white children."[37] Perhaps overstated, this analysis reveals that racialization is a process—not a readymade—taking place in fits and starts during the life cycle. The key moment of intensification—whether under slavery's iron fist or the more diffuse tyranny of capitalism—occurs as the individual is readied for and enters the labor market. The recent deluge of "whiteness" studies (those biased toward "social structure," on the one hand, and toward "cultural representation," on the other) do not account well for doo-wop.[38]

The two major fronts of the whiteness project at this moment—labor history and literary criticism—have barely begun to address racial formation as it unfolds over an individual's lifetime. Popular music, doo-wop especially, might provide critical materials for helping us determine the differential achievements of racialization. Doo-wop's polymorphous sexual dynamics, in short, might have been possible because the black men who performed them did not yet have to be "black men" as prescribed by the normative structures and signifying strictures of their culture.

As we begin to explore such complicated moments—for example, young black men singing audibly "white" roles—it is important to ask ourselves why we have become accustomed to ignoring them. After all, organizing "whiteness" as an academic field (in universities and by publishers) is in itself what Omi and Winant call a "racial project": "simultaneously an interpretation, representation, or explanation of racial dynamics, and an effort to reorganize and redistribute resources along particular racial lines."[39]

"Whiteness" work—much of which would have been called Afro-American studies a decade ago—has been done mainly by white people (with some major exceptions, including bell hooks and Toni Morrison).[40] Also of interest is that a major strand of this work investigates "white" subjects experimenting with "black" expressivity. We know little about the reverse, however: What does "white" sound like coming out of a black singer, and what cultural work might it accomplish or embody?[41]

Doo-wop groups often fantasized romantic utopias: "Island of Love" and "Lovers Island" are not just song titles but statements of purpose, too. Even so, I do not mean to suggest that doo-wop inhabited or created some kind of racial utopia in which young black men had complete freedom to explore and give voice to countless racial, gender, and sexual roles. For starters, it was a society of young men that did not just accidentally exclude women but responded—as Susan McClary has written about castrati—to a social need for men "who sounded like women."[42]

One content analysis of mid-1950s popular songs finds that male singers often seemed "powerless and helpless in the face of the girl, who appears to hold the key to the relationship."[43] Whatever the specific valences of such performances of weakness were, they tend to call attention most to the social mobility of men. Coming on the heels of the increased female presence in the workforce during World War II, it was at least a happy coincidence for the major American gender project of the postwar era that a popular art form developed in the 1950s could conjure up women without employing them.[44] But black women—as should be clear from my descriptions of the music and its makers—were almost off the radar in regard to the production of doo-wop.

The "relatively innocent bad boys" of doo-wop (as Gribin and Schiff call them—The Shangri-Las just said "good–bad" but "not evil") found a place where as adolescent males, they could experiment with pliant gender roles.[45] If doo-wop was any kind of utopia, it was a doomed utopia. The "whiteness" of this black music was temporally bound by the fact that these teenagers had to grow up in a labor economy heavily invested in racial division.

Since doo-wop relied on "teenage" production, perhaps the way that people often refer to the legacy of the music in our own time is to play a round of "Where Are They Now?" Mark Halliday, in his poem "Little Star," and Fred Pfeil, in his story "Plus You," are able to imagine comfortable white-collar jobs for their white singing protagonists. On the other hand, when Greil Marcus hears four black men singing "Earth Angel" outside a supermarket while they load boxes into a van, he concludes that this is the only thing The Penguins could be doing "thirty years after their one hit."[46]

The complicated racial and sexual signification of doo-wop also ripened it for appropriation by white people. In an earlier generation, Jews explained their fluency in blues and jazz as an outgrowth of the minor-keyed pathos of their cantorial music. Some Jews kept on saying this. Now they were joined by Italian Americans who explained, not cantors but bel canto.[47]

The year 1957 might look quite different if we shifted our scholarly attention away from Norman Mailer's "White Negro" and toward Lee Andrews and The Hearts' "Teardrops." Although white people have certainly used their social power to experiment with a variety of racialized expressive practices, they are not the only people who have done so. If we mean to dislodge "white" as the normative center of an oppressive racial system, we could contemplate how African Americans (from the early days of the cakewalk to our own time) have manipulated multiple, and often unexpected, "racial" postures. Thinking about the young African American men of doo-wop—their overall theatrics, lyrical concerns, and vocal articulations of sexuality and gender—might help us see that Mailer's imagined White Negro was not the only one finding a home in postwar America through racial masquerade.[48]

NOTES

This chapter owes its title and much else to Rachel Rubin, without whose intellectual guidance and used-record store camaraderie it could not have been written. Thanks also to Scott Fabozzi and Dan Melnick, who still shop for vinyl, and Fred Pfeil and Hazel Carby, who read and commented on earlier versions of it.

1. See, for instance, Russell A. Potter, *Spectacular Vernaculars: Hip-Hop and the Politics of Postmodernism* (Albany: State University of New York Press, 1995); Houston A. Baker Jr., *Black Studies, Rap, and the Academy* (Chicago: University of Chicago Press, 1993); Tricia Rose, *Black Noise: Rap Music and Black Culture in Contemporary America* (Hanover, NH: Wesleyan University Press/University Press of New England, 1994).

2. See, for instance, Eileen Southern, *The Music of Black Americans: A History* (New York: Norton, 1983); LeRoi Jones, *Blues People: Negro Music in White America* (New York: Quill/William Morrow, 1963); Nelson George, *The Death of Rhythm & Blues* (New York: Pantheon, 1988); Charles Hamm, *Yesterdays: Popular Song in America* (New York: Norton, 1983).

3. Ntozake Shange, "just as the del vikings stole my heart," in her *Nappy Edges* (New York: St. Martin's Press, 1978), p. 54.

4. Pedro Pietri, "The Last Game of the World Series," in his *Puerto Rican Obituary* (New York: Monthly Review Press, 1973).

5. Pinsky's poem is in his *The Want Bone* (New York: Ecco, 1990), pp. 10–13.

6. See Mark Halliday, "Little Star," in his *Little Star* (New York: Quill/William Morrow, 1987), pp. 58–60, and "Ode: The Capris," in his *Tasker Street* (Amherst: University of Massachusetts Press, 1992), pp. 23–24.

7. This can be found on *The Five Keys: Classic Rhythm and Blues Recordings* (Gusto/King 50134, 1968).

8. Hear also Vernon Green and The Medallions' "A Lover's Prayer" available on their *Golden Classics* (Collectable Records, CD-5047). "The Masquerade Is Over" was performed by The Five Satins and Nolan Strong and The Diablos, among others. Strong's version is on *Mind over Matter* (Fortune LP 8015).

9. *The Doo Wop Box* (Rhino Records 71463, 1993), liner notes, p. 9. On the other hand, Greil Marcus argues that doo-wop was the "first form of rock & roll to take shape, to define itself as something people recognized as new, different, strange, theirs." "Is This the Woman Who Invented Rock & Roll: The Deborah Chessler Story,"

Rolling Stone, June 24, 1994, p. 43. Gus Gossert and Wayne Stierle did much of the work surrounding the naming and defining of doo-wop.

10. Charlie Gillet, who counts doo-wop as one of the five major strands of rock and roll in the 1950s, adds that the singers were generally more concerned "with rhythmic and percussive impact than with harmonic sophistication." *The Sound of The City: The Rise of Rock and Roll* (London: Souvenir, 1983), p. 31. Aside from Gribin and Schiff, there have been few serious studies of doo-wop; See Bernard Gendron's essay, "Theodor Adorno Meets the Cadillacs," in Tania Modleski, ed., *Studies in Entertainment: Critical Approaches to Mass Culture* (Bloomington: Indiana University Press, 1986), pp. 18–36.

11. On the importance of this store, see Lenny Kaye, "The Best of Acappella" (1970), reprinted in Clinton Heylin, ed., *The Penguin Book of Rock & Roll Writing* (New York: Viking Press, 1992), pp. 22–37.

12. W. T. Lhamon, *Deliberate Speed: The Origins of a Cultural Style in the American 1950s* (Washington, DC: Smithsonian, 1990), p. 76; but also see Philip Ennis, *The Seventh Stream: The Emergence of Rock 'n Roll in American Popular Music* (Middletown, CT: Wesleyan University Press, 1992), pp. 193–228.

13. Andrew Ross, *No Respect: Intellectuals and Popular Culture* (New York: Routledge, 1989), pp. 75–76.

14. Billy Joel's song "The Longest Time" is on his album *An Innocent Man* (Columbia QC 38837, 1983). Paul Simon's "Rene and Georgette Magritte with Their Dog After the War" (featuring spectral vocals by The Harptones) can be found on *Hearts and Bones* (Warner Bros. 23942-1, 1983); and Simon's "Was a Sunny Day" is on *There Goes Rhymin' Simon* (Columbia KC 32280, 1973). As I write, rumor has it that Paul Simon is casting a doo-wop musical to open on Broadway.

15. Many soul performers, including Marvin Gaye, appeared in doo-wop groups early in their careers.

16. Albert Murray, *The Omni-Americans: Black Experience and American Culture* (New York: Vintage Books, 1983). See also Lawrence Levine, *Black Culture and Black Consciousness: Afro-American Folk Thought from Slavery to Freedom* (New York: Oxford University Press, 1977); Gerald Lyn Early, "Pulp and Circumstance: The Story of Jazz in High Places," in his *The Culture of Bruising: Essays on Prizefighting, Literature, and Modern American Culture* (Hopewell, NJ: Ecco, 1994), pp. 163–205.

17. On The Harptones versus The Dreamers, see Philip Groia, *They All Sang on the Corner: New York City's Rhythm and Blues Vocal Groups of the 1950's* (Setauket, NY: Edmond Publishing, 1974), p. 63, n. 5.

18. George, *The Death of Rhythm & Blues,* p. 35; Anthony Gribin and Matthew Schiff, *Doo-Wop the Forgotten Third of Rock 'n Roll* (Iola, WI: Krause, 1992), p. 86.

19. Gerald Early, *Tuxedo Junction: Essays on American Culture* (Hopewell, NJ: Ecco, 1989), p. 98.

20. See the liner notes to Sonny Til and The Orioles, *Hold Me, Thrill Me, Kiss Me* (Dr. Horse, RBD800).

21. See Charles Keil's *Urban Blues* (Chicago: University of Chicago Press, 1966).

22. For great group photos, see Groia, *They All Sang on the Corner.*

23. Lhamon, *Deliberate Speed,* p. 9. Also see Karal Ann Marling, *As Seen on T.V.: The Visual Culture of Everyday Life in the 1950s* (Cambridge, MA: Harvard University Press, 1994).

24. Gribin and Schiff, *Doo-Wop,* pp. 425–28.

25. Suzanne Moore, "Getting a Bit of the Other—The Pimps of Postmodernism," in S. Rowena Chapman and Jonathan Rutherford, eds., *Male Order: Unwrapping Masculinity* (London: Lawrence and Wishart, 1988), pp. 166.

26. Charlie Gillet, "Black Market Roots," in R. Serge Denisoff and Richard Peterson, eds., *The Sounds of Social Change: Studies in Popular Culture* (Chicago: Rand McNally, 1972), p. 275. The imitative play at the heart of doo-wop has led a number of historians to take The Platters' "The Great Pretender" as the representative song of the decade. See Lhamon, *Deliberate Speed,* p. 76; and Wini Breines, *Young, White, and Miserable: Growing up Female in the Fifties* (Boston: Beacon Press, 1992), p. 125. Marjorie Garber also notes that a magazine for male transvestites is called *Great Pretenders.* See her "Spare Parts: The Surgical Construction of Gender," in Henry Abelove, Michele Aina Barale, and David Halperin, eds., *The Lesbian and Gay Studies Reader* (New York: Routledge, 1993), p. 323.

27. Kobena Mercer, "Black Masculinity and the Sexual Politics of Race," in his *Welcome to the Jungle: New Positions in Black Cultural Studies* (New York: Routledge, 1994), p. 133.

28. Groia, *They All Sang on the Corner,* p. 81; Gribin and Schiff, *Doo-Wop,* p. 384. See also Gribin and Schiff, *Doo-Wop,* p. 121, for examples of groups that combined racial burlesque with Orientalism, as in The Quinns' "Hong Kong." The phrase "compulsory heterosexuality," now in common use, was popularized by Adrienne Rich in her essay "Compulsory Heterosexuality and Lesbian Existence," republished in Abelove et al., eds., *The Lesbian and Gay Studies Reader.*

29. See Clive Richardson's notes to The Spaniels, *Stormy Weather* (Charly CRB 1114). See also Riggs's *Tongues Untied,* Lasley's *Missin' Twenty Grand* (EMI America, ST17066, 1982), and The Flirtations' eponymous 1990 record on Significant Other Records (SO 902).

30. This song can be found on *The Best of Frankie Lymon and The Teenagers* (Rhino R2 70918). Obviously this leads to the question of what can be read out of the "nonsense" so central to doo-wop vocalizing. See Greil Marcus, *Ranters & Crowd Pleasers: Punk in Pop Music, 1977–1992* (New York: Doubleday, 1993), p. 31.

31. Wayne Koestenbaum, "The Queen's Throat: (Homo)sexuality and the Art of Singing," in Diana Fuss, ed., *Inside/Out: Lesbian Theories, Gay Theories* (New York: Routledge, 1991), pp. 218–20. See also Moore, "Getting a Bit of the Other."

32. Wayne Koestenbaum, *The Queen's Throat: Opera, Homosexuality, and the Mystery of Desire* (New York: Poseidon Books, 1993), p. 165.

33. Angus Heriot, *The Castrati in Opera* (New York: Da Capo, 1974), p. 26.

34. See Donn Filetti, notes, *The Best of the Kodaks: Featuring Pearl McKinnon* (Fury 5083); and Marcia Vance "A Fan Remembers," in *Frankie Lymon/The Teenagers, For Collectors Only* (Murray Hill 000148).

35. See Marcus, *Ranters & Crowd Pleasers,* pp. 84–85.

36. Gribin and Schiff, *Doo-Wop,* p. 41.

37. John Blassingame, *The Slave Community: Plantation Life in the Antebellum South* (New York: Oxford University Press, 1972), p. 94.

38. Michael Omi and Howard Winant, *Racial Formation in the United States: From the 1960s to the 1980s* (New York: Routledge, 1986), p. 56.

39. Ibid., p. 56.

40. See bell hooks, "Representing Whiteness in the Black Imagination," in Lawrence Grossberg, Cary Nelson, and Paula Treichler, eds., *Cultural Studies* (New York: Routledge, 1992), pp. 338–46; Toni Morrison, *Playing in the Dark: Whiteness and the Literary Imagination* (Cambridge, MA: Harvard University Press, 1992).

41. I am thinking here of Eric Lott's *Love and Theft: Blackface Minstrelsy and the American Working Class* (New York: Oxford University Press, 1993); Michael Rogin, "Blackface, White Noise: The Jewish Jazz Singer Finds His Voice," *Critical Inquiry* 18 (1992): 417–53; and Shelley Fisher Fishkin, *Was Huck Black? Mark Twain and African-American Voices* (New York: Oxford University Press, 1993).

42. Susan McClary, *Feminine Endings: Music, Gender, and Sexuality* (Minneapolis: University of Minnesota Press, 1991), p. 181, n. 31.

43. James Carey, "Changing Courtship Patterns in Popular Song," in Denisoff and Peterson, *The Sounds of Social Change,* p. 210.

44. See Greil Marcus, *Lipstick Traces: A Secret History of the Twentieth Century* (Cambridge, MA: Harvard University Press, 1989), p. 258.

45. Gribin and Schiff, *Doo-Wop,* p. 57.

46. Mark Halliday, "Little Star," and Fred Pfeil, "Plus You," in his *What They Tell You to Forget* (Wainscott, NY: Pushcart, 1996); Greil Marcus, *Lipstick Traces,* p. 94.

47. On Jewish involvement with African American music, see Jeffrey Melnick, "Ancestors and Relatives: The Uncanny Relationship of African Americans and Jews" (Ph.D. diss., Harvard University, 1994).

48. Michael Rogin, "Making America Home: Racial Masquerade and Ethnic Assimilation in the Transition to Talking Pictures," *Journal of American History* 79 (1992): 1050–77.

10

One of the Boys? Whiteness, Gender, and Popular Music Studies

Gayle Wald

In the annals of made-for-television interviews, surely one of the oddest single encounters of 1995 was that between Courtney Love, lead singer of the predominantly female rock band Hole, and Barbara Walters, a journalist best known for her ability to elicit sentimental, often tearful, self-revelation, on Walters's "Most Fascinating People of 1995" television special. On the surface, except for the fact that Love wore a beige suit rather than her trademark baby-doll dress, there was little about the interview that seemed particularly unusual. With the kind of Jackie O–style grit that such occasions demand, Love faced down Walters's questions about her recovery from heroin addiction, her negotiation of single motherhood in the wake of her husband Kurt Cobain's 1994 suicide, and her status as the most visible member of a group of commercially successful female musicians making loud, "angry" rock music. Yet just as Love uses her trademark smudged red lipstick to parody conventional femininity and bourgeois tastefulness, so there was something oddly askew about her rehearsal of female virtue: a curiously compelling disjunction between composure and

151

distraction, propriety and vulgarity, that suggested nothing less than the specta-cle of bourgeois white femininity in drag. Or as Love sings in the song "Doll Parts" from *Live Through This,* Hole's major-label debut: "I fake it so real I am beyond fake."

Love's parody of telegenic white femininity more often associated with her host Barbara Walters parallels several recent notable trends among women in rock. Since the early 1990s, a wide variety of female musicians, including women in female-centered rock bands (Hole, Babes in Toyland, L7, the Breed-ers, Belly, Elastica, Veruca Salt, Luscious Jackson) and female singer-songwriters (k. d. lang, Melissa Etheridge, Tori Amos, Liz Phair, Polly Harvey) have achieved commercial popularity despite—and perhaps because of—their per-formance of various defiant stances against normative femininity.

Similarly, although the ongoing girl-style "revolution" has made it possible to imagine both corporate and independent rock cultures as realms in which white women may play with, challenge, or redefine femininity (e.g., Love's determined promotion of an image of fallen womanhood or Riot Grrrls' canny recuperation of girlhood), the corporate success, beginning around 1991, of the Seattle-area punk-inspired music that eventually came to be known as grunge spurred a parallel interest in the potential emergence of new masculine subjectivities within "alternative" rock.[1]

A great deal of attention has been focused on young rock musicians' highly visible experimentation with gender, but considerably less notice has been paid to the fact that these "new gendered subjectivities," as Angela McRobbie dubbed them, also are new (or potentially new versions of old) racialized subjectivities. With notable exceptions—for example, Fred Pfeil's deft reading of the white "working-class" masculinities of Bruce Springsteen and Axl Rose[2]—the tendency has been to celebrate the gender transgressions of white rock performers in the 1990s without attempting to understand how these transgressions—from Liz Phair's aggressive yearning to be her lover's "blow job queen" on her archly feminist debut album *Exile in Guyville,* to Smashing Pumpkins vocalist Billy Corgan's displays of punky androgyny—signal the emergence of new cultural modes of expressing, displaying, and performing whiteness, with the understanding that these modes represent both formal innovations and cultural responses to changing social and economic conditions. At the same time, although there has been considerable interest in the (paradox-ically) media-friendly spectacle of Riot Grrrls, much of the recent work on the intersectionality of race and gender in contemporary rock music has concen-trated on young men. As signaled by the upsurge in contemporary cultural studies of interest in male groups like Nirvana, white men continue to be viewed (implicitly or otherwise) as this realm's primary producers, just as black men have drawn most of the attention for their participation in hip-hop.[3]

In a parallel manner, traditional ways of theorizing the play of racial identities in rock music cultures have not adequately addressed gender. Accordingly, many of the best analyses of the "racial unconscious" of popular music cultures center on the complex articulation of whiteness among male rock icons—for example, the impressive, often brilliant, body of work on Elvis—and we are left wondering whether these analyses apply equally to women.[4]

This chapter asks a series of interrelated questions: If cross-racial appropriation as embodied by the "white Negro" has been the dominant model for understanding the race-ing of white male rock performance, what is the racial logic of white women's performance? What historical continuities or discontinuities shape the relations between an earlier generation of pioneering white female rock musicians and the current "generation" of young women rockers, both inside and outside the corporate mainstream? How has the racial identity of white women, with their attendant access to the social rewards associated with conventional femininity, affected their staging of defiance toward patriarchal gender expectations in and through their musical performance?

Although Love was not invited to sing or play guitar during her "Most Fascinating People of 1995" appearance, her interview with Walters provides a starting point for understanding the racialized performance of gender among white women rock musicians. Just as Love's trademark image of fallen womanhood unhinges the traditional equation of white femininity with sexual purity, so her apparent recuperation of normative femininity during the interview with Walters attests to white women's ability to reclaim such images—if only to caricature them, as Love frequently does.

In this reading, which equates white subjectivity with a social entitlement to experiment with identity, Love's subtle mimicry of Walters's more conventionally feminine demeanor and "look" demonstrates her ability, as a white woman, to displace/display femininity—an enterprise that could be compared with the putting on and taking off of ripped baby-doll dresses or elegant beige suits. And yet if Love's behavior with Walters speaks to the privileges associated with white womanhood, various elements of the interview nevertheless undermine Love's carefully crafted impression of being in control. For example, Walters's pursuit of questions about Love's previous flagrant refusal to perform the functions associated with good (i.e., bourgeois) motherhood seems significant, especially since the media's discourses of "single motherhood" have disproportionately focused on the "failures," in this regard, of poor women of color.

Although Love was clearly able to draw on her celebrity status to redress her previous, well-publicized deviations from this norm, her need to engage in defensive posturing about her musical and maternal competence—and implicitly the links between them—reveals crucial fissures in her command over the terms of gender. Ultimately, Love, one of 1995's "most fascinating" women, was reduced to pointing out that she had risen to rock stardom by her own merits, not by riding on the coattails of her famous husband.

Love is hardly the first white woman in rock to have been the object of equally intense media fascination and scrutiny on account of her outrageous (read "unfeminine") appearance or behavior. In recent memory, Sinead O'Connor also faced down questions about her status as a single mother and her defiance of corporate beauty culture (although once, after chiding her for her baldness, *Tonight Show* host Jay Leno broke down and confessed that he found her beautiful anyway). Like other Riot Grrrl musicians, Bikini Kill's Hanna has had to fend off criticism that she is a "man hater" merely because her songs express undiluted anger at patriarchal abuses of girls and women, and out lesbian performers such as k. d. lang are treated in a manner that combines homophobic wariness of sexual "deviance" with popular curiosity about lesbian sexual practices.

The fact that so much is made of the sexual frankness of, and parodic display of femininity by, rockers like Love (particularly in comparison with a similar frankness or display of femininity among New Jill R & B artists such as Mary J. Blige or women in hip-hop) is significant, however. Indeed, rock journalism's ambivalent love affair with Love says more about the social expectations of white and black women (i.e., the racialized constructions of gender/gendered constructions of race) than it does about the formal expectations attached to the various musical genres. Given that long-standing associations between women's sexual degradation and their performance or display are as old as women's participation in the popular music culture, we might well ask why white women rockers are subjected to interrogation—or, as is more likely of late, celebration—for acting "unladylike." Have all women had the same access to the transgressive pleasures associated with rock performance and rock rebellion?

The work of black feminist intellectuals provides insight into the relation between women's assigned place in the dominant social order and their ability to draw on cultural symbols to stage their critique of social norms, including conventions of gender. As nineteenth-century black women repeatedly pointed out in a variety of contexts, middle-class white women—that is, those women who tend to benefit most from social discourses of race and class—are, by virtue of their position, accorded the greatest access to prevailing notions of "womanhood."[5] Hence, and in a patriarchal context in which women's social value is conflated with their sexuality and sexual conformity, middle-class white women are deemed "naturally" virtuous, whereas black women, especially poor black women, are deemed "naturally" degraded or corrupt or are removed from the realm of adult sexuality altogether.

Although white supremacy accords white women social privilege on the basis of race, such privilege is fundamentally self-divided, since it rests on white women's acquiescence to patriarchal and class oppression. As long as these other forms of oppression are not challenged, middle-class white women's "rights" remain unquestioned, but as soon as they are confronted, white women's ability to draw on the social cachet of white racial identity weakens. In short, whereas black women's marginality on account of race and gender renders them uniquely vulnerable to patriarchal and white supremacist abuse, white women's racial entitlement and their gender vulnerability go uneasily hand in hand.

The career of Janis Joplin, the performer usually acknowledged as rock's first female superstar, illuminates how the contradictions that both underscore and constitute white women's racial subjectivity are translated in and through their musical performance. Moreover, although Joplin's musical repertoire, which consisted primarily of blues or blues-inflected rock, ostensibly bears little formal relation to the punk-derived rock of many contemporary female musicians, her expression of outlaw femininity/sexuality prefigured the defiant stances of many of today's white women rockers and hence could shed light on their own articulations of gender and race.

"Discovered" at the 1967 Monterey Pop Festival, Joplin achieved national visibility as the lead singer of Big Brother and the Holding Company, a band that released its major-label debut album *Cheap Thrills* (Columbia) in 1968. The first female rock star ever to be subjected to intense media scrutiny (her rise to fame coincided with the founding of *Rolling Stone* and the beginning of professional rock music journalism), Joplin occupied the spotlight for less than three years, dying of a heroin overdose in October 1970, although whether her death was a suicide has never been established.

In an industry based on the commodification of images of eternal youth, death proved to be a predictably effective marketing device. The posthumously released *Pearl,* featuring the number one single "Me and Bobby McGee," was Joplin's biggest commercial achievement.

Joplin's several dueling biographers—the best of whom is Myra Friedman, Joplin's former publicist—paint a complex picture of her life and death.[6] There

is Joplin the prototypical outsider, a shy and chronically pimply faced girl from
Port Arthur, Texas, whose college peers, in an act of breathtaking cruelty, once
voted her "Ugliest Man on Campus."[7] There is Joplin the "smart girl" and
closet bookworm who passed her spare time on tour reading and who once
instructed a friend to make her a handbag "big enough for a book and a
bottle."[8] Most important in this context is Joplin as "Pearl," the alter ego she
fashioned based on an identification, nurtured since adolescence, with "Em-
press of the Blues" Bessie Smith. Under the guise of Pearl, Joplin cultivated
aspects of her own character that correlated with what she knew of Smith's: a
taste for alcohol, a fondness for ornamenting herself with feathers and beads,
bisexuality, and a reputation as a "good-time girl" who talked frankly about
her sexual needs.

Joplin cultivated her most revealing and meaningful connection with Smith
through voice.[9] It was while attempting to emulate the qualities that distinguished Smith's singing—her timing and well-placed phrasing, her ability to
tease out the emotional complexities of a blues lyric, her emphasis on musical
structure—that Joplin discovered her own country-blues style, which she then
ratcheted up a few notches to compete with the rhythm and volume of a rock
band.[10] You can hear her striving for something like Smith's controlled intensity on her rendition of "Piece of My Heart" (especially in the part where she
sings "And each time I tell myself/That I think I've had enough/What I'm
gonna show you baby/Is that a woman can be tough"), but the performance
achieves little of Smith's melodic intensity or the irony, humor, and gravity that
infuse famous pieces such as "Young Woman's Blues." Instead, the impression
is of a singer working very hard to convey the emotion the song demands,
which is a well-honed balance between vulnerability and nerve.

Rock music journalists frequently used the phrase "whiskey voice" to
describe Joplin's work, in apparent reference not to her drinking (which indeed
hastened the deterioration of her vocal chords) but to the deep, gravelly quality
of her vocals, whose technical imperfections she compensated for with a
fervent (some would say maudlin) emotionalism. More than any other quality
it was this emotional fervor—fashioned after the model provided by blues
singers like Smith and Odetta and, later, Tina Turner and soul singer Otis
Redding—that distinguished Joplin's singing and that listeners today tend
either to love or to despise.

Such striving to "let it all hang out"—through voice, gesture, dress, hair-
style, and the like—was at best a paradoxical project for Joplin, one containing
the same ambivalent economy of cross-racial desire that Eric Lott calls "love
and theft" and that he argues was foundational to the articulation of turn-of-

the-century white working-class subjectivities.[11] In part, of course, Joplin's "free and easy" personal/performance style reflected the dominant aesthetic of late-1960s San Francisco hippie youth culture, with its emphasis on spontaneity, experimentation, and unfettered self-expression.

My argument here, however, is that Joplin's style also reflected an ambivalent disidentification with whiteness and femaleness, which Joplin equated with estrangement from authentic emotion, particularly sexual desire. Joplin's screaming and screeching (all assiduously rehearsed and practiced, as Friedman tells it) were thus not only her formal incorporation of a politicocultural stance, however sincerely felt, but also the source of an admittedly problematic oppositional practice—a means by which to critique southern white bourgeois femininity and its insistence that women act "little and pretty."[12] Joplin's mother is reported to have once asked her, "Why do you scream like that when you've got such a pretty voice?"[13]

Her question cuts to the heart of what fascinated contemporary white fans and detractors alike: Joplin's conspicuous break with the more conventionally "sweet" or "silky" vocal style of 1950s white female pop singers such as Anita O'Day, Peggy Lee, and Lita Roza, the last one famous for "How Much Is That Doggie in the Window?"[14] In the decades preceding Joplin, record companies had often used white women singers to "domesticate" R & B songs in order to market them to white audiences, much as white male rock musicians from Elvis Presley to the Beatles interpreted African American R & B in a way that proved highly marketable to white teenagers. Joplin also made a career out of covering songs originally performed by black musicians—most famously Big Mama Thornton's "Ball and Chain" and Erma Franklin's "Piece of My Heart" (which landed up in Billboard's Rhythm and Blues Top Ten). Yet in contrast to earlier white female vocalists—those "nice girls" who "cleaned up" the blues—Joplin, through her own interpretations of a blues idiom, pioneered for white women a sexually assertive performance.

She did so, as her self-fashioning as "Pearl" reveals, by capitalizing on the historical links between blues performance and black women's cultural construction of sexual agency—an agency lived out through song as well as personal example. Blues have often been falsely characterized as a musical expression of African American sorrow or victimhood, but as Rosetta Reitz notes, blues lyrics like "I bake the best jelly roll in town" and "I got the sweetest cabbage" gave female artists a pleasurable, metaphorical, and yet easily accessible language of sexual desire.[15] Hazel Carby reinforces this position, arguing that black women blues vocalists were "organic intellectuals" who articulated the social, political, and spiritual needs of their overwhelmingly poor and working-class black audiences.[16] As did soul singers in the 1960s, blues singers in the 1920s sought to create a resonant, dynamic relationship between audience and vocalist, one encouraging the audience to respond to the singer's performance of emotional authenticity and "depth."

Equally important to Joplin, whose very rise to rock stardom indexed the entrenchment of the youth/music culture industry by the late 1960s, black female blues singers such as Mamie Smith and Bessie Smith were among the first artists to confront the commodification of their cultural practices as well as the manufacture, by means of the "race record," of a new category of the "black consumer," who eventually came to represent a distinct market for capital expansion.[17] Recording before the industry was fully professionalized and corporatized, women like the Smiths, Ida Cox, and Alberta Hunter had a degree of artistic control that Joplin—who was as much as anything the product of an intensive marketing campaign by Columbia Records—never could have hoped to have.

In short, Joplin did not simply look to blues singers such as Smith for artistic inspiration; she also mediated her own feelings of outsidership from the 1950s-era "feminine mystique" through her appropriation of a blues aesthetic that decades earlier had supported the production of a critical, oppositional, and public discourse of black female sexuality. In giving birth, as it were, to Pearl, Joplin was engaging in what George Lipsitz calls (using a term from film theorists Douglas Kellner and Michael Ryan) "discursive transcoding," or the process by which white artists "disguise" their own subjectivities in order to "articulate desires and subject positions" that they cannot express in their own voices.[18] As Lipsitz explains, white artists traditionally have looked to black cultures as sources of cultural self-fashioning because these cultures have nurtured and sustained "moral and cultural alternatives to dominant values" and served as an "important source of education and inspiration to alienated and aggrieved individuals cut off from other sources of oppositional practice."[19] This was precisely the case for Joplin, who used blues to negotiate the gender and racial taboos that she had found simultaneously alienating and alluring during her Texas girlhood.

Yet just as Lott discovers in nineteenth-century white minstrel performance "a simultaneous drawing up and crossing of racial boundaries" and a "mixed erotic economy of celebration and exploitation," so in Joplin's rock performance we can detect an emulation of black female blues artists that borders on a reactionary romanticization of their artistic achievement and a reification of the notion of racial difference.[20] "You know why we're stuck with the myth that only black people have soul?" Joplin once asked a white male reporter.

"Because white people don't let themselves feel things. Man, you and any housewife have all sorts of pain and joy. You'd have soul if you'd give in to it."[21] Joplin's critique of white bourgeois "inauthenticity" echoes that of Norman Mailer in his infamous 1957 "White Negro" essay, which invests black men with the sexual potency, emotional resourcefulness, and disruptive, oppositional power that Mailer finds lacking in the dominant culture. As does Mailer's essay, Joplin's comment imagines the inversion of traditional racial hierarchies so that black people not only are mythologically more soulful but in fact are "on top" of white people in their capacity for emotional surrender.

In addition, Joplin's comment implies a self-negating thesis of black performance that rests on stereotypical assumptions of black artistic naïveté. Hence any implied tribute to black female blues singers contained in Joplin's disparagement of the white bourgeoisie is evidence of, in inverted form, a patronizing belief in female blues singers' fundamental lack of craft. Such a nonperformative thesis of blues performance is ironic given Joplin's historical knowledge of Smith, as well as her own experiences as a performer who always projected sexual confidence on stage and then anxiously searched for tricks after shows.[22]

Mediated through her romanticization of black women blues singers, Joplin's de-idealization of bourgeois white femininity (i.e., the housewife of the preceding quotation) primarily served her need to justify her own tendencies toward hard drinking, hard living, and hard singing. Friedman and Joplin's sister Laura Joplin both describe a brief period in summer 1965 when Joplin, who had been living in San Francisco, returned abruptly to Port Arthur, where she covered the needle tracks on her arms with long-sleeved dresses, made plans to get married, and began "a ten-month period of attempted conformity that even surpassed, as her friends saw it, the demanded conventions of the town."[23]

Although Joplin apparently constructed this penitential phase of her life to gain control over her substance abuse, Friedman argues that Joplin's impulsivity resulted from her own unresolved desires. Such an interpretation supports the relevance of Lott's thesis of "love and theft" to Joplin's own self-fashioning. On the one hand, she drew inspiration from the historical example provided by black women blues singers; on the other hand, she projected onto these adopted historical "role models" her own fascination with and hatred of white bourgeois femininity. The "split" in Joplin's subjectivity predictably resulted in crushing artistic insecurities, self-doubts that for Joplin were exacerbated when the white music press compared her with Aretha Franklin, over whom she was once, to her horror, voted "Queen of Soul."[24]

Joplin's fetishization of Smith recalls the fetishization of Louis Armstrong by white Jewish jazz musician Mezz Mezzrow in a way that sheds light on the gendering of cross-racial desire and its relation to white musical performance. As he recounts in his 1946 autobiography *Really the Blues,* Mezzrow devoted his life to emulating Armstrong (and, to a lesser degree, clarinetist Sidney Bechet), to the point that he believed that after years of immersion in black musical culture of the 1930s and 1940s, he had become a "voluntary Negro," much as Joplin near the end of her life imagined herself to be Pearl. Even more than Joplin, whom he outlived, Mezzrow was a strict blues purist who spent his later years organizing "classic blues" revival concerts throughout Europe. Drugs were important to both artists (especially Mezzrow, who gained access to men like Armstrong by keeping them supplied with marijuana), both expressed an erotically charged admiration for black performers, and both tended to camouflage their artistic self-doubt under the veil of a stringent work ethic.

Mezzrow, who was also a prototype for Mailer's "white Negro," returns us to the question of the "racial unconscious" of white popular musical perfor-mance, which historically has been figured in terms of symbolic commerce among men, mediated by and through "the power of the black penis in white American psychic life."[25] Although the permutations of this traffic across the color line are too numerous to cite here, generally speaking white male rock performers' "translation" of black music styles and associated black perfor-mance styles into an oppositional practice for white youth has also enhanced their ability to attain what Herman Beavers calls "successful" masculinity in the public sphere: to construct themselves as sexually powerful, physically poised, stylish, aloof, self-sufficient, street smart, and "hip."[26]

Lipsitz, Peter Guralnick, Greil Marcus, and Andrew Ross, among others, describe this process as one in which white male performers seek to "own" the qualities they romantically ascribe to black male performers while simultane-ously projecting these qualities onto black performers in the depreciated form of "natural" talent or "biologically-driven urges,"[27] a tendency that recalls Joplin's belief in the nonthetic aspects of black experience and, by extension, black women's blues performance. At the same time, the concealment of this symbolic commerce is fundamental to white male performers' ability to main-tain control over the terms of the "real" economic commerce—in other words, to sustain the impression of owning, and therefore justly profiting from, certain black cultural practices. White performers' sublimation of the erotic intricacies of such cross-racial mimetic desire (desire fueled by state-mandated segregation, which invested prohibited bodies and acts with erotic significance) also helps explain why white male rock cultures have traditionally been so rigidly homophobic while remaining open to various forms of homoerotic play or display.

In short, white male rock musicians did not compromise their hegemonic masculinity by appropriating black cultural practices; on the contrary, and as the trajectory of so many careers makes clear, normative heterosexual masculinity may even be reclaimed through such appropriations. As my own narrative of the development of Joplin's artistic practice suggests, however, the results of a loosely analogous enterprise may ultimately be mixed for white female performers who confront, on account of gender, both the pleasures and the dangers of cross-racial appropriation.

Such was the case for Joplin, who gained authority over her audiences and notoriety in the music press for wringing "the last drop of sex from every song" (as a 1969 *Newsweek* article put it), even as such straightforward erotic display further distanced her from hegemonic white femininity.[28] "Pearl," Joplin's name for a set of artistic practices that she evolved through a series of cross-racial and homoerotic desires, not only facilitated Joplin's success as a performer; she/they also enabled Joplin to negotiate the contradictions of a music industry that was simultaneously hostile to women and yet eager to market the "unselfconscious sexuality"[29] of its first nationally known white female star.

If the "rock 'n' roll tragedy" narratives that have never ceased to circulate around Joplin have any validity in this context, they support the notion that it was Joplin's inability to reconcile the apparent contradictions among her social location, her location in the music industry, and her ambitions as a performer that contributed to her self-destruction. (This is why even Joplin's most vehement rejections of bourgeois white femininity circumvented the cheap misogyny of some of her peers, as evidenced in Rolling Stones songs such as "[Here Comes Your] 19th Nervous Breakdown" or "Mother's Little Helper.") Shut out of the "aloof sorority" of the middle-class southern white womanhood that she simultaneously admired and despised, Joplin attempted to resolve at the level of artistic praxis the social contradictions of her own subjectivity.[30]

Joplin's career is interestingly juxtaposed with that of Tina Turner, a contemporary of Joplin's who had a string of R & B hits in the late 1950s fronting for Ike Turner and the Kings of Rhythm. In the decades before the release of her 1984 album *Private Dancer,* which went triple platinum and became the fifth best-seller of all time, Turner spent years as a battered wife who sang all night and then at 4 A.M. cooked breakfast for the band.[31] Although her vocal versatility put her in a league with Gladys Knight and Aretha Franklin, who were equally at home with gospel, soul, and R & B, Turner pursued rock music for her "comeback" as a solo artist, in part because rock carried fewer personal associations with a past marred by abuse and neglect. "I realized," she said, "I liked the way people like Eric Clapton and the Rolling Stones had mixed white and black music, taking feeling from black people and adding it to their own. Blues to me is depressing. White music has a liberating feeling about it, and I needed a change."[32] Turner's comment brings to mind a number of relevant comparisons: In contrast to Joplin, who sought her "liberation" in blues, Turner pursued the opposite artistic trajectory, "crossing over" to the commercial mainstream with hits like "What's Love Got to Do with It?" and a role in the postapocalyptic film *Mad Max III: Beyond the Thunderdome,* for which she contributed the theme song.

Turner signified this artistic conversion as a matter of personal transformation, working out on the "plane of aesthetics" and through the "rhetoric of style"[33]—that is, through newly dyed and teased hair and a newly toned body—her newfound commercial "muscularity" and personal and musical "control." Whereas Joplin signified her rejection of white bourgeois femininity through "unkempt" hair and far-out hippie ensembles, Turner, then in her forties, appeared in music videos in short dresses and high heels designed to draw attention to her legs. Turner's aggressive self-commodification points to black women's relative lack of power in the music industry.

If record-label executives had shown little interest in Joplin before her success at the Monterey Pop Festival made it apparent that even a somewhat disheveled hippie girl singer could be marketed, they were notoriously less generous with black female singers, whose careers often languished from neglect or who were denied visible roles because they were deemed unattractive. Such was the case with Florence Ballard, the original "third Supreme" who was bumped from the group in 1967 to make room for the more photogenic, if less vocally skilled, Diana Ross. Unlike Ballard, who never recovered her career, Turner, after living in poverty in the late 1970s and raising four children on food stamps, began recording again and eventually earned the curious title of rock's "sexy godmother."[34]

The phrase "sexy godmother" reveals the suspect foundations on which rests the sort of capitalist story of resurrection that Turner's career exemplifies. "Godmother" in this context is not only or primarily a respectful acknowledgment of Turner's artistic longevity; it is also or rather a radically ahistoricizing term suggesting that Turner bears no legitimate relation to rock, a music that she in fact helped pioneer. Such forgetfulness is part of the narrative strategy by which the music industry continually gives birth to "new" commodities, whether these commodities be musical genres (e.g., in the transatlantic revival of 1960s soul music) or musical performers like Morissette who, before being heavily marketed as a singer with just enough tough-girl rebelliousness to appear appropriately nonconformist, was a Canadian teen pop idol.

Most crucially, these capitalist narratives of resurrection tend to erase the very racialized institutional practices that obstruct black performers' mobility while facilitating opportunities for white performers. Through these practices, the music industry is able to fashion markets and products around categories of race while simultaneously rendering invisible the "race" of white performers. Whereas Joplin, who died at age twenty-seven, was posthumously commodified as rock's preeminent tragic heroine, her contemporary Turner (who was just four years older) became an icon of rock culture's "eternal youth" and, perhaps even more predictably, a paragon of "strong black womanhood."

Rejecting Joplin's association with the excesses of 1970s-era hippie rock and Turner's frank marketing of her sexuality, today's young white female rockers do not claim either artist as an important musical forebear, despite the different ways that both innovated the scream as a rebellious vocal style for women. Even Riot Grrrls, who have made the reclaiming of "lost" rock heroines a central part of their cultural practice, look to other sources for inspiration and instruction. The current generation's preference for germinal girl rockers such as Pat Benatar and Joan Jett or more avant-garde musicians such as Sonic Youth's Kim Gorden or Yoko Ono produces an alternative to the capitalist narrative of artistic resurrection that I have been describing—one in which younger women's support of earlier performers has actually helped reinvigorate the latter's careers, often through collaborative efforts. Joan Jett, for example, has been actively involved with Riot Grrrls since at least 1993, when she recorded and contributed second guitar and vocals to Bikini Kill's single "Rebel Girl," released on the independent Kill Rock Stars label. Yoko Ono, who in 1992 put out her own "greatest hits" compilation, *Walking on Thin Ice* (Ryko), lent her support to the girl duo Cibo Matto, who toured recently with Ono's son Sean Lennon on guitar.

This promotion of selected women in rock by some of today's young musicians, who have grown up in what Kimberlé Crenshaw calls the post–civil rights era, raises questions about how white women's racial and gender subjectivities are differently articulated in the latter half of the 1990s than they were thirty years ago, when Joplin began performing. To date, the tendency in popular music studies has been to use "appropriation" as the dominant intellectual paradigm through which to understand the articulation of white racial subjectivity. Even though such a strategy may illuminate aspects of Joplin's career, "appropriation" may be an inherently less useful model for discerning the racialized performance of gender among today's young white women in rock, who tend to cultivate an attitude of ironic self-consciousness in their videos, music, and live performances. Joplin staged her defiance of white bourgeois femininity through a process of racial projection, introjection, and disavowal, demonstrating that a disidentification with whiteness cannot necessarily be equated with antiracism. Yet this process seems outmoded as a way of describing the artistic practices of contemporary white female performers.

Today's young women rockers are more likely to express their rejection of normative white femininity through postmodernist strategies of parody, of which Love's slightly tight baby-doll dresses are but one example. When Love hoarsely declares "I'm Miss World, somebody kill me" in the Hole song "Miss World," she is not only critiquing patriarchal beauty culture, with its emphasis on the hierarchical display of female bodies; she is also expressing a jaded weariness with conventional forms of femininity and a recognition of her own place in an industry that can readily absorb and market her mockery of feminine grace. When she rocks her guitar suggestively back and forth on her pelvis (as she did when Hole appeared on the television show *Saturday Night Live*), she is not only satirizing the phallic symbolism of old-fashioned rock 'n' roll; she is also playfully caricaturing a previous era's gender-bending "girls with guitars."

Likewise, when Polly Jean Harvey, her face gaudily made up and her small gaunt frame draped in a satin sheath, manically shouts that she is a "50-Foot Queenie" (a phrase derived from the sci-fi film *Attack of the 50-Foot Woman,* about a housewife's revenge against her husband), she is simultaneously invoking notions of "monstrous" female sexuality and parodying her own performance of phallic femininity.

At the same time, however, white women rockers' "refusal of the gaze"—a refusal literalized, for example, in the Breeders' live performances and music videos, in which they typically avoid smiling at or for the camera—belies the rapid success of the music industry in marketing images of disenfranchised, alienated white femininity. Among white male rock stars, the analogy is the relatively recent emergence of the "loser"—men such as Corgan, Cobain, Beck, Thurston Moore of Sonic Youth, or even Eddie Vedder of Pearl Jam, who display vulnerability, introversion, androgyny, bisexuality, or sexual passivity and who sometimes (as in the case of the "token boys" in Bikini Kill and Hole) allow themselves to be upstaged by charismatic women, including female instrumentalists. If the loser's display of abject white masculinity draws attention away from his phenomenal commercial success, it must also be said that the results of such capitalist incorporation for understandings of whiteness are complex. Whereas in a regional independent music scene, proclaiming oneself a "loser" reflects a punk-inspired critique of corporate capitalism, the same gesture on MTV comes off more like a residual, rather than an anticipatory, put-down.

It remains to be seen whether there is value in such performances of self-loathing, outside their ability to entertain. For as with "white guilt," the source of another kind of abject subjectivity, it is not clear that in the context of capitalist appropriation, the "loser" can be the source of any sustained—or sustaining—progressive politics, especially a racial politics that rises above narcissistic white self-contempt. Similarly, if critiques of femininity in recent rock performance also are racialized, as I have been arguing, then what an admittedly unsympathetic male friend of mine disparagingly characterizes as "white women complaining" reveals that for young white female rockers, membership in the "boy's club" has its difficulties, but membership also has its privileges.

NOTES

1. Cobain's refusal to conform to an image of strutting masculinity associated with male rock stars, together with his personal links to Riot Grrrl bands in and around Olympia, Washington, put him at the center of this speculation about new rock masculinities. Only days after Cobain's memorial services, Ann Powers, now a senior editor at the *Village Voice* and one of few prominent female rock music journalists, made the case that Cobain at his best drew on punk values to critique rock culture's own tendencies to bolster patriarchal masculinity, if not straight-out, hard-core misogyny. For Powers, Cobain's frank experimentations with gender—for example, his donning of a yellow satin ball gown for a November 1991 episode of MTV's "Headbanger's Ball"—represent important departures from the homophobic traditions associated with glam rock and its cross-dressing, gender-bending progeny.

2. See Fred Pfeil, *White Guys: Studies in Postmodern Domination and Difference* (London: Verso, 1995), esp. pp. 71–104.

3. Such oversights have important implications for the writing of rock histories and for the theoretical project of understanding how race, gender, and class subjectivities are expressed through and shaped by popular cultural practices. On the one hand, the persistent focus on young men as the central authors of youth music cultures tends to ignore women's contributions and to produce "universal" models of rock rebellion that, in effect, perpetuate the marginalization or exclusion of women. For important statements of this argument, see Angela McRobbie, "Settling Accounts with Subcultures: A Feminist Critique," in her *Feminism and Youth Culture* (Boston: Unwin Hyman, 1991), pp. 16–34, and "Feminism, Postmodernism and the 'Real Me,'" in her *Postmodernism and Popular Culture* (New York: Routledge, 1994), pp. 61–74; and Dick Hebdige, *Subculture: The Meaning of Style* (London: Methuen, 1979). Simon Reynolds and Joy Press's more recent contention that contemporary rock rebellion takes the form of

"gender tourism" paradoxically reiterates this exclusion of women, constraining white women to equally unsatisfactory roles as outsiders or "one of the boys" and denying black women historical agency as artistic innovators, role models, or mediating influences. See Reynolds and Press, *The Sex Revolts: Gender, Rebellion and Rock 'n' Roll* (Cambridge, MA: Harvard University Press, 1995).

4. See, for example, Greil Marcus, *Dead Elvis: A Chronicle of a Cultural Obsession* (New York: Doubleday, 1991); and Peter Guralnick, *Last Train to Memphis: The Rise of Elvis Presley* (Boston: Little, Brown, 1994).

5. See, for example, Ida B. Wells-Barnett, *On Lynching* (1892; reprint, Salem, NH: Ayer, 1991); and Harriet Jacobs, *Incidents in the Life of a Slave Girl* (New York: Oxford University Press, 1988). It is precisely because of racialized and class-inflected hierarchies of gender that Jacobs, writing in her 1863 autobiography, entreated her Northern white abolitionist "sisters" to judge slave women's virtue by standards different from those applied to middle-class white women.

6. On Joplin, see especially Myra Friedman, *Buried Alive: The Biography of Janis Joplin* (New York: Harmony, 1992); and Laura Joplin, *Love, Janis* (London: Bloomsbury, 1992).

7. Friedman, *Buried Alive*, p. 40.

8. Lucy O'Brien, *She Bop: The Definitive History of Women in Rock, Pop and Soul* (New York: Penguin Books, 1995), p. 102.

9. Ibid., p. 104.

10. Ibid., p. 12; Friedman, *Buried Alive*, p. 74.

11. See Eric Lott, *Love and Theft: Blackface Minstrelsy and the American Working Class* (New York: Oxford University Press, 1993), esp. pp. 3–31.

12. John Poppy, "Big Brother's White Soul," *Look*, September 3, 1968, p. 61.

13. Ibid.

14. O'Brien, *She Bop*, p. 38.

15. Ibid., p. 12.

16. Hazel Carby, "It Just Be's Dat Way Sometimes," *Radical America* 20 (June–July 1986): 8–22.

17. The rage for race records was spurred by the phenomenal and unforeseen success of Mamie Smith's "Crazy Blues," recorded for Okeh in 1920. The record sold 500,000 copies in six months—primarily to black consumers. Bessie Smith signed with Columbia in 1923.

18. George Lipsitz, *Dangerous Crossroads* (New York: Verso, 1994), p. 53.

19. Ibid., p. 54.

20. Lott, *Love and Theft*, p. 6. I borrowed the term *racial unconscious* from Harry Stecopoulos.

21. Poppy, "Big Brother's White Soul," p. 61.

22. Lott, *Love and Theft*, p. 39.

23. Friedman, *Buried Alive*, p. 58.

24. Ibid., p. 334.

25. Lott, *Love and Theft*, p. 9.

26. Lipsitz, *Dangerous Crossroads*, p. 54. I first heard Beavers use this term in his talk at the American Studies Association's "Toward a Common Ground Conference," November 10, 1995.

27. Ibid., p. 54.

28. "Rebirth of the Blues," *Newsweek,* May 26, 1969, p. 83. Such frankly sexist and exotic language had previously been used—by black and white observers alike—to describe black musical practices (e.g., Harlem cabaret shows in the 1920s). What makes such a sentence extraordinary here is the fact that it describes a white woman.

29. Charlie Gillett, *The Sound of the City: The Rise of Rock and Roll,* 2nd ed. (New York: Da Capo Press, 1996), p. 356.

30. O'Brien, *She Bop,* p. 100. In many ways, this is similar to the story often told about Cobain. Like Joplin, Cobain was known for experimenting with the terms of gender, and like her, he fashioned himself as an outcast and a "loser."

31. Cathleen McGuigan, "The Sexy Godmother of Rock," *Newsweek,* March 4, 1985, p. 50. The drudgery, agony, and excitement of these years are documented in *I, Tina,* written by Turner with Kurt Loder, now of MTV News (New York: Avon Books, 1987).

32. Turner, *I, Tina.*

33. Hebdige, *Subculture,* pp. 44–45.

34. Ibid.

11

What Is "White Trash"? Stereotypes and Economic Conditions of Poor Whites in the United States

Annalee Newitz and Matthew Wray

"White trash" is, in many ways, the white Other. When we think about race in the United States, we often find ourselves constrained by categories we have inherited from a kind of essentialist multiculturalism, or what we call *vulgar multiculturalism*.[1] Vulgar multiculturalism holds that racial and ethnic groups are "authentically" and essentially different from one another and that racism is a one-way street: it proceeds out of whiteness to subjugate nonwhiteness, so that all racists are white and all victims of racism are nonwhite. Critical multiculturalism, as it has been articulated by theorists such as those in the Chicago Cultural Studies Group, is one example of a multiculturalism that tries to complicate the dogmatic ways in which vulgar multiculturalism has understood race, gender, and class identities.[2] A "white trash" identity is one that a critical multiculturalism should address in order to advance its project of reexamining the relationships between identity and social power. Unlike the

Adapted from *the minnesota review* 47 (Spring 1997): 61–77.

"whiteness" of vulgar multiculturalism, however, the whiteness of "white trash" signals something other than privilege and social power.

The term *white trash* points up the hatred and fear undergirding the American myth of classlessness. Yoking a classist epithet to a racist one, as white trash does, reminds us how often racism is in fact directly related to economic differences. As a stereotype, white trash calls our attention to the way that discourses of class and racial difference tend to bleed into one another, especially in the way that they pathologize and lay waste to their "others." Indeed, "subordinate white" is such an oxymoron in the dominant culture that this social position is principally spoken about in our slang in terms like *white trash, redneck, cracker,* and *hillbilly.*

We don't say things like *nigger trash* precisely because "nigger" often implies poverty.[3] Are some African Americans "niggers" because they are black or because they are poor? There is no one answer to this one; it is difficult to distinguish between race and class when discussing the derogatory meanings of "nigger." In this way, *nigger* is a term like *white trash.* This conflation of race and class in America often is confusing, as are most ideologies that perpetuate injustice. When people are kept guessing about what kinds of social forces oppress them, they are less able to defend themselves. Naming the connections between race- and class-based inequalities, however, clarifies the overlapping interests of marginalized groups seeking recognition and social justice.

White trash needs to be considered in any analysis of whiteness, and our intention is not merely to critique the project of deconstructing whiteness; rather, we wish to extend it. We strongly agree with what we consider to be the motivation behind this project, namely, the recognition that allowing whiteness to remain invisible or unmarked makes it difficult, if not impossible, to develop antiracist and anticlassist forms of white identity. However, we are suggesting that an alternative and as yet unexplored way to deconstruct whiteness is to examine the differences within whiteness. We thus argue for the necessity of breaking down whiteness by examining how, for instance, discourses of differences among whites tend to de-stabilize and undermine any unified or essentialized notion of white identity as the primary locus of social privilege and power.

Unlike unmarked hegemonic forms of whiteness, the category of white trash is marked as white from the outset. But in addition to being racially marked, it is simultaneously marked as trash, as something that must be discarded, expelled, and disposed of in order for whiteness to achieve and maintain social dominance. Thus, white trash must be understood as both an external and an internal threat to whiteness. It is externalized by class difference but made the same through racial identification. White trash lies simultaneously inside and outside whiteness, becoming the difference within, the white Other that inhabits the core of whiteness.

Finally, the term *white trash* reminds us that one of the worst crimes of which one can accuse a person is poverty. If you are white, calling someone "white" is hardly an insult. But calling someone "white trash" is both a racist and classist insult. Why is this so? Perhaps the scar of race is cut by the knife of class, although this is not to say that race is in any way reducible to class. Clearly, the knife cuts both ways. Yet all too often in discussions of racial identity, class is ignored, dismissed, and left untheorized.[4] We argue that leaving class out of antiracist criticism not only creates a theoretical blind spot but also can lead to class prejudice. We cannot understand many types of social injustice without using theories that wed antiracist agendas to anticapitalist ones. Analyzing white trash is one way to begin launching, and ultimately popularizing, such theories.

SOME DEFINITIONS OF WHITE TRASH

The earliest recorded usages of the term *white trash* are found in references to "poor white trash" dating back to the early nineteenth century. Historical dictionaries of Americanisms typically ascribe the term's origins to black slaves. If we are to believe these dictionaries, the term originated as a black-on-white labeling practice and was quickly appropriated (by 1855) by upper-class whites.[5] Both terms appear to have remained in use by blacks and whites throughout the nineteenth century, and although today, *white trash* seems to be more widespread and to be used more frequently, the term *poor white trash* remains with us, a reminder that it is, after all, an explicitly economic as well as a racial identity.

For this reason, white trash presents us with the possibility of a radical transvaluation of what it means to be white, poor, or both. For contemporary writers and activists like Dorothy Allison or Jim Goad,[6] white trash becomes a potent symbolic gesture of defiance, a refusal of the shame and invisibility that come with being poor. It also becomes a way to call attention to a form of injustice that is often ignored, given popular conceptions of the United States as a meritocracy. Even if calling oneself "trash" seems to smack of self-loathing, it nevertheless serves to reveal the prejudice against the impoverished in America. Sometimes it is better to be named something terrible rather than to have no name at all.

It is difficult to determine just exactly whom or what we are talking about when we use the term *white trash*. The questions "How do you define white trash?" and "Whom are you talking about?" demand answers. These questions are basically ways of asking whether or not we think the stereotypical images of white trash America as violent, incestuous, and criminal are true. That is, most people understand white trash not as a clearly defined socioeconomic stratum or as a cultural group but, rather, as a complex set of social representations, an amalgam of well-known stereotypes. White trash as we know it is both an economic identity and something imaginary, or iconic.

When we talk about white trash, we are discussing a discourse that often confuses cultural icons and material realities and, in effect, helps establish and maintain a complex set of moral, cultural, social, economic, and political boundaries. To explore this discourse, we need to ask where its representations and stereotypes come from, what motivates them, how they are produced and taken up, and by whom. From this perspective, we can begin to see how the category "white trash" is used to blame the poor for both their poverty and their social problems, which can be found at all levels of the economic ladder. For example, stereotypes of white trash and "hillbillies" are replete with references to dangerous and excessive sexuality; rape (both heterosexual and homosexual), incest, and sexual abuse are supposed to be common practices among poor rural whites. Yet we know that sexual abuse occurs in all segments of the population. But white trash is associated with and blamed for the kinds of sexuality that people may experience no matter what their class background. This is likewise the case when poor whites are stereotyped as virulently racist in comparison with their wealthier white counterparts. As long as the poor are said to possess such traits, people can convince themselves that the poor should be cast out of mainstream society, that they deserve what they get.

Having established that we need to question these representations, it is important to return to the problem of just whom we think we are talking about. Even those of us who would lay claim to some white trash past (say, those of us from impoverished and/or undereducated white families or communities) might find it hard to claim this identity now, owing to the considerable social distances we have traveled to reach our various locations in the academy. How do we represent the material realities, the real-life experiences of poor, undereducated, and otherwise marginalized whites in our own discourses and practices?

One way to answer this question is to examine how we explain the marginal status of these whites. Is it genetic? People like Charles Murray and other proponents of the "bell curve" theory of intelligence believe that poor whites are poor simply because they are not as smart or as educable as their genetically well-endowed fellow whites. Murray and his ilk are reviving an old idea about race dating back to the early-twentieth-century eugenics theory described by Nicole Hahn Rafter.[7]

More recently, other conservative cultural critics, known collectively as the "angry white males," have argued that impoverished whites are largely the product of misguided social policies. According to this view, government programs associated with the War on Poverty have failed the poor and have thereby led to generations of welfare-dependent whites. Affirmative action policies are singled out here as well, as these critics contend that they function as little more than racial quota systems that exclude the white underclass. The end result of these programs and policies, they conclude, is a growing class of poor, disenfranchised whites who share a culture of poverty that makes it nearly impossible for them to enter mainstream American life.

From our perspective, both of these explanatory models demonstrate the tendency of the social sciences and policy studies to pathologize certain behaviors or groups, thereby completely misdiagnosing the problem. For example, both liberal and conservative sociologists view poverty as a kind of sickness, a social ill resulting from either individual or cultural deficiencies (i.e., "the poor are just lazy" or "they live in cultures of poverty") or from the history of liberal welfare-state planning. In either case, poverty is not understood to be endemic to capitalist social relations. However, as is a Marxist commonplace, asymmetrical class relations and class exploitation—as well as the maintenance of a large reserve army of the unemployed—are structural aspects of any functioning capitalist order. A critique of capitalist social relations enables us to understand white trash as twofold: it is a way of naming actually existing white people who occupy the economic and social margins of American life, and it is a set of myths and stereotypes that justify their continued marginalization.

WHITE IDENTITY IN MULTICULTURALISM

For centuries, whites in and out of the United States have formed their identities in largely negative terms. That is, they have known themselves not to be savages like aboriginals; they have known themselves not to be foolish and emotional like women; and they have known themselves not to be decadent heathens like "Orientals." Their self-image was thus often formed from the lack of certain cultural or characterological traits—and the universality or "obviousness" of their moral righteousness. But in an era when "globalization" is occurring on all levels of social relations, from the economy to popular culture, whiteness has suddenly come to seem like the only identity not associated with a rich and specific historical tradition or like some type of separatist space sanctioned as authentically white. In a multicultural, multinational global civilization, some whites—oddly enough—feel anachronistic and displaced.

We are not attempting a kind of crude psychologization of contemporary white identity, but merely suggesting that historical developments in social relations have now made it obvious to many people that there can be no universal identity as whites once described it. Furthermore, many postcolonial nations and oppressed minority groups have seriously undermined white confidence—and also white actions—associated with the idea that being good imperialists automatically makes them a morally superior group. Doubting, sometimes unconsciously, that universal superiority constitutes their character, some whites in the United States are beginning to use a different narrative to explain their identities. This narrative is borrowed from the very groups that whites once defined themselves against: those marginalized peoples who, taken together, are described as multicultural.

The rise of the term *white trash* in the mass media follows closely on the heels of highly publicized debates about multiculturalism and multicultural identity. As we see it, there are two principal reasons that a sudden interest in the idea of a white trash identity might be associated with a multiculturalist discourse. First, white trash can function as a politically conservative white protest against so-called multiculturalist agendas such as affirmative action, revisionist education, and social welfare programs. Second, white trash may represent the first wave of white assimilation to multiculturalist identity, since it is a way of articulating racial disempowerment and whiteness together. For some people, the category of white trash essentially brings into focus the way in which whites are interpreted to be the victims of racism and minoritization as much or in the same ways as their fellow multicultural U.S. citizens. Whether white trash is used to signal a breaking or a joining with the tenets of multiculturalism, it is principally a way of explaining white identity through narratives of victimhood.

As its critics have noted, a multicultural identity is often authenticated through stories about personal or historical injury at the hands of dominant groups. Indeed, as Cornel West points out in *Race Matters,* black identity is largely constituted by its relationship to potential racist oppression. "After centuries of racist degradation, exploitation, and oppression in America, being black means being minimally subject to white supremacist abuse and being part of a rich culture and community that has struggled against such abuse."[8]

Multicultural techniques of identity formation often are associated with the so-called victim mentality decried by Charles Sykes in his *A Nation of Victims,*[9] in which he argues that U.S. citizens seem to feel that they all, no matter how privileged, deserve to be pitied—and compensated—as victims in some situations. In the terms of multiculturalism, being the victim of racism, sexism, and homophobia often grants you a special and even sanctified identity. We believe that this is what some whites may be seeking when they lay claim to the label *white trash* or, more generally, *white victim.*

One kind of white victimization narrative comes out of "white power," and it holds that affirmative action, immigrants' rights, and social welfare programs are racist attacks on whites. Generally conservative and reactionary, such stories are told by white groups that are marginal in their own right: skinheads, some Christian fundamentalist churchgoers, members of the Ku Klux Klan, and allies of politicians like David Duke. More mainstream versions of the white power story, such as California Governor Pete Wilson's antiaffirmative action policies or House Speaker Newt Gingrich's extolling the benefits of a welfare rollback, are less virulent but nevertheless demonstrate a trend toward whites finding their identities once again through lack. Because they lack multicultural cachet, whites allegedly endure social disempowerment. By painting themselves as the victims of multiculturalism, whites can go multicultural identity one better. As the victims of victims, whites can believe that they have the richest and most marginalized identities around.

Another type of white victimization narrative discovers in whiteness an identity that is capable of joining with multiculturalism rather than claiming to be its victim. The white trash identity as we know it in the late twentieth century—even as it complicates the idea of multiculturalism—has learned to talk about itself by hearing, reading, and seeing members of oppressed minority groups talk about themselves and their identities. In their longing for the kinds of coherent and strong identities that they see minorities presenting in the mass media or common culture, some whites try to make their own racial identities conform to models they find in multiculturalism. Certainly, many representations of multicultural people in the media are negative or incomplete. But Hollywood has recently had something of a romance with movies by and about African Americans.[10] Popular music forms like hip-hop and rap also are multicultural.

Multicultural products like movies and music appeal to a mainstream white audience in part because their characters or contents can express a deep and enduring sense of community and purpose forged by racial or ethnic ties. Often, the positive aspects of identity in multicultural productions are represented as inextricably linked to the experience of racial injustice. Calling themselves white trash is one way that whites can see themselves as both racially marked and oppressed, and it also is a way to begin excavating a uniquely white version of what Cornel West calls "a culture and community that has struggled against [racist] abuse."[11]

A growing number of mainstream products and representations offer whites (and nonwhites) a version of white identity that can be integrated into a multiculture, either by choice or through social marginalization. A recent and highly popular film about multicultural drag queens on a road trip, *To Wong Foo Thanks for Everything, Julie Newmar* (1995), is about how the citizens of a rural "redneck" town visited by the drag queens are able to cross both racial and gender lines in order to form bonds of friendship and gain strength. In this movie, whiteness and maleness are not privileged in the usual sense and are indeed most seductive when they seem mixed up with nondominant forms of identity.

In addition, we are currently witnessing something of a resurgence of stories about impoverished whites who are degraded and traumatized by the dominant culture. Fiction and autobiographies by E. Annie Proulx, Carolyn Chute, and Harry Crews address what it means to be white and marginal. Likewise, self-identified "Okie" Roxanne Dunbar, like many critics of whiteness, discusses her own life experiences in the context of historical migrations of poor whites from farmlands to industrial factory towns. Dunbar creates a personal and political history that calls attention to poor whites as part of a community with a complex background of oppression and subversive practices.

TRASH IN THE MASS MEDIA

As we have repeatedly argued, one thing that separates trash from the rest of white people is class. But class in the United States has always been a tricky category, often used metaphorically to designate forms of pathology and taste rather than literally to designate economic position. In the popular imaginary, there is often a confluence between white poverty and white criminality, deviance, or kitsch. Tobe Hooper's famous 1974 cult horror movie *The Texas Chainsaw Massacre* portrayed poor, rural whites as cannibalistic, deformed, and homicidal. Another cult director (who has since gone mainstream), John Waters, got his start making satirical movies about the kitschy, disgusting habits of Maryland white trash. *Pink Flamingos* (1972), one of his best-known art-house hits, is named for the lawn ornaments in front of protagonist Babs's trailer park home, a cliché fixture of white trash living. Played by cross-dressing actor Divine, Babs and her family vie with another couple to earn the title of "the filthiest people alive." Being filthy, in Waters's movie, means being poor, stealing, raping, engaging in bestiality, enjoying tacky clothes or furniture, and generally embodying many of the stereotypical attributes of "white trash." Babs finally wins the contest by exuberantly killing her competitors and then eating dog shit while making "yummy" noises.

During the 1980s and 1990s, white trash stories went mainstream. This was at roughly the same time that the essentialist identity of 1970s politics was giving way to new ideas about social constructivism in the academy and multiculturalism was becoming a staple of mass media discourses on liberal education and minority concerns. Two "celebrity" stories of these decades seem to us to epitomize the way that white trash has come to be understood as a marginalized white identity that nevertheless is reluctant to disclose its own class-based origins and experiences of injustice. The stories we refer to are those of the infamous victim of castration, John Wayne Bobbitt, and popular TV star Roseanne.

During the summer of 1993, Bobbitt made headlines—and punch lines—in the United States and beyond. After he allegedly raped and physically abused her for years, his wife Lorena cut off his penis with a carving knife while he was sleeping. She then drove off in their car and, at an intersection, tossed her husband's penis out the window. Found a few hours later by police, Bobbitt's severed penis was taken on ice to the hospital, where it was sewn back on him. Much of his reconstructive surgery was paid with funds raised during a cable television special hosted by "shock jock" and author Howard Stern. A year later, Bobbitt decided to appear as the star of a pornographic movie called *John Wayne Bobbitt Uncut* (1994), essentially to prove that he was still potent despite Lorena's surgery. The movie is largely unremarkable regarding pornography; rather, its entire appeal seems to depend on its audience's fascination with Bobbitt's reattached penis.

The Bobbitts' story and Lorena's and John's subsequent trials for assault and rape, respectively, focused almost entirely on issues of gender and race. John Bobbitt was often represented as a "macho man," and Lorena, as his timid, Venezuelan bride who naively married him in her pursuit of the American dream. A *Vanity Fair* article about the couple is typical, describing John as "a martial-arts buff who would sign in at the apartment pool as 'Jean-Claude Van Damme.'"[12] Accompanying this somewhat tongue-in-cheek account is a picture of Lorena in a pool, hands clasped under her chin, hair wet, with eyes gazing upward at the camera in a position that makes her appear prayerful and seductive at once. She looks like a travel ad for Latin America—all Catholic innocence and Latin sexiness.

Underlying these representations of the tough guy and his demure Third World bride is an implicit discussion of lower-class behavior in America, especially among men. Bobbitt met his wife at a Virginia club frequented by enlisted men. A marine, he made so little money that their honeymoon consisted of breakfast at a Bob's Big Boy restaurant. They then moved into a studio apartment with no furniture, where they lived with one of Bobbitt's cousins, a drug addict. Bobbitt himself was often drunk and was fined several times by the Marine Corps for showing up late to work. After leaving the marines, Bobbitt held nineteen different jobs in two years, according to Lorena's lawyer. He often beat his wife and flaunted the fact that he was having affairs with other women. Bobbitt's life story reads like a textbook case of white trash; incapable of holding a job, he turned to boozing, promiscuous sex, and wife beating.

During their marriage, Lorena worked at a nail salon, from which she stole thousands of dollars because Bobbitt spent the family income on alcohol and parties. At the same time, Lorena admits she was trying to get money so that she could have the middle-class life she had seen on American television when she was growing up in Venezuela. One of the things she bought with this stolen money was a satellite dish. If we look at the Bobbitts' marriage through Lorena's eyes, we see John as low class and hence a failure—he provided her with so little and hurt her so much that she was forced to steal.

Much of the coverage of the Bobbitt case focused on so-called feminist reactions to it. Television and the newspapers talked about women who showed up at court to cheer Lorena on or who proclaimed her violent act as a victory for women in the war between the sexes. There were no stories about men championing John Bobbitt or even feeling sorry for him (unless it was in the context of comedy, such as the Howard Stern special). Ultimately, Lorena was the victim and John was the joke.

As much as we might want to, however, it would be foolish to think that the "pro-Lorena" stories were a result of some kind of feminist consciousness raising, for other factors aroused much glee in women and men alike when hearing about John's predicament. Instead, we suggest that part of this glee came—perhaps unconsciously—from a sense that Lorena's blow was struck not for women but for the middle class, against underclass men.

Antiwelfare critics such as Charles Murray and George Gilder describe the "rogue male" as one of the major problems produced by the welfare state.[13] The rogue male is essentially a counterpart of the "welfare mother," dependent on government checks or underemployment—and socially destructive as a result. Bobbitt embodies the myth of the rogue male exactly: incapable of committing to a job or a family, he becomes a criminal or a public nuisance. If we see him in this light, we might understand the Bobbitt jokes and "feminist" celebrations of Lorena as something far more vicious and sinister than they appear on the surface.

Rather than a skirmish in the sex war, Bobbitt's unelected surgery was a casualty of the class war in America. Public fascination with the Bobbitts might then be associated with a middle-class distaste for underclass physicality, sexuality, and supposed inability to conform to the "work ethic." As a manual laborer and marine, Bobbitt's masculine body was his source of work and income. Cutting off his penis therefore symbolically robbed him of his identity as a member of the (potential) working class. Interestingly, once his penis had been restored, Bobbitt was again able to get work, starring in *John Wayne Bobbitt Uncut.* Because Bobbitt's class position is so closely bound up with his gender and sexuality, it is all too easy to confuse our laughter at his compromised machismo with a snicker at the weaknesses and inferiority of the white male underclass.

"WHITE TRASH WITH MONEY"

Whereas Bobbitt's castration and subsequent fame represent lower-class white identity in connection with sexual victimization and humiliation, the 1980s and 1990s success story of TV star Roseanne offers an image of white trash identity as hinging on marketable style rather than economic class. Roseanne's smash hit television show *Roseanne,* along with shows like *Married with Children* and, more recently, *Grace Under Fire,* helped make white trash a new form of chic. Roseanne is a star who openly identifies herself as white trash (contrast this with John Bobbitt, who identified himself as "Jean Claude Van Damme," a movie star). Indeed, Roseanne's former husband Tom Arnold once described himself and Roseanne as "America's worst nightmare: white trash with money."

The idea that white trash can have a lot of money and yet still somehow remain "trash" seems contradictory, particularly when we consider that trash are marked by their position at the bottom of the white socioeconomic ladder. However, "trash with money" is precisely the way in which white trash have been made accessible to Americans as a kind of cultural group with whom they might like to identify.

For example, Roseanne's work demonstrates how white trash identity comes across simultaneously as a form of class consciousness and a campy, stylized set of consumer items or taste preferences. Both Roseanne's early comedy act and her self-publicized autobiography emphasize her status as poor, vulgar, and proud.[14] In an HBO comedy special, Roseanne poked fun at middle-class white culture by stressing that she felt left out of it: "There's Malibu Barbie, but there's no abused trailer park Barbie," she commented. Her sitcom, centering on the working-class Conner family, is likewise notorious for featuring issues associated with the working class, including episodes dealing with the characters' unemployment, financial difficulties, and lack of education. Recently, the show has concentrated on the economic fates of the Conner daughters, one of whom, Becky, has moved into a trailer park with her husband while the other, Darlene, is going to art school on a scholarship. In one episode, Roseanne expresses sadness that she was unable to help her daughters "get a head start" and blames herself for Becky's living circumstances. At the same time, proud but ironic references to their status as white trash—or to their community as white trash—are common on the show.

Of course, Roseanne is not the only celebrity to claim a white trash identity as a form of personal style. "Alternative" and grunge rock musicians such as the late Kurt Cobain (of Nirvana) often perform a kind of camp white trashiness even if they do not overtly claim the label. As if to underscore the connection between campy "trash" performance and a more familiar camp tradition, Cobain was often photographed in drag wearing white trash rayon, floral-print dresses. These costumes, coupled with his much-discussed childhood in the industrial ghost town of Aberdeen, Washington, gave Cobain what can only be described as an air of "white trash chic."

The hugely successful Nirvana album *Nevermind* not only revolutionized alternative rock but also changed youth fashion. Featured on MTV in torn jeans, thermal underwear, faded flannel, engineer's boots, and thrift store "unstyle," Nirvana and other alternative bands like Pearl Jam, Alice in Chains, and Dinosaur Jr. popularized a kind of "trash drag" style known as *grunge*. White trash identity was packaged as a series of commodities that one could buy at Urban Outfitters, The Gap, or Tower Records. *My So-Called Life,* a short-lived but critically acclaimed TV series about middle-class high school students in the mid-1990s, consistently dressed its heroine Angela in bulky work boots, several layers of flannel, and faded T-shirts. Certainly, this was the show's attempt to represent youth fashion accurately, and indeed it did. Like teenagers across America, Angela was dressing up like someone who might be a manual laborer and "getting grungy."

Although "dressing down" in grungewear does feed class stereotypes, this particular fad also acts out the middle class's confusion regarding the origins of class identities. One might read the grunge craze as an example of how the middle class interprets poverty as a consumer choice rather than an economic condition of scarcity and deprivation. If a popular TV star like Roseanne can be white trash with money, then it would seem that money could buy white trash culture and style. Dressing up in white trash drag is a strategy of denial that allows the middle class to think about class difference in terms of images rather than material realities. If the middle class can buy white trash style, then class is merely an image, and real impoverished people can be understood as happily hip or even secretly members of the middle class in trash drag. White trash cultural commodities are in many ways an appropriate ideological development for post-Reagan America, in which the Republican party line is, in effect, that the poor want to be poor and could recover if they really tried. That anyone can choose to look like trash seems—illogically—to prove their point.

MAPPING WHITE TRASH AMERICA: CLASS MATTERS

Understanding the social structures and the processes of representation that produce a group of people is difficult. As cultural materialists, we hold that economic structures and conditions are crucial to shaping and forming identities of individuals and groups. Certainly, racial, ethnic, gender, and sexual differences all are deeply embedded in class formation. But these notions of difference, so often foregrounded by postmodern social theorists, often serve as a means for talking about class difference without actually using a language of class analysis.[15]

Put in another way, class difference is often read through these other discourses of difference, and vice versa. This is not to say that class is the principal determining structure of domination in American life. But it is all too often neglected and ignored by some academics, activists, and public intellectuals in favor of discussions and movement building around other forms of difference. The result of this neglect of class has been to overlook the workings of capitalism as a system of domination and oppression. And to the extent that identity-based political movements and social theory have not been consciously critical of capitalism, they have reproduced and perpetuated capitalist structures of domination.

As minority groups enter the middle class, markets targeted specifically at African Americans, women, Latinos, and the like have been very successful. Clearly, engaging in capitalist consumer culture and, by extension, enjoying a standard of living that helps perpetuate class difference are not activities limited to white people. In her recent *Fire with Fire: The New Female Power and How to Use It,* power feminist Naomi Wolf encourages women who feel marginalized in public life to embrace capitalism as a form of empowerment. She urges women to get in touch with their "will to power," and by this she means their desire to take control over "the weak," just as white men historically have done. Like other procapitalist members of minority groups, Wolf promotes one form of liberation—specifically, feminism—by encouraging a system of economic inequality that marginalizes a large proportion of the population. In other words, freedom for racial, gendered, or sexual minority groups does not necessarily equal freedom for everyone, especially the underclasses.

Another obvious and persistent form of economic domination can be seen in the global geography of uneven capitalist development. The massive and widening gap between rich and poor countries is a direct result of long histories of colonial and imperialist exploitation of the Third World by industrialized First World nations. Historically, the rise of capitalism as a global phenomenon has been marked by this uneven development, by both territorial expansion and contraction, bringing economic booms and busts to different geographic regions at different times.

Similar patterns of uneven development have shaped U.S. history and society. The long post-Depression boom that gave U.S. industrial workers a chance to lead middle-class lifestyles of relative luxury is just one example of the cyclical movement of capital involving tremendous regional and even national economic growth. During this time, hundreds of thousands of American workers left home to find good-paying jobs in heavy industries in northern cities like Chicago and Detroit and western cities like Oakland and Los Angeles. These vast internal migrations of millions of mostly white American workers, prompted by the new flow of capital from the economic restructuring of the 1930s, resemble in many ways a twentieth-century American working-class diaspora.

Often, the idea of a diaspora has been used effectively to describe how racial groups find themselves scattered across the globe in contemporary life, unbound to the country or continent of their origin (perhaps by many generations as well as many thousands of miles). Scholars and critics who describe postcolonial racial and religious identities use the term *diaspora* as a way of articulating the sense of homelessness and loss felt by minority groups who find they have no extended communities or places to call their own.

These diasporic identities are forged in the fires of capital—Asian immigration to the United States throughout the twentieth century, for example, was largely a response to economic opportunities of the sort that mobilized the white working-class populations already living here. Certainly, African American populations in the United States were forcibly created in order to support the southern agrarian economy. Furthermore, without the imperialist expansion associated with the early stages of capital accumulation, the United States would not have been able to obtain an African slave population in the first place. Because it requires class division and uneven development to function, capital is a social system that encourages formerly whole communities to become diasporic, like capital itself. If workers wish to stay afloat on the seas of economic change, they must be prepared to follow capitalist wealth from region to region or country to country.

In keeping with our understanding of whites as a racialized group and our desire to understand the economic and social construction of different forms of whiteness, we see these economically driven internal white migrations, these poor white diasporas, as important to the shaping of white identities. Since at least the mid-nineteenth century, generations of white (usually male) workers have left their families and communities in search of jobs and the promise of economic prosperity, following the dispersal of capital and establishing new identities, communities, and families in faraway regions and distant states. As economic restructuring brought previously separate and distinct groups and communities into contact with one another, as southerners met northerners and new white immigrants met white "natives," new tensions and conflicts began to form. Out of these tensions, new prejudices and new stereotypes arose. White trash was just one of the many hateful names given to those who seemed out of place, who seemed to pose a threat to the existing economic and social order.

The Dust Bowl migrations of poor whites from Oklahoma and the Southwest to California's agricultural fields and the subsequent wave of "defense Okies" who flooded California's burgeoning defense industry in the 1940s are prime examples of newly arriving whites who became scapegoats for unwanted changes created by both economic boom and bust. To this day, many of our most familiar stereotypes of poor white trash emanate from this historical period and these places. In this way, these migrating white workers have had a profound effect not only on California's political and social life (to this day, in the minds of many Californians, "Okie" is synonymous with "white trash") but on the nation as a whole.[16]

Currently in the United States, this inconstant geography of capitalism we have been describing has caused tremendous pain and suffering for those left in the wake of this capitalist growth. The Rust Belt cities of Cleveland, Pittsburgh, Gary, and, above all, Detroit are tragic examples of the effects of the de-industrialization that began in the early 1970s. Capital and new production technologies have proved to be far more mobile than the auto and steel workers for whom the "American dream" of a middle-class lifestyle has quickly turned into a living nightmare.[17] Whole communities that bloomed around regional growth centers have withered as corporations, struggling to maintain profitability in the face of increasing global competition and productivity, have abandoned those same communities, locales, or regions in their ceaseless search for new resources, new markets, and new labor pools.[18] Workers of all races have found themselves physically dislocated from their homes, used as cheap labor, and abandoned.

As Barbara Ehrenreich points out in her book *Fear of Falling*,[19] the arriviste American middle classes are generally fearful about losing whatever level of status and economic privilege they have gained, and Americans facing economic decline are especially anxious about the threat of downward mobility. This fear and dread of falling into the lower classes is, she argues, what lies behind many of the stereotypes of and prejudices against poor Americans.

Images of the poor are used in mainstream culture as repositories for displaced middle-class rage, excess, and fear. These images and representations are then sold to the public as the real poor whites, thus effectively hiding who the actual poor people are and what their struggles might be. Because images of the poor in the media seem so rich and fascinating, the social causes of poverty and economic neglect are easily overlooked. We are left with provocative stereotypes, stripped of their historical and social context. White trash is clearly one such stereotype, and from this perspective, it should not surprise us that images of and fantasies about low-class whites are enjoying such popularity at this particular juncture in American history. During times of economic uncertainty or downturn, poor white trash is the ghastly specter that haunts the white middle class.

NOTES

1. *Vulgar multiculturalism* is a term we (along with our colleagues on the *Bad Subjects* electronic mailing list) coined to refer to essentialist multiculturalism and racial theory, which posits that whites are a monolithic and unified group wielding absolute, racist power across lines of class, gender, sexuality, and other forms of difference.

2. See David Theo Goldberg, "Critical Multiculturalism," in David Theo Goldberg, ed., *Multiculturalism: A Critical Reader* (Oxford: Blackwell, 1994); and the Chicago Cultural Studies Group.

3. If conservative African American media entrepreneur Ken Hamblin has his way, "black trash" could become a household word. He uses it frequently in interviews and on his syndicated radio show, making explicit the class dimensions of racist slurs. See Hamblin's exchange with filmmaker John Singleton, "Who Will Save the Black Man?" *New York Times Magazine,* December 4, 1994, pp. 16–24.

4. Various critics, such as bell hooks and Cornel West, have discussed race in terms of class, but whiteness and class are not their main concern. Race and class have been connected principally in studies of African Americans.

5. According to one dictionary, "poor white trash" dates back to 1833: "The slaves themselves entertain the highest contempt for white servants, whom they designate as 'poor white trash.' " For other references to these terms, see Mitford Matthews, ed., *A Dictionary of Americanisms* (Chicago: University of Chicago Press, 1951).

6. See, for example, Dorothy Allison's preface to her *Trash* (Ithaca, NY: Firebrand Books, 1988); also see Jim Goad's "Statement of Intent," in his *ANSWER Me!: The First Three* (San Francisco: AK Press, 1994).

7. Like IQ theory, eugenics states that certain "characterological deficiencies" are a result of biological inheritance; for example, a tendency toward poverty or manual labor might be genetic. On this, see Nicole Hahn Rafter, *White Trash: The Eugenic Family Studies 1877–1919* (Boston: Northeastern University Press, 1988).

8. Cornel West, *Race Matters* (Boston: Beacon Press, 1993), p. 25.

9. See Charles Sykes, *A Nation of Victims* (New York: St. Martin's Press, 1992).

10. Nearly all of Spike Lee's movies, *Menace II Society* (1993), *Boyz n the Hood* (1991), and *Straight out of Brooklyn* (1991); and Asian Americans *The Joy Luck Club* (1993).

11. West, *Race Matters*, p. 25.

12. Kim Masters, "Sex, Lies, and an 8-inch Carving Knife," *Vanity Fair*, November 1993, pp. 168–72.

13. George Gilder, *Wealth and Poverty* (San Francisco: Institute for Contemporary Studies Press, 1981). Murray offers slightly different accounts of the kinds of men produced by welfare, but in both works, they are characterized as animalistic, violent, uncontrollable, and connected to mothers on welfare. Charles Murray, *Losing Ground: American Social Policy 1950–1980* (New York: Basic Books, 1984).

14. In her biography, Roseanne discusses her history of poverty and abuse. She then explains how she recovered from drug and spousal abuse but continues to enjoy the "trash" culture that she associates with her life as a poor white. Roseanne Arnold, *My Lives* (New York: Ballantine Books, 1994).

15. As anthropologist Sherry Ortner puts it: "Class is central to American life, but it is rarely spoken in its own right. Rather, it is represented through other categories of social difference: gender, ethnicity, race, and so forth." See her "Reading America: Preliminary Notes on Class and Culture," in Richard Fox, ed., *Recapturing Anthropology* (Santa Fe: SAR Press, 1991).

16. For an extended analysis of Okies, see James Gregory, *American Exodus: The Dust Bowl Migration and Okie Culture in California* (New York: Oxford University Press, 1989).

17. See Mike Davis, *Prisoners of the American Dream* (London: Verso, 1986).

18. For an excellent discussion of post-Fordism and economic globalization, see Andrew Sayers and Richard Walker, *The New Social Economy* (Oxford: Blackwell, 1992).

19. Barbara Ehrenreich, *Fear of Falling: The Inner Life of the Middle-Class* (New York: Harper Perennial, 1989).

WHITE BODIES

12

The Unexamined

Ross Chambers

WHO WAS THAT MARKED MAN?

A long time ago, perhaps 1963, I took a flight from Sydney to Rome. It's a long flight, so there's time to chat with your neighbor. On this occasion, mine was a fellow Australian, a bit younger than I and smartly dressed. Although his accent was proletarian, I judged him to be a successful businessman (in Australia there's no real incompatibility). I was even a bit intimidated, as his cool urbanity contrasted more than favorably, I thought, with the veneer of citified ways I had recently picked up after spending my early years in "the bush." (There must have been sexual attraction, too; why else would I remember all this so vividly?) We chatted pleasantly, breaking the ice—since he was from Melbourne and I from Sydney, then as now rival cities—with well-tried pleasantries (Melbourne's unaccountable passion for Aussie Rules football, the difficulty of finding decent beer in Sydney). Oh, I forgot to tell you that we both

Adapted from *the minnesota review* 47 (Spring 1997): 149–65.

were white, male, and English speaking—but you knew that, didn't you? Some things can be taken for granted.

As the flight approached Rome, my companion reached into a bag and pulled out his disembarkation card; could I help him with it? My first thought was that he needed assistance with a document in Italian—but then I suddenly realized the problem was of another order. He could read and write, but only very laboriously, and it quickly came out that after emigrating to Australia in early adolescence, he was now returning for the first time in more than ten years to visit his family in Sicily and demonstrate his wealth and social success. I couldn't have been more surprised. But now I looked again: yes, how had I failed to notice the black hair, the olive complexion, the dark eyes? Suddenly my companion had slipped from the unexamined, all-purpose category of (male) "Australian" into another, *marked* group, one that could not so easily be taken for granted and instead invited examination. In the awkward government-sponsored euphemism of the day, he was now a "New Australian."

At that moment, I began to learn about the contingent, context-bound character of social classification, but I confess that my first feeling, along with surprise, was one of reassurance. The man's "whiteness" was not (quite) at issue, but it was more compromised by his Mediterranean origins than mine could ever be by my countrified crudeness, since I belonged to the "naturally" superior category of the native born. The quality of my whiteness was enhanced, in other words, to the same degree that his was damaged. He was a marked man in a way that I was not, even though we both were soon to emerge into the streets of Rome where he would pass unnoticed and I would stick out like the proverbial sore thumb.[1]

Markedness and unmarkedness, then, are relative categories; who is marked and who not is ultimately a matter of context. In linguistics, from which social semiotics borrowed the concept of markedness, there is no sense that the unmarked/marked pair lines up with concepts like normalcy and deviation or unexaminedness and unexaminability. Those linguistic features designated as marked or unmarked form part of a single paradigm, so that a zero-degree feature (e.g., the unpronounced ending of the French verb *j'aime*) is in differential relation not with the general category of marked features but with each member of the paradigm, whether marked or unmarked. Thus, *j'aime* contrasts with *tu aimes* or *il/elle aime,* in which the ending also is unpronounced, in a way no different from its contrast with, say, *j'aimais* or *j'aimerai* with their marked endings.

In the social sphere, however, things work otherwise. The differential structures that mediate social relations are themselves mediated by the phenomena we call power and desire. One of the effects of such phenomena is to distribute to unmarkedness the privileges of normalcy and unexaminedness and to reserve for markedness the characteristics of derivedness, deviation, secondariness, and examinability, which function as indices of disempowerment (although, oddly, not always of undesirability).

There are plenty of unmarked categories (maleness, heterosexuality, and middle classness being obvious ones), but whiteness is perhaps the primary unmarked and so unexamined—let's say "blank"—category. Like other unmarked categories, it has a touchstone quality of the normal, against which the members of marked categories are measured and, of course, found deviant, that is, wanting. It is thus (unlike linguistic unmarkedness) situated outside the paradigm that it defines. Whiteness is not itself compared with anything, but other things are compared unfavorably with it, and their own comparability with one another derives from their distance from the touchstone. In other words, unmarked or "blank" categories are *aparadigmatic.* Only the marked categories form part of the paradigm and may therefore be compared with one another.

As a result, the marked categories' relation to the unmarked ones that define their paradigmaticity is that of a *plural* (having the characteristic of comparability) to a *singular* (having the characteristic of incomparability). For example, in championship tennis, as Freadman and Macdonald point out, men's singles (there being no "mixed singles") is the touchstone game. Men's singles is in a different category, since it alone determines who the "top" players are from the various other singles and mixed games that (together with men's singles, however) constitute the field of "tennis." In the field of "race," whiteness occupies the position of men's singles with respect to the many categories of nonwhite, determining who the "top" people are.

Something similar could be argued for all the big binaries, whose unmarked-versus-marked structure is more frequently bound up with a singular-versus-plural (or indivisible-versus-divided) distinction than is generally recognized. Like the difference between white and nonwhite, that between masculine and nonmasculine or metropolitan and nonmetropolitan (notice that I don't say white and black or masculine and feminine or metropolitan and colonial) is the difference between an incomparable singular and a plural—the plural of "colors" and "ethnicities," of straight women/lesbians/gay men, of the different kinds of colonies, "client states," and provinces—whose members are subject to comparison among themselves. Thus, gay men are "like women"; Asians are "better immigrants" than Latinos; Thailand is "third world," even though it was never strictly a colony.

Notice also that this result is produced by a certain "contamination" among the binaries themselves. To enable the pluralization of the nonmasculine other, it is necessary for the gender binary (masculine/feminine) to be contaminated by sexuality (heterosexual/homosexual), so that it becomes what is familiar to us as the sex–gender system. Similarly, the configuration of the postcolonial world results from a contamination of the metropolitan/colonial binary with a European/non-European or West/rest binary that is itself modeled on the city/country or capital/provinces distinction.

In the same way, in a country such as the United States, the racial binary (white/colored) is contaminated by the concept of ethnicity (with whiteness constituting the "blank"—nonracial and nonethnic—category). It thus becomes a race-ethnicity system in which Jews and "white ethnics" mingle with Latinos, Asian Americans, and blacks to form a variegated class of "others." By means of a similar system, a young Australian of Anglo-Celtic ancestry (the blank category) was able, in 1963, to put a young Australian of Mediterranean extraction into a category that might have been labeled "off-white," where he began to rub shoulders with *who knows whom?* (that was my mother's catchall phrase for the innumerable set of marked groups from which our white, lower-middle-class family knew itself to be significantly different). The class contamination according to which—at that time and in that culture—it was better to be a white, urban, working-class businessman than a white, countrified, middle-class teacher, a contamination that might in other circumstances have made me the marked category and compromised my social status, faded into insignificance by comparison with the power of the race-ethnicity system to determine prestige, privilege, and power.

I am arguing that the difference between white and nonwhite depends in crucial ways on there also being differences among the multiple categories that constitute the paradigm of the nonwhite, since it is only by differentiation from a pluralized paradigm that the singularity of whiteness as nonparadigmatic, its undivided touchstone character, can be produced. Thus, the fact that non-whiteness can be black or coffee colored or yellow or olive, African, Asian, or Latino, mestizo, or "pure" is, according to this argument, the essential feature by which whiteness enjoys its privileged, aparadigmatic status. In short, to pluralize the other is to produce one's own singularity.

The case of the countrified white Australian and the new Australian from Sicily on that Qantas flight demonstrates that the tactic of pluralization (like all scapegoating tactics)[2] can backfire. A singularity that is the product of the pluralization of its other can be vulnerable, in turn, to a pluralization, a divisibility of its own. There are "degrees" or "shades" of whiteness, which is a quality that can be inflected by the same operators (of color, ethnicity, class, and the like) needed to pluralize the other.

Mine is an argument from example, but it is confirmed by deconstructive philosophy, which teaches that there is no difference without mixture. The equation "whiteness is to nonwhiteness as the aparadigmatic is to the paradigmatic" implies a sense in which the supposedly aparadigmatic category actually forms part of the paradigm, and whiteness—thus brought within the purview of difference—is therefore "tinged" with nonwhiteness. Only if whiteness were opposed to an equally homogeneous category of nonwhiteness and only if there were no other systems of social classification could an absolute distinction between the categories be maintained and the purity of each sustained.

Questions arise, however, as they did on that Qantas flight. Is a Jewish lesbian as white as a straight male WASP? How does southern white "trash" measure up against a light-skinned, blue-eyed, college-educated, second- or third-generation, non-Spanish-speaking Cuban American? In South Africa under apartheid, visiting Japanese businessmen enjoyed the status and perks of honorary whites. Light-skinned, middle-class, educated African Americans in the United States can seem well on the way to becoming white by comparison with cousins or even siblings who may be darker skinned or have remained working class, rural, or poor. In the end, identity becomes a bit like a poker hand, in which the value of the ace (whiteness) can be enhanced, if one holds a couple of face cards or another ace (masculinity, heterosexuality, middle classness) or, alternatively, depreciated by association with cards of lower value (ethnicity, color, lack of education, working classness).

My question now is why these facts are so widely ignored, misrepresented, and misrecognized. How does whiteness retain its mythic status of aparadigmaticity? It is not enough, it seems, for whiteness to pluralize its other. It must also protect itself from scrutiny, for fear that it will lead to the kind of awkward questions asked on my Sydney-to-Rome flight. In addition to singularity, whiteness needs another quality to ensure that its highly vulnerable claim to the indivisibility of an aparadigmatic norm will not be examined. That is, it needs to be not only indivisible but also invisible.

EXAMINABILITY AND IN(DI)VISIBILITY

Indivisibility ensures that whiteness is considered to be, contrary to the evidence, a uniform quality that one either possesses or does not, whereas the pluralization of the other produces nonwhiteness as a multiplicity of different ways of being (of being nonwhite). The invisibility of whiteness, however—its ability to elude examination—depends on a further dichotomization of the white/nonwhite relation, one that inverts in an apparently contradictory way the relation of white singularity to the pluralized other. Whereas the other is *pluralized* in order to produce whiteness as indivisible and singular, the groups that compose this pluralized other are *homogenized* in this new relation, through what is called *stereotyping,* that is, the belief that "all Xs are the same" (where X refers to the members of marked, examinable groups and perhaps, at a certain horizon, to the whole set of members of all such groups).

In contrast to those whose identity is defined by their classificatory status as members of a given group, whites are perceived as individual historical agents whose unclassifiable difference from one another is their most prominent trait. Whiteness itself is thus atomized into invisibility through the individualization of white subjects. Whereas nonwhites are perceived first and foremost as a function of their group belongingness, that is, as black or Latino or Asian (and then as individuals), whites are perceived first as individual people (and only secondarily, if at all, as whites). Their essential identity is thus their individual self-identity, to which whiteness as such is a secondary, and so a negligible, factor.[3]

The pluralization of the *other* and the homogenization of *others* are not contradictory, however, because each depends on the classification of non-whites into groups. The nonwhite is pluralized by being divided into groups, each of which is homogenizable through stereotyping, either as an autonomous group or in association with other groups with which it may be thought to have an affinity (thus, at some official level in the United States, "Asians and Pacific Islanders" are thought to be "all the same"). In contrast, the category of the individual is the key to white hegemony, that is, to the unexaminedness of the degrees and divisions in whiteness (its own forms of nonwhiteness). The reason is that whiteness's indivisibility (as a function of the pluralization of the other) can be maintained only through the production of an invisibility that depends on atomizing whiteness (as a function of the homogenization of others), distributing it among individual historical agents whose common whiteness thus is unperceived and escapes examination.

Since the category of the individual shares with the singularity of whiteness the quality of undividedness (that is what "individual" means etymologically) and is simultaneously the factor of white invisibility, we can encapsulate the secret of whiteness's unmarked, unexamined quality in a single word, *in(di)visi-bility.* We also can state that in(di)visibility has as its opposite the examinability resulting from the pluralization of the other (its divisibility), in conjunction with the homogenization of the others resulting from pluralization. What does it mean, then, to be examinable—what form of visibility, as well of divisibility, does this imply—and what does it mean to be unexamined?

First, the category of examinability has not one but two alternatives: one can either be unexaminable (out of reach of examination) or examinable but nevertheless be unexamined (which is the case, I claim, of whiteness). Christopher Miller points out that in European "Africanist" discourse, Africa was perceived as a place of "blank darkness."[4] It was so other that other was not the word; there was nothing to be perceived there and no knowledge to be had of it. According to this definition, "blank darkness" exemplifies the category of the unexaminable, and in(di)visibility can therefore be said to produce, at the other end of the spectrum, something like "blank whiteness." It is as much outside the paradigm of divisible otherness as blank darkness is, but normalized into familiarity rather than exoticized and taken for granted rather than posing a challenge by virtue of its extreme otherness. Blank whiteness is therefore in the category of the unexamined. It is as if the system encompassed two mythic (or incomparable) categories, blank whiteness and absolute blackness, each of which is held to lie outside the sphere of examinability. One is unexamined "norm," and the other is unknowable "other" (or extreme of otherness), and between them lies the pluralized area of the multiple categories that come under scrutiny, constituting the knowable others of whiteness as the domain of the examinable. These in-between categories are disqualified for their otherness from the status of the unexamined, but they are not consigned, beyond the limits of the knowable, to the category of unexaminability.

As a result of a long history of European colonization, "darkest Africa" has moved from its status of absolute and unexamined alterity to the category of the examinable other. One may think that blackness, as the category diametrically opposed to whiteness, has retained from this history a certain characteristic of extremity that gives it a particular status among whiteness' pluralized others. In the United States, for example, it is clear that the system of racial categories is bookended by whiteness and blackness, as if the in(di)visibility of whiteness were matched by the blank inscrutability of blackness.[5]

This category of absolute blackness is necessary, it seems, only so that there can be, for symmetry, a category of unexamined whiteness, since blacks do not enjoy the same privilege of aparadigmaticity as whites do and are included in the general mix of the pluralized other even as they are viewed as the polar opposite of whiteness. In other words, the special status of blackness derives from an ambiguity: it forms part of a (white/black) dichotomy while simultaneously functioning as only one category—the "extreme" one—among those that constitute whiteness's pluralized other.[6] The special status of whiteness derives from its being opposed to blackness as an absolute term, and so it lies (unlike blackness) outside the pluralized group that constitutes its others.

As a product of in(di)visibility, blank whiteness escapes examination by being unexamined, but all other nonwhite categories, including blackness, belong to the field of examinable others. Examinability, as I am using the term here, refers to the unfavorable attention to certain groups that is recognized, in its overtly hostile forms, by terms like *misogyny, homophobia,* and *racism* but that has many other more covert, polite, hypocritical, and even sanctimonious forms. It is not in principle the same as the practice of examination that Foucault identified as the key practice of disciplinary knowledge, which is thought of as an objective scrutiny characterized by the supposed neutrality of the examiner and based on the false assumption of the separability of the examining subject and the object of examination.[7] Historically, the disciplinary examination of marked categories (nonwhite, women, homosexuals, criminals, the insane) has been difficult to distinguish from the prejudiced attention paid to socially marked others, so illusory is the alleged neutrality of examination as a practice.

Examination, furthermore, is not solely an operation performed by members of unexamined groups on members of examinable groups, as the phenomena of "internalized" misogyny, homophobia, and racism demonstrate. What all these cases of examination (disciplinary, prejudiced, internalized) have in common, however, is the examining subject's desire not to be confused with those who, because of their examinability, are its objects, even when the subject and the object of examination are housed in the same person. It is as if the practice of examination itself resulted in the desired separation of the (unexamined) examiner from the (examinable) examined, by producing as its object an area of examinability that can imply a space exempt from examination that is occupied by the examiner. Examining thus turns out to have the structure of scapegoating: one classifies oneself as a member of the category of the unexamined through the very act of examining others.

If this analysis is correct, examination expresses a desire for the separation of examiner and examined that is itself an acknowledgment that the two are in fact connected. Examinability, in other words, is a device of disconnection: it presupposes the denegation of contexts—that is, of a history—in which the relatedness of the subjects and objects of examination becomes apparent. The act of examining (think of this next time you have a medical, or academic, or judicial examination) is a device for denying the contexts that join people. As it happens, the idea that such disconnectedness, as the denial of historical context, is what defines both the familiarity of the "everyday" and the strangeness of the "exotic" is something that I have argued elsewhere.[8]

A radical disconnection of subject and object causes the object-world to fade into insignificance and become unworthy of examination, so that only the doings and concerns of the subject (to the extent that they are separable from the mere "decor" that surrounds them) are perceived as interesting and important. This is the structure of the "everyday," which is unexamined as an object (like the invisibility of whiteness) because it is presumed to be already known, as opposed to the concerns, tasks, and negotiations in which the subjects of history engage.

The "exotic," on the other hand, results from a disconnection that brings the object-world into prominence and visibility, with a concomitant backgrounding of the viewing subjectivity. Its examinability is proportionate to the degree to which the subject and object are connected (otherwise it would simply be "blank darkness," the unknowable). These disconnections of subject and object are what permit historical contexts to be forgotten, ignored, or at least backgrounded (in short, denied), because the stories that actually connect the subject and the object come to be identified exclusively with either the overlooked object (in the case of the everyday) or the underrated subject (in the case of the exotic).

My claim is now, therefore, that at the two extremes, unexamined whiteness can be mapped onto the familiar invisibility of the everyday, and unexaminable blackness (as blank darkness) can be projected onto the strange unknowability of the exotic. Each is a product of disconnectedness and of the denial of those historical contexts by virtue of which we all are brought together. If so, in light of this mapping, it becomes possible to describe the intervening area of whiteness's pluralized and examinable other(s) as one that has mixed characteristics. It is neither wholly familiar nor completely exotic because it is at one and the same time both familiar and exotic. We can then understand the trick of othering—from the point of view of ensuring the unexamined in(di)visibility of whiteness—as the production of forms of disconnectedness that correspond, on the one hand, to the homogenized other's status as familiar and already known and, on the other, to the pluralized other's status as exotic. More particularly, the pluralization of the other is a practice of exoticization, and the homogenization of others is a practice of familiarization, with the outcome of the two being examinability.

By relation to the exoticization of the plural other as a multitude of diverse and colorful forms and practices, the normalcy of singular, undivided whiteness is produced as part of the familiarity of the everyday, unworthy of examination.

At the same time, because of the homogenization of marked categories, these categories are themselves produced as familiar and always already known (since "all Xs are the same"). They become part of the ordinary surroundings and trappings, the decor of everyday life. In contrast, the individuality of white subjects—their essential difference from one another as the markers of history—is highlighted, their common whiteness receding into the invisibility of the unexamined. The exotic quality of the pluralized other produces white indivisibility as something relatively unworthy of note, and the actual invisibility of whiteness is a function of the foregrounding of white subjects as active and diverse agents, in contrast to their homogenized and so already familiar others.

The pluralization of the other and the homogenization of othered groups are thus part of the same ploy—the ploy of in(di)visibility. The ploy in turn is possible because of the definitional fact that the other is constitutively split between familiarity and strangeness (as in the Freudian understanding of the unconscious as un/heimlich). Finally, this split furnishes the means by which corresponding fissures in the category of whiteness are able to escape examination. Whiteness—like other "blank" categories—is the denial of its own dividedness through the production of its other(s) as examinable, because they are split. Examinability, producing the separation of the unexamined and the examined, is the scapegoating device through which the distinction between the in(di)visible (those individuals whose whiteness is simultaneously invisible and undivided) and the (di)visible (those groups whose visibility is a function of their split identity as others and produces them as examinable) is enforced.

The (di)visibility of the examinable other has more obviously "political" advantages as well. Groups that are produced, through pluralization, as different from one another while simultaneously sharing a relatively small proportion of the available power, wealth, and social prestige can readily become mutually suspicious, envious, and hostile. These qualities are enhanced as the hegemony of whiteness breeds specific subforms of racism (such as "black anti-Semitism"), and the differential system that governs the identity of homogenized others can be used to justify an unequal distribution of the relatively few social advantages that are available. The pluralization of the other translates, in other words, into political disunity and competitive victimhood and forces disadvantaged groups, whose common interests are obscured by their pluralized differences, into the complexities and frustrations of alliance politics.

Meanwhile, white people, whose solidarity is ensured by the singularity and indivisibility of whiteness, have little trouble identifying their common interests and pursuing the policies that those interests dictate. (This does not preclude the possibility of internal divisions between groups of white people—say, white feminists against white male chauvinists—but it predicts the difficulty of their being perceived as divisions among white people as opposed to divisions among [kinds of] "people.")

Such difficulties, bred as they are by the pluralization of the other, are exacerbated by the effects of homogenization and stereotyping. To internalize the doctrine that "all Xs are the same" is to produce forms of chauvinism (e.g., racial "pride") that can obscure people's common interests across the lines of social categorization, producing in many cases conflicts of "loyalty" (should my lesbianism, my feminism, or my racial allegiance take political priority?) and the kinds of "loyalty oath" that activists sometimes extract. Political chauvinisms are readily identified (from the point of view of a white politics that passes for "mainstream" because its whiteness is unexamined) as "special interests" and their insistent claims can be all the more easily ignored because of the principle that "all Xs are the same," so whatever a given X may have to say can always be assumed, like women's "nagging," either to have been heard before or else to be entirely predictable, given one's foreknowledge of Xs.

It is against this picture of disunity and militancy that white politics comes to look democratic, reasonable, and (not "white" at all but) mainstream. The in(di)visibility of whiteness ensures that white people doing what is in effect their own brand of special-interest politics look like so many individual agents getting on with the business of expressing, exploring, negotiating, and even settling their legitimate differences—differences that define them not as white people (a classificatory identity) but as "people." Identity politics is alien to white people as white people (I'm obviously not talking about white women as women or white gay men as gay men) because whiteness is not a classificatory identity but just the unexamined norm against which such identities are defined, compared, and examined. Their whiteness (our whiteness) being too in(di)visible to define them (us), they (we) have only the self-identities of individual agents. Whereas others may have group identities, white people as a group are just the unexamined. But there is more political strength in that than in all the identity politics in the world.

BUZZING AT THE GLASS DOOR

What must be done? I have been describing, in a too schematic and abstract way, the operation of a hegemony, and I would not have been able to describe it if it weren't already beginning to come under attack, to falter, and to fail. (As I write, Nelson Mandela is being sworn in as president of South Africa.) But the hegemony is far from dead, and the question is how to hasten its demise. In which direction should we push? Should the breakdown of the power differential separating the unexamined from the examinable take the form of bringing the pluralized/homogenized other(s), with their group identities, into the capacious mansion of whiteness, where individuality reigns and racial identity becomes invisible? Or should it take the form of bringing whiteness out of its aparadigmaticity and having it join those whose differences form a paradigm, in which it would become one group—a classificatory, not a normative, identity—among many other, comparable groups? Can both these operations be pursued at the same time? Are they incompatible, or are they in a relation of solidarity with each other? Whatever the theoretical issues, the actual structure and distribution of power, which make the attributes of whiteness widely desirable, suggest that the priority is likely to go toward bringing nonwhite others into the sphere previously defined by whiteness, in which individuality defines subjects as historical agents, regardless of racial or ethnic identity. If so, the story of Patricia Williams's attempt to enter the Benetton's store in SoHo has a certain emblematic significance.[9]

Patricia Williams is a black woman law professor. To judge by the photo on the cover of her book, she also is quite light skinned. As an African American woman, she still has a couple of face cards in her poker hand. One day she saw a sweater in the window of a Benetton's store and, thinking of buying it as a Christmas present for her mother, buzzed—"Buzzers are big in New York City"—for admittance.

> A narrow-eyed, white teenager, wearing running shoes and feasting on bubble gum glared out, evaluating me for signs that would pit me against the limits of his social understanding. After about five seconds, he mouthed: "We're closed," and blew pink rubber at me. It was two Saturdays before Christmas, at one o'clock in the afternoon; there were several white people in the store who appeared to be shopping for things for *their* mothers.[10]

The buzzer, of course, signified that admission to the store was conditioned on a test of examinability, a test that Patricia Williams failed. Through a homogenization ("all Xs are the same") that made her excludable on the strength of a classificatory identity, she was denied the unexamined status that would have made her welcome in the store as an individual member of the buying public. Her examinability meant that she and her desire to buy a sweater could be ignored, referred back to the everyday decor of a New York City street where they "belonged," while the white people in the store went on with the important business of shopping. "No words, no gestures, no prejudices

of my own would make a bit of difference to [the clerk]; his refusal to let me
into the store was an outward manifestation of his never having let someone
like me into the realm of his reality." And so she was left pressing "[her] round
brown face to the window and [her] finger to the buzzer," [11] an exemplary
victim of the glass divide—a window for some, a door for others, a partition
for all—that separates, as a form of apartheid without segregation, the unexamined from the examinable in American society.

As Williams observes, the exclusion of blacks from the marketplace has its
historical roots in slavery, when they (like sweaters) were the objects of transac-
tions between historical white subjects to whom they were simply chattel:

> Blacks went from being owned to having everything around them owned by
> others. In a civilization that values private property above all else, this means a
> devaluation of the person, a removal of blacks not just from the market but from
> the pseudo-spiritual circle of psychic and civic communion. As illustrated in
> microcosm by my exclusion from Benetton's, this limbo of disownedness keeps
> blacks beyond the pale of those who are entitled to receive the survival gifts of
> commerce, the life, liberty and happiness whose fruits our culture locates in the
> marketplace. [12]

Notice that Williams refers quite naturally here to "our culture"—of which
she is part—even as she laments the exclusion of blacks from its fruits. They
have a function in the culture, which is to be excludable, on the grounds of
examinability, from those historical activities the culture holds to be central;
they thus help define those activities as historical and central.

Our analysis could be extended (minus the heritage of slavery, a large
omission) to the various other groups whose markedness—similarly, but in
different ways and to different degrees—justifies their reclusion behind the
glass door that divides the national culture of the United States into those who
partake and those who, at best, are permitted to buzz for admission. In her role
as X, Patricia Williams, testing the salesclerk's "social understanding," stood for
the homogenized category of blacks in general. But also and by extension—in
the way that Asian American and Pacific Islanders can be "all the same"—she
stood for all the examinable/excludable social categories that Benetton's did
not wish to admit "into the realm of [its] reality."

The role played by the buzzer in Williams's story interests me. It is provided
as a means to get attention so that the owner of the face and the finger behind
the glass can, on occasion, be excluded from attention, ignored. Ironically
enough, it means that white people, as the unexamined, are subject to a prior
examinability that establishes their "unexamined" status. But for others, the

buzzer stands for examinability as a form of noticeability that serves to mark certain people as not worthy of notice—a truly curious form of attention. It is a bit like the hypocritical slide of the eyes performed in the street (I know, I've done it) by those who identify, say, a homeless or handicapped person only to look immediately away, as if the person had not been seen at all. Had I been in that Benetton's on that December Saturday afternoon, intent on selecting a sweater or engaged in making a purchase, would I have allowed the buzzer to distract me? Would I have noticed the "round brown face" pressed to the glass or perceived the "saleschild's" mouthed (unspoken, silent) words: "We're closed"? Maybe I would have—but it is possible, more than possible, that I would just have vaguely looked up and gone straight back to the sweaters.

In this case, the buzzer is not so much about averting the gaze as about not hearing messages, about selectively not hearing messages. A glass door permits visibility (Williams can see the white shoppers inside; the saleschild can subject her to scrutiny) while by promoting inaudibility, it makes communication—in particular, two-way communication—problematic. The clerk's rather straight-forward message can be "mouthed" (it doesn't need to be spoken in order to be understood), whereas any of the necessarily more complex arguments Williams might try to make in reply will be—literally as well as figuratively—unheard, given the glass and the hum of commerce inside the store and the street din outside.

In her account of the incident, Williams quite logically talks about the difficulty she had in publishing her story in a law review that insisted on neutralizing it into aspecificity and pointlessness; and then of how, when she told the story in a public lecture, it was misheard and misreported in the press, its meaning distorted into a critique of affirmative action. A system of apartheid without segregation is one in which people share cultural "space" but communication between them is seriously muffled.

Examinability in this context—the buzzer system—means, as I mentioned, producing certain groups of people as noticeable in the sense that they, their desires and projects, and their messages can be ignored. To return to my previous analysis of otherness as split, their noticeability is a function of their relative strangeness, and their ignorability results from the relative familiarity of their otherness, its everyday, already known quality. Examinability in this sense is the metaphorical glass in the door that separates the members of a racially divided society, as sharers in a common history whose relevance is denied by the practice of examination, so that communication is basically limited to the one-way message: "We're closed." But the system cannot work without a buzzer; a shared (but denied) history implies the necessity of a means for sorting the candidates for admission into those—the unexamined—who will be admitted and the examinable, who will be excluded (so that the "unexamined" is itself a category subject to examination).

Conversely to the way that examinability presupposes a shared history that it is the function of examination to deny, the buzzer therefore figures all the inescapable reminders of shared historical context—those that enable, for example, a Patricia Williams, excluded from Benetton's, to refer nevertheless to "our culture." And people who are not allowed in and whose argument may be inaudible can still keep on buzzing, buzzing, and buzzing again.

That is, they can exploit cultural commonality in order to assert their status as individuals, the status implied by shared history, as opposed to the classificatory identity and the excludability that examinability foists on them. Patricia Williams's book, with its insistence on her singularity as a person and its analysis of shared U.S. history, but taken also as a rhetorical performance (its foregrounding of her personality, its performance of "craziness"), is a fine example of what it takes to be heard when one is on the wrong side of the glass, pressing one's face to the window and one's finger to the buzzer, in a society in which "the rules may be colorblind but people are not." [13] The trick is to convert the background buzz of speech that, like nagging, attracts attention only to be ignored, to a claim for admission that cannot be denied.

But this puts the whole burden on the excluded to demonstrate their admissibility, as individuals, into the world of the unexamined. Would it be too much to expect that the unexamined themselves might dismantle the glass doors and disconnect the buzzers? Thus, they (we) might substitute for the attention characteristic of examinability—quick-to-notice classificatory identities so that their bearers can be relegated behind the glass—a form of attention that would watch for signs of individuality, signs that would be indistinguishable from the evidence of a given person's historical relevance and so the legitimacy of her or his participation in whatever the business at hand might be. For all of her criticism of the law, Williams puts her faith in affirmative action: "It is thus that affirmative action is an affirmation, the affirmative act of hiring—and hearing—blacks as a recognition of individuality that re-places blacks as a social statistic, that is profoundly connected to the fate of blacks and whites either as sub-groups or as one group." [14]

But given a world of apartheid without segregation, in which the rules may be color blind but the people are not, the success of affirmative action itself depends on the fulfillment of a cultural precondition, one that the law itself cannot legislate. The recognition of individuality that Williams seeks presupposes the abandonment of both the categories of examinability and the practices of examination.

In their place, we need to substitute the concept of readability and modes of reading, understanding "reading" to name a relational practice that does not deny but actually recognizes the mutual dependence of subject and object, the relevance, therefore, of context, and finally the particularity of social interactions, mediated as they may be by the codes and conventions without which sociality itself would be impossible.

A reader does not "examine" a text, presumed to be disconnected from the reading subject, but enters into an interaction in which the other (the text) is understood as relevant to (connected with) the self. And finally, reading does not imply a distinction between the readable and the unread in the way that examination presupposes the separability of the examinable and the unexamined. Rather, the act of reading, as I have discussed elsewhere,[15] presupposes the possibility of the readers being read in turn. Such an understanding would be the condition, I suggest (with an apology for bringing this idea so suddenly and so briefly out of my hat; I plan to return to it on another occasion), for social relations of genuine mutuality, as opposed to the glass doors and the buzzers, the system of marked and unmarked, examinable and unexamined categories, that still plagues even the best-intentioned relations today.

But how to achieve this? I hear you ask. Well, we're just going to have to work at it, that's all.[16]

NOTES

1. I begin with a story that illustrates my own racism, among other reasons because in my experience it's rare for the critics of racism to confess the racist structure of their own subjectivity. Yet it's impossible to live in a racist society, that is, to be subject to a racist culture, without being a racist cultural subject. It is ourselves we are trying to change, and it does no good, therefore, to begin by pretending that we are ourselves exempt from the problems we describe.

That said, the date of the story is important: few contemporary Australians, I surmise, are likely to recognize themselves in it. Particularly offensive is the conflation of whiteness with Australianness, as if the country had not been inhabited for forty thousand years before the white people came. But an elderly aunt of mine, born at the turn of the century (about the same time as modern Australia) and recently deceased, steadfastly refused to take a taxi unless it was driven by an "Australian," by which she meant a person, preferably male, of Anglo-Celtic extraction.

2. Scapegoating consists of singling out for blame and exclusion an individual or group that is charged with the evils of a community. It follows that scapegoaters are, by

definition, guilty of that with which the scapegoat is charged, as it is the general function of the act of scapegoating to produce a kind of magical exemption of the scapegoater—a pseudoinnocence that can always be called into question.

3. For a similar argument (with less stress on individualization as such), see Richard Dyer, "White," *Screen* 29 (Autumn 1988): 46. "White people—not there as a category and everywhere everything as a fact—are difficult if not impossible to analyze *qua* white" because they are always represented as something else instead (middle-class English people, the lesbians who live around the corner, or a "boy from the bush"). My thanks to Ian Leong for directing my attention to this article.

4. Christopher Miller, *Blank Darkness: Africanist Discourse in French* (Chicago: University of Chicago Press, 1985).

5. The word *inscrutability,* which I use here as a synonym for unexaminability, has a parallel colonial and racist history of its own, as witness the cliché of "oriental inscrutability."

6. The same analysis applies to the dichotomization of masculine–feminine or metropolitan–colonial in conjunction with the pluralization of the (nonmasculine or the nonmetropolitan) other.

7. Michel Foucault, *Discipline and Punish: The Birth of the Prison* (New York: Vintage Books, 1979).

8. Ross Chambers, "Pointless Stories and Storyless Points: Roland Barthes Between 'Soirées de Paris' and 'Incidents,' " *L'Ésprit créateur* 34 (Summer 1994): 12–30.

9. Patricia Williams, *The Alchemy of Race and Rights: Diary of a Law Professor* (Cambridge, MA: Harvard University Press, 1991), pp. 44–51.

10. Ibid., pp. 44–45.

11. Ibid.

12. Ibid., p. 71.

13. Ibid., p. 120.

14. Ibid., p. 50.

15. Ross Chambers, "Reading and Being Read: Irony and Critical Practices in Cultural Studies," *the minnesota review* 43/44 (Fall 1996): 113–30.

16. An enabling step would consist of substituting an understanding of the (negotiable) genre of specific social interactions for that of the (nonnegotiable because pregiven) identity of the participants in interactions. Genre is the mediator of reading, whereas identity is the object of examinability. It would take a long essay to explore this idea. See Anne Freadman and Amanda Macdonald, *What Is This Thing . . . "Called Genre"?* (Mount Nebo, Qsld: Boombana Publications, 1992).

13

Outing Whiteness: A Feminist/ Lesbian Project

Kate Davy

On their way to perform in the Miss Make Believe Contest—a benefit for a neighboring theater—two of the WOW Cafe's Five Lesbian Brothers, Maureen Angelos and Peg Healey, talk about what to do for the talent section of the contest. Three of the troupe's performers have bowed out at the last minute, leaving Angelos and Healey without a repertoire; there are no duets in this quintet. They decide to do something related to the film *Basic Instinct,* since it had recently opened in New York and debates were raging in the press and on the street over Sharon Stone's portrayal of an ostensibly lesbian character. Later, when the emcee introduces two of the Five Lesbian Brothers, Angelos and Healey walk slowly and purposefully on stage. Drawing deeply and excessively on lit cigarettes hanging from the corners of their mouths, they drop a block of ice on the stage, reach in their back pockets for ice picks, and throw themselves on the block, ravaging it. As the ice is decimated, smoke billowing, wave on wave of squeals and laughter rise and fall as the metaphoric potential is realized and drained from the image.

This chapter was born out of a desire to explore and come to terms with a major and long-standing concern of the women who make up a theater collective, the WOW Cafe, in New York's East Village.[1] WOW is an acronym for Women's One World. Its membership is made up predominantly of middle-class, white lesbians, a few working-class, white lesbians, and an occasional heterosexual woman. In its fifteen-year history, however, very few women of color have participated in its productions, and still fewer have belonged to the collective itself. This is especially worrisome considering that a number of African American women participated in the two international festivals in New York (1980 and 1981) that constituted WOW's founding moments.

Billed as "celebrating the diversity of women," these Women's One World festivals included work from other U.S. cities and several countries, as well as work by local African American women.[2] As the theater space developed, however, virtually no African American women became involved in the collective, and WOW has grappled with the issue ever since. One attempt to address it in recent years was to set aside a substantial block of time each year for African American women to present their work. Members of the collective provide the staff for these shows in the form of technical, promotional, and house management support. Although this approach has worked well, it is considered less than satisfactory, indeed ghettoizing, and the collective continues to struggle with the larger issue.[3]

I asked novelist and critic Jewelle Gomez what she thought the problem might be, not only because she is an African American lesbian, but also because she attended WOW's inaugural festivals and has been a frequent WOW audience member. "It's the same problem," she said, "that black women and white women have had with each other for three hundred years,"[4] a dynamic between black women and white women in their shared history.

Lynda Hart suggests that in the modern portion of this history, the hegemonic culture has attempted to enforce a strict separation of the "white lesbian" from the "single woman of color" as symbolic categories. But she maintains that they are nonetheless linked to each other "in the white masculine imaginary as figures who constitute serious threats to the reproduction of white men—both fail to reproduce *him,* even when they do reproduce." She argues that beginning with nineteenth-century sexology and criminology, "the lesbian" has been constructed as white. She then shows why this strategy is an effective means of maintaining a division between the constructions of the lesbian and the single woman of color, driven by a fear of the possibility that these bodies might align to perform together.

"The *single* woman" is a phrase so overdetermined with connotations of both African American motherhood and lesbianism that . . . where one is implicated, the other is not likely to be far away. The threat of their proximity constitutes a sufficient danger in patriarchal fantasies; the fact that they can and often do inhabit the same space appears to be a possibility so terrifying that it is constantly erased. The resulting historical product has been an entrenched separation of the two.[5]

Although Hart's argument provides a useful and promising way to analyze the phenomenon at WOW, I want to explore a concomitant operation at work, one equally embedded in history but generated by the nature of WOW's work itself. In order to get at the significance of this three-hundred-year history in relationship to WOW, I begin with the collective's early years to determine whether there is something about the aesthetics and the strategies of the work that implicates the dynamics of whiteness as central to the issue of participation by women of color.

MAKING GIRLS AND COMMUNING WITH CULTURE

We don't kill them [men] because they're bad; we kill them because we're bad.
                                                                    "The Secretaries"

This section is entitled "making girls," first, because the women of WOW have always referred to themselves and to one another as girls, WOW girls. This is somewhat ironic since WOW was founded at the end of a decade-long struggle by some feminists to end the hegemonic culture's infantilization of women in part by altering rhetorical conventions, insisting, for example, that women be addressed as adults and henceforth referred to as women, not girls. Making girls, second, is meant not only to foreground as forcefully as possible the point that all girls are socially and culturally constructed but also to indicate that many of the strategies used in WOW work are aimed at (re)making girls or making girls anew, that is, intervening in the normative, naturalizing, and mystifying representational codes that produce "woman" as an ideological construct and heterosexuality as a psychological, social, and cultural imperative.

For the most part, the members of WOW's collective have been far more concerned with intervening in the processes that produce the subjectivities of female-sexed bodies as gender-marked "woman" than with representing the experiences of women and lesbians in the hegemonic culture. Joan W. Scott argues that "it is not individuals who have experiences, but subjects who are constituted through experience."[6] In other words, experience is not a product of subjectivity but a process that constructs subjectivity. Even if experience were something that individuals "had," most WOW practitioners would be interested in having new or alternative experiences, producing alternative subjectivities rather than making visible those experiences of women indicating that psychosocially they have been "had."

Because sexuality is the locus of these interventions, I intend the sexual connotations that making girls carries, for sex and sexuality are the central preoccupations of much WOW work. Certain eccentric, excessive, deviant enactments of gender in some WOW work signal alternative sexualities and have their roots in a variety of sources. In the early days, WOW sponsored a number of all-girl parties where racks of costumes were made available, from strapless gowns to leather pants and jackets and black lace underwear and bedtime wear. Party goers were encouraged to indulge their desires and erotic fantasies by making themselves into whomever they most secretly wanted to "be," in both costume and impromptu performances, some of which found their way to the WOW stage.[7]

At a time when many feminist circles frowned on butch/femme role playing, not only were a number of WOW productions built on the dynamics of butch/femme desire, but the collective also sponsored separate butch and femme workshops to explore the histories, meanings, practices, iconographies of dress, and subversive possibilities of these sexual and performative categories. More remarkably, perhaps, during the period when the infamous "sex wars" on a number of fronts were being waged over lesbian sadomasochism, WOW unabashedly and unapologetically presented work that included S/M references and iconography, as well as performances explicitly focusing on S/M ideologies and practices.

There is generally no "party line" at WOW with regard to the content or ideology of a piece. Work is rarely challenged from within the group, but when it is, the ensuing debates remain just that—debates, not doctrine. Ultimately, a desire to explore multiple performative modes for women in search of an autonomous sexuality overrides other concerns in much of WOW's work. WOW's recuperation of "girl" flies in the face of feminisms that tend to de-sexualize women and can be read as a move toward examining how one might refunction gender through embodied performances of alternative sexualities.[8] Since its inception, the operating principles of many collective members and their work have been informed by an impulse to thwart the "good girl" syndrome in its many dominant cultural, as well as feminist, forms. But who gets to claim good girl status in the first place?

The bit of shtick by two of the Five Lesbian Brothers that begins this piece is a quick example of a central feature of much WOW work, which can be characterized as a kind of communing with (Western) culture by way of the hegemonic culture's artifacts or products.

In this comic bit, Angelos and Healey—the brothers (as they call themselves)—refer to a moment in the film *Basic Instinct* when "the lesbian" (Sharon Stone), in an otherwise perfectly genteel act of making cocktails, hacks away at a block of ice. The moment is designed to make the detective (Michael Douglas) and the film's audience wonder what this woman is capable of doing, especially since the authorities have already surmised that the murder weapon was an ice pick. The brothers take the image a step further by enacting— and thereby revealing—the moment's subtext, which smacks of something profoundly "not right" or unnatural about this woman. For starters, a normal household (and movie) would have a bucket of ice cubes. Their crazed, murderous bludgeoning of the ice block makes clear the point that this beautiful, blonde, immaculately dressed, upper-class woman hacking away is indeed a bad woman and not, as her wealth would suggest, a lady. As lesbians, Angelos and Healey echo her status as a woman who sleeps with other women, lending the crucial symbolic dimension to her violent hacking, one that seals her fate as an evil woman, a homicidal woman, or, as Lynda Hart calls her, a fatal woman.[9]

At the same time and in contrast to Sharon Stone, the brothers position themselves as the "real thing," by enacting a hilarious parody of the horror that lesbian sexuality evokes and, as self-described "lesbian brothers," making themselves the epitome of the perverse, the ultimate in "bad womanhood." In appropriating a mass-culture image, Angelos and Healey fashion themselves a new one and in the process construct themselves as the antithesis of middle-class propriety as lodged in the image of the good girl. This is a hallmark of early WOW performances, and it is through the performers' race that this site of resistance is readable and, therefore, possible at all.

When WOW performers commune with (Western) culture, "culture" is invoked. In James Clifford's definition, culture is "always relational, an inscription of communicative processes that exist, historically, *between* subjects in relations of power."[10] The "nature" of the culture that WOW invokes, then, cannot be taken for granted but must be described in terms of the relations of power that historically have mobilized processes/experiences between subjects. To thwart the good girl syndrome is to call forth those historical processes that produced the good girl construct.

As a form of embodied representation, performance enacts race, class, gender, and sexuality. Even when these categories are culturally "unmarked"—

to borrow from Peggy Phelan[11]—they are nonetheless (presumptively) read and produce meanings. In hegemonic Western cultural economies, good girls are straight-middle-class-white girls; they emerge at the intersection of all four categories. As I have argued over the last several years, WOW's performative strategies have been enormously important to the project of challenging the hom(m)osexual frame of reference,[12] but as I contend here, some of these strategies depend on whiteness to do so and so throw into relief certain performative dimensions of whiteness and so concern the "one" in women's one world.

MAKING MONSTERS AND WHITE WOMANHOOD
AS INSTITUTIONS

> White avant-garde artists must be willing to openly interrogate work which they or critics cast as liberatory or oppositional. That means they must consider the role whiteness plays in the construction of their identity and aesthetic visions, as well as the way it determines reception of their work.   bell hooks, "Representing Whiteness"

As the work of many critical theorists of African American womanhood indicates, a presumptive good girl status has not been a prerogative for African American women in the dominant culture. White women and black women may share the last three hundred years, but from crucially different sociohistorical spaces. As Kimberlé Crenshaw observes, "the stereotypes and myths that justified the sexual abuse of black women in slavery continue to be played out in current society."[13] These stereotypes and myths foster images of black women as sexually promiscuous and sexually voracious.

Regarding the roots of these images, Hazel Carby notes that the association of black women with overt sexuality and taboo sexual practices allowed the white male to be "represented as being merely prey to the rampant sexuality of his female slaves."[14] Crenshaw brings the continuing saliency of these images to bear, among other dynamics, on the dilemma of Anita Hill during the Clarence Thomas hearings, citing examples like the "familiar stereotypes of black women as hardier than white women, and more accustomed to aggressive, gritty, even violent sex." In the end, she asks, "To what authority can women who have been consistently represented as sexually available appeal?"[15]

Patricia Hill Collins examines the differing ways in which black women and white women are constructed in heterosexual pornography as another way of unmasking the difference that race makes in representation. Following Alice Walker's formulation of white women as objects in pornography and black women as animals, Collins shows how race becomes the distinguishing feature in determining the type of objectification that women encounter.

> As objects white women become creations of culture—in this case, the mind of white men—using the materials of nature—in this case, uncontrolled female sexuality. In contrast, as animals Black women receive no such redeeming dose of culture and remain open to the type of exploitation visited on nature overall.[16]

Lest anyone think that such rank notions circulate only in pornography and congressional hearings, let me remind you of the 1992 mass-distribution film *Peter's Friends* written by stand-up comic Rita Rudner and her husband. The only African American in this *Big Chill*–like film of gathered friends is a woman who plays the only character with an excessive, insatiable sexual appetite, a character who is either screwing or attempting to screw every man in sight. Rudner, a white woman, plays a character in the film who derisively refers to the black woman, not once but twice, as a "fuck monster."

Again, white women and black women share an enforced embodiment, but with important differences. Three hundred years of history ensures the naturalness of both the hypersexuality inscribed on the body of the black woman in *Peter's Friends* and the high road of moral rectitude momentarily invoked by the white woman who marks it. In order to label the black woman a sexual monster, the white woman must assume a position of sexual propriety authorized by the dictates of white womanhood, a descendant of the cult of true womanhood, which functioned historically to exclude some groups of white women and all women of color. Performing sexuality excessively as an oppositional strategy, as is the case at WOW, depends on racial encoding, and as Carby points out, "The ideology of true womanhood was as racialized a concept in relation to white women as it was in its exclusion of black womanhood."[17] The form communing with culture takes in WOW work is an exclusionary practice in which WOW performers participate in a process of racialization that produces whiteness. This whiteness is manifest and performed at the intersection of class.

Vincente L. Rafael asked, "What would whiteness be without middle-class respectability?"[18] Authors of "white trash" narratives, like Dorothy Allison's *Trash* and *Bastard out of Carolina,* have answered this question and contested its premises.[19] But Rafael's question is about an institutional whiteness, the kind of whiteness used to rationalize white domination and privilege, the kind of whiteness against which white trash is measured and from which it is distanced.[20]

To describe this kind of whiteness both ideologically and performatively,

Richard Dyer analyzes certain classical films and notes that "whiteness" is enacted in terms of rationality, rigidity, gentility, order, stability, and the capacity to set boundaries.[21] He argues that whites exemplify "an over-investment in the brain" (p. 63), manifest in acts of calm and control that are so extreme, he contends, that whites represent the ability to repress life to the point of death or a kind of pure abstraction. "Whites," he suggests, "are the living dead" (p. 59).[22] In contrast, not surprisingly, black people are represented as having more "life" than whites, more emotion and sensuality derived from their perceived (closer) proximity to nature, the same ideology that positions blacks to represent backwardness, irrationality, chaos, and violence (pp. 55, 49).

As Dyer's argument progresses, he qualifies the characteristics of whiteness with regard to gender. "Thus, whites and men (especially) become characterized by 'boundariness' " (p. 51). Even though white women also have these characteristics, they are especially true of—in fact seem to belong to—white masculinity. Dyer's notion of whiteness in its institutionalized form gestures toward a disembodied or beyond-the-body state of abstraction, a state that is not entirely available to white women, since femininity itself is characterized by embodiedness. Because of gender, white women also are closer to nature, also embodied, and therefore less "dead" and less deadly empowered. Tracing the construct of white womanhood historically is important to understanding the duplicitous positioning of white women and the racializing process that produces whiteness.

White womanhood is the consequence of a racialization process played out on multiple fronts, but perhaps most ironically and certainly most enduringly in the role that the cult of true womanhood played in facilitating the transition from the ideology of possessive individualism in the nineteenth century to what Gillian Brown calls "domestic individualism." In a complex argument that I am massively reducing here, Brown describes possessive individualism as a form that reflects a masculine selfhood, and then she shows how it became associated with the feminine sphere of domesticity to the point that individualism itself was constituted in the domestic. Moreover, Brown maintains that it was the domestic cult of true womanhood, which is already white womanhood, that facilitated the transition to the ideology of domestic individualism. In other words, white womanhood came to signify a selfhood that, although constituted in the domestic, was denied to women or, more accurately, to which white women had access only in their relationship with white men. Brown writes, "Far from a account of the female subject, domesticity signifies a feminization of selfhood in service to an individualism most available to (white) men."[23]

In the absence of an alternative model of selfhood, white feminists were inextricably aligned with white patriarchy even as they attempted to reform its effects. This feminization of individualism, as well as what I mark as its racialization, also was inflected by class and sexuality, producing a construction of white womanhood that allows white women to signify and enact the whiteness that Dyer describes, without inhabiting the subject position reserved for white man. White women signify hegemonic, institutionalized whiteness through their association with a pure, chaste, asexual before-the-fall-womanhood (a next-to-man-and-godliness womanhood), attained and maintained via middle-class respectability with its implicit heterosexuality. At the same time, white women signify an uncontrolled after-the-fall-sexuality, or fallen-woman status, embodied by some white women (prostitutes, white trash, lesbians) and all women of color. As Kimberlé Crenshaw puts it, "Given their race, black women have . . . always been within the fallen-woman category."[24]

In her book *Beyond the Pale,* Vron Ware explains how, depending on the social and historical context, white women can be constructed as both civilized and savage.

> Civilization . . . is the other side of the coin to savagery. In some contexts, white women might indeed be associated with the idea that female nature is inherently uncivilized, primitive when compared to men, and lacking in self-control. In the context of imperialism or modern racism, the dominant ideology would place white women firmly in the civilized camp, in opposition to non-European women whose lack of social and political rights are to be read as a mark of cultural savagery. This means that white women can occupy both sides of a binary opposition.[25]

I disagree that white women can unproblematically occupy that side of any binary opposition reserved for white, heterosexual masculinity, and I propose instead the more fluid notion of a continuum. White women can travel from the end of this continuum reserved for those most embodied—that is, those most encumbered by nature and, therefore, understood to be least civilized or most degenerate—to the other end of the continuum representing culture and civilization, that is, the (abstract) mind of heterosexual white masculinity, creative and creating, unburdened by the constraints of embodiment. The white woman's privilege, then, can be understood in terms of her mobility. Because of race, she is able to travel this continuum, moving further away from savagery toward enlightenment. Insofar as she is white, heterosexual, and of middle- to upper-class status, she moves closer to the civilized end of this sociosymbolic order. But she never quite reaches the most privileged end of this continuum/world order; she can never, paradoxically, fully embody the unembodied dimension of white masculinity, for "to embody" is still her definition and destiny. And it is crucial to recognize that women of color, because of their status as both racially and gender marked, do not have the mobility to go far from the end of the continuum that represents materiality.

Some white women have more mobility than others; it is at the intersection of class privilege that whiteness is fully mobilized. The symbology of white womanhood is not that of the fallen, disenfranchised white woman but that of the respectable white woman; it is at the intersections of gender and race with "middle classness" that white women embody and perform an institutionalized whiteness. Rather than a totalizing notion of universal whiteness, this intersection produces the form that whiteness takes in its function as the raison d'être of white supremacy. The category of middle class carries far more symbolic weight than merely that of economic status.

I agree with Marilyn Frye when she says of her concept of "whiteliness" that it is not "just middle-class-ness misnamed."[26] I maintain that the meanings of "middle classness" are virtually the same as the meanings that constitute an institutionalized whiteness.[27] Middle classness denotes a kind of hard-earned, as opposed to birthright, "gentility" in the form of civility (a bedrock concept of imperialism) that encompasses a plethora of values, morals, and mores that determine sexual propriety, as well as the tenets of respectability in general, all of which are lodged, for signifying purposes, in the Western ideological phantasm "white womanhood." This is a phantasm only in the sense that the full force of its effects exceeds an embodiment of it, which is not to deny or ameliorate the complicity of white women in an ongoing project to instrumentalize its privileges.

White womanhood needs to be theorized as an institution in the service of white control and supremacy in the same way that heterosexuality has been used as an institution in the service of patriarchy.[28] White womanhood has long been understood as an ideology of white supremacy. Ida B. Wells, a black woman, was one of the first activist scholars to delineate this dimension of the construct.[29] In calling for a broader understanding of it as an institution, I mean that white womanhood contains a number of sometimes conflicting ideologies used differently and differentially depending on the historical needs of white control. Like any institution, white womanhood is not a totalizing force, but one that shifts and changes in response to historical conditions.

When the last three hundred years is understood as white women's history as well as black women's, gender ideologies can be searched for their racial specificity, and whiteness can be examined as a racial category embedded in material circumstances and wielding far-reaching effects in both the social and symbolic orders.[30] The terror in *Basic Instinct* is that of white womanhood run amok; it is the peril of the white woman detached from middle-class respectability. Although deviant sexual behavior unfastens the Sharon Stone character from the constraints of white womanhood, the ultimate punishment is exacted from the far more disturbing figure of the white psychologist (Jeanne Tripplehorn) with her abject masochism—her dying words to the man who has just shot her point-blank are "I love you"—precisely because her status as inside what deserves protection, that is, white womanhood, has been thrown into question by the film's narrative.[31] Marking the invocation of white womanhood is critical to dismantling its privileges, punishments, and exclusions.

WOW artists' performative strategies challenge white womanhood when they undermine the ontological propriety of white woman, creating a discursive and performative space of not-virgin, not-mother, not-whore, not-woman. These strategies have been enormously productive, but at the same time that they challenge white womanhood, they depend on it and once again circumscribe and consign to erasure those bodies that white womanhood nullifies historically and continues to negate. Representational strategies built around performing alternative notions of sexuality excessively are not necessarily strategies that black women would employ to enact counterhegemonic disruptions. The histories inscribed on the bodies of African American women ensure a circulation of meanings quite different from those assigned to the bodies of other women of color, as well as white women.

In a review of a WOW production entitled *Queer Justice* (1990), Alisa Solomon describes two of the ten solo pieces—each performed by a different woman—that made up the show:

> A woman introduces herself as a "lesbian truck driver extraordinaire" and croons a country-western paean to life on the road, an eighteen inch vibrator dangling from her belt. "Driving my truck is like a good fuck," she sings. "What do you say we set cruise control? We can rock till we drop and continue to roll." The audience hoots, howls, and swoons playfully in response to this open celebration of a sexuality that is represented rarely. . . . [A] woman in a short tight, black leather skirt gyrates and grinds, curling her ruby-red mouth into baby-doll kisses as she lip-synchs along with a recording of the old pop tune, "Pretty woman, walking down the street. . . ." As she twists toward the floor, her skirt hikes up her thighs, revealing red satin panties. Once again, the audience hoots, howls, and swoons.[32]

Solomon no doubt chose these two pieces to examine in detail in part because they are typical of much WOW work. She also briefly describes those of three other white women in the show. She does not mention the performances of two African American women who were among the cast; their pieces were serious in approach, reflective in tone, and had nothing to do with performing an excessive sexuality to the hoots and howls of the audience.

Performative strategies that challenge the institution of white womanhood are not inherently antiracist. In order to function in ways productive to an antiracist project, challenges to white womanhood must be foregrounded as such; that is, they must be marked in such a way that the institutional apparatus of white womanhood in its effacing, obliterating mode is, at the very least, exhumed from its status as unremarkable to be remarked.

THE POLITICS OF RESPECTABILITY
AT THE SATURATION POINT

> The white girl learns that whiteliness is dignity and respectability. . . . Adopting and cultivating whiteliness as an individual character seems to put it in the woman's own power to lever herself up out of a kind of nonbeing (the status of woman in a male supremacist social order) over into a kind of Being (the status of white in white supremacist social order).
>
> Marilyn Frye, *Willful Virgin*

In the spring of 1994, at the University of California at Irvine, I directed a play entitled *Brave Smiles . . . Another Lesbian Tragedy,* written by the Five Lesbian Brothers. The play is a parody of the "tragic end" that every lesbian must meet in any form of dominant representation that deigns to represent her. In *Brave Smiles,* lesbians are hanged, hit by trucks, electrocuted, blown up in airplanes, and felled by alcoholism and brain tumors. It is a play not just about lesbians but very much about *white* women. Indeed, the show's tragedies are a consequence of the intersection of an outlawed sexuality with an especially white womanhood. In addition to foregrounding the play's homoeroticism, then, I wanted the production to address the ways in which the ideologies of white womanhood work to produce the play's dilemmas. In this context, I discovered that the notion of white womanhood as an institution is not very useful if its dynamics are not identified and articulated. The following section of this chapter attempts to take a step in that direction.

White womanhood is a racialization process in which middle-class respectability functions as a structuring principle. Respectability as a notion seems somehow quaintly old-fashioned, in the sense that it has a long history in feminist and civil rights movements. An analysis of the historical function of respectability is one way to understand whiteness as dynamic rather than as merely an unmarked category.

The work of Evelyn Brooks Higginbotham on the women's movement in the black Baptist Church between 1880 and 1920 is especially useful for getting at this notion of respectability, because she casts her argument in terms of the "politics of respectability" and shows how it operated in a movement committed to both women's rights and the rights and empowerment of black people. Her argument makes clear that although black Baptist women engaged in a politics of respectability that had a decidedly accommodationist and assimilationist dimension, it also had a decidedly resistant dimension, one with subversive implications. Indeed, her conception of the "politics of respectability" is characterized in part by "black Baptist women's opposition to the social structures and symbolic representations of white supremacy." For Higginbotham, adherence to the principles of respectability enabled black women to counter racist discourses and images of black women as immoral, that is, as the very embodiment of deviance and, hence, unworthy of respect and protection. By using a politics of respectability, black women also launched an attack on the structures of white supremacy, "an attack on the failure of America to live up to its liberal ideals of equality and justice and an attack on the values and lifestyle of those blacks who transgressed white middle-class propriety." One of the reasons that Higginbotham's work is so important is that she delineates not only what a politics of respectability in the hands of black women means at particular historical moments but also the complex ways in which it works.[33]

Any politics that has an assimilationist dimension necessarily invokes the hegemonic culture and, hence, those processes that produce the othered subject or culture. The assimilationist component of the politics of respectability invokes whiteness through its appeal to bourgeois characteristics, which Higginbotham describes as a kind of conglomerate of middle-class ideals, including "temperance, industriousness, thrift, refined manners, and Victorian sexual morals."[34] Although she locates and discusses respectability in the context of class, her particular configuration of class invokes the dominant regime of whiteness.

Instead of an intersection, it might be more helpful at this point to think of the link between bourgeois middle classness and whiteness in terms of Hortense Spillers's concept of *saturation,* which Robyn Wiegman reads as an "insistence that categories don't simply overlap but so thoroughly saturate one another that gender . . . rarely refers to the same constellation. Differences in racial positioning must therefore be understood to produce quite different (feminine) genders."[35] Spillers's point is that when the marked-category woman is saturated with certain racial positionings, specifically those of the female captive under slavery, it produces something else, something not only greater than but different from the sum of gender and race.

My point is that when the unmarked category of white is saturated with bourgeois middle classness, it too produces something else, that is, an ideal of whiteness or an epitome of whiteness, whose dynamics bestow privilege on all white people and justify white supremacy. Played out in the politics of respectability, whiteness becomes the dynamic underpinning a process of racialization that feeds privilege to all whites, so to speak, without letting all white people sit at the table.[36] Those middle-class people of color invited to sit at the table are assigned a status that is always, already, and only honorary, contingent, itinerant, and temporary. As Hazel Carby puts it, "Black entry into the so-called mainstream has been on the grounds of middle-class acceptability and not the end of segregation."[37]

To follow Higginbotham's lead and trace the historical workings of a politics of respectability in the hands of white women is an endeavor with vastly different meanings and outcomes. Carby writes, "The texts of black women . . . are testaments to the racist practices of the suffrage and temperance movements and indictments of the ways in which white women allied themselves not with black women but with a racist patriarchal order against all black people."[38] Of the myriad historical examples of white women participating in the politics of respectability, the most telling instances are those distancing white women from black women in the context of the very organizations that white women formed to advance the cause of justice for women and blacks.[39] When black women were not allowed to join these organizations, the rationale was that white women could better serve the interests of black women by maintaining their respectability and hence credibility, something that they could accomplish only by distancing themselves from black people.

In this and many other ways, white women were able to serve the cause of justice while simultaneously maintaining their allegiance to whiteness. An organization called the Association of Southern Women for the Prevention of Lynching (ASWPL) is a later but nonetheless representative example. Founded in 1930 by Jessie Daniel Ames, a white woman who had been a leader in the suffrage movement, the ASWPL occasionally invited black women to attend its meetings and give presentations, but they were not allowed to become members.

In her book *Revolt Against Chivalry,* Jacquelyn Dowd Hall explains that this policy was justified by the contention that allowing black women into the organization would undermine white women's respectability and therefore jeopardize the cause. This exclusionary policy "eliminated the very participants who could keep the organization accountable to changing black agendas for reform," and it reinscribed white supremacy as well. According to Hall, "white women were viewed *collectively* as the repositories of white racial legitimacy," and thus "as absolutely inaccessible sexual property, white women became the most potent symbol of white male supremacy." The protection of white middle-class respectability was used to justify exclusionary feminist political moves in the name of a greater good and at the same time protected the vehicle through which white women come to symbolize white supremacy, further consolidating and solidifying the institutional power of white womanhood. Hall makes it clear that Jesse Daniel Ames, like other feminists, "manipulated rather than directly challenged the symbolism of white southern womanhood" to achieve her ends.[40]

White women continue to engage a politics of respectability. For instance, wouldn't it be far more difficult for women's studies programs to maintain their institutional credibility if activism inside and outside the academy were to become a priority? The conflict and controversy that such activism engenders denote a certain rowdiness unseemly for women who want to be taken seriously. When we as white women let an investment in institutional credibility take precedence over the action agenda needed to change the power structures and processes that produce elitist and exclusionary conditions, aren't we as white women making an(other) investment in whiteness, renewing, as it were, our allegiance to the race? Instead of viewing the institutionalization of women's programs as a recent phenomenon born of white women's newly found position of legitimacy in the academy, we might understand it as the function of a current politics of respectability grounded in our very real historical investment in whiteness.[41]

In recent years, sex-radical lesbians have challenged "old guard" lesbian feminists, whom they perceive as preoccupied with gender. Sex-radical lesbians have called these lesbian feminists to accountability for prescribing "appropriate sexual practices" to complement a non–male-identified gender identity and thereby policing the borders of identity and desire. Sex-radical lesbians represent themselves as "bad girls" and accuse those lesbian feminists who aspire to "good girl" status of creating painful silences and exclusions in lesbian communities with different social identities, ideologies, and practices. Are some lesbian feminists engaged in an assimilationist project in an attempt to hang onto some remnant of "good girl" status, that bourgeois construct giving white women full access to the privileges of white womanhood? And on the sex-radical side of the debate, which social subjects have access to a presumptive good girl status, that is, who can demand the right to be "bad" without reinscribing an already naturalized deviance?

I am not trying to reduce these debates to a single issue but, rather, to complicate them and suggest that the dynamics of race and class operate in them. Examining the ways in which white women engage in and use a politics of respectability "outs" whiteness, makes it manifest by revealing its investments, operations, and relations of power. My use of "outing" here is in no way meant to appropriate or eschew the critical meanings of the closet for lesbians and gays. Rather, I use it for the sense of forced disclosure it portends. Whiteness, not gay and lesbian people, should be "outed."

In whiteness, bourgeois values are naturalized in ways that use and justify the relations of power that ensure a strict social stratification seemingly based solely on the dynamics of class while masking its own operations that ensure and provide the care and maintenance of racial boundaries. This masking marks the function of whiteness in the concept of multiculturalism, a concept that Michaela DiLeonardo calls "a stupidly obfuscating frame . . . that never penetrate[s] to the roots of power."[42]

In "The Multicultural Wars," Carby asks, "Is the emphasis on cultural diversity making invisible the politics of race in this increasingly segregated nation, and is the language of cultural diversity a convenient substitute for the political action needed to desegregate?"[43] An analysis that uses the politics of respectability helps make visible the politics of race and makes room for further exploration and intervention.

This is what we attempted to accomplish in the Irvine production of *Brave Smiles*. Briefly, the first act is a parody of the Weimar film *Mädchen in Uniform*, which is set in a girls' boarding school between the wars and has an explicitly lesbian story line. The second act is a series of vignettes that follow the girls through the 1940s, 1950s, and 1960s to their tragic ends while parodying films like *The Children's Hour* and *The Killing of Sister George*. A cast of five women play some nineteen different characters; the white girls and women among them were played with a vengeance. The idea was both to queer white womanhood and expose it as racialized. By the show's opening, I felt that white womanhood emerged as a distinctive performative dimension of the piece. I think, however, that if it was read as such, it was because there was an African American woman in the cast.

After dozens of roles in which she was subsumed into whiteness without so much as a nod toward the meanings of her always already racialized status in a racist culture, Lisa Colbert, an African American woman, relished the opportunity to play a white woman as a white woman. Her parody of Audrey Hepburn was so brilliant performatively that the white woman playing the Shirley MacLaine role opposite her, in a parody of the hand-wringing confession scene from the film version of *The Children's Hour,* looked like she was playing a white woman too. Moreover, by playing the Shirley MacLaine of *Sweet Charity,* rather than the MacLaine of *Children's Hour,* Demetra Tseckares used class performatively to distance her MacLaine a little further from the ideal of white womanhood that Audrey Hepburn so perfectly enacts.

In the first act, when one of the boarding school's girls admits to being a Jew, the girl played by Lisa Colbert does not participate in the ensuing gawking and gaping and lines like "I've never seen a Jew before." But when one of the girls puts a proprietary arm around the Jewish girl and says, "You're my first Jewish friend ever," Colbert shakes her head derisively and says knowingly, "White girls." The Jewish girl nods in agreement; in Weimar Germany, Jews were the subject and targets of a racial, as well as an ethnic, discourse.

Of course, all this can be seen as enormously problematic because ultimately whiteness was foregrounded in the production in the way it always is, by constructing racial others that carry the burden of difference. At the same time, we did not want to pretend, in high liberal humanist fashion, that African American women's bodies and white women's bodies don't carry meanings, which we attempted to expose and fly in the face of, in part by marking whiteness. It didn't entirely work, and I can't help but wonder that if we had been thinking more dynamically about the operations of whiteness, we could have come up with more effective strategies for exposing the politics of race.

NOTES

1. WOW is not a collective in the sense of a unified theater organization. Instead, it is primarily a space where women can present work in progress. Any woman can become a member of the collective simply by showing up at meetings and working in different capacities on the season's shows. For more details on how WOW is organized, how it functions, and the kinds of work presented there, see my interviews with Peggy Shaw and Lois Weaver in W. B. Worthen, ed., *Modern Drama: Plays/Criticism/Theory* (Fort Worth: Harcourt Brace, 1995), pp. 1003–8. Shaw says, "The basis for WOW [is] the built in system of anarchy . . . it's very hard to build in a system of anarchy. Everyone wants to make something something" (p. 1004).

2. At the 1981 festival, work was presented by women's groups from England, Finland, Italy, Sweden, and New Zealand, as well as from the east coast cities of Baltimore; Boston; Ithaca, NY; Northampton, MA; and Washington, DC. Work by African American women from New York City included the Flamboyant Ladies Theatre Company (Brooklyn) with Gwendolen Hardwick, and "Edwina Lee Tyler and a Piece of the World," which was billed as "an all black women's percussion and dance

troupe." Programs from both festivals and from virtually every subsequent WOW performance are on file at the Lesbian Herstory Archives in Brooklyn, NY.

3. WOW's concern about the participation of women of color has focused primarily on African American women, not because WOW collapses all women of color into black women, but because of the precedent set by WOW's original festivals and also because some other women of color have participated over the years (certainly more so than African American women have, though not in significant numbers), like Alina Troyano a.k.a. Carmelita Tropicana, Reno, and the group East Coast Asian Lesbians. At the same time, as Elizabeth Abel has suggested, white women need to examine their desires and investments vis-à-vis women of color. See Elizabeth Abel, "Black Writing, White Reading: Race and the Politics of Feminist Interpretation," *Critical Inquiry* 19 (1993): 470–98. In the case of WOW, this would mean examining where the desire to include African American women comes from, and why, or to whom it is important that African American women participate in the collective.

4. Interview with Jewelle Gomez, New York City, August 6, 1992.

5. Lynda Hart, *Fatal Women: Lesbian Sexuality and the Mark of Aggression* (Princeton, NJ: Princeton University Press, 1994), pp. 117, 112 (italics in original). Hart discusses this distinction in her analysis of the film *Single White Female*.

6. Joan W. Scott, "Experience," in Judith Butler and Joan W. Scott, eds., *Feminists Theorize the Political* (New York: Routledge, 1992), pp. 25–26. See also Teresa de Lauretis, "Semiotics and Experience," in her *Alice Doesn't: Feminism, Semiotics, Cinema* (Bloomington: Indiana University Press, 1984), pp. 158–86.

7. One of the events at the 1981 Women's One World International Festival was listed in the program as follows: "Sex and Drag and Rock 'n' Roles (NYC). Jordy Mark presents her fantasies, her songs, her friends, *and* her wardrobe in a cabaret. With Pamela Camhe, The Sexaphones and many guests. You are encouraged to attend as your drag fantasy."

8. See Hilary Harris, "Toward a Lesbian Theory of Performance: Refunctioning Gender," in Lynda Hart and Peggy Phelan, eds., *Acting Out: Feminist Performances* (Ann Arbor: University of Michigan Press, 1993), pp. 257–76.

9. For her reading of this film, see Hart's chapter entitled "Why the Woman Did It: *Basic Instincts* and Its Vicissitudes," in her *Fatal Women*, pp. 124–34.

10. James Clifford, "Introduction: Partial Truths," in James Clifford and George E. Marcus, eds., *Writing Culture: The Poetics and Politics of Ethnography* (Berkeley and Los Angeles: University of California Press, 1986), p. 15 (Italics in original).

11. For an analysis of the operations of whiteness, among many other things, see Phelan's chapter entitled "The Golden Apple: Jennie Livingston's *Paris Is Burning*," in her *Unmarked: The Politics of Performance* (London: Routledge, 1993), pp. 93–111.

12. See my essays "Fe/male Impersonation: The Discourse of Camp," in Janelle G. Reinelt and Joseph R. Roach, eds., *Critical Theory and Performance* (Ann Arbor: University of Michigan Press, 1992), pp. 231–47, and "From *Lady Dick* to Ladylike: The Work of Holly Hughes," in Hart and Phelan, eds., *Acting Out*, pp. 55–84. References in both of these pieces will lead to additional sources for information on the WOW Cafe and work by the collective's members.

13. Kimberlé Crenshaw, "Whose Story Is It Anyway? Feminist and Antiracist Appropriations of Anita Hill," in Toni Morrison, ed., *Race-ing Justice, En-gendering Power:*

Essays on Anita Hill, Clarence Thomas and the Construction of Social Reality (New York: Pantheon, 1992), p. 412.

14. Hazel V. Carby, *Reconstructing Womanhood: The Emergence of the African American Woman Novelist* (New York: Oxford University Press, 1987), p. 27.

15. Crenshaw, "Whose Story Is It Anyway?" pp. 423, 429.

16. Patricia Hill Collins, *Black Feminist Thought: Knowledge, Consciousness, and the Politics of Empowerment* (New York: Routledge, 1990), p. 170.

17. Carby, *Reconstructing Womanhood*, p. 55. For conceptions of both black and white womanhood in the antebellum South, see Elizabeth Fox-Genovese, *Within the Plantation Household: Black and White Women of the Old South* (Chapel Hill: University of North Carolina Press, 1988), esp. pp. 50–66, 230–41, 292. She writes, "From slave women's perspective, the slaveholders' behavior arrogantly assimilated the essence of womanhood to the prerogatives of class and racial status" (p. 324).

18. Vincente L. Rafael posed this question during a closed session of the minority discourse resident fellows at the University of California Humanities Institute, Irvine, California, May 25, 1993. He was kind enough to allow me to quote him.

19. Dorothy Allison, *Trash* (Ithaca, NY: Firebrand Books, 1988), and *Bastard out of Carolina* (New York: Dutton, 1992). See also Mary Childers and bell hooks, "A Conversation About Race and Class," in Marianne Hirsch and Evelyn Fox Keller, eds., *Conflicts in Feminism* (New York: Routledge, 1990), pp. 60–81.

20. In "Demarginalizing the Intersection of Race and Sex: A Black Feminist Critique of Antidiscrimination Doctrine, Feminist Theory and Antiracist Politics," *University of Chicago Legal Forum,* 1989, pp. 139–67, Kimberlé Crenshaw gives an example of what I'm calling institutionalized whiteness in action, that is, in its role of rationalizing white control/domination at the intersection of class (a point I, not Crenshaw, am making). She writes, "During a recent and memorable discussion on the public policy implications of poverty in the Black community, one student remarked that nothing can be done about Black poverty until Black men stop acting like 'roving penises,' Black women stop having babies 'at the drop of a hat,' and they all learn middle-class morality" (p. 164, n. 70).

21. Richard Dyer's essay, entitled "White," appeared originally in *Screen* 29 (Fall 1988): 44–64. It is reprinted in his book *The Matter of Images: Essays on Representations* (London: Routledge, 1993), pp. 141–62. Page numbers cited in the text are from the *Screen* version.

22. Although this seemingly evokes the vampire, Dyer's "living dead" are the zombies that inhabit the film *Night of the Living Dead*. Unlike the passion and sensuousness typically associated with at least the male vampire, these zombies represent a more catatonic state.

23. Gillian Brown, *Domestic Individualism: Imaging Self in Nineteenth-Century America* (Berkeley and Los Angeles: University of California Press, 1990), pp. 3, 7.

24. Crenshaw, "Whose Story Is It Anyway?" p. 414.

25. Vron Ware, *Beyond the Pale: White Women, Racism and History* (London: Verso, 1992), p. 237.

26. Marilyn Frye, *Willful Virgin: Essays in Feminism, 1976–1992* (Freedom, CA: Crossing Press, 1992), p. 159. See the sections "Whiteliness and Class" and "Feminism and Whiteliness," (pp. 158–63), in which she draws different conclusions from some of the same points I address here.

27. If this is true and the meanings that adhere in "middle classness" are virtually the same as the meanings of a kind of institutionalized, "media-tized" whiteness, would it help to explain the criticism leveled at, for example, television programs that portray middle-class African American life (like *The Cosby Show*), for in some sense "being" white or aspiring to whiteness?

In "Passing for White, Passing for Black," *Transition: An International Review* 58 (1992): 6, Adrian Piper tells about walking through a black working-class neighborhood one day when a black teenager called out to her, "Hey, white girl! Give me a quarter!" She answered, "I'm not white and I don't have a quarter!" He replied, "You sure look white! You sure act white!" Piper is often mistaken for white because people think she looks white, but the perception (and, emphatically, not any notion of a performance) of acting white, it seems to me, is a function of the staunch middle-class background that Piper describes as hers. Middle classness may be mistaken for whiteness.

28. In her essay "Eccentric Subjects: Feminist Theory and Historical Consciousness," *Feminist Studies* 16 (Spring 1990): 129, Teresa de Lauretis writes, "The understanding of heterosexuality as an institution is a relatively recent development in feminist theory and not a widely accepted one among feminists." The apparatus and operations of heterosexuality as an institution are so fundamental a ground of feminist/lesbian theorizing that it is difficult to comprehend the categories "man" and "woman" without them. Lynda Hart takes it a step further when she contends that "heterosexuality, as an institution, is also an economy that maintains white supremacy" (*Fatal Women*, p. 117). I'm suggesting that white womanhood as an "institutional arm" of heterosexuality is the vehicle through which heterosexuality maintains white supremacy, as well as the venue where it is staged.

29. For example, Vron Ware writes, "Ida B. Wells was not interested in criticizing the behavior of the white women who were implicated in lynchings; her argument was based on the perception of white womanhood as an ideological component of American racism" (*Beyond the Pale*, p. 197).

30. Ruth Frankenberg's *White Women, Race Matters: The Social Construction of Whiteness* (Minneapolis: University of Minnesota Press, 1993) is an excellent example of this project of examining and questioning the racial specificity of whiteness.

31. Jennifer DeVere Brody pointed out to me that in contrast to Sharon Stone's "blonde Venus," Jeanne Tripplehorn has dark hair, dark features, and full lips. This strikes me as an enormously interesting reading of the film. Extrapolating from Brody's observation, I venture a racialization process in which Tripplehorn, although white, gestures toward and in some sense makes manifest what Toni Morrison calls an "Africanist presence" or a "theatrical presence of black surrogacy" that is the ground against which all portrayals of whiteness are constructed. See Jennifer DeVere Brody, *Playing in the Dark: Whiteness and the Literary Imagination* (New York: Vintage Books, 1992), pp. 3–28.

Although Stone's character's licentiousness is legendary, Tripplehorn's character is portrayed as the even scarier escapee from white womanhood so that, in the terms of the film, her punishment/death is "understandable." Tripplehorn's character invokes the sexual and moral degeneracy of the historically configured black woman.

It would be productive to examine such "racializations" in other films as well. For instance, I'm thinking of the lesbian "classic" *Desert Hearts,* in which the "innocent" straight women is blonde and fair and the "corrupting" lesbian who brings her into "the life" is dark haired with dark features. How do such imagings function to maintain an "Africanist presence" while excluding African American women?

32. Alisa Solomon, "Queer Justice," *Theatre Journal* 42 (1990): 366.

33. Evelyn Brooks Higginbotham, *Righteous Discontent: The Women's Movement in the Black Baptist Church 1880–1920* (Cambridge, MA: Harvard University Press, 1993), pp. 186, 15. I'm grateful to Amy Robinson for bringing Higginbotham's work to my attention.

34. Ibid., p. 14.

35. Robyn Wiegman, "Introduction: Mapping the Lesbian Postmodern," in Laura Doan, ed., *The Lesbian Postmodern* (New York: Columbia University Press, 1994), p. 18, n. 10. Wiegman suggests that this notion of "saturation" (for which I am indebted to her) is implicit in Spillers's essay "Mama's Baby, Papa's Maybe: An American Grammar Book," *Diacritics* 17 (Summer 1987): 8. "This problematizing of gender places her [female captive] . . . *out* of the traditional symbolics of female gender, and it is our task to make a place for this different social subject" (italics in original).

36. Lynda Hart writes, "Because the 'real' of female homosexuality was historically displaced onto women of color and working-class women, the white middle-class lesbian was considered an impossibility. And yet the lesbian, like the whore, is perceived as 'not-woman' and therefore also not 'really' white" (*Fatal Women*, p. 119).

37. Hazel V. Carby, "The Multicultural Wars," in Gina Dent, ed., *Black Popular Culture* (Seattle: Bay Press, 1992), p. 197.

38. Carby, *Reconstructing Womanhood*, p. 6. See also Paula Giddings, *When and Where I Enter: The Impact of Black Women on Race and Sex in America* (New York: Bantam Books, 1984), esp. pp. 46–55, 64–83, 119–31, 199–215.

39. For excellent histories, see Nancy F. Cott, *The Grounding of Modern Feminism* (New Haven, CT: Yale University Press, 1987); and Marjorie Spruill Wheeler, *New Women of the New South: The Leaders of the Woman Suffrage Movement in the Southern States* (New York: Oxford University Press, 1993). Cott writes, "Despite links between early woman's rights and anti-slavery reformers, the suffrage movement since the late nineteenth century had caved in to the racism of the surrounding society, sacrificing democratic principle and the dignity of black people if it seemed advantageous to white women's obtaining the vote" (p. 68). Wheeler not only cites multiple instances of white feminist betrayal of black women and their causes (pp. 21, 79, 101, 111–18, 131), but throughout her book she links upper- and middle-class ideology, historically, to white supremacy. I would argue that her work supports my notion that "middle classness" is a defining feature of (institutionalized) whiteness. Wheeler writes, "White suffragists believed that blacks were best served by deferring to the leadership of the best classes of Southern whites, who would represent their interests and protect them from the abuse of less enlightened whites" (p. 108).

40. Jacquelyn Dowd Hall, *Revolt Against Chivalry: Jesse Daniel Ames and the Women's Campaign Against Lynching* (New York: Columbia University Press, 1979), pp. 182, 155 (italics in original), 249.

41. See Chandra Talpade Mohanty, "Cartographies of Struggle: Third World Women and the Politics of Feminism," in Mohanty, Ann Russo, and Lourdes Torres, eds., *Third World Women and the Politics of Feminism* (Bloomington: Indiana University

Press, 1991), pp. 1–47; see also Ruth Farmer, "Place but Not Importance: The Race for Inclusion in Academe," in Joy James and Farmer, eds., *Spirit, Space & Survival: African American Women in (White) Academe* (New York: Routledge, 1993), pp. 196–217. Farmer writes: "[The] essential discussions which could lead to structural changes within academe do not take place. This necessary dialogue is avoided under the guise that it is too political for the educational forum. Problems shaped by racism, sexism, class oppression, heterosexism, and other forms of domination will only be solved through analysis of power dynamics and a commitment to altering power bases" (p. 198).

42. Michaela DiLeonardo, "White Fright," *Village Voice* 18 (May 1993): 40.

43. Carby, "The Multicultural Wars," p. 194.

14

If Uncle Tom Is White, Should We Call Him "Auntie"? Race and Sexuality in Postbellum U.S. Fiction

Warren Hedges

The andrometer was an impeccably Foucauldian device. During the Civil War, the U.S. Sanitary Commission used it to derive statistical standards for a variety of racial types, and as the accompanying illustration suggests, it both measured and confined.[1] Or rather, it confined *by* measuring. The discipline of anthropometry was also a means to discipline its subjects: by defining the boundaries of the normal, it implicitly consigned whatever lay beyond those bounds to categories like "abnormal" or "degenerate."[2] Consequently, the Sanitary Commission studies became the "scientific" basis for much of the racism that followed the Civil War.[3] Taking the findings about white men to represent the healthy norm, later theorists used the studies to "prove" the inferiority of Negroes, the atavism of Native Americans, and the degeneracy of mulattos.[4] In a dynamic central to racist thought, character traits were deduced from physical ones.

The attempt to link character traits to physical ones was also directed at white men, even if the aim was to underwrite white supremacy. In a society

226

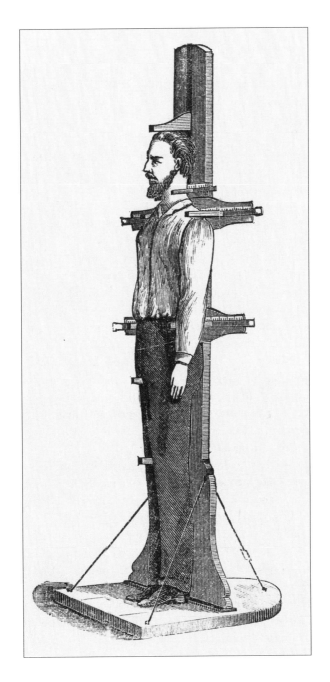

(White) man in andrometer. Picture taken from Benjamin Apthorp Gould, *Investigations in the Military and Anthropological Statistics of American Soldiers* (New York: Hurd and Houghton, 1869).

that equated African Americans with unbridled impulse, the portrayal of white men's bodies became ever more identified with their supposedly superior capacity for self-regulation. Then as now, the white norm depended not only on subordinating racial others without but also on expunging their supposed traits within. Racial norms operated by a double action, by violently excluding racial others from definitions of normalcy while simultaneously narrowing the range of acceptable white behavior. In this chapter, I illustrate the importance placed on eliminating the racial other within by examining an image that haunted men of the emerging Anglo middle classes: the white dissolute.

My examples of dissolutes are drawn primarily from nineteenth-century American realism, the genre of norms, standards, and middle-class experience.[5] I also am confining myself to discussing males to foreground the role that a nascent homophobia played in regulating white identity.[6] If white Anglo men were discouraged from acting "colorfully" in the late nineteenth century, the images of dissolution that discouraged them laid the cultural groundwork for the consequences of acting "flamboyantly" during the twentieth century. It has long been recognized that the late nineteenth century was a crucial period for creating the notion of "the" homosexual.[7] My work suggests that in the United States, the homophobic imagery structurally intertwined with the emergence of this new "species" (to use Foucault's term) had as much to do with racial norms as it did with norms of sex and gender. Behind the images and definitions defining and suppressing sexual "deviance," there was a legacy of images attempting to regulate racial deviance.[8]

To regulate the body politic, it was not enough for discourses like anthropometry to use white men as a standard and see racial others as imperfect and secondary. There also had to be a way of accounting for "irregular" white men. In particular, there was a need to explain white Anglo men who acted "colorfully" and thus called into question the "natural" differences between supposedly self-regulated white men and undisciplined racial and ethnic others. One way was to appeal to class distinctions, to claim that white men lacking discipline were not "really" white at all but a more soiled "white trash." Yet the white "dissolute" posed a problem (to racist ideology) precisely because his class credentials were impeccable but his self-discipline was not. Such characters were especially troubling to male realists, who based their claim of empirical authority on a professionalized notion of discipline that supposedly subordinated their own narrow interests (racial, class, and otherwise) to a set of professional procedures and self-restraints.[9]

Perhaps not surprisingly, a white dissolute is present in what is often taken to be the first realist novel in the United States, *Miss Ravenel's Conversion from*

Secession to Loyalty, by John William De Forest.[10] In it, Colonel Carter, a Union commander of Southern extraction, marries Miss Ravenel, fathers a child by her, then succumbs to drink, speculation, and an affair with another woman. These character flaws, and the cultural fears they evoked, are condensed in an almost allegorical description of Carter early in the novel:

> In some Arabian Nights or other, there is a story of voyagers in a becalmed ship who were drifted by irresistible currents towards an unknown island. As they gazed at it their eyes were deceived by an enchantment in the atmosphere, so that they seemed to see upon the shore a number of beautiful women waiting to welcome them, whereas these expectant figures were really nothing but hideous apes with carnivorous appetites, whose desire it was to devour the approaching strangers.
>
> As Miss Ravenel drifted towards Colonel Carter, she beheld him in the guise of a pure and noble creature, while in truth he was a more than commonly demoralized man, with potent capacities for injuring others. (p. 150)

The passage is striking for the equivalencies it implies: Carter = enchanter = woman = ape. It takes little more than a cursory knowledge of racism in the United States to name the next link in this chain, ape = black man. The images also capture the difficulty the dissolute posed to the mainstream racial logic of the time. He is a white man, too well educated to be dismissed as "trash," who behaves the way a black man, in racist discourse, is "naturally" supposed to behave.

In *Miss Ravenel's Conversion,* temperance discourse provides a way out of this ideological dilemma by suggesting that for an educated white man to act like the racist notion of a black man, some external, corrupting influence must be involved. Drink, the novel repeatedly stresses, is Carter's undoing. But although alcohol explains Carter's colorful behavior, it also raises the specter that many, perhaps all, white men could be similarly corrupted, causing a widespread breakdown in racial boundaries.

This worry frequently surfaces in the opinions of the heroine's father. Speaking of "the bibulous gentry of Louisiana," Dr. Ravenel remarks, " 'to think of those whiskey-soaked, negro-whipping, man-slaughtering ruffians, with a bottle of Louisiana rum in one hand and a cat-o'-nine-tails in the other . . . drunken, swearing, gambling, depraved as Satan, with their black helpmeets and mulatto children—to think of such ruffians prating about their sacred honor!' " (p. 47).

Here, drink breaks down character, leads to miscegenation, and destroys distinctions between black and white, civilization and savagery, sacred honor and inevitable decline. Similarly, Dr. Ravenel repeatedly refers to Southerners with metaphors emphasizing either savagery—as "Ashantee" idolaters (p. 50) who have a "redskin fury" (p. 123)—or paganism—the South as "Tyre and Babylon" (p. 114). These tropes of barbarism and Old Testament decadence dispute proslavery comparisons between the South and ancient slaveholding civilizations like Rome. Rather than defending slavery by equating white Southern interests with the protection and promulgation of "civilization," as proslavery apologists were wont to do, Ravenel portrays the South in Gibbonesque terms of imperial excess and decline, substituting "Ashantee" and intermarriage for Visigoths and Vandals. In other words, Ravenel attacks drink and slavery by evoking a racist fear of miscegenation and a subsequent breakdown in distinctions between "civilization" and "savagery."[11]

Temperance imagery like Dr. Ravenel's reflected both capitalist needs and an emerging racial standard. As John Rumbarger reports, temperance movements were influenced by "men of power and substance [who] . . . articulated and refined a utopian vision of society at the heart of which lay an abstemious and cooperative workforce perpetually manufacturing wealth for others."[12] The attack on alcohol was the flip side of the attempt to create a workplace with little room for precapitalist behaviors like taking unscheduled breaks or missing work to celebrate a saint's feast day. This was particularly true for recent immigrants being consolidated into the workforce and being pushed, as David Roediger persuasively argues, to give up precapitalist habits in exchange for racial privileges.[13] The regulation that temperance promoted was cultural as well as physical, as it attempted to shear off immigrant practices in order to create an increasingly bland notion of white respectability well suited to the industrial workplace.

Ravenel's comments illustrate how the imagery of white dissolution was a part of these disciplinary trends rather than a site of resistance to them. The specific terms he uses reflect both an indictment of the antebellum South and a horrified anxiety of what the republic might become if there were white privilege without self-discipline, and miscegenation without slavery. He ultimately unites the unholy trinity of drink, barbarism, and doom with the metaphor of Sodom:

> "Well, they [Southerners] are rushing to their doom," resumed the Doctor. . . .
> "They couldn't wait for whiskey to finish them, as it does other barbarous races. They must call on the political mountains to crush them. Their slaveholding Sodom will perish. . . . It must be razed and got out of the way, like any other obstacle to the progress of humanity." (p. 48)

If the call to raze Sodom goes out, can the accusation of sodomy be far behind?[14] To explore a time period when such an accusation might be made and to understand what it might mean, we must turn from De Forest's novel, with its heavy engagement with temperance and abolitionist imagery, and look to realist novels written later, during the rise of Jim Crow and a racially specific homophobia.

Mark Twain's *Pudd'nhead Wilson* and Charles Chesnutt's *The Marrow of Tradition* have several things in common.[15] Both were published during a time of increasing segregation and represent, in differing ways, the authors' attempts to come to grips with black disenfranchisement. Both are set in the South and have plots involving race, inheritance, and murder. And most significantly for our purposes, both feature dissolutes who, perhaps not coincidentally, are named Tom.

Although set in the antebellum South, the tensions that Twain's novel examines are results of the 1890s.[16] To summarize the plot: Two indistinguishable children, one legally white and one mulatto, are switched at infancy. Tom, the mulatto child, grows up believing that he is white, and Chambers, who legally should be Tom's master, lives as a slave.[17] To pay his gambling debts, Tom commits a series of robberies that culminate with the murder of his uncle. While investigating the murder, Pudd'nhead Wilson, a lawyer with a hobby of taking people's fingerprints (still a novelty when the story was written), discovers not only that Tom is the murderer but also that Tom and Chambers were switched at infancy. In a climatic trial, Wilson's evidence convicts Tom and restores Tom's and Chambers's proper racial and legal categorizations. Chambers, albeit awkwardly, moves into white society, and Tom is sold down the river.

Tom incarnates many of the fears of racial confusion expressed by antimiscegenationists like Dr. Ravenel in De Forest's novel. He differs from other "tragic mulattos" who discover their hereditary background in that he passes for white and, furthermore, passes for a specific kind of white person—a dissolute who drinks, gambles, and robs. In other words, he is a legally black person passing for a white person who acts like the racist idea of a black person. To complicate matters still more, when Tom commits some of his crimes, he does so in blackface. Specifically, when he murders his uncle, he escapes the house disguised as a black woman. At the very least, this profusion of categories and doublings is a parody of the legal definitions and distinctions of Jim Crow.[18] More important to our purposes, Tom's portrayal indicates that a disruption in racial categories also destabilizes categories of gender; blackface and cross-dressing, it seems, went hand in hand.[19]

To fully appreciate these connections between race and homophobia, we must consider Twain's novel in relation to Samuel Clemens's past life. Like the cultural distance between the treacherous, but hardly murderous, Colonel Carter in De Forest's 1867 novel and Tom Driscoll's violence, there is a distance between Clemens's behavior in the 1860s and his attitude toward it thirty years later. In the 1860s, heavy drinking, gender indeterminacy, and even blackface were a part of his environment that Clemens viewed as pleasurable and harmless. In the 1890s, he wrote a tale in which an alcoholic fop in burnt cork commits murder and is sold into slavery. Comparing these two moments illustrates how deeply the cultural links among dissolution, race, and male intimacy changed in the years between *Miss Ravenel's Conversion* and *Pudd'nhead Wilson*.

In a meticulously researched article, Twain biographer Andrew J. Hoffman details the gender flexibility that characterized Clemens's surroundings during his years in San Francisco and Virginia City, Nevada. The Bohemians with whom Twain identified and shared rooms, Hoffman writes, "lived marginally, drank excessively, espoused effete literary aesthetics, and boasted an especially high tolerance for sexual ambiguity" and even "lived in a social context which relished gender-role confusion." Using his evidence cautiously, Hoffman reconstructs a series of close relationships between the men in Twain's set and between Twain and a series of men with whom he shared rooms and often a bed, an unusual practice at the time for men with a fixed residence. When he was living with Dan De Quille, for instance, their relationship was close enough for a local newspaper to print the following spoof: "TO BE MAR-RIED—Dan De Quille and Mark Twain are to be married shortly. About time." Clemens also modeled his writerly and performance persona partially on the foppishly dressed, man-loving Artemus Ward, who visited Virginia City in 1863 and spent many a drunken night with De Quille and Clemens, at least one of which ended with the three of them in bed. Using this and other evidence, Hoffman suggests—and only suggests—the possibility that Clemens had sexual contact with other men during this period of his life. Although this possibility would advance my argument, what concerns me is easier to establish—that the period Hoffman documents, when Clemens's companions celebrated gender ambiguity, was also characterized by heavy drinking and a concern with racial crossings.[20]

Alcohol played an integral part in the intimacy that Clemens enjoyed with men like Ward and De Quille during the 1860s. Associates later boasted that Clemens consumed "gallons" of whiskey, and one of his (poorly chosen) character references for his fiancée's family predicted that he "would fill a drunkard's grave."[21] In *Mark Twain: The Bachelor Years,* Margaret Sanborn describes the nightly "cruises" that Clemens, De Quille, and other reporters took in search of news, food, and drink, and the general mix of alcohol, male intimacy, and professional rivalry that characterized Clemens's life as a reporter.[22] While in Virginia City, Clemens and De Quille belonged to an informal drinking club first dubbed Companions of the Jug and then, later, The Visigoths.

In fact, the nickname Mark Twain may be traced back to these drinking days. Although Clemens later claimed a boatman's sounding as the inspiration, there is some evidence that the pseudonym originally referred to the chalk marks that bartenders used to keep track of Clemens's drinks, which it was a trademark of sorts for him to take "in twain."[23] During this period Clemens also encountered Neil Moss, a figure from his past who was a partial model for Tom Driscoll in *Pudd'nhead Wilson.* Like Tom, Neil had gone to Yale and returned to Missouri sporting affectations and fine clothing, but when Clemens ran into him in the West, he had descended to a life of drifting and begging.[24]

Although the Mark Twain that modernists celebrated was known for his drinking, Clemens's attitude toward alcohol after the 1860s may have been more ambivalent.[25] He sometimes marched in temperance parades;[26] both his mother and sister were involved in the Women's Christian Temperance Movement;[27] and his portrayals of heavy drinkers are often tinged with a repugnance linked to race.

In *The Adventures of Huckleberry Finn,* Pap is a dissolute who also repels because of his whiteness: "There warn't no color in his face, where his face showed; it was white; not like another man's white, but a white to make a body sick, a white to make a body's flesh crawl—a tree-toad white, a fish-belly white."[28]

Later, Pap's drunken monologue against a "govment" that allows a freed black college professor to vote parodies the notion that white privilege rests on an innate capacity for self-regulation. During his speech, Pap acts "black," whereas the well-dressed professor to whom he refers is a model of civilized deportment. What then, are we to make of Tom Driscoll, a dissolute who not only acts "black" but turns out to be black and is not above wearing his mother's dresses to boot?

Among other things, Driscoll may be a doppelgänger for a younger Clemens. Tom's drinking leads to a miscarried duel that recalls a similar duel that Clemens claimed forced him to leave Nevada but may actually have been a cover story for a falling-out with Dan De Quille. In the novel Tom accompanies Luigi and Angello, the Italian twins, to an antitemperance rally. While there, he becomes "almost idiotically" merry with alcohol, insults the twins, and finds himself booted off the stage by the irate Luigi. When Tom takes Luigi to court rather than dueling him, it so offends his uncle's aristocratic pretensions that he disinherits his nephew and challenges Luigi himself, initiating a rivalry that will allow Tom to frame Luigi for his uncle's murder.

Just as drunkenness and a duel challenge precipitated Judge Driscoll's break with Tom, they apparently played a role in De Quille's break with Clemens, although in this case the duel challenge arose because of a racial insult. While living with De Quille in Virginia City, Clemens attended a fund-raiser in Gold Hill for the same U.S. Sanitary Commission that conducted the anthropometric studies mentioned earlier. According to a local paper, Clemens and other "bibulous reporters . . . came in a free carriage, ostensibly for the purpose of taking notes, but in reality in pursuit of free whiskey." [29] Later that evening Clemens jotted down a report repeating a joke he had heard about a fund-raiser for the commission: "It was stated that the money raised at the Sanitary Fancy Dress Ball, recently held in Carson . . . had been diverted from its legitimate course, and was to sent to aid a Miscegenation Society somewhere in the East." [30]

This remark may have been a dig at some of the Carson City nobs' pro-Confederacy sentiments, for by this time in California—following a logic not unlike Dr. Ravenel's account of Southern depravity—"miscegenationist" functioned as a label for Southern sympathizers. [31] (There is also the intriguing possibility that part of the crowd in which Clemens heard the remark made might have been in blackface.) [32] Clemens probably had no intention of publishing the article. According to his account, he laid it aside, and a foreman, mistaking it for copy, printed it without his knowledge. In any case, the slur created enough of an uproar to involve him in a duel challenge with James Laird, the editor of a rival paper. Whether or not an actual duel nearly took place is uncertain, but just as in *Pudd'nhead Wilson,* the original insult was the inadvertent result of drunkenness. In a letter to his sister-in-law, Clemens confessed that he "was not sober" when he composed the article. [33]

Most Twain biographers assume that Clemens left Nevada at this time to avoid running afoul of the territory's antidueling laws. Yet Hoffman notes that after Clemens left with another companion named Steve Gillis, De Quille cut Clemens off entirely, refusing to answer his letters and taking up with the reporter Alf Doten. Quotations from Doten's journals are Hoffman's most convincing evidence that romantic involvements in Clemens's former set went considerably beyond nineteenth-century conventions of male friendship. [34] But whatever De Quille felt for Clemens seems to have been terminated when

Clemens left Nevada with Gillis, and the account of his departure that Clemens later encouraged (with Gillis's help)[35] highlighted alcohol and dueling, perhaps to downplay the possibility of a dispute, maybe a jealous one, between Clemens and De Quille.

If alcohol, male intimacy, and a rhetoric of racial crossings underlay events surrounding Clemens's falling out with De Quille, these factors were equally integral to his interactions with Artemus Ward. Shortly after his stay with Clemens and De Quille, Ward sent Clemens the following note:

> My dearest Love,—I arrived here yesterday a.m. at 2 o'clock. It is a wild, untamable place, but full of lion-hearted boys. . . .
>
> Why did you not go with me and save me that night?—I mean the night I left you drunk at that dinner party. I went and got drunker, beating, I may say, Alexander the Great in his most drinkinist days, & I blackened my face at the Melodeon, and made a gibbering, idiotic speech. . . .
>
> Why would you make a good artillery man? Because you are familiar with Gonorrhea (gunnery). . . . Some of the finest intellects in the world have been blunted by liquor.
>
> Whiskey, Sir, is your bane. But no doubt you have derived a good deal of pleasure from your bane.[36]

In the intimate tone of the letter, Ward moves from drink to minstrelsy before alluding to Clemens's sexuality and the pleasures that accompany whiskey, almost as if alcohol were the medium that made such intimacy possible. Furthermore, on at least one occasion, Clemens appears to have been the one corking Ward's drunken face. Writing in the *Overland Monthly* in 1915, William Corey recalled that "it was hardly fair in Clemens, with the lecture hour drawing near, to get Ward hopelessly drunk, black his face with burnt cork and then thrust him out before his waiting audience."[37] If alcohol was a medium of intimacy between the men, blackface may have been one of its markers.

Historians like W. C. Green and David Roediger have written that Irish and German characters' giving way to black ones on the minstrel stage helped consolidate formerly distinct European ethnicities into a common whiteness. But Roediger also contends that blackface gave mechanics—a designation that included printers and reporters like the young Clemens—a means of embodying, at least temporarily, preindustrial behaviors without sacrificing their emerging racial privileges. "The growing popular sense of whiteness," he writes, "represented a hesitantly emerging consensus holding together a very diverse white working class and that part of that consensus derived from the idea that blackness could be made permanently to embody the preindustrial past that they scorned and missed."[38] If blackface was a strategy to indulge temporarily in preindustrial pleasures, Clemens's and Ward's behavior suggests that one of those vanishing pleasures may have been an undisciplined intimacy between men. This would also be compatible with Eric Lott's impressive account of how minstrelsy served as a structuring vehicle for desire both between white men and by white men toward black men.[39]

For Clemens in the 1860s, the pleasures of heavy drinking and male companionship included, at least once, blacking up a companion. Thirty years later, after he married into an abolitionist family and was living in an upper-class community, blackface played a far different role in his fiction. Tom Driscoll, who was white in early drafts of the novel's opening chapters,[40] not only dons blackface but turns out to be black and is sold down the river with ruthless efficiency.

Critics have debated the extent to which this ending and the fact that Tom is partially African American compromise the novel's critique of Jim Crow. More to our purpose, however, is the way that the temperance imagery on which Clemens draws to critique Tom himself resembles the homophobia that would build on and succeed temperance as a primary means of surveilling and controlling white Anglo male behavior. Writing about the historical development of racism in the context of an increasing emphasis on (white) self-discipline, Roediger states that "Americans cast Blacks as their former selves."[41] For Clemens in the 1890s, Tom may need to be discarded and sold down the river not because he is a black man but because he is a drunken man in blackface representing a time of Clemens's life—indeed, a former self—that had become increasingly threatening, especially in a book published the same year in which Oscar Wilde's trial began.

Published six years after *Pudd'nhead Wilson,* Charles Chesnutt's *The Marrow of Tradition* is in some ways a response to the earlier book. Instead of Tom Driscoll, we have Tom Delamere, who also drinks heavily, has gambling debts, lives with a scion of Southern gentility who is not his father (in this case, his grandfather), is worried about losing his inheritance, and dons blackface to commit a robbery that ends in the murder of a prominent white citizen. Rather than depicting the antebellum South, Chesnutt's novel refers to a historical event, the 1898 riots in Wilmington, North Carolina, that left at least eleven African Americans massacred, scores of others wounded, and still more homeless. This contemporary referent allows Chesnutt to detail the lethal consequences of black disenfranchisement more directly than *Pudd'nhead Wilson* does. Moreover, since Delamere has no African ancestry, Chesnutt can use him as a clear example of the hypocrisy underlying white supremacy's equation between "pure" blood and "civilization."

As Eric Sundquist notes, "Against the common charge that postbellum blacks and especially mulattos were a retrogressive or 'degenerate' species, likely without careful regulation by white civilization to revert to the purported savagery of their African ancestors, Chesnutt ranges the obvious degeneration of the Old South's aristocratic descendants, particularly Tom Delamere." Chesnutt's novel, Sundquist goes on to argue, focuses on the violently farcical role that "pure" bloodlines and inheritance played in the context of white men's ability to father unacknowledged children by black women.[42]

In fact, the editorial by black newspaper publisher Alexander Manly that helped spark the Wilmington massacre pointed out this very contradiction: "You [white men] set yourselves down as a lot of carping hypocrites. . . . You cry aloud for the virtue of your women while you seek to destroy the morality of ours. Don't think ever that your women will remain pure while you are debauching ours. You sow the seed—the harvest will come in due time."[43]

Chesnutt's portrait of Delamere, the dissipated offspring of a once upright family, captures with devastating accuracy the white anxieties about vitality, birthright, and power that helped fuel massacres like the one in Wilmington. His first appearance in blackface comes at a cakewalk where neither the white audience nor the other performers, who are black, recognize his disguise. The cakewalk is staged for Northern visitors, who earlier in the day were treated to their hosts' thoughts on black racial decline. Specifically, the prominent citizens of "Wellington" lament "the disappearance of the good old negro of before the war, and . . . the degeneracy of his descendants" and sigh over the sad "spectacle of a dying race, unable to withstand the competition of a superior type."[44]

Chesnutt's emphasis on the persecution that is the real cause of any decline in black vitality makes it impossible to understand these remarks without an irony underscored by Tom's blackface performance. If the new generation of African Americans are reputedly "degenerate," then what future for white Anglo men does Tom represent? Similarly, the novel opens with the aged wife of Major Carteret, another fixture of the white gentility, unexpectedly giving birth to a long-hoped-for heir. A sickly infant, Theodore Carteret is imperiled throughout the novel and lies in danger of death at its close. Although Tom may have "breeding" by right of birth and social position, his ability to breed— to hold onto wealth and transmit it to a white heir—is doubtful, as is the vitality of children like Theodore. In Chesnutt's account, the "inevitable" decline of the black race is a farce maintained by violence, a murderous projection of white Anglo anxiety about race suicide and cultural decline onto imperiled bodies of African Americans.

The specter leading to these white anxieties has a shape that should, by now, be recognizable. After Tom wins the cakewalk with his antics, he celebrates by doing an impromptu "buck dance" (p. 118). This label has an irony of which even Chesnutt was probably unaware, for earlier in the century, "buck" was a designation for a (white) fop and only gradually came to be applied to black men.[45]

Like *Pudd'nhead Wilson's* Tom Driscoll, and blackface performers more generally, Tom Delamere's actions recall earlier, preindustrial behavior now prohibited by an equation between self-discipline and racial privilege. But even more than with Driscoll, Delamere's lack of discipline is associated with deviating from masculine norms: "Tom Delamere . . . was easily the handsomest young man in Wellington. But no discriminating observer would have characterized his beauty as manly. It conveyed no impression of strength, but it did possess a certain element, feline rather than feminine, which subtly negatived [*sic*] the idea of manliness" (p. 16).

The language here is important: Delamere is presented not in terms of gender inversion, as when Driscoll dons a dress along with his blackface, but as possessing something that "subtly negatived the idea of manliness." The unease occasioned by the white dissolute has begun to shift from behavior and gender convention to something more intangible, a question of addictive compulsion and also a subtle inclination that attacks the idea of manliness from within. To understand this shift from regulating external agents (alcohol and gambling) to scrutinizing internal characteristics and motivations, we must turn to that great late-nineteenth-century text of racialized discipline and interspecular male desire, Melville's *Billy Budd*.

No dissolute, Billy is drawn into a mechanism of intermale scrutiny that nonetheless renders him suspect, drives him to commit a murder, and hangs him for his lack of discipline. Because I cannot discuss *Billy Budd* in detail here, I will draw on Eve Sedgwick's account of the text as an exemplary one for understanding the contradictions that shape North Atlantic sexual definitions in the modern era.[46] What interests me is that this pivotal text for understanding emerging dynamics and contradictions of male sexuality is also saturated with the imagery of race.

First, we should note that Billy is a figure of exemplary whiteness, or to use Melville's more frequent term, rosiness. We are introduced to Billy by way of a meditation on the "handsome sailor," but the prior example of this category is not white, rather, a man "so intensely black that he must needs have been a native African of the unadulterate blood of Ham."[47] Yet unlike Billy, the black sailor's crewmates' veneration contains little possibility of tragedy.[48] Billy, in contrast, is not white but is "cast in a mold peculiar to the finest physical examples of those Englishmen in whom the Saxon strain would seem not at all to partake of any Norman or other admixture" (p. 1360). Despite his "rose-tan," Billy is "welkin-eyed" with "curled flaxen locks" recalling primitive Britons (pp. 1422, 1354, 1423–24). These passages also demonstrate Melville's use of a British ship to emphasize the specifically "Anglo-Saxon" purity undergirding white supremacy in the United States.[49]

Billy's racial purity encourages metaphors of femininity, but the implied narrator stresses that these comparisons are analogies and not equivalencies. Budd's face is "all *but* feminine in purity of natural complexion." His situation is "*analogous* to that of a rustic beauty transported from the provinces," although he "has as much of masculine beauty as one can expect anywhere to see; nevertheless, *like* the beautiful woman in one of Hawthorne's minor tales, there was just one thing amiss in him" (pp. 1359, 1360, 1362, italics added). Like Chesnutt, Melville struggles to define something akin to, but different from, gender inversion, although unlike Chesnutt he places this something in the context of interactions between men and not in Billy's character itself.

Billy's innocence is repeatedly stressed by images such as Captain Vere's opinion that "in the nude [Billy] might have posed for a statue of young Adam before the Fall" (p. 1400). But whatever racial and theological purity Billy may embody, he finds himself subject to a scrutiny that eventually results in his death. Or to put it more accurately, the racial purity that Billy embodies invites an intense scrutiny, which in turn invites disciplinary action. As Sedgwick points out, Billy is subject to two tiers of disciplinary surveillance: a one-on-one, paranoiac scrutiny epitomized by Claggart's desires and the logic of entrapment that structures them, and a more "spectacular one of exemplary violence, the male body elevated for display."[50]

In regard to the ship's master of arms, we should note that the quality in Billy that so rouses Claggart's envious desire is packaged in a racialized form:[51] "to him [Claggart] the spirit lodged within Billy, and looking out from his welkin eyes as from windows, that ineffability it was which made the dimple in his dyed cheek, suppled his joints, and dancing in his yellow curls made him preeminently the Handsome Sailor" (p. 1385). Similarly, when Claggart insinuates to Captain Vere that Budd may be guilty of mutinous sentiments, he calls attention to racial characteristics: "You have but noted his fair cheek. A mantrap may be under the ruddy-tipped daisies" (p. 1400). A mantrap indeed, but for whom? Billy's comeliness may captivate others' admiration, but he is the one who ends up in irons. His very aesthetic distinctiveness elevates his rosy body to a visibility that is dangerous.

At the moment of Billy's maximum elevation, when he is hanged for inadvertently killing Claggart, Melville's theological imagery is colored with an Anglo-Saxon palette:

> [When the signal was given,] it chanced that the vapory fleece hanging low in the East was shot through with a soft glory as of the fleece of the Lamb of God seen in mystical vision, and simultaneously therewith, watched by the wedged mass of upturned faces, Billy ascended; and ascending, took the full rose of dawn. (p. 1427)

Later, when Billy is buried at sea, "the fleece of low-hanging vapor had vanished, licked up by the sun that late had so glorified it. And the circumambient air in the clearness of its serenity was like smooth white marble in the polished block not yet removed from the marble-dealer's yard" (p. 1431). This transition, from rosy martyr to a standardized, unremarkable mortuary white, captures the return to anonymity and colorlessness that discipline, now restored, on the *Bellipotent* entails. It also highlights the links between homophobia and Jim Crow: a white man who is too visible, undisciplined, or colorful can almost at any time, and regardless of his intentions, become a white man lynched.

Melville's text is especially disturbing because it underscores the point that Billy's own character and desires have a negligible effect on the disciplinary mechanism that surrounds and destroys him. Instead, disciplinary structures themselves generate and depend on homophobia. And when this homophobia is coupled with the racist equivalency between white Anglo manhood and self-governance, white men rightly or wrongly identified as refusing to endorse a rigid, colorless self-control become homophobia's most visible, although hardly sole, target.

Let me be clear—I do not mean to insinuate that white men are more likely to be the objects of homophobic violence than other men are. On the contrary, it is white men's normative privileges that make so distinctive the spectacle of one homophobically punished (Oscar Wilde on trial, Billy swaying from the yardarm). It shocks to the degree that it underscores the narrow base on which white male privilege rests, an apprehension all the more anxious because, like Billy, one can never be certain that one is not alarming a companion or failing to live up to what Chesnutt perceptively called "the idea of manliness." [52] The price of white Anglo privilege, it seems, is conformity to a kind of blandness (I cannot help thinking of fraternity boys with their T-shirts and baseball caps) that is simultaneously a defense against homophobic scrutiny.

If Billy, the white man lynched, functions as both martyr and warning, it seems to me that the most comparable figure today occurs in the popular imagery of AIDS, which normatively focuses on a tubercularly white, dying, gay male. Despite activists' repeated attempts to remind the general public that HIV/AIDS strikes people of many nations and orientations, the mass gaze in the United States always seems to swing back to this figure. For example, consider that one of the first prominent discussions of combating HIV/AIDS in the African American community was entitled "AIDS in Blackface."[53]

My work indicates that this iconography may have deep cultural roots. To choose just two examples: The horrifying belief that gay men deserve to die as punishment for their lack of sexual restraint seems linked to notions that most gay men are white, unrestrained in their desires, and, like the images of the white dissolute, always and already associated with death. Similarly, many African Americans, discussed even in Chesnutt's time as "a dying race, unable to withstand the competition of a superior type,"[54] are confronted with a general public indifference to their deaths in any case, much less deaths from a disease that few of their kind are widely represented as having. Or whose deaths—in a metaphorics stretching back to at least the nineteenth century—are written off as part of a naturalized affinity for addictive substances (alcohol then, crack and intravenous drugs now) or as a genocidal antidote to an imagined unrestrained fecundity that reflects white Anglo fears of reproductive competition from darker-skinned people. Although associations such as these are not hegemonic, they are enduring. I hope that by understanding their history, we will not be doomed, literally, to repeat them.

NOTES

1. The U.S. Sanitary Commission studies were distinguished by their scope and the consistency of their equipment and procedures. Using standardized equipment, researchers took "anthropometric" measurements of almost nineteen thousand soldiers— "1,146 white sailors, 68 white marines, 2,020 full-blooded Negroes, 863 mulattos, and 519 Indians"—recording proportions such as the "breadth of the pelvis," the "ratio of leg to arm," the "height to Pubes," and the slope of the forehead. Benjamin Apthorp Gould, *Investigations in the Military and Anthropological Statistics of American Soldiers* (New York: Hurd and Houghton, 1869), pp. 218–320. See also John S. Haller, *Outcasts from Evolution: Scientific Attitudes of Racial Inferiority, 1859–1900* (Champaign-Urbana: University of Illinois Press, 1971), pp. 27–28; and Charles J.Stilli, *History of the United States Sanitary Commission: Being the General Report of Its Work During the War of Rebellion* (Philadelphia: Lippincott, 1866), pp. 451–69.

At first it might seem surprising that these studies were carried out by the Sanitary Commission, but on reflection it makes sense. Sanitation, after all, attempts to regulate bodies and their behavior. With its metaphors of health and pollution, cleanliness and contagion, integrity and dissolution, sanitation has a long history in the discourse of social control, cordoning off external threats to the body politic and policing its internal behavior. Tropes of sanitation typically venerate an ideal of impossible purity—the contagion eliminated, the foreign pollutants ejected, the boundaries of the body secure and impregnable. Consequently, sanitation metaphors have played a part in a variety of pogroms in the United States, whether to quarantine the immigrant "hordes," round up "degenerate" prostitutes, deprive "lascivious" black men of their rights, or ward off an endless succession of nebulous threats to the nation's boundaries. If cleanliness is next to godliness, frequently the ideal is to identify and eliminate all traces of dirt, darkness, or other irregularities.

2. For more on how the accumulation of knowledge is simultaneously an expression of power, see Michel Foucault, *The Order of Things: An Archaeology of the Human Sciences* (New York: Vintage Books–Random House, 1973), and *Discipline and Punish*, trans. Alan Sheridan (New York: Vintage Books–Random House, 1979).

3. Haller, *Outcasts from Evolution*, pp. 26–27.

4. Ibid., pp. 3–40. See also Thomas F. Gosset, *Race: The History of an Idea in America* (New York: Schocken Books, 1975), pp. 54–83.

5. Literary realism is an especially appropriate starting point for this inquiry because it, no less than anthropometry, tried to define what Mark Seltzer calls "statistical persons"—normative types or case studies illustrating how the social acts on or through the body. See Mark Seltzer, *Bodies and Machines* (New York: Routledge, 1992), pp. 91–118.

6. This is not to suggest that homophobia was new at the time, only that it was beginning to enter a modern phase tethered to notions of "the" homosexual, an identity in which sexual desires were thought to play a pervasive and determinative role.

7. As Foucault famously put it, "The psychological, psychiatric, medical category of homosexuality was constituted from the moment it was characterized—Westpahl's famous article of 1870 . . . can stand as its date of birth. . . . The sodomite had been a temporary aberration; the homosexual was now a species." Michel Foucault, *An Introduction*, vol. 1 of *The History of Sexuality*, trans. Robert Hurley (New York: Vintage Books–Random House, 1980), p. 43. Even if, as Eve Sedgwick has pointed out, the search for an exact paradigm shift is fruitless, the late nineteenth century nonetheless remains the period when predominant twentieth-century notions of sexuality and identity were first formally reified.

8. I by no means wish to claim that racial images are the only genealogy for later homophobic ones, only that this aspect has been previously overlooked.

9. For more on realism, class, and professionalism, see Warren Hedges, "Howells's 'Wretched Fetishes' ": Character, Realism, and Other Modern Instances," *Texas Studies in Literature and Language* 38 (Spring 1996): 26–50.

10. John William De Forest, *Miss Ravenel's Conversion from Secession to Loyalty* (New York: Harper, 1939) (subsequent page references to this book are cited in parentheses). Amy Kaplan, "Nation, Region, and Empire," in Cathy N. Davidson, Patrick O'Donnell, Valerie Smith, and Christopher P. Wilson, eds., *The Columbia History of the American Novel* (New York: Columbia University Press, 1991), pp. 240–41; Robert E. Spiller et al., *Literary History of the United States* (New York: Macmillan, 1953), p. 881.

11. The fictional doctor's particular combination of abolitionism and racism was by

no means atypical. For a discussion of similar attitudes in abolitionist circles, see Michael Fellman, "Theodore Parker and the Abolitionist Role in the 1850s," *Journal of American History* 61 (1974): 666–84. Like Ravenel, Parker and his peers viewed Southerners as "degenerate" because of their practice of "diluting" Anglo-Saxon blood through miscegenation, and they compared their impending decline with that of Rome. See also Gosset, *Race,* p. 60.

12. John J. Rumbarger, *Profits, Power, and Prohibition: Alcohol Reform and the Industrializing of America, 1800–1930* (Albany: State University Press of New York, 1989), p. xxii.

13. David R. Roediger, *The Wages of Whiteness: Race and the Making of the American Working Class* (New York: Verso, 1991), pp. 1–17, 95–132.

14. Recently, much excellent work has been done to historicize and explicate the meanings and rhetorical functions of the terms *Sodom* and *Sodomy.* In "New English Sodom," *American Literature* 64 (1992): 19–47, Michael Warner writes that Sodom functioned as a shadow image of the New English Zion that could never be banished entirely because of the way that the community was structured by affective, contractual ties between men (to vastly oversimplify his argument). Ed Cohen's equally helpful "Legislating the Norm: From Sodomy to Gross Indecency," *South Atlantic Quarterly* 88 (1989): 181–217, details the role that changing conceptions of sodomy played in consolidating the very kind of male norm that I discuss here with a greater emphasis on race.

15. Mark Twain, *Pudd'nhead Wilson* and *Those Extraordinary Twins,* ed. Sidney E. Berger, *Norton Critical Edition* (New York: Norton, 1980). Charles Chesnutt, *The Marrow of Tradition* (Ann Arbor: University of Michigan Press, 1969). For an excellent discussion of both novels as responses to Jim Crow, see Eric Sundquist, *To Wake the Nations* (Cambridge, MA: Belknap–Harvard University Press, 1993).

16. See Susan Gilman, *Dark Twins: Imposture and Identity in Mark Twain's America* (Chicago: University of Chicago Press, 1989), pp. 14–53; Sundquist, *To Wake the Nations,* pp. 225–71; and Arthur G. Pettit, "The Black and White Curse: *Pudd'nhead Wilson* and Miscegenation," in *Pudd'nhead Wilson* and *Those Extraordinary Twins,* pp. 346–60.

17. Technically, the mulatto child is really Chambers, instead of Tom, the child he replaces, and vice versa. However, since he is referred to as "Tom" for most of the story, I will refer to him as "Tom" as well.

18. Although Twain's novel reflects a contemporaneous confusion about the role that heredity might play in Tom's actions, I agree with Fishkin's and other critics' reading that the novel disputes and complicates, rather than simply endorses, racist notions of hereditary determinism. Indeed, Twain's original manuscript at the Pierpont Morgan Library indicates that if heredity plays any role in Tom's actions, "that which was base was the white blood in him debased by the brutalizing effects of a long-drawn heredity of slave-owning, with the habit of abuse which the possession of irresponsible power always creates & perpetuates, by a law of human nature." Shelley Fisher Fishkin, *Was Huck Black? Mark Twain and African American Voices* (New York: Oxford University Press, 1993), p. 122. See also Gilman, *Dark Twins,* pp. 53–95.

19. Marjorie Garber writes about the ways that "the possibility of crossing racial boundaries stirs fears of the possibility of crossing the boundaries of gender, and vice

versa," in *Vested Interests: Cross-Dressing and Cultural Anxiety* (New York: Harper, 1993), p. 274, and the frequent female impersonation in minstrel troops (pp. 276–77). See also Eric Lott, *Love and Theft: Blackface Minstrelsy and the American Working Class* (New York: Oxford University Press, 1993), pp. 26–30, 53–54, 159–168.

While I am exploring the meaning of Tom's cross-dressing and blackface, I do not want to subsume his actions under a rubric of transvestitism and/or minstrelsy, or at least not subsume them too quickly. Doubtlessly, Tom's blacking his face and donning a dress addresses cultural concerns similar to those mediated by minstrels dressing up as black women. But the episodes about Tom are also motivated by highly specific concerns about dissipation, inheritance, and heredity. I also have some hesitation about applying the label *transvestitism* to every episode of cross-dressing, especially one to commit robbery, because I feel that it obscures the profoundly different meanings that cross-dressing carries in different communities and historical contexts.

Finally, we should note that Tom's foppishness as a white man destabilizes racial and gender categories, too. When he returns from Yale decked out in his finery, the town's response is to equip a black man in Zip Coonish attire to follow him (*Pudd'nhead Wilson and Those Extraordinary Twins*, p. 24). And although railing against foppishness has a long history in English letters (perhaps most paradigmatically in Carlye's *Sartor Resartus*), the 1890s also saw the emergence of the foppishly dressed "fairy" as a predominant opposition to "normal" male sexuality. See George Chauncey, *Gay New York: Gender, Urban Culture, and the Making of the Gay Male World, 1890–1940* (New York: Basic Books–HarperCollins, 1994), pp. 1–99. For an account of the conflicted and proliferating taxonomies of sexuality in late nineteenth and early twentieth centuries in the United States and Europe, see Jonathan Katz, *The Invention of Heterosexuality* (New York: Dutton–Penguin Books, 1995), pp. 1–112.

20. Andrew J. Hoffman, "Mark Twain and Homosexuality," *American Literature* 67 (1995): 27, 34, 32. Besides presenting his research, Hoffman's article discusses the ad hominem arguments that have been applied to him personally (instead of his evidence) and the motives and positions that have been irresponsibly assigned to him for presenting what is, on examination, an extremely cautious discussion of a possibility that, if it cannot be proved, cannot either, in light of the evidence, be ignored.

21. Paul Fatout, *Mark Twain in Virginia City* (Bloomington: Indiana University Press, 1964), p. 37; Justin Kaplan, *Mr. Clemens and Mark Twain: A Biography* (New York: Simon & Schuster, 1966), p. 91.

22. Margaret Sanborn, *Mark Twain: The Bachelor Years* (Garden City, NY: Doubleday, 1990), pp. 183–220.

23. Fatout, *Mark Twain in Virginia City*, pp. 34–39.

24. Sanborn, *Mark Twain: The Bachelor Years*, pp. 195–96. Later in life, Clemens noted that "at 30 [Moss] was a graceless tramp in Nevada, living by mendicancy and borrowed money. Disappeared." See Samuel Clemens, *Huck Finn and Tom Sawyer Among the Indians & Other Unfinished Stories*, The Mark Twain Library (Berkeley and Los Angeles: University of California Press, 1989), p. 94.

25. Except for a brief period when he was courting his wife-to-be Olivia, Clemens drank throughout most of his life, even celebrating his fondness for whiskey. The image of Mark Twain that has come down to us is of a man who took a genial pleasure in shocking his uptight contemporaries with his fondness for drinking, smoking, and

swearing. This enduring image, however, may mask a more ambivalent attitude on Clemens's part after the 1860s, one obscured by the critics and artists who accepted, elaborated, and helped propagate "Mark Twain" as a national icon and cultural hero. As early-twentieth-century critics and authors wrote about Twain, they almost uniformly celebrated and created a "western" Twain who drank heavily, debunked genteel vapidity, and resisted the "feminine" enervations of bourgeois culture. See Guy Cardwell, *The Man Who Was Mark Twain: Images and Ideologies* (New Haven, CT: Yale University Press, 1991), pp. 1–45, 97–122.

This image can be further historicized when we consider that the revolt against temperance and prohibition was a fundamental element of American modernism. Modernist writers and critics largely portrayed prohibition as the design of sectarian killjoys and middle-class prudes, but they failed to appreciate the role of temperance in eradicating immigrant customs and work habits, in attempting to produce a well-ordered industrial workforce, and in serving as a forum for women's concerns. See John William Crowley's *The White Logic: Alcoholism and Gender in American Modernist Fiction* (Amherst: University of Massachusetts Press, 1994); Rumbarger, *Profits, Power, and Prohibition*; and Barbara Leslie Epstein, *The Politics of Domesticity: Women, Evangelism, and Temperance in Nineteenth-Century America* (Middletown, CT: Wesleyan University Press, 1981).

26. Justin Kaplan, *Mr. Clemens and Mark Twain,* pp. 101–3.

27. See Laura Skandera-Trombley's excellent account of the Twains' connections to temperance and other reform movements, in her *Mark Twain in the Company of Women* (Philadelphia: University of Pennsylvania Press, 1994), pp. 105–30.

28. *The Adventures of Huckleberry Finn,* The Mark Twain Library (Berkeley and Los Angeles: University of California Press, 1985), p. 23.

29. Gold Hill *Daily News,* May 11, 1844. Cited in Fatout, *Mark Twain in Virginia City,* p. 188. See also chapter 45 of *Roughing It,* The Mark Twain Library (Berkeley and Los Angeles: University of California Press, 1993), which describes the Sanitary Commission's fund-raising auctions in the West; and Stilli, *History of the United States Sanitary Commission,* pp. 188, 236.

30. Reprinted in Fatout, *Mark Twain in Virginia City,* p. 196.

31. See ibid., pp. 197–98.

32. In her work on public gatherings in Philadelphia, Susan Davis comments on the practice of using blackface in parades and processions in the 1830s and 1840s. See her *Parades and Power: Street Theater in Nineteenth-Century Philadelphia* (Philadelphia: Temple University Press, 1986), pp. 105–11, and "Making Night Hideous: Christmas Revelry and Public Order in Nineteenth-Century Philadelphia," *American Quarterly* 34 (Summer 1982): 185–99.

Whether the processions surrounding the fund-raiser that Clemens attended (in which a sack of flour was paraded from town to town and then auctioned off, attracting large and festive crowds) generated similar practices half a continent away and a decade or two later is uncertain, but if they did, it would have given Clemens's remark about miscegenation an additional bite.

Margaret Watson describes several minstrel shows and troupes in Virginia City and Washoe County, in her *Silver Theatre: Amusements of the Mining Frontier in Early Nevada, 1850 to 1864* (Glendale, CA: Arthur Clark Co., 1964), pp. 185–86, 196–97; and

Anthony Berret reports that Twain listened to the San Francisco Minstrels during his western years, in his "Huckleberry Finn and the Minstrel Show," *American Studies* 27 (1986): 37–49. In fact, even the Mormons staged minstrel shows and blackface processions. See Michael Hicks, "Ministering Minstrels: Blackface Entertainment in Pioneer Utah," *Utah Historical Quarterly* 58 (1990): 49–63.

33. Edgar Marquess Branch, Michael B. Frank, and Kenneth M. Sanderson, eds., *1853–1866,* vol. 1 of *Mark Twain's Letters,* The Mark Twain Papers (Berkeley and Los Angeles: University of California Press, 1988), p. 288.

34. Andrew Hoffman conservatively states that "we can claim to know that Alfred Doten and others in his circle slept with both men and women quite freely, but we can only guess at what they did together or what they thought they meant by doing whatever they did." Hoffman, "Mark Twain and Homosexuality," p. 38.

35. See Sanborn, *Mark Twain: The Bachelor Years,* p. 237; and John Lauber, *The Making of Mark Twain: A Biography* (New York: American Heritage, 1985), p. 133.

36. Charles Farrar Browne (Artemus Ward) to Samuel L. Clemens, January 4, 1864. Although Hoffman quotes passages from the letter, the full text of it, and the source of my quotation, is David E. E. Sloane, "A Revisionist Perspective on Mark Twain," *Studies in American Humor* 2 (October 1975): 135–36.

37. William Corey, "Memories of Mark Twain," *Overland Monthly,* September 1915, p. 265.

38. Roediger, *The Wages of Whiteness,* pp. 118, 97; W. C. Green, " 'Jim Crow,' 'Zip Coon': The Northern Origins of Negro Minstrelsy," *Massachusetts Review* 11 (1970): 385–97.

39. See Lott, *Love and Theft,* pp. 51–55, 138–53, 159–68, and esp. pp. 147–48.

40. Hershel Parker, *Flawed Texts and Verbal Icons: Literary Authority in American Fiction* (Evanston, IL: Northwestern University Press, 1984), p. 129.

41. Roediger, *The Wages of Whiteness,* p. 95.

42. Sundquist, *To Wake the Nations,* pp. 408, 408–53.

43. Cited in H. Leon Prather Sr., *We Have Taken a City: Wilmington Racial Massacre and Coup of 1898* (Toronto: Associated University Presses, 1984), p. 73. Prather and other historians of the massacre make it clear that Manly's editorial was merely fodder for a larger, carefully orchestrated campaign against both African Americans and the Populist Party.

44. Chesnutt, *The Marrow of Tradition,* p. 114 (subsequent page references to this book are cited in parentheses).

45. See Roediger, *The Wages of Whiteness,* p. 99.

46. This is, of course, an oversimplification of numbing proportions. The first section of Eve Kosofsky Sedgwick's *The Epistemology of the Closet* (Berkeley and Los Angeles: University of California Press, 1990) is built around an extended reading of *Billy Budd* and should be read in full to understand her argument (or mine, for that matter).

47. Herman Melville, *Pierre; Israel Potter; The Piazza Tales; The Confidence Man; Uncollected Prose; and Billy Budd* (New York: Library of America, 1984), p. 1353 (subsequent page references to this book are in parentheses).

48. Here we might note the tendency in U.S. literature to have darker-skinned men serve as acceptable objects for white men's extended visual attention because of their

"exoticism" (Chingatchgook's striking features, Queequeg's tattoos). And although these same men often become targets of violence, this violence does not seem to implicate the white men who watch them, as it does with Claggart and Billy. In fact, racist discourse often figures watching men of color—whether to supervise slaves or workers, to "protect" white women, or to patrol for hostile Indians—as white men's primary function.

49. For example, *The Leopard's Spots: Romance of the White Man's Burden* (New York: Doubleday, 1902), Thomas Dixon's novel that helped reinvigorate the Ku Klux Klan, has the recurring refrain "You can not build in a Democracy a nation inside a nation of two antagonistic races. The future American must be an Anglo-Saxon or a Mulatto" (p. 383). For more on the Anglo-Saxon in Anglo-Saxon supremacy, see Gosset, *Race,* pp. 84–122.

50. Sedgwick, *The Epistemology of the Closet,* p. 104.

51. Some might argue that these categories are simply aesthetic, but such an argument would obscure the degree to which aesthetic categories of that time (and ours) are racial to begin with. See, for example, Sander Gilman, "Black Bodies, White Bodies: Toward an Iconography of Female Sexuality in Late Nineteenth-Century Art, Medicine, and Literature," in Henry Louis Gates Jr., ed., *"Race," Writing, and Difference* (Chicago: University of Chicago Press, 1986).

52. Eve Sedgwick sums up the dynamic underlying such homophobic terrorism: "Not only must homosexual men be unable to ascertain whether they are to be the object of 'random' homophobic violence, but no man must be able to ascertain that he is not (that his bonds are not) homosexual. In this way, a relatively small exertion of physical or legal compulsion potentially rules great reaches of behavior and filiation." Eve Sedgwick, *Between Men: English Literature and Male Homosocial Desire* (New York: Columbia University Press, 1985), p. 89.

53. The fact that an African American activist like Harlon Dalton could wander into this metaphor so blithely only underscores how deeply such imagery often operates.

54. Chesnutt, *The Marrow of Tradition,* p. 114.

15

Performing Men of Color: Male Autoperformance, Highways Performance Space, the NEA, and the White Right

Robert H. Vorlicky

America's art and culture are, more and more, openly anti-Christian, anti-American, nihilistic. . . . While the Right has been busy winning primaries and elections, cutting taxes and funding anti-communist guerrillas abroad, the Left has been quietly seizing all the commanding heights of American art and culture. . . . A nation absorbs its values through its art. A corrupt culture will produce a corrupt people, and vice versa; between rotten art, films, plays, and books—and rotten behavior—the correlation is absolute. The hour is late; America needs a cultural revolution in the 90's as sweeping as its political revolution in the '80s.

Patrick Buchanan, *Washington Times,*
May 22, 1989

EARLY AUGUST 1995

I received a donation request from the artistic leadership of Highways Performance Space in Santa Monica, California. It was an urgent call for funds in order to help Highways, an alternative arts environment, in their words, to "solidify our local base of support." Why? Highways' 1995 Ecco Lesbo/Ecco Homo Summer Festival programming, "specifically by artists of color, is being used as proof that the National Endowment for the Arts [NEA] must be eliminated." The opposition's strategy: The "radical Christian right . . . have sent copies of our calendar to every member of Congress. . . . For the first time ever, only one organization is being targeted—Highways"—for defunding.[1] Senator Nancy Kassebaum (Republican, Kansas), a "long-time leader in the fight for the NEA" and the current chair of the influential Senate Labor and Human Resource Committee (which makes direct recommendations to

A shorter version of this essay appeared in *the minnesota review* 47 (Spring 1997): 167–77.

congressional committees about the awarding of NEA funds), was quoted in Highways' appeal as having told the *Washington Post* that grants to Highways, specifically, had eroded her support: "I find it offensive to me . . . I strongly criticize using taxpayer dollars. It was not what we intended."

Although I'm neither a member of Congress nor a California resident, I've been receiving Highways' calendar, its schedule of events, for several years now. A quick glance at earlier calendars (which are characterized by their stylish graphics, captions that are tongue-in-cheek, campy, or provocative, and photographs of performers or production stills that are unadorned, playful, or tantalizing) suggests that a popular venue is the solo performance, as several are presented monthly at Highways by a range of artists. Among the various kinds of material that find their way into solo work, autobiographical content is noticeably favored in Highways' offerings. Although it is a predominant mode in the lesbian and gay summer schedule, autoperformance is also highly visible throughout the year. As an organization, Highways offers numerous workshops for Southern Californians that encourage any artist (gay, lesbian, bisexual, straight, transsexual, transgendered) to explore and develop autobiographical material into public performance. At Highways, the (speaking) subject is not only not dead, it is speaking out as though her or his life depended on it.

But it is the public claim to space by men's autoperformative voices—unlike the women's voices, which continue to strengthen and diversify a historically grounded, ongoing feminist movement of women's autoperformance—that seems, paradoxically, an unfamiliar, if not completely new, occurrence. After all, the control of public space has historically been claimed by men. But cultural mythologies and gendered codings, not personally defined autobiographies of diversified subjectivities, have generally grounded and determined men's experiences in these spaces. Highways, therefore, affords men the opportunity to redefine their place in public space through the performance of their lives.

> We know what that wonderful National Endowment for the Arts has been doing, that upholstered playpen of the arts and crafts auxiliary of the Eastern liberal establishment. They have been subsidizing both filthy and blasphemous art.　　　　　　　　　Patrick Buchanan, *Washington Times,*
> February 21, 1992

"We" know, don't we, about the NEA? And "we" know, don't we, the premises that shape Pat Buchanan's rhetorical style, his performance strategies?

Elin Diamond's paraphrase of Helene Cixous offers a way to understand the thinking behind Buchanan's 1992 remarks against the NEA (as well as those on the presidential campaign trail in 1996), a position echoed in the "logic" of Speaker of the House Newt Gingrich's conservative Republican–dominated Congress during the NEA debates of 1995–1996: "I lose nothing—there is no loss of self—rather I appropriate you, amplifying my 'I' into an authoritative 'we.' " This appropriation of "you" into "I" as "we," an "annihilation of difference," Diamond suggests, is also "violence to the other," including, of course, those whose gender, sexuality, race, class, religion, and so forth are different from those of the speaking "I" subject.[2]

By deconstructing the process underlying such an appropriation, we can also begin to understand, as Richard Dyer observes, "whiteness as a culturally constructed category," how the white "I" has been positioned as the universal "we." But as Dyer argues, "If the invisibility of whiteness colonizes the definition of other norms—class, gender, heterosexuality, nationality, and so on—it also masks whiteness as itself a category."[3]

Through a solo performance by a white body, a teasing out of its racial categorization is possible, if not self-evident. An identification of such a "category" is not solely dependent on language to define it, however; the body "speaks" (i.e., represents) itself. It is visible, it is marked, and it is susceptible to the scrutiny and gaze of the spectator. Its racial, sexual, or gendered "otherness," according to the conventions of solo performance, remains invisible and unmarked in current time and space.

Focusing their attack on the Ecco Lesbo/Ecco Homo Summer Festival at Highways in order to advance their political agenda, the vocal conservative right-wingers in Gingrich's Congress—most of whom are white, straight, and male—centered their attention on their movement's predictable, inflammatory objects: gays, lesbians, and people of color. But even though this particular festival—a program marked by its artists' race and sexual orientation—has galvanized the opposition's interests, it is no surprise that Highways and other such alternative spaces remain sitting ducks for the (white) reactionaries. Their ability to continue to get any federal funding has always hinged on how long a conservative majority could be kept from the elected ranks of lawmakers.

Among the range of their unconventional theatrical offerings that challenge traditional power structures, nonmainstream theater venues encourage, develop, and produce male autoperformers who—like their female counterparts—question the authority and reality of gender socialization and racial categories in America. Their embodied difference from white heteronormativity is clearly marked, and so they draw attention to the ruse of white neutrality by bringing race—as well as sexuality—into dialogue with gender. Race and sexuality become the markers by which the men can identify, can speak about the differences among themselves while, presumably, still collectively identifying as gendered men (or perhaps more accurately as biologically identified men). It is through the singular body of an autoperformer, whether explicitly or implicitly, that whiteness is marked, as Dyer notes, as a "category." It is also a category that contributes to the defining positionality of each spectator who witnesses the performing body.

On the initial level of the confrontation between socialized gender codings and male subjectivity, the work of Highways cofounder and "NEA Four" alumnus Tim Miller (who is Anglo American) intersects, for instance, with other men who have found an artistic home at Highways, including Dan Kwong (Asian American), Keith Antar Mason (African American), and Luis Alfaro (Latino). (To this I would add that some straight white male autoperformers—Scott Carter in his *Heavy Breathing* series at Dixon Place in New York City readily comes to mind—also are beginning to push against the boundaries of conventionally coded gender representation in their work, although others are not, like Rob Becker in *Defending the Caveman,* a revolutionary work that closed in January 1997 after Becker had broken the record for number of performances on Broadway for a solo artist.)

At Highways, an informal coalition of men that is not segregated on the basis of race and sexual orientation develops individuals' work amid an extended, artistic community committed to exploring the range of male diversities, of male subjectivities. This is an exploration that in itself speaks to the dismantling of gender codings that foster social conventions of (white, heterosexual) male authority and power. In other words, Highways is a space in which people not only practice what they preach; they also push themselves to understand and acknowledge the complex connections between "self" and "communities," a decidedly different feature from those works produced by most men during the 1970s and 1980s.

Inherent in this type of exploration is a reconfiguration—initially in terms of the narrative exploration and possibility—of the constitution of power and authority in American life. Later would come the deeper psychic level of determining the connection between "self" and "other." By examining and valuing one's relationship to the "other"—by addressing what Jessica Benjamin identifies from a psychoanalytic feminist perspective as the "fragile, unenclosed space of intersubjectivity," one can "recuperate difference and respect for otherness along with agency . . . account[ing] for the impact of the other on the self—a negation that is at once determinate and irreducible to the subject's own mental world, thus not the subject's own constructed Other, even through related and interdependent with it." What intersubjectivity postulates, according to Benjamin, is that "the barbarism of incorporating the other into the same, the cycle of destructiveness, can only be modified when the other intervenes. Therefore, any subject's primary responsibility to the other subject is to be her intervening or surviving other." "The condition for the other being recognized," Benjamin concludes, "is that the other also be a subject, an ego, capable of negating."[4]

As Drucilla Cornell puts it, "The strangeness of the Other is that the Other is an 'I.' But, as an 'I,' the Other is the same as 'me.'" Without this moment of universality, the otherness of the Other can be only too easily reduced to mythical projection.[5]

The recognition of the intersubjective relationship between a subject and an other effectively counters the moralist, political agenda of the reactionary Right. Autoperformance, paradoxically, is not wholly unlike the act of witness by the faithful that resides at the core of fundamentalism. Yet the (male) autoperformer who links his subjectivity with his sense of community, who explores his misogyny, homophobia, and racism, and who deepens the links between his own diversities and those of others in order to transform the quality of his life into one of mutual respect for his choices and those of others, steps boldly in a different direction than do those who continue to mark individuals by gender in a hierarchical, compulsory heterosexual power structure (whether that structure is defined by the state or church).

The theatrical representation of men talking about their lives in ways that challenge the parameters of conventional gender codings in an effort to redefine those codings is a radical action. Arguably, a rethinking of gender representation—a project that is urgent in a way quite different from a rethinking of race and sexual orientation—may mark the more haunting threat to the white Right, who are aggressively committed to maintaining power and privilege in American society. The lesbian and gay festival was really an easy target amid the more broadly defined features of Highways' monthly calendars. Through its advocacy of male autoperformance, Highways offers the spectator pinups of live males, in all their diversities, who represent the changing bodies and voices of American men. And this is not the stuff of pure fun[ding] in Newt's House.

> In a sexually grieving culture, conservative politicians exploited rampant homophobia under the guise of fiscal restraint to restrict the spending of the National Endowment for the Arts (NEA). Nonreproductive perfor-

mance art dovetailed with the nonreproductive ontology of homosexuality: conservatives used one to attack the other. All four performers "defunded" during the NEA scandal in 1990 [Holly Hughes, Karen Finley, John Fleck, and Tim Miller] make work which incorporates a sympathetic, if not evangelical attitude towards homosexuality.

Peggy Phelan, Unmarked

LATE AUGUST 1995

During a brief stay in Los Angeles, I attended one of the programs during the infamous festival in question at Highways that featured solo performances: *Copping a Feel: Gay Men of Color and Their Bodies.* Of the six performers who presented material that evening, four self-identified the centrality of autobiographical material to their pieces: Luis Alfaro's *Mirror, Mirror: Four Exercises in Futility,* Jorge Ignacio Cortinas's *Temple Drums,* joel b. tan's *In His Arms,* and James E. Sakakura's *James at 36.* Within this group, Mr. Sakakura, a *yonsei,* or fourth-generation Japanese American, offered the most vivid example of the kind of experience—textually, visually, and politically—that can be created in the interactive dynamics of autobiographical text, actor's body, and performance strategies (Alfaro's piece, I should note, also illustrates well the following points). The experience prompted by Sakakura's work is arresting—certainly to me—because, most notably, it was presented by a solo male performer.

The roots of this immediately "gendered" experience are located in nearly thirty years of feminist performance art that heralded the public, dramatic declaration or presentation of female subjectivity and difference through many groundbreaking (i.e., those from the 1960s and 1970s) and contemporary female autoperformers (e.g., the works of Rachel Rosenthal, Beatrice Roth, Leeny Sack, Holly Hughes, Robbie McCauley, Blondell Cummings, Marga Gomez, Darci Picoult, Susan Miller, Lisa Kron, and the lesbian talent at Highways' festival). What is striking at this moment in history is that some male autoperformers are shadowing or adopting performance strategies—in form and content—from feminist performance artists able to disrupt conventional codes of representation, the least of which are not the gender codings that inform stage dialogue: what one says and how one says it.

Current male autoperformance has spawned the post–Spalding Gray era of solo male representation. Whereas many diverse examples of women's autoperformance flourished during the 1970s and 1980s theater scene, Spalding Gray epitomized the culture's commodified concept of—and the artistic community's definition of—male autoperformance during this time as white and heterosexual. Near the end of the 1980s, autoperformer Tim Miller edged toward a national reputation in the theater and gay communities, yet his visibility in popular culture remains restricted next to the national exposure of Gray, who has become a commercial stage, TV, and film artist of some notoriety.

As implied in her criticism of Gray's work (in particular, of *Swimming to Cambodia*), Peggy Phelan identifies the kind of work that would, in fact, emerge out of the next generation of male autoperformers (features, again, that have been evident for years in the work of feminist autoperformers):

> Gray's "speaking" is not in any way an authentic exposure, nor is it a sincere attempt to "share" his selfhood. . . . I am disappointed that he has not faced the truly radical innovative edge in his project . . . explor[ing] his own misogyny, racism, colonialism, and economic imperialism. . . . Such an exploration would not abandon irony, but it would add to it a more challenging intelligence.[6]

The four autoperformances I saw at Highways broke through the barriers of representation to a "selfhood," a kind of individualization (albeit to varying degrees of success) that Phelan identifies as missing in Gray's work. The fact of their races as men of color may have served as an originating point for the narrative exploration of self-identification. This, however, is not the case with Gray. Gray never questions his whiteness, choosing to assume a racially un-marked, "colorless" subjectivity in his narrative, in his language. But his body's visible color counterpoints his dialogue—one cannot escape the fact that his effort at straight boy talk is also the talk of a white guy. His actual color, which remains unactualized through the submerged or recoded dialogue of more "universalized" (or male gendered) narrative assumptions, is vividly present front and center. His whiteness, therefore, is not neutralized; his racial markings suggest "how" he chooses to tell his story, and of course, they define—they emphasize—the inescapable color of the body from which the story emanates.

The Highways performers, however, relatively quickly shifted their narrative foci to gender codings, a confrontation that actually links their thematics (however tangentially) to Gray's. The issue of what it means to be a man in America appears repeatedly to be the point toward which the narrative text of male autoperformance is moving, as gendered codes linked to the identities of all colored bodies are shifting.

At Highways, one does not lose sight of the performers' racialized bodies during the evening's performance because the men insist, in both language and movement, that we hear and see them. Their bodies are the "queer," "colored" ones whose theatricalized life stories conservative white politicians did not want to endorse through NEA funding. After all, "queer," "colored" male autoperformers cannot reproduce the ("real" stories of) "straight," "white" male (politicians). The contested ground boldly reveals that the white hetero-sexuals in power are eager to support only that legislation guaranteeing their reproduction, whether it be antiabortion legislation or NEA funding to artists who will reproduce their "stories"—complete with the racial, sexual, and gendered markings that have hitherto guaranteed white men's socially con-structed base of authority. Highways men, it seems, have different stories to tell than those that the legislators are willing to hear or, at least, to allow to circulate in the culture at large.

Contemporary autoperformers are pushing the boundaries of self-explora-tion toward deeper levels of insight, revelation, and transformation than is apparent in Gray's writing. In order to confront the reality that a pervasive semiotic of maleness determines how a "man" is defined or defines himself in American culture, more men (both gay and straight) of color (including white) in the post-Gray era are "exploring their own misogyny, racism, colonialism, economic imperialism," and homophobia in contemporary autoperformance. They are demanding of themselves a level of self-expression and investigation unparalleled in previous generations of male autoperformers.[7]

Let us turn to James Sakakura—to the striking features of his performance and the reasons that the presentation of those features (apparent in his and others' work performed at Highways) is being used by the Right as evidence of inappropriate funding by the government, which, in turn, is contributing—from their perspective—to the decline in America's family values and moral fabric.

Sakakura's work both startles and energizes (some) spectators because the (male) body (which here is also Asian American) is speaking personally and revealingly, all the while challenging each spectator to recognize and value the contradictions inherent in the essentialist categorizing of men and women vis-à-vis gendered socialization (i.e., a man is not to threaten the stability of his gendered power base by becoming vulnerable through personal disclosures). Whether or not the spectator chooses to confront issues raised by gendered essentialism is another issue, one complicated by the tension created between the spectator's relationship to his own gender, race, and sexual markings com-pared with those markings manifested by the performer.

Nonetheless, the contradictions that surface become a basis from which one's subject position begins to self-identify and through which the subjectivity of the "other" also begins to materialize—a relationship that includes the associative tension between performer and spectator. How does one distinguish between the unmarked position established by the white congressmen voting on NEA funding that supports the works of gays and lesbians of color, and the white spectator, including the healthy straight white male spectator, who sees and hears Sakakura's *James at 36?*

Benjamin's notion of intersubjectivity is again a useful means of identifying the connection between performer and spectator when each embodies—when each "owns," as it were—his own racial, sexual, and gendered codings. Sakakura's subjectivity exists because of the othered nature of the spectator's subjectivity; the spectator's subjectivity becomes Sakakura's "other," through which he realizes his own subjectivity. One's "examinability" facilitates—permits—the other's examinability as well, initiating a kind of circuitry between autoperformer and spectator. It is within this intersubjective dynamic that the potential political import of autoperformance can be identified.

This notion of autoperformance as a circuitry of mutual, albeit implied, examinability between performer and spectator is heightened theatrically during Sakakura's performance. His narrative (i.e., the emotional and psychological depth that his personal storytelling explores) is complicated by the final visible stage image of a man who, upon dropping his pants on stage, reveals a lower body that is covered with KS lesions. Speaking as a man who once was robust and unself-conscious about his body and now as one who finds himself living with and physically marked by AIDS, Sakakura provides in *James at 36*—first and foremost—a snapshot narrative of life in America for a boy/man: moving between the gender privileges afforded him in this culture as a male and the levels of marginalization he experiences as an Asian American, as a homosexual, and as a seriously ill person. His piece remains in the frame of maleness, of masculinity, of gender codings while intentionally rupturing (or perhaps enlarging) that frame with admissions of his own subjectivity.

Sakakura's fluid movement inside and outside the frame of socially constructed maleness sparks, for some spectators, a short-circuiting of the possible intersubjective relationship between autoperformer and spectator. A spectator who is most likely to resist Sakakura's work, one might argue, is a healthy straight white man who considers himself "unmarked" (to be distinguished from a man with the same features who considers himself "marked"). For such an unremarkable spectator, Sakakura is not only the "other"; he is the other who must never realize his own subjectivity, because from that spectator's perspective, Sakakura exists only as an object through which the spectator defines his own subjectivity. Sakakura's story cannot reproduce the story of the unmarked spectator. Thus, to the eyes and ears of the unmarked, Sakakura's story does not need to be seen or heard. Or to be funded.

Sakakura's articulation of his subjectivity—which, in turn, he positions in and among the various "community" identities with which his own diverse features intersect—distinguishes his voice from Gray's while aligning it in the dynamics characteristic of other post-Gray male autoperformers. By exposing and exploring the deeper levels of his conscious sense of self, Sakakura tackles the contradictions and challenges one faces when reaching for a more complicated representation of "selfhood"—what Phelan identifies as "an authentic exposure." But Sakakura also provides the visual and verbal ammunition for the opposition's cannons: to the fundamentalist Right, he is the queer whose diseased body is the price he must pay for his "filthy" stories—the stories that are his life. He, positioned on a continuum of NEA targets from Tim Miller to Ron Athey, easily translates into the Right's anti-ideal poster boy in its raging war on "others."

> Buchanan is the only man who will address the issue of the proliferation of gay legislation and say what he believes.
> Dick Huggs, farmer in Carroll, Iowa,
> February 10, 1996

> When Buchanan speaks, I hear the driving, urgent undershadow of menace (promises of dark things, of retribution) that Senator Joseph R. McCarthy conjured; their voices are eerily similar, and like Pat, Joe McCarthy had considerable personal charm.   Lance Morrow, *Time,*
> February 26, 1996

MARCH 13, 1996

Today, Ralph Regula (Republican, Ohio), chair of the House Appropriations Subcommittee on the Interior (which allocates money for the NEA) confirmed that the "majority of the majority" of House members remain committed to shutting down the NEA by fiscal 1997. The NEA's chairwoman, Jane Alexander, passionately and forcefully defended the NEA's centrality as a sign of federal commitment to the arts, to the enhancement of the quality of American life and its diverse cultures. Dates for the final votes in the House and Senate on the NEA's future existence have not been scheduled.[8]

Yesterday, Senator Bob Dole all but wrapped up the GOP presidential nomination after his clean sweep in the "Super Tuesday" primaries. Some people have credited his consolidated support from the Christian Coalition as a major reason for his victories. From all indications, Steve Forbes will soon drop out of the race, leaving only Patrick Buchanan—who has vowed to stay in the race through to the national convention in San Diego—to dog Dole and to hound the architects of the party's platform. Buchanan's fundamentalist Christian platform: antiabortion, antihomosexual, anti-immigration, anti-NEA . . . "we" know the rest.

Buchanan has restored "real" color, for the time being at least (as did General Colin Powell during the fall of 1995), to the theater of American presidential politics. His visibility to the media is not wholly unlike the personal exposure of Louis Farrakhan, who masterfully put the "black" back into the consciousness of African Americans in October 1995 when he staged the "Million Man March" in Washington, D.C.[9]

According to most polls, Buchanan has found "whites" to be his most ardent supporters, the majority of whom are Anglo American blue-collar workers and religious fundamentalists—groups that also believe they are marginalized in American society. Both Farrakhan and Buchanan have forcefully and willfully grabbed (or perhaps they have been handed) the national stage as the space in which to perform their racial and religious identities, to express their sexist, homophobic politics.[10] Each man's public persona is unmistakably marked as a "guardian of the race." Farrakhan and Buchanan assume their guardianships as the rightful duty of a man. Of a straight man. Of a straight man of color.[11]

Buchanan claims his whiteness—and his maleness, his spirituality, his educational background, and his privileged class status as he mines his personal history—through his bold autoperformances on the campaign trail and in the media, with a style that has rarely been seen in twentieth-century presidential politics. Experienced as a syndicated columnist, a radio and TV program host, Buchanan, like former actor President Ronald Reagan, is comfortable with the self-creation of image in print as well as in live and filmed performances. Like Reagan, his former boss, Buchanan oozes self-confidence, charisma, conviction, wit, and the oratorical style to grab spectators' attention and demand that he be heard and his body be seen. Yet there is a tension between the "visible" and the "invisible" in Buchanan's performance.

Phelan explains the nature of performance in general:

> Performance implicates the real through the presence of living bodies. . . . Without a copy, live performance plunges into visibility—in a maniacally charged present—and disappears into memory, into the realm of invisibility and the unconscious where it eludes regulation and control. . . . Performance art is vulnerable to charges of valuelessness and emptiness. Performance indicates the possibility of revaluing that emptiness; this potential revaluation gives performance art its distinctive oppositional edge.[12]

The visible presence of Buchanan's white body in conjunction with a "dialogue" that suggests the "we" and the "our" of his American references are somehow fixed in an intercultural and interracial frame—such as "We've got to have a new conservatism of the heart that looks on all Americans as brothers and sisters. We've got to be concerned about all of our folks" (Manchester, NH, February 13, 1996)—is constantly disrupted by the varied contexts in which the same words/dialogue resurface only to shift in the specificity of their referents. During the South Carolina primary, for instance, Buchanan defended the state's right to fly the Confederate flag below the American flag at its state capitol building because "we have to stand up for our heritage." Who, one might ask, are the "we" and the "our" to whom he is referring? "We" certainly are not the black men and women of South Carolina whose ancestors lived in bondage to white masters during slavery. "We" certainly are not the gay men of color, "copping a feel," who performed at Highways Performance Space in August 1995. Buchanan clearly thinks of himself and presents himself as "white."[13]

Buchanan's white body performs as a marked site of health, vigor, stamina, determination, willfulness, invincibility in the face of adversity (albeit by a kind of "divine right"), and power—a kind of immortality—that is clearly unlike the marked racialized body (by its Asianness) of James Sakakura. Nonetheless, the public, visible presence of James's colored, queer, ill body remains in "dialogue" with Pat's "colored," straight, healthy body. And the latter is obviously threatened by the former. What it/he represents. What it/he is saying. What it/he is doing. And how it/he threatens, through time, to shift the balance of power in America away from Pat. After all, the James Sakakuras of the world undoubtedly embody the "promises of dark things" to come, the feared punishment Buchanan promises for some of his listeners, including Lance Morrow. Pat has the nation's attention; James has the attention of his various communities—those who are Asian American, those who are gay, those who are living with AIDS, those who are artists. But to a greater or lesser extent, both men share a similar feature: Pat's and James's bodies and their words are circulating in the real and the memory, in the visible and the invisible of America's culture and psyche.[14]

As a consummate autoperformer, Buchanan has become the premier white heterosexual man to fill in the color left by Spalding's "gray," although he and Gray would not fill in "whiteness" in quite the same way. Nonetheless, Buchanan has unabashedly inhabited, if not invaded, the otherwise emptied body of the white straight male as represented in, as staged before, the public eye, and he has done so in order to name him, to claim him, and to control him as his own—and in his own image. During the last decade of his political career, Buchanan consciously constructed a powerful racial category, one in which he can stand at the center of its harsh spotlight. He presents himself as the universal American "white" colored person, who presumably speaks for "us," for all colorless whites. Fortunately, his candidacy has prompted some white citizens (and noncandidates) who disagree with his political stance to speak out, many of whom otherwise might have remained silent.

> Racial identities are not only black, Latino, Asian, Native American and so on; they are also white. To ignore white ethnicity is to redouble its hegemony by naturalizing it. Without specifically addressing white ethnicity, there can be no critical evaluation of the construction of the other.   Coco Fusco, "Fantasies of Oppositionality"

EARLY SUMMER 1996

Pat Buchanan's show remains on the road, and it will continue to engage audiences long after the battle over the Republican platform is waged in San Diego. It's actually beside the point that Buchanan will not win the GOP nomination. It certainly hasn't stopped him from drafting the "McLean Manifesto," which "lays out the philosophy and positions he believes the Republican Party should adopt."[15] Rather, like Farrakhan, Buchanan already has captured the country's attention and imagination.

As A. M. Rosenthal suggests, Buchanan has nonetheless become a "steadily increasing political and moral liability," and the Republican leadership is to blame:

> By selective silence they helped him build national standing and, save our souls, acceptability. They criticized his economics but refused to say why he had no place in political life, when they knew exactly why. In the primary campaign, he showed himself as he has for years—intelligent enough to exploit real problems troubling many Americans and superciliously ignored by the mainstream [read white] politicians, a rousing orator, and a bigot.[16]

Pat's act is tight and it will not vanish completely from memory. He believes deeply in his power as an autoperformer—as a white, straight male performer whose mission, whose life story, is to warn "us" about "dark things." He is confident that his version of whiteness, maleness, and straightness constructs the voice of America. From his perspective, his "I" is the "we" speaking for all the people. Yet his message is racially nostalgic, one that appeals to, among others, those who yearn for the days when whiteness was wholly unmarked, a mythic past, as Mike Hill notes, of "white directed equality, which depoliticizes whiteness."[17] Nonetheless, the specificity that characterizes Buchanan's message in performance—one that is pregnant with reactionary right-wing ideology that laces religious doctrine with class, gender, sexual, and racial overtones—reveals Buchanan, the autoperformer, as a model of postmodern America's embodiment of the religious Right's politicization of whiteness. Buchanan's own whiteness is implicit in the way he codes his rhetoric and is explicit through his material body. The "role" of Pat Buchanan cannot, realistically, be cross-culturally cast. His autoperformances dictate the primary importance that his body is the one to theatricalize his text.

Joining Pat in this distinction are other white religious right-wingers Pat Robertson and Ralph Reed, executive director of the Christian Coalition. It is from a comparable reductionist, arrogant, fascistic position as activated by these white religious Right politicians that their supporters in Congress fight the battle against public funding for "other," marginalized voices through NEA support. To them, the work of these other voices is wasteful, blasphemous, and un(white) American.

The national and local stages, however, remain open. The spectators are scattered but can be quickly gathered. Other male autoperformers, in art and life, remain to be seen and heard—in particular, straight men of white color who neither presume to speak for the rest of "us" nor dismiss the urgency to participate in meaningful, progressive dialogue with the rest of "us." On the political scene, neither Bob Dole nor Ross Perot is such a man. For the Democrats, Bill Clinton, though less offensive than his Republican challengers, continues to disappoint.

Nonetheless, worthy visions are arising from the performances of Jane Alexander (a white woman and the chair of the NEA) and from the autoperformances that appear and disappear nightly in theaters across America—work by brave men and women like those at Highways Performance Space. Their visions urge the rest of us not to give up hope, as they put their bodies behind this message: each day, we must work toward and speak out for the cultural changes that will lead to the recognition and integrity of human diversity.

NOTES

1. For a history of the turmoil surrounding the awarding of National Endowment funds to those involved in American not-for-profit theater, see the government coverage

in *American Theatre,* a monthly magazine published by the Theatre Communications Group. This periodical has faithfully documented the decade-long battle among the National Endowment for the Arts, Congress, and the American nonprofit arts world (which began under Ronald Reagan's presidency), most forcefully since 1989 when Senator Jesse Helms (Republican, North Carolina) complained about spending the public's tax dollars on the NEA's grants, on museums displaying the "obscene" works of Andrew Serrano and Robert Mapplethorpe.

The groundswell behind Helms's initiative, one that was/is aggressively supported and funded by the fundamentalist Right, directly influenced the denial of NEA fellowships in 1990 to four performance artists—Holly Hughes, Karen Finley, John Fleck, and Tim Miller (who cofounded Highways Performance Space with Linda Frye Burnham in 1989)—whose solo performance works push the boundaries of identity and community politics by foregrounding—often through frank, raw language and visual imagery—such issues as sexuality, prochoice and AIDS activism, nontraditional views of religion, and attacks on right-wing political and religious public figures.

The "NEA Four," as the quartet has come to be known, had been recommended for fellowships by the peer review panel. John Frohnmayer, then the NEA's chairman, and the National Council of the Arts, appointed by President George Bush, overruled the peer decision. For an insightful analysis of each of these NEA controversies, see Peggy Phelan, "Money Talks," *Drama Review* 34 (1990): 4–15, and "Money Talks, Again," *Drama Review* 35 (1991): 131–42.

The most recent demonstration of an ever increasing national grassroots movement for uncensored and fully supported arts, ARTNOW, was held on April 19, 1997, in Washington, D.C. ARTNOW, a celebration of the arts, turned the national spotlight on the stark diminishment of federal backing for the arts—evidenced by Congress's continuing efforts to shut down the NEA—and the crippling effect that the lack of funds has had and will have on the preservation and growth of the arts in America's cultures.

2. Elin Diamond, "The Violence of 'We': Politicizing Identification," in Janelle G. Reinelt and Joseph R. Roach, eds., *Critical Theory and Performance* (Ann Arbor: University of Michigan Press, 1992), p. 390.

3. Richard Dyer,"White," *Screen* 29 (1988): 44, 46.

4. Jessica Benjamin, "The Shadow of the Other (Subject): Intersubjectivity and Feminist Theory," *Constellations* 1 (1994): 247, 239, 243, 244.

5. Drucilla Cornell, *Philosophy of the Limit* (New York: Routledge, 1992), p. 55.

6. Peggy Phelan, "Spalding Gray's Swimming to Cambodia: The Article," *Critical Texts* 5 (1988): 29.

7. Notably, Spalding Gray intersects with the post-Gray generation of male autoperformers in his latest solo, *It's a Slippery Slope,* which premiered at New York's Vivian Beaumont Theater on November 10, 1996. In this autoperformance, his sixteenth solo since 1979, Gray exposes and explores, uncharacteristically, "the deeper pains and consolations of his life over the last several years," cites Peter Marks: "the death of his father, the breakup of his relationship with his wife and collaborator, Renee Shafransky, and the birth of his first child, a son, by another woman." See Peter Marks, "Negotiating the Twists in Skiing and Life," *New York Times,* November 11, 1996, pp. C11–C12.

8. Judith Miller, "Future of Arts Agency Unclear," *New York Times,* March 14, 1996, p. C15.

9. In his profile of Farrakhan that appeared in the *New Yorker* six weeks after the Super Tuesday primaries, Henry Louis Gates Jr. quotes Eldridge Cleaver on the leader of the Nation of Islam and his march: "We have the worst leadership in the black community since slavery. Farrakhan saw that vacuum, saw nothing motivating the people, no vision being projected to the people, and he came up with the defining event for a generation of people" (p. 128). Gates notes, however, that "at the helm of the mainstream black-advocacy groups are men and women who may say conciliatory things about the Nation of Islam, but their jaws are tense and their smiles tight. They assure themselves that Farrakhan is bound to remain a marginal phenomenon because of his extremism. . . . [Nonetheless] from all indications, the underclass is continuing to expand, [and] Farrakhan's natural power base will only increase" (p. 129). Henry Louis Gates Jr., "The Charmer," *New Yorker,* April 29 and May 6, 1996, pp. 116–31.

In their recognition of Buchanan as a political force of potential consequence, mainstream white Republican leaders also have adopted a similar strategy, especially among those whites who consider themselves to be disenfranchised. Republican leadership tends to speak of Buchanan as a marginalized factor while not forgetting that his supporters, like those who promoted Christian fundamentalist Pat Robertson during his bid for the presidency, are fiercely loyal and vocal.

10. For a discussion between Essex Hemphill and Isaac Julien on the kinds of complications that (might have) informed a black gay man's relationship to "Farrakhan's spectacle" of the Million Man March, see Don Belton, "Where We Live: A Conversation with Essex Hemphill and Isaac Julien," in Don Belton, ed., *Speak My Name: Black Men on Masculinity and the American Dream* (Boston: Beacon Press, 1995), pp. 209–19. According to Julien, "If you want to be a black version of white supremacy, of course you end up with a Farrakhan" (p. 215). Also see Michelangelo Signorile, "Queer in a Million," *Out,* February 1996, pp. 30, 32–33. For an analysis of Farrakhan's post-MMM activities, in particular the World Friendship Tour and its relationship to the MMM, see Adolph Reed Jr., "Defending the Indefensible," *Village Voice,* April 23, 1996, p. 26; Gates, "The Charmer."

11. By pairing Buchanan and Farrakhan as self-proclaimed spokesmen for their races, I am thinking of Buchanan in much the same way that Gates critiques Farrakhan's dualist tendencies that mark him—that split him—as a black supremacist and a liberal universalist (such a split would not characterize white supremacist David Duke, for instance, thus distinguishing Duke from Buchanan). Gates concludes that for Farrakhan, "the two tendencies, in all their forms, are constantly in tension" (p. 118). His shifting attitudes toward Jews, Gates suggests, best illustrate Farrakhan's characteristics of "psychological obsession" (p. 128). Although both Farrakhan and Buchanan are well known for their anti-Semitic remarks, each is also an outspoken critic of homosexuality and a woman's right to choose—beliefs that each directly connects to Islamic and Christian doctrines. Each man's racial "supremacist" leanings, I believe, are subtly (or not so subtly) revealed through his public persona and presentations as a man of God or Allah vis-à-vis the more expansive, metaphorical rhetoric of religious doctrine and spiritual interpretation. Gates, "The Charmer."

12. Peggy Phelan, *Unmarked: The Politics of Performance* (New York: Routledge, 1993), p. 148.

13. Dyer, "White," p. 47.

14. Distinguishing between erotica and pornography, Jill Dolan suggests that "making visible gay male or lesbian bodies in motion, engaged in sex acts, is perhaps one most radical way to disrupt dominant cultural discourse on sexuality and gender." Jill Dolan, "Practicing Cultural Disruptions: Gay and Lesbian Representations and Sexuality," in Reinelt and Roach, eds., *Critical Theory and Performance,* p. 267.

From this viewpoint, we might hypothesize that some spectators watching Sakakura's marked, unhealthy, singular body in motion imagine the sex acts that they presume to be the "cause" of his AIDS. Sakakura's imagined gay sex acts, therefore, might be more radical in their political impact on dominant cultural discourse than the "acts of empowering verbalization" (ibid., p. 270) that are a prominent feature of his single-bodied autoperformance.

15. James Bennet, "Buchanan Backing off with Curt Nod to Opponent," *New York Times,* April 18, 1996, p. B6.

16. A. M. Rosenthal, "Buchanan and the Fish," *New York Times,* March 22, 1996, p. A27.

17. Conversation with Mike Hill, April 17, 1996.

Conditions of Immigration

Amitava Kumar

And it's very hard to recognize that the standards which have almost killed you are really mercantile standards. They're based on cotton; they're based on oil; they're based on peanuts; they're based on profits.

James Baldwin, *James Baldwin and Nikki Giovanni: A Dialogue*

Immigrants and faggots
They make no sense to me
They come to our country —
And think they'll do as they please
Like start some mini-Iran
Or spread some fuckin' disease

Guns n' Roses

The illegal immigrant is the bravest among us. The most modern among us. The prophet.   Richard Rodriguez, "Prophets Without Papers"

It need not have anything to do with a newspaper report about a Mexican couple being clubbed by two white policemen on a California highway. For example, I could be lying in bed — as I was only half an hour ago — reading a poem whose opening lines are "Today you are wearing a white body marked vertically and/horizontally with the stripes of underwear, garter belt,/stockings. You move unsteadily on the two black bars of/your heels."[1] The poem is written by a writer whose name is Evelyn Lau, and it appears in an anthology of Asian American poetry. In the poem, a bald man sits on the side of the bed playing with spoons and baking powder and cocaine.

Is he white? Clearly she isn't, I tell myself. I work through a small, scattered drama of sexuality and power that burns close over the words and gathers like smoke. I inhale. I quickly decide that the narrator "wearing the white body" is a woman of Asian origin. The bald male, the client, is white. "Through brown slits he watches you/open your legs. Wider, he says. You gather one breast/up in two hands and place your nipple into your mouth./Good girl, he says."

265

To be white is to be able to say "Good girl" when a woman puts a nipple in her mouth.

That man has a beach towel under him to protect his sheet when he comes. But I'm not taking any precautions at all. By the time I reach the end of the page, I can hear the loud noise of helicopter blades, which are actually in another poem three pages away.

The sum of my responses to Lau's poem reminds me that encounters with race, characteristically clichéd or not, are often colored by fantasy. In those dark chambers, what is revealed always hides something else. These experiences are also always irreducibly gendered and engage varieties of complicities and contradictions.

In this chapter I want to trace some of these impulses, linking them in a broad domain of the aesthetic, for it is in the field of writing that I hope to offer road maps to immigrant conditions. In memoirs and daily journalism, in the fictive space of novels by writers of Asian origin, in poems written to celebrate or condemn hybrid existences, how is white racism constructed and critiqued? In a space beyond scholarly discussions, defined by codes other than those of academic political correctness, in the routine flows of the everyday, identities stall—or stumble. And often, with a dull and somewhat tiresome brutality, they extract a terrible price from those most unaware of having been drawn into an exchange.

I am a figure in your dream.

When the sun rises over the skyscrapers of New York City, darkness has already fallen in the land of my birth, India. In that area of darkness, the head of the New Delhi bureau of the *New York Times* discovers the face of otherness that offers the comfort of absolute difference. "Shackled by Past, Racked by Unrest, India Lurches Toward Uncertain Future" is the title of a story filed by Edward R. Gargan. From that remote wasteland of meaning, the journalistic Indiana Jones files his report on his reading of the runes of frozen time. "More than 70 percent of India's people live in villages, where their habits, customs and traditions have changed little over the centuries, even as economic, religious and political forces have changed around them." [2]

The report is lengthy (hence authoritative) and undeniably human (hence believable). The changes that are announced seem all the more illusory because we are returned so relentlessly to the unchanging condition. By the article's end, it has become possible to pyschologize current struggles and fit them into a vision of the eternal, fixed psyche. The conclusion reads: "The Indian temperament is not democratic enough." Let me engage in a bit of psycholo-gizing myself. In this article, we are back in the nightmare space of an American childhood memory of the 1950s and 1960s. It is dinnertime in a white, middle-class American home. The child, who is refusing to finish the food on his plate, is remonstrated by his mother, "Eat your food, Billy. There are children in India going to bed hungry."

Never mind the fact that enough grain is being produced in India to feed its entire population. Never mind that there still is widespread hunger. Never mind that prosperity under the auspices of the U.S.-guided Green revolution was designed to block the "Red" revolution and managed to make the rich richer and the poor more desperate. Never mind that there is something called contradiction and that its complex attritions have nothing to do with the monumentalization of stasis.

I am riding in a New York subway car, reading a literary article about a Brazilian poet, João Cabral de Melo Neto. The review mentions that Cabral had reached a dead end as a poet "until he happened to read one day that life expectancy in his native Recife was even lower than India."[3] As a result of this new knowledge, the poet made a turn from speculative poetry to a social one. He wrote *The Dog Without Feathers*. "With that poem he rediscovered the city of his birth, its river, the rio Capibaribe, and the people who survive however marginally along its banks."

Shortly thereafter, I search for and find Cabral's poem about the river in his birthplace. "And I never saw it seethe/(as bread when rising/seethes)./In silence/the river bears its bloating poverty,/pregnant with black earth."[4]

I am held by the poem's presentation of this image of the river that "never opens up in fish." Even in the description of its stagnation, Cabral conveys the dynamism of his inquiry. The sluggishness of the river and its poverty evoke a response very different from that incited by the closed mindedness or the complacency of the bourgeosie on its banks. "(It is there,/with their backs to the river,/that the city's "cultured families"/brood over the fat eggs/of their prose./In the complete peace of their kitchens/they viciously stir/their pots of sticky indolence.)"

For Edward A. Gargan of the *New York Times*, however, Indian poverty has not meant what it has for Cabral. Rather, it has only signaled a racist desire to seize the stereotype and refurbish it with the kind of detail that makes good copy. Beyond the repetition of the same, there is no further interest or self-criticism. I imagine Gargan climbing into the back of a yellow cab in New York City, and it is against what he does, I think, that three South Asian cabdrivers offer the following testimony: " 'Where do you come from?' All of them have begun to hate the question. They feel that the person asks the question out of a ghoulish desire to confirm their origins as the starving and poor country of Bangladesh." [5]

The words we choose carefully to describe ourselves rely sometimes on the words you use to talk about us.

A female poet, an Indian immigrant in the United States, looks for the right words that will describe her. These descriptions inevitably engage politics too; otherwise, she says, evoking Frantz Fanon, one will remain "merely a walking wound, a demilitarized zone, a raw sodden trench." This writer, Meena Alexander, walks us through an exercise in which she explains where she is coming from, so to speak:

> As much as anything else, I am a poet writing in America. But American poet? What sort? Surely not of the Robert Frost or Wallace Stevens variety. An Asian American poet then? Clearly that sounds better. Poet, *tout court,* just poet? Will that fit? Not at all. There is very little that I can be *tout court* just by itself in America, except perhaps woman-mother. But even there I wonder. Everything that comes to me is hyphenated: a woman-poet, a woman-poet of color, a South Indian woman-poet who makes up lines in English, a post-colonial language, as she waits for the red light to change on Broadway, a third world woman-poet, who takes as her right the inner city of Manhattan, making up poems about the hellhole of the subway line, the burnt out blocks so close to home on the Upper West Side. Oh confusions of the heart, thicknesses of the soul, the borders we cross tattooing us all over. [6]

Every time the detailed map of her country—the terrain of its difference but also its links with other nations of the Third World as well as its history's complex implicatedness with the history of the First World's dominance—is essentialized into the barren image of her nation as an empty bowl, this poet suffers the violence of the dominant American ideology.

"When are you going back?" which means, of course, its opposite, "You're dying to live here." Our poet is sitting, a magazine in her hand, at her hairdresser's. Someone might say, trying to be kind, "You all have beautiful black hair." Or with the extravagant certainty of the stereotype, "You must be Indian. I know that from the dot on your forehead." If the magazine our poet is holding in her hands happens to be the *National Geographic,* the hunger of the empty bowl is replaced by the mystical aura, in color no less, of a contented people, tigers, the striped patterns of a land diverse in its ancient natural beauty. "I saw this program about India, I think it was on *Sixty Minutes.* Y'all have problems with women." A primal landscape dotted with snakes and elephants gives way to the horrifyingly primitive scenario of women being burned for dowry. This singular image blocks any elaboration; all the hyphens are quickly crushed into a dot. It would be futile for our poet to say, "We do, and you don't?" or "Yes, and what are we, especially women, doing about that? Would you really want to know?" Our poet feels tired. Bad hair day . . .

All this also doesn't allow us to begin measuring the distance that separates our well-educated, published poet from the Punjabi woman who does not have a job, cannot speak English with any confidence in her Queens neighborhood, and finds herself trapped in an abusive marriage. Or even the Bangladeshi cabdriver who dislikes being asked where he's from. Or the lines that both join and divide the poet who so scrupulously lists her hyphens from the male Pakistani organizer who is both a cabdriver and an activist, savvy in the business of subverting the dominant codes in order to question New York City's Mayor Rudolph Guiliani and his ilk:

> I want to say 42 cab drivers have been killed. If they are the best police, how many killers have they arrested? The mayor gets concerned about cop murders. But cab drivers are also ambassadors of goodwill. They take passengers from JFK and introduce them to the city. We are also the finest. New York's yellow cab drivers are famous all over the world and no one cares. Have you ever seen the mayor go to a driver's family who has been killed?[7]

Small solidarities are found in the passages in books that speak of immigrant conditions.

I read the first lines of his poem: "I will die one day, in Kashmir,/and the shadowed routine of my veins—/the blood censored—will still be news," and I murmur my assent.[8] Because this poet, Agha Shahid Ali, writes of "the country without a post office" and because his "letters are cries that break like bodies/in prisons," I recognize the appeal to a community that is at once there—and absent. On Immigration Street, writing often goes knocking on empty doors.

Meena Alexander's similarly anguished question, "How could I dream of paper filled with light?" is laden with hurt because a community has indeed been shaped in her writing, a community of shared pain: "I am here in Isamu's garden, by an old warehouse,/by a children's park, by the East River—rusty gasoline tanks,/the packed cars of new immigrants, the barbed wires/of Meerut, Bensonhurst, Baghdad, strung in my brain."[9] In another place, she speaks of what the immigrant writer's response ought to be: "in our writing we need to evoke a chaos, a power equal to the injustices that surround us."[10] That power, Alexander writes, is rooted in its capacity to engender communities. "The notion of ethnicity is exciting because already we are making alliances, and therefore our works will be refracted against that of each other. . . . The present for me is the present of 'multiple anchorages.' "

When Alexander writes, "It is these multiple anchorages that an ethnicity of an Asian American provides for me," the possibility of a community of difference is opened up. For immigrant intellectuals and writers of color, to speak of this community is to confront the white imaginary with the challenge of Third Worlds other than the ones fixed as sites of terror and the exotic. Our task is to make visible the links between our different worlds, including the First and the Third. Often, it is also to announce the presence of the Third World inside the First.

In my own writing, for example, as an op–ed writer, I choose to speak of the fifty thousand people, mostly Asian and Latina women, who, according to a General Accounting Office report, work for slave wages in unsafe, unsanitary conditions in New York City's 4,500 sweatshops. "Ying Yi Deng Chan, a 56-year-old Chinese immigrant woman who has worked in New York City's sweatshops for six years, is reported to have told the secretary of labor, Robert B. Reich, that she now gets 30 cents for stitching a waistband to a skirt that she said she once saw on sale for $80."[11]

The sense of what Alexander calls "multiple anchorages" makes me pause in my reading on an airplane during the Thanksgiving weekend when I encounter a description of life for Mexican boys at the Tijuana border. I stop to consider the contradictory imbrication of racism, sexism, and violent poverty; this complexity is irreducible to the stereotypical and not unaffected by the impulse toward anti-imperialist critique:

> Daily life revolved around prostitution and drugs. Soon the boys realized that the thousands of *gringos* who came down to party on the weekends made easy targets—especially once they'd had enough to drink. The boys lured the tourists away from the disco lights. All it took was a promise: girls—*muchachas bonitas*. They were sly enough to know that we still believed the racist myth of *fock my seester,* and they said it. And the gringos followed. Or they offered dope, cheap. Or themselves. Or watches. The point was to get the victim alone. Then the one boy magically became three, four. Eight arms, eight legs lashed out of the dark and pummeled, with fists, shoes, rocks, pipes.[12]

I must return briefly to the space of my own fantasy. How, in the pages of the immigrant writings that I'm most familiar with, is an identity being forged in opposition to the more strident claims of the dominant white ethos?

Well I was good at doin' what I was told
Kept my uniform pressed and clean
At night I chased their shadows
Through the arroyos and ravines
Drug runners farmers with their families
Young women with little children by their
    sides
Come night we'd wait out in the canyons
And try to keep 'em from crossin' the line"
               Bruce Springsteen
          Photo: Amitava Kumar,
      Tijuana, Christmas, 1995.

At the close of Hanif Kureishi's latest novel, *The Black Album,* in the London of 1989 rocked by the *fatwa* against Salman Rushdie, the protagonist Shahid Hasan sits down to write and discover his own endangered communities. It is in the practice of writing, I want to suggest very strongly, that the limits of community are revealed—pace Rushdie—and explored—pace Kureishi. As Kureishi writes of the young Shahid:

> Among unmarked essays, letters, and newspaper clippings he found a fountain pen with a decent nib, and began to write with concentrated excitement. He had to find some sense in his recent experiences; he wanted to know and understand. How could anyone confine themselves to one system or creed? Why should they feel they had to? There was no fixed self; surely our several selves melted and mutated daily? There had to be innumerable ways of being in the world. He would spread himself out, in his work and in love, following his curiosity.[13]

For Shahid, writing very early on begets opposition—from those closest to him. His first story written in school, "Paki Wog Fuck off Go Home," is discovered by his mother who immediately slips into a denial-induced intolerance of any talk of the racism meted out by whites. Even when her son vomits and defecates in his pants for fear of going to school and returns assaulted by blows and knives, she chooses to act "as if so appalling an insult couldn't exist." Shahid also meets with very hostile responses from fellow Muslims in London. His writing thus becomes a way of turning away from fundamentalism. He writes a book to get away from the absolute power of The Book. Shahid advises a fellow Asian Muslim: "Surely, brother, there must be more to living than swallowing one old book? What men and women do, and the things they make, must be more interesting than anything that God is supposed to do?"[14]

In other words, immigrant art functions in this case as the domain for what Paul Gilroy, following Seyla Benhabib, calls "the politics of transfiguration."[15] As Shahid proclaims rather grandly and a bit desperately in Kureishi's novel, "A free imagination ranges over many natures. A free imagination, looking into itself, illuminates others."[16] It would be a mistake to think of this as an expression of some kind of universal humanism. Rather, even its universalism is a specific one.

As an examination of the implication of the *fatwa* in the immigrant Asian community in Britain, *The Black Album* might be described in terms of the specific universalism of Rushdie's own defense of *The Satanic Verses:* "It is written from the very experience of uprooting, disjuncture and metamorphosis (slow or rapid, painful or pleasurable) that is the migrant condition, and from which, I believe, can be derived a metaphor for all humanity."[17] I call this *specific* universalism because Kureishi's—and Rushdie's—portrayals of the immigrant conditions turn on a historical understanding of difference.

For instance, Kureishi objects to the white media's description of immigrant folk being "constantly in-between":

> We are all torn people—in many directions. But they like to see us as being particularly torn. You know, as if some people particularly belong and we don't. And I think that's a construction and, I think, it's a cliché. And I really think it's stupid, to be honest. It's a way of marginalizing us as well. They like to put Martin Amis in the middle. He's white. He's male. He comes from a literary family. He's the head guy and we're the little guys around the edges, in between, with particular kinds of problems of identity. But he's the main man.[18]

It is precisely this clear-eyed calculation of political interest—more genuinely hybrid than random invocations of that term—that is reduced, indeed flattened, in the debates over the question of Third World peoples immigrating to the United States. In closing, let me take up the more poisonous aspects of that discussion.

Very early on in *Alien Nation*—in what he flatters himself is an exposé of the immigrant conditions in the United States—its author, Peter Brimelow, a *Forbes* magazine hack, confronts the horror of the Third World in the heart of darkness that is New York City. "Just as when you leave Park Avenue and descend into the subway, when you enter the INS waiting rooms you find yourself in an underworld that is not just teeming but is almost entirely colored." After complaining that in 1990 only 8 percent of the legal immigrants to the United States are from Europe, Brimelow addresses what he supposes are his like-minded readers: "You have to be totally incurious not to wonder: where do all these people get off and come to the surface?"[19]

Brimelow, an Englishman who is now a naturalized American citizen, froths at the mouth when witnessing the demographic changes in his adopted country, because he believes that "the American nation has always had a specific ethnic core. And that core has been white."[20] This race enthusiasm pushes Brimelow to offer bigoted advice to his ordinarily conservative colleagues when they happen to disagree with him. For instance, A. M. Rosenthal of the *New York Times* wrote that "this country should have the moral elegance to accept neighbors who flee countries where life is terror and hunger, and are run by murderous gangs left over from dictatorships we ourselves maintained and cosetted." To Rosenthal's conclusion, "If that were a qualification for entry into our golden land, the Haitians should be welcomed with song, embrace and memories," Brimelow responds, "Be careful about those embraces, Mr. Rosenthal, sir. Some 3 percent of the Haitian refugees at Guantanamo tested HIV-positive." [21]

From George Washington who said, during the Revolutionary War, "Put none but Americans on guard tonight" to Theodore Roosevelt who declared, "There is no room in this country for hyphenated Americans," Peter Brimelow finds loose examples for inspiring racial prejudice. And in a text that's nearly three hundred pages long, he spews contempt for "all those endless newspaper columns about Vietnamese valedictorians and the delights of ethnic cuisine." [22] The reality, of course, is that more newspaper columns are written about immigration as a problem to be rationally solved—rather than as a systemic issue linked with the structure of global capitalism. [23] And yet a major publishing company like Random House can actually publish a tract like *Alien Nation* which— apart from wrongly claiming that all dominant institutions in this country support immigration—can suggest that dogs be set on people trying to cross the U.S. border illegally to find work. (To be fair to Brimelow, he is not entirely insensitive. He points out that "the dogs don't have to *eat* the illegals.") [24]

At one point, Brimelow quotes Raoul Lowery Contreras, a columnist writing for the Sacramento weekly paper *El Hispano*. Contreras was contesting a point raised by George Will, who in turn was using Brimelow's critique of the 1965 Immigration Act, which allowed foreigners, including people of color, to emigrate to the United States. George Will wanted immigration supporters to "explain why they wish to transform the American nation as it had evolved by 1965." Here's the lengthy quotation from Contreras that Brimelow cites:

> In their precious 1965, I was 24 years old and, though I was a veteran of six years service in the American armed forces and a life-long U.S. citizen, I could not vote in some Texas counties. Fellow Marines, black Marines, couldn't vote in at least ten states of the land of the brave and of the free. . . . In 1965, black children were murdered by white males in many ways, in many places, in the South. Black male adults were beaten, killed and castrated in Mississippi, Alabama, Arkansas and other Southern states for the crime of having black skin. . . . In 1965, though a veteran, college graduate and political professional, a bartender refused to serve me a drink in a Texas bar because, he said, "We don't serve foreigners." That was Brimelow's and Will's 1965 America. Unfortunately, it was my 1965 America also. *That's the America that needed to be transformed and that's exactly what's happening,* Brimelow, Will and Metzger notwithstanding. [25]

To all this, Brimelow can only say defiantly, "Even at the height of Jim Crow Era, the United States was not Hitler's Third Reich." He then faults

Raoul Contreras for "his profound alienation from America—and his conscious support of immigration as a way of striking back."[26] More than 150 pages later, Contreras's name comes up again. This time it is in response to Brimelow's suggestion that racial intermarriage might be a good way to ensure the assimilation of aliens into the shared, national fold. But here Brimelow mentions Contreras, reminds readers of their disagreements, and tells us that Contreras is part Anglo. The conclusion the reader is to draw from this information is as follows: "Intermarriage cannot guarantee social harmony. That can only be done by an American majority that is confident and strong."

Welcome to the United States of Amerika. Give me all your tired, your poor, huddled masses, and I will join them under one race, one nation, and one father.

We are treading the fantasy landscape of whiteness. Lawlessness and disease are, for Brimelow, immigration's chief gifts to the United States. To top it, there is, he claims, "increased mismatching with the U.S. Labor market."[27] Here, as in almost all other aspects of Brimelow's arguments, it is important to recognize that commonsensical assumptions—or, rather, racist prejudice— form the basis of a predetermined conclusion. And the wide disparity between what is commonly believed and what the reality is, is best expressed by these facts cited in an article in the *New York Times:*

Percentage of the United States population that white Americans think
   is Hispanic: 14.7.
Percentage that is Hispanic: 9.5.
Percentage that white Americans think is Asian: 10.8.
Percentage that is Asian: 3.1.
Percentage that white Americans think is black: 23.8.
Percentage that is black: 11.8.
Percentage that white Americans think is white: 49.9.
Percentage that is white: 74.[28]

In the end, this is what it comes down to. The poverty of the immigrant condition is that its differences have to be doled out in a parsimonious economy of numbers. Immigrant writing loses all form here, nothing more defined than a blur moving on the infrared scopes of those guarding the borders of fixed identity. Homi Bhabha writes: "The enchantment of art lies in looking in a glass darkly—a wall, stone, a screen, paper, canvas, steel—that turns suddenly into the almost unbearable lightness of being."[29] As the case of Fauziya Kasinga reminds us—the young woman who fled Togo to avoid genital mutilation and was held in detention for an unconscionably long time by the U.S. Immigration authorities—the real persists in its unenchanting rudeness. What is truly unbearable is its persistence in places where to speak is only to declare it a station of loss.

I brought two bags from home, but there was a third that I left behind./In this new country, apart from the struggles that made me a stranger,/were your needs, of the ones who bid me goodbye, those I left behind./Among the papers I collected, you had put a small bag of sweets, I left behind./There were divisions at home, there were other possibilities;/there were communities in my town, there were communities where I came;/I found a job, called it a struggle for survival, everything else I left behind./I didn't want to forget my traditions, the tradition of forgetting I left behind./Bags, passport, my shoes crossed the yellow lines, something was left behind./Here I am, a sum of different parts; travel agents everywhere are selling ads/for the parts that were left behind.[30]

NOTES

1. Evelyn Lau, "Crack," in Walter K. Lew, ed., *Premonitions: The Kaya Anthology of New Asian North American Poetry* (New York: Kaya Productions, 1995), pp. 135–36.

2. Edward A. Gargan, "Shackled by Past, Racked by Unrest, India Lurches Toward Uncertain Future," *New York Times,* February 18, 1994, p. A4.

3. Thomas Colchie, "The River Wild: Cabral's Catchall Museum," *Voice Literary Supplement,* April 1995, p. 25.

4. Joâo Cabral de Melo Neto, "O cao sem plumas," trans. Richard Zenith, in Djelal Kadir, ed., *Selected Poetry, 1937–1990* (Middletown, CT: Wesleyan University Press, 1995). pp. 53–61.

5. Anannya Bhattacharjee, "Yellow Cabs, Brown People," *Samar* (Summer 1993): 61–63.

6. Meena Alexander, "Is There an Asian American Aesthetics?" *Samar* (Winter 1992): 26–27.

7. S. Shankar, "Ambassadors of Goodwill: An Interview with Saleem Osman of Lease Drivers' Coalition," *Samar* (Summer 1994): 44–47.

8. Agha Shahid Ali, "The Last Saffron" and "The Country Without a Post Office," in Lew, ed., *Premonitions,* pp. 456–62.

9. Meena Alexander, "Paper Filled with Light," in Lew, ed., *Premonitions,* pp. 88–90.

10. Alexander, "Is There an Asian-American Aesthetics?" pp. 26–27.

11. Amitava Kumar, "Immigration's Good vs. the Evil," *Gainesville* [FL] *Sun,* September 30, 1995, p. 6A.

12. Luis Alberto Urrea, *Across the Wire* (New York: Anchor Books, 1993), p. 66.

13. Hanif Kureishi, *The Black Album* (New York: Scribner, 1995), p. 285.

14. Ibid., p. 283.

15. Paul Gilroy, *The Black Atlantic* (Cambridge, MA: Harvard University Press,

1993), p. 37. Gilroy's discussion in this context is related chiefly to the recombinant qualities of music. See also George Lipsitz, *Dangerous Crossroads* (London: Verso, 1994). My argument, only sketchily developed here, is to find those resources in some examples of immigrant writing.

16. Kureishi, *The Black Album,* p. 194.

17. Salman Rushdie, "In Good Faith," in his *Imaginary Homelands* (New York: Granta Books, 1981), p. 394.

18. Hanif Kureishi, " 'I'm Not Going to Write About Eighteen Year Olds or Twenty Year Olds Anymore': Hanif Kureishi Speaks with Jessica Hagedorn," *Samar* (Summer 1996): 34–38.

19. Peter Brimelow, *Alien Nation* (New York: Random House, 1995), p. 28.

20. Ibid., p. 10.

21. Ibid., p. 113.

22. Ibid., pp. 192, 203, 181.

23. I cannot really want to remind readers of a Leadership Education for Asian Pacifics report that informs us that fifteen of the most successful high-tech companies in the United States were founded by Asian American immigrants, which now have a combined revenue of $22.25 billion (reported in *India News Network Digest,* April 6, 1996). I cannot do so because the point isn't really to say, "Look, immigration can also work for white America." Real education will begin when white America begins to take stock of its unequal gain from such phenomena as "brain drain" from the nations of the Third World or its disproportionate share of savings from legal immigration, when immigrants pay $90 billion in taxes and get only $5 billion in services.

24. Brimelow, *Alien Nation,* p. 237 (italics in original).

25. Ibid., p. 106 (italics added by Brimelow).

26. Ibid., p. 107.

27. Ibid., p. 146.

28. Priscilla Labovitz, "Immigration—Just the Facts," *New York Times,* March 25, 1996, p. A15.

To ease the residual disquiet of any reader of this chapter, let me cite the views on immigration of a mainstream economist:

> Almost without exception the behavioral characteristics of immigrants are conducive to economic advancement for the community as well as for the immigrants themselves. Compared to natives of the same sex and age, immigrants work harder, save more, have a higher propensity to start new business, and are more likely to innovate. Two frequent allegations—that immigrants are more disposed to crime, and that they have large numbers of children which are a burden upon the native community—have no basis in fact. Julian L. Simon, *The Economic Consequences of Immigration* (Cambridge: Blackwell, 1989), pp. 103–4.

29. Homi K. Bhabha, "Unpacking My Library . . . Again," in Iain Chambers and Lidia Curti, eds., *The Post-Colonial Question* (New York: Routledge, 1996), p. 205.

30. Amitava Kumar, *No Tears for the NRI* (Calcutta: Writer's Workshop, 1996), pp. 25–26.

WHITE MINDS

17

The Universalization of Whiteness: Racism and Enlightenment

Warren Montag

On December 12, 1774, a mere eighteen months before the American Revolution, Janet Schaw, a Scottish "lady of quality" (whose ultimate destination was her brother's plantation in North Carolina) stepped onto a wharf at the port of St Johns, Antigua, still "giddy" from a long and difficult voyage from the Firth of Forth. As she walked with the rest of her party into the narrow lane that led to their hotel, an astonished Schaw reported that "a number of pigs ran out at a door, and after them a parcel of monkeys. This not a little surprised me, but I found that what I took for monkeys were negro children, naked as they were born."[1]

Schaw is obviously far from the world in which Aphra Behn (another "lady of quality" who visited the colonies and observed chattel slavery first-hand) could write *Oroonoko* (1688), a world in which it was still possible to imagine African slaves as physically and morally superior to their European masters. The conceptual divide that separates the two representations of colonial slavery testifies to the emergence, in an interval of less than a century,

281

of what Theodore W. Allen calls that "truly peculiar institution":[2] the white race.

This interval corresponds almost exactly to the time that separates Bacon's rebellion in 1676 in which African and English bond laborers in Virginia united to demand an end to their servitude[3] and the American Revolution, by which time "the white race" had become the linchpin in the strategy of the Anglo-American plantation owners to maintain their domination over the surplus-producing classes, both African and English. Indeed, Schaw's otherwise forgotten narrative, marginal almost to the point of invisibility, has survived thanks exclusively to the brief passage just cited, which appeared in a number of examinations of "the changing image of the negro," to use David Brion Davis's characterization[4] or, conversely, what Leon Poliakov labels "the Aryan myth."[5]

Schaw's two brutal sentences exhibit with remarkable economy the set of specific differences that historically constituted whiteness as an ontological as well as an epistemological category. The need to separate white from black and to establish an irreducible distance between them appears to be so overwhelming that Schaw has to retreat into a momentary delusion in order to defend against any feelings of kinship or commonality. The fact that she lets stand her erroneous assumption, placing it next to its "correction," establishes for all time the connection between the black children and the monkeys for whom she mistook them.

Before we dismiss this "observation," as other commentators have done, as an example, and a particularly egregious one, of a racism so crude (and, in this case, literally hallucinatory) that Schaw's words need only be repeated for their historical significance to be grasped, it might be productive to examine the place of these two sentences in the work from which they are taken and, in turn, the place of this work in the discursive network of which it is a part.

We would be wrong to think that Schaw's attitudes, as they are expressed in this passage, are typical or representative of the racism to which the slave-owning class could descend, in opposition to the more "enlightened" views of ruling classes in the metropolitan centers of Europe. Janet Schaw was neither ignorant nor vicious. On the contrary, she was both a product and an exemplar of the Scottish Enlightenment; so much so, in fact, that her traveling companion read to her from Kames's *Elements of Criticism* instead of the Bible during a particularly stormy moment in the transatlantic crossing. Her journal itself is an expression of what Habermas calls the public sphere, that zone of social interaction and cosmopolitan conversation made possible by the emergence of a civil society outside and opposed to the state, as well as by global trade and colonization.[6] According to this perspective, Schaw's journal even testifies to a tendency to level gender distinctions in the emergent public sphere, an effect of the new democratic social interaction.

Schaw's moral sentiments were indeed finely tuned. When she discovers, for example, shortly after the ship sails, that a group of impoverished Highland exiles have been smuggled on board, her first reaction is one of disgust at their wretched appearance and the stench they exude. But the moment she sees them look with longing, as the homeland to which they will never return recedes into the distance, her disgust melts into the tenderest sympathy. She reflects critically on her initial reaction and recognizes it to have been the product of the "dirty passions" that arise from the artificial, material differences of social rank, a particularism of class extinguished by the universalizing current of sympathy that surges through her. She values above all else "pity," that "fellow-feeling" as Adam Smith called it, uniting individuals into a community of sentiment. "The fairest social virtues derive their being" from pity, according to Schaw, virtues that "melt, soften and humanize the soul."[7]

We are thus compelled to recognize that Schaw's narrative exhibits a striking contradiction. The description of her encounter with the "negro children" seems incompatible with her repeated expressions of a universalist humanism before the encounter. Schaw is indisputably a standard-bearer of the cause of the universal against the particular and of the identical against the different in the social world. How then can we reconcile her endorsement of the cardinal Enlightenment virtues, her conscious universalist humanism, with her reduction or degradation of the "negro children," even if only for an instant, to a "parcel of monkeys?"

Such a "mistake" is, of course, in no way arbitrary. On the contrary, its condition of possibility is the presumption, grounded in the natural histories characteristic of the Enlightenment epoch (Maurpetuis, Linnaeus, Buffon) and in the early racist literature of the colonial period,[8] of an anatomical resemblance between the African people and the apes. The explanation of the apparent contradiction haunting the narrative takes us far beyond Schaw's journal and into the heart of contemporary debates about the Enlightenment and the meaning of universalism. Is the historical construction of whiteness, or even of the white race, incompatible with universalism?

The most obvious way to address this problem would be to argue that Schaw (and with her every "enlightened" exponent of white supremacy—and there were, and are, many) was simply an inconsistent proponent of universalism who failed to extend it to the entirety of its proper domain. According to such an argument, the equation of blacks with monkeys (and Schaw's discussion of Africans throughout the text) should be seen as a lapse in the rigorous application of a universalizing judgment and thus as an element foreign and even opposed to the humanist sentiments that dominate the journal.

We should not judge universalism and Enlightenment by the failures of a single person (even if her failures are expressions of a contemporaneous collective "invention of the white race"). Perhaps, at least on the question of race, Schaw (and her fellow white supremacists) suffers from what Kant in "What Is Enlightenment?" termed "an immaturity of the understanding," the inability to identify and criticize one's own prejudices or to understand what conditions one's experience. Although Schaw admittedly overcame some of the prejudices contributing to particularistic social thought, she "lacked the resolution," to use Kant's terminology, to think critically about her experience of certain peoples, to think for herself, entirely "unaided" by the racist prejudices of others, which are only so many strings by which we are led: *encore un effort!*[9] This would be the "exceptionalist" explanation of the coincidence of the Enlightenment and the emergence of whiteness as a practical–discursive construct. The latter can be understood only as an exception or even a resistance to the former.

Indeed, the text may allow us to go even further in this direction, for when we examine the two sentences that comprise Schaw's report, they appear to offer no normative judgment at all, communicating nothing more than a moment of perceptual confusion succeeded by clarity. Schaw presents her lapse as nothing more than a perceptual error, and so we are left to infer that the dark color of the children's skin (they were, after all, naked)—as well, perhaps, as their contiguity to "a number of pigs"—allowed her, for no more than a blink of an eye, to mistake the children for monkeys. Once the mistake is rectified, they are restored to their properly human status and promptly forgotten.

The apparently different is restored to its place in the identical. Isn't the activity of the understanding embodied in the movement of these two sentences an enactment of the criticism that constitutes the Enlightenment: the questioning of oneself, one's faculties, the removal of prejudices so that one may see clearly, see things as they really are? The critical gaze is thus the gaze that looks again, after looking at itself looking, so that it may distinguish between what it brings to the experience of reality and the reality as it is independently of the act of knowing.

But the notion that Schaw's mistaking black children for monkeys is merely an inconsistency, a momentary failure. Thinking in a universalist spirit itself rests on the position that the universal is incompatible with the debasement to the inhuman or an animal of certain human beings, whether groups defined "phenotypically" or culturally or even individuals defined by their speech or actions.

To put the question in the terms of Schaw's text: Can whiteness be understood not as one possible human attribute or property, distinct from and in opposition to other human attributes of the same class, such as blackness, but instead as the very condition of one's humanity, one's species being? We can begin to glimpse the existence of what would otherwise be a paradox: that the (or, rather, a) universal was one of the forms in which the white race historically appeared. In a certain sense, one of the moments in the invention of the white race was its universalization in a movement that replaced the distinction between the black and white "races," "varieties of the human species" according to Buffon, with the distinction between the human and the animal. To be white is to be human, and to be human is to be white. In this way, the concept of whiteness is deprived of its purely racial character at the moment of its universalization, no longer conceivable as a particularistic survival haunting the discourse of universality but, rather, as the very form of human universality itself.

Thus this late-eighteenth-century text that emerged within a much larger discursive network (and its practical conditions: capitalist surplus extraction as well as colonialism and slavery) allows us to ask whether, since whiteness is not logically confined to the status of a particularism but can be conceived as one possible form of universalism, the category or attribute of whiteness has functioned historically in opposition to universalism. To consider such a possibility is, of course, to question universalism not merely in its historical actuality but even in its ideal form, a form perhaps not yet (fully) realized. Janet Schaw's lapse assumes the character of a symptom determined not simply by the conflicts underlying the journal but by the conflicts forming the very concept of universality as it actually functioned in the epoch of the Enlightenment.

As Etienne Balibar argues in his essay "Racism as Universalism," there are weak and strong versions of the idea of universalism as racism. According to the weak version, "universalism was used in a Machiavellian way to cover and implement racist policies, to justify in a fake scientific manner racist ideologies, to rationalize institutional racism, to impose the domination of some cultures on others in a racist way." In contrast, the strong version "questions the notions of universalism, universality, or universal with respect to their internal constitution and their implications, preferably in a historical manner." It is precisely this second, "strong" version of universalism that allows us to see that the contradiction dominating Schaw's text is not the contradiction between universalism and particularism but, instead, the antagonism(s) internal to universalism itself. According to Balibar, every universalism, or at least every humanist universalism, is forced to undertake "a definition of the human species, or simply the human," that leads to an "infinite process of demarcation between the human, the more than human and the less than human (or *Supermen* and *Untermenschen*) and the reflection of these two limits within the imaginary boundaries of the human 'species.' "[10]

And it is this that is crucial about Schaw's journal: it stumbles at the border, which separates the identical and the different or, to characterize this opposition in the concrete terms of the text, the limit between the human and the nonhuman. It seems that the children's negritude places them at outermost limit of the human species. We might even say that their negritude is that limit, the site of an oscillation between the human and the nonhuman that—despite the apparent resolution of the second sentence, Schaw's finding that what she took for monkeys were in fact children—repeats itself several times later in the text, thus emerging as a kind of undecidable or even uncanny moment in which the familiar never ceases to be haunted by the strange, always internal to it.

Later in the narrative, Schaw has an opportunity to observe slave gangs cutting sugarcane. Although she can clearly see where the whip has been applied on the slaves' naked backs, she comforts herself and her more delicate readers by observing that

> when one comes to be better acquainted with the nature of the negroes, the horrour of it must wear off. It is the suffering of the human mind that constitutes the greater misery of punishment, but with them it is merely corporeal. As to the brutes it inflicts no wound on their mind, whose natures are made to bear it, and whose sufferings are not attended with shame or pain beyond the present moment. (p. 127)

It is important to note here that Schaw differentiates the observable characteristics of Africans not from those of Europeans or even from those other non-European cultures or racial groups but, rather, from humans per se. Africans' suffering is merely corporeal, not the suffering characteristic of the human mind, a shame or pain that transcends the physical and that would persist long after the sensation of the whip ceased to be felt. The fact that they live a merely physical existence in which memory and history play no part renders them "brutes" to whom pity cannot be extended. In the face of Schaw's universalizing "social virtue," if the racial hierarchies internal to humanity disappear, it is because irreducible difference has been moved to the periphery of the species beyond which the universal no longer applies. The universalization of whiteness has made the question of the Africans' humanity a permanent, insoluble problem.

It might be imagined that in contrast to an admittedly marginal figure like Schaw, the "great philosophers" of the Enlightenment—those who posited the original equality of all men (and women) without exception, from European monarchs to solitary savages wandering through the empty wastes of America—were innocent of the effort to universalize whiteness by adjusting the boundaries of the human species. Their texts, however, exhibit in exorbitant ways what Balibar names the "paradoxes of universality."[11]

It is well known that Locke, to take one important example, refused any notion of a natural hierarchy internal to the human order, declaring in opposition that all men in the state of nature (a universalist concept if there ever was one, denoting the condition common to all people before their division into nations, races, and classes) were naturally free and equal. Locke's questioning of the received ideas concerning the boundaries of the human species at precisely the same moment has received far less attention, and the possible connection of such questioning to his political doctrines remains, with a few exceptions,[12] unexplored. His radical interrogation of the limits of the human species can in no way be seen as some atavistic survival marring the otherwise egalitarian nature of both his epistemology and his political theory. On the contrary, his questioning is very much in the spirit of the Enlightenment.

More than two centuries earlier, the Spanish debated the question of the Native Americans' humanity, rather quickly resolving, with the aid of King Charles V (Proclamation of August 2, 1530) and Pope Paul III (papal brief of June 9, 1537) that the Indians were indeed human and thus possessed of immortal souls: All men are sons of Adam and made in God's image.[13] This debate, however, differed in essential ways from the concerns of the eighteenth century and was in a fundamental sense opposed to the concerns of the Enlightenment. The Spanish debate centered not on the problem of defining the precise boundaries of the human species but on the correspondence of the Indians to a model spelled out in Scripture and therefore not open to question (except in the limited form of exegesis). Locke's refusal to be guided by dogma—whether religious dogma or even the dogma of opinion, a hallmark of the Enlightenment (at least as defined by Kant)—led to the recognition that the boundaries between species were indeterminate, set not by nature but by human convention concealing itself as nature. After all, in order to declare all men naturally free and equal, isn't it first necessary to determine what a "man" is, or rather, which phenomena do or do not correspond to the name "man"?

On what rational grounds were these limits established? Were they justifiable? Could they stand up under scrutiny? Were they too inclusive or too narrow?

In *An Essay Concerning Human Understanding* (1690), Locke asked about humanity:

> Wherein, then, would I gladly know, consist the precise and unmovable boundaries of that species? It is plain, if we examine, there is no such thing made by nature and established by her amongst men. . . . So uncertain are the boundaries of species of animals to us who have no other measures than complex ideas of our own collecting: and so far are we from knowing what a man is; though perhaps it will be judged great ignorance to make any doubt about it. And yet I think I may say, that the certain boundaries of that species are so far from being determined, and the precise number of simple ideas which make the nominal essence so far from being settled and perfectly known, that very material doubts may still arise about it.

And if there were any doubts about the social and political direction of this line of inquiry, Locke makes it quite clear that the question of boundaries arises as one moves outside the realm of whiteness. He imagines that a child in its innocence and naïveté might "demonstrate to you that a negro is not a man because white colour was one of the constant simple ideas of the complex idea he calls man."[14]

Furthermore, for Locke, the question of the limits and definition of humanity was not simply a question of establishing the proper classificatory boundaries, demarcating the outermost periphery of the species. It was also a political question, for there was a limit or threshold internal to the human order that a person by virtue of an action voluntarily undertaken might cross and, in so doing, cease to be a man. Locke reminds us that not merely murderers but even criminals who would "invade others rights" and threaten their liberty or goods "having renounced reason, the common rule and measure God hath given to mankind, hath, by the unjust violence and slaughter he hath committed upon one, declared war against all mankind and therefore may be destroyed as a lion or a tiger." Thus Locke may kill the thief who seeks only to rob him of his coat, the thief by his voluntary renunciation of reason and God's law (of property) having equally renounced his humanity with all the privileges pertaining to it. It is not simply what a man is, his physical appearance, that may serve as the basis for a questioning of his humanity; it is even more what a man (or group of men or people) does, his actions, practices, customs, and manners that may, insofar as they depart from reason, disqualify him as a man. Locke offers a hypothetical example of this latter form of exclusion in the *First Treatise*: Native Americans who have inflicted some injury on a West Indian planter.[15]

At this point, we might object that even if we grant that a universalist humanism like Locke's must define the human, setting by empirical, logical, or juridical–moral means the limits between the human and the nonhuman, such a definition might function as the guarantee of what we might call the universality of the (human) universal, of the universal extension of the universal, a universal without a remainder, without an outside. Such a definition might exclude once and for all any attempt to dehumanize a variety of the human.

The case of Rousseau who, even more rigorously than Locke, rejected any notion of a natural inequality among men is instructive in this regard. Although Locke's search for an adequate definition of the human seemed destined to lead to a narrowing of the species and the exclusion from the human of the pseudohuman (of which the only example offered is that of blacks) and the men who by their voluntary actions ceased to be men (Native Americans), Rousseau sought to expand the definition of the human to encompass species that his contemporaries regarded as beasts. The philosophers of his time (including and perhaps especially Locke) who "examined the foundations of society have all felt the necessity of going back to the state of nature, but none of them has reached it . . . they carried over to the state of nature ideas that they had acquired in society: they spoke of savage man and described civil man." [16] They generally failed to consider the accounts of explorers and naturalists, content to explicate human nature in the light of their own nation, with its peculiar manners and characteristics: "individuals may well come and go: philosophy, it seems, does not travel" (p. 210). [17] In ascribing to savage man not only such "civil" passions as greed and avarice, as well as a primordial desire to dominate others, and such civil institutions as property—but even speech, reason, and any thought apart from instinct and reflex—they arrived at too absolute a distinction between the human and the animal. Even travelers, less encumbered than philosophers with prejudices concerning the variety of the human species, often take for beasts the various "anthropomorphic animals" who exhibit "striking similarities to the human species and fewer differences than those that may be found from man to man" (p. 207).

Rousseau imagines that they have arrived at such conclusions because of these animals' "stupidity" and the fact that they do not speak. But to assume that these qualities do not pertain to humanity even in its natural state is to fail to take into account "to what point his perfectibility may have raised civil man above his original state" (p. 207). We need only observe the great variety of the human species produced by innumerable causes (among them "the diversity of climate, atmosphere, food, way of life and habits in general," p. 203) to

wonder if a number of animals similar to men taken by travellers for beasts . . .
are not in fact true savage men whose race, dispersed long ago into the woods,
did not have the occasion to develop any of its virtual faculties, having acquired
no degree of perfection, and finding itself still in a primitive state of nature.
(p. 204)

Rousseau's inclusivity—his proposal to extend the boundaries of the human
species to a point well beyond any limit assigned by his contemporaries,[18]
together with his apparent denial that actions, practices, or customs serve to
distinguish the human from the animal—appears to offer the antidote to
Locke's restrictive definition. He thus seems to provide an anthropological
ground for a universalism that, if anything, exceeds what we now think of as
humanity, providing a margin of error that guarantees that no human variety
can be placed outside its jurisdiction. Rousseau's anthropology, however, rests
on a paradox that prevents him from ever drawing a clear line of demarcation
between the human and the animal and thus excluding any bestialization of the
human. On the contrary, a regression to the nonhuman or the less-than-human
is a possibility insofar as the origin of humanity lies outside itself in a realm of
pure animality from which every properly human characteristic is absent. At
the beginning, then, for Rousseau (and before Hegel), man is the negation of
himself, and this negation must itself be negated for man to become himself.

But what is the human if its initial form cannot be distinguished from
animality? The specificity of the human, the difference that separates it from
the animal, is not any actually existing set of characteristics but a mere potential
that may never be realized. What makes human the beasts dispersed long ago
into the woods is not what they are but what they are not (yet). Their essence
is what will be or could be: they are men degree zero. According to Rousseau,
the "specific character of the human species" consists almost exclusively of the
principle of perfectibility. The blurring of distinctions between the human and
the animal means that just as we cannot know to what degree humanity may
rise in perfecting itself, so it is difficult to recognize how far below us are our
origins, in the nearly unimaginable alterity of "those who have acquired no
degree of perfection."

What are the implications of Rousseau's anthropology for the universalization of whiteness? It allows us to see that Hume's often cited theses (which, as
in the case of Rousseau's proposal to expand the limits of the human, are stated
outside the bounds of the text in a footnote, an "afterthought" that, whatever
its chronological relation to the arguments whose appendix it forms, may
logically precede them) on the natural inferiority of blacks to "the whites"—

deduced, as David Theo Goldberg reminds us, from the strictest empirical observation (of the negative correlation between men of "that complexion" and civilization)—represent a relatively primitive form of the philosophy of white supremacy, easily seen for what it is and just as easily refuted.[19]

In contrast, Rousseau does not even use the term *white:* he does not need to. Whiteness is no longer conceivable as one human attribute or property (or even, *avant la lettre,* phenotype) the presence or absence of which determines one's place in an anthropological taxonomy or, conversely, the privileges that one is accorded or denied in a given legal order). Rather, whiteness functions as a norm in the sense defined by Georges Canguilhem (who reminds us that the term *normal* first appears in French in almost the same year as the "Discourse on the Origin of Inequality"):

> A norm draws its meaning, function and value from the fact of the existence, outside of itself, of what does not meet the requirement it serves. . . . To set a norm, to normalize is to impose a requirement on an existence, on a given whose variety, whose disparity is offered as more hostile than foreign to the requirement.[20]

Given that humanity is not originally human but nonhuman and that the humanness of the human species is not to be found in its actual condition, an ideal emerges out of and against actuality that allows us to assign descending "degrees of perfection" to the individuals or groups we consider. It is the principle not external to humanity but immanent in it as an internal distance that separates humanity as it is from humanity as it ought to be, that receding horizon of perfectibility in relation to which specific anthropological cases may be hierarchized in order of failure. Thus, in appearing to homogenize the human species (in conformity with the ideals of universalism), such a norm instead furnishes the criteria of its internal differentiation all the way down to the animal who possesses not a single human characteristic except a perfectibility always to be realized. The human norm, of course, is always glimpsed only negatively: it is what allows us to see the deficient and the abnormal without itself being seen.

The secret of whiteness, as David Roediger argues, is that it is empty, defined only negatively by what it is not,[21] a rule or norm established only after the phenomena that it came to define as inadequate or abnormal. Accordingly, in its most historically effective forms, whiteness does not speak its own name. It may be nothing more than the principle in relation to which all (other) races, nations, and peoples are classified and hierarchized, the principle of perfection, to use Rousseau's phrase, established to measure the degree to which all (other) races have fallen short of it, a definition of the human that renders them subhuman. Whiteness is itself the human universal that no (other) race realizes. In theory, no (other) race is, or need be, inferior (it is only the contingent and the accidental that make them so). In fact, all (others) are inferior, having fallen short of the universal and therefore of humanity.

The gaze that, in the brilliant light of a Caribbean morning, played between children and monkeys, unable finally to decide the humanity of the dark beings on which it settled, was not the gaze of Janet Schaw alone; it was a gaze that enveloped her, a gaze that saw through her, the gaze of an implacable whiteness confronted with beings that it could not reduce to its truth. It is the gaze of a universal that stumbles on what it has left out, on the remainder that it cannot acknowledge except by projecting it beyond the limits whose existence it is designed to mask. We are, of course, still imprisoned in these limits. To reveal their existence is the first step toward their destruction and the abolition of the white race.

NOTES

I would like to thank Gabrielle Foreman, G. Elmer Griffin, and Ben Swire for their comments and suggestions.

1. Janet Schaw, *Journal of a Lady of Quality; Being the Narrative of a Journey from Scotland to the West Indies, North Carolina and Portugal, in the Years 1774 to 1776* (New Haven, CT: Yale University Press, 1927), p. 78 (subsequent page references to this book are in parentheses).

2. Theodore H. Allen, *The Invention of the White Race: Volume One* (London: Verso, 1994), p. 24.

3. See ibid.; and Edmund S. Morgan, *American Slavery, American Freedom* (New York: Norton, 1975).

4. David Brion Davis, *The Problem of Slavery in Western Culture* (Ithaca, NY: Cornell University Press, 1966).

5. Léon Poliakov, *The Aryan Myth* (New York: Basic Books, 1971).

6. Margaret C. Jacob, "The Mental Landscape of the Public Sphere: A European Perspective," *Eighteenth-Century Studies* 28 (Fall 1994): 95–113.

7. Adam Smith, *The Theory of Moral Sentiments* (Indianapolis: Liberty Fund, 1976), pp. 36, 10, 36.

8. Davis, *The Problem of Slavery,* pp. 446–82.

9. Immanuel Kant, "What Is Enlightenment," in *Kant's Political Writings* (Cambridge: Cambridge University Press, 1970), p. 54.

10. Etienne Balibar, "Racism as Universalism," in his *Masses, Classes, Ideas* (New York: Routledge, 1994), pp. 195, 197.

11. Etienne Balibar and Immanuel Wallerstein, *Race, Nation, Class: Ambiguous Identities* (London: Verso, 1991), p. 54.

12. Wayne Glausser, "Three Approaches to Locke and the Slave Trade," *Journal of the History of Ideas* 51 (1990): 199–216.

13. Louis Sala-Molins, *Le Code noir ou le calvaire de canaan* (Paris: PUF, 1987), pp. 35–41.

14. John Locke, *An Essay Concerning Human Understanding* (New York: Dover, 1959), vol. 2, pp. 77–78, 289.

15. John Locke, *Two Treatises of Government* (Cambridge: Cambridge University Press, 1963), pp. 314–15, 321, 276.

16. Jean-Jacques Rousseau, *The First and Second Discourses* (New York: St. Martin's Press, 1964), p. 102 (subsequent page references to this book are in parentheses).

17. I have slightly modified the translation of this and the following passages from Rousseau's *Second Discourse.*

18. Michèle Duchet, *Anthropologie et histoire au siècle des lumières* (Paris: Maspero, 1971).

19. See David Theo Goldberg, *Racist Culture* (Oxford: Blackwell, 1993).

20. Georges Canguilhem, *The Normal and the Pathological* (New York: Zone, 1989), p. 239 (translation slightly modified).

21. David R. Roediger, *Towards the Abolition of Whiteness* (London: Verso, 1994), p. 13.

──── 18 ────

Racial Politics and the Pedagogy of Whiteness

Henry A. Giroux

YOUTH AND THE POLITICS OF WHITENESS

Central to any pedagogical approach to race and the politics of "whiteness" is the recognition that race is a set of attitudes, values, lived experiences, and affective identifications. However arbitrary and mythic, dangerous and variable, the fact is that racial categories exist and shape the lives of people differently within existing inequalities of power and wealth.[1] As a central form of difference, race will not disappear, be wished out of existence, or somehow become irrelevant in the United States and the larger global context. Howard Winant argues:

> Race is a condition of individual and collective identity, a permanent, though tremendously flexible, element of social structure. Race is a means of knowing and organizing the social world; it is subject to continual contestation and reinterpretation, but it is no more likely to disappear than any other forms of human inequality and difference. . . . To rethink race is not only to recognize its permanence, but also to understand the essential test that it poses for any diverse society seeking to achieve a modicum of freedom.[2]

294

As a pedagogical device, Winant suggests providing the conditions for students to address how their "whiteness" functions in society as a marker of privilege and power and also how it can be used to expand the ideological and material realities of democratic public life. All students should understand how race functions systemically as it shapes various forms of representations, social relations, and institutional structures. Rather than proposing the eradication of the concept of race itself, educators and other cultural workers need to take a detour through race in order to decide how "whiteness" might be renegotiated as a productive force in a politics of difference linked to a radical democratic project. Doing this means considering the differences in "whiteness" and the political possibilities that can be opened up through a discourse of "whiteness" articulated in new forms of identity, new possibilities for democratic practices, and new processes of cultural exchange.

Analyzing "whiteness" as a central element of racial politics becomes useful in exploring how "whiteness" as a cultural practice promotes race-based hierarchies, how white racial identity structures the struggle over cultural and political resources, and how rights and responsibilities are defined, confirmed, or contested across diverse racial claims.[3] "Whiteness" in this context becomes less a matter of creating a new form of identity politics than an attempt to rearticulate "whiteness" as part of a broader project of cultural, social, and political citizenship.

I want to begin this challenge pedagogically by building on James Snead's observation that the emergence of mass visual productions in the United States requires new ways of seeing and making visible the racial structuring of white experience.[4] The electronic media—television, movies, music, and news— have become a powerful pedagogical force, veritable teaching machines in shaping the social imaginary of students regarding how they view themselves, others, and the larger society. Central to the formative influence of the media is a representational politics of race in which the portrayal of black people abstracts them from their real histories while reinforcing familiar stereotypes ranging from lazy and shiftless to the menacing and dangerous.

Recent films from a variety of genres, such as *Pulp Fiction* (1995), *Just Cause* (1995), and *Ace Ventura: When Nature Calls* (1996) offer no apologies for using racist language, depicting black men as rapists, or portraying blacks as savage or subhuman. Antiracist readings of these films often position white students to define and critique racism as the product of dominant racist stereotypes that unfairly depict black identities, experiences, histories, and social relations. As important as these critiques are to any antiracist discourse or pedagogy, they are limited theoretically because they do not make problematic how "whiteness" as a racial identity and social construction is taught, learned, experienced, and identified in certain forms of knowledge, values, and privileges. Hollywood films rarely position audiences to question the pleasures, identifications, desires, and fears they experience as whites viewing dominant representational politics of race. More specifically, such films rarely make problematic either the structuring principles that mobilize particular pleasures in audiences or how pleasure as a response to certain representations functions as part of a broader public discourse. At worst, such films position whites as racial tourists, distant observers to the racist images and narratives that fill Hollywood screens. At best, such films reinforce the liberal assumption that racism is something that gives rise to black oppression but has little or nothing to do with promoting power, racial privilege, and a sense of moral agency in the lives of whites.[5]

In this chapter, I want to explore the pedagogical implications for examining representations of "whiteness" in two seemingly disparate films, *Dangerous Minds* (1995) and *Suture* (1993). Although I will focus primarily on *Dangerous Minds*, it is through a juxtaposition and intertextual reading of these films that I hope to provide some insights into how "whiteness" as a cultural practice is learned through the representation of racialized identities, how it opens up the possibility of intellectual self-reflection, and how students might critically mediate the complex relations between "whiteness" and racism, not by having them repudiate their "whiteness," but by grappling with its racist legacy and its potential to be rearticulated in oppositional and transformative terms. I also want to stress that I am not suggesting that *Dangerous Minds* is a bad film and *Suture* is a good film given their different approaches to "whiteness." Both have notable weaknesses. What I am suggesting is that these films are exemplary in representing dominant readings of "whiteness" and as cultural texts that can be used to address the shortcomings of the recent scholarship on "whiteness," in particular, ways to move beyond the view of "whiteness" as simply a trope of domination.

At first glance, these films appear to have nothing in common in terms of audience, genre, intention, or politics. *Dangerous Minds*, a Hollywood blockbuster starring Michelle Pfeiffer, was produced for a general audience and, in its first week, grossed millions for its producers. The film's popularity can, in part, be measured by the creation of a pilot television series called *Dangerous Minds* that began in the fall of 1996. In contrast, *Suture* is an independent film that played primarily to highbrow audiences with a penchant for avant-garde cinema. Although some people may argue that *Dangerous Minds* is too popular and too unoriginal to be taken seriously as a cultural text, it is precisely because of its popularity and widespread appeal that it warrants an extended analysis.

Like many Hollywood films, *Dangerous Minds* is offensive not only for its racial politics but also for its debased depiction of teaching and education. The 1995 summer hit is symptomatic, as well, of how seemingly "innocent" entertainment gains its popularity by taking part in a larger public discourse on race and "whiteness" largely informed by a right-wing and conservative notion of politics, theory, and pedagogy.

DANGEROUS MINDS AND THE PRODUCTION OF WHITENESS

Dangerous Minds resembles a long tradition of Hollywood movies recounting the sorry state of education for dispossessed kids who bear the brunt of poverty, crime, violence, and despair in the inner cities of the United States. Unlike earlier films such as *Blackboard Jungle* (1955), *To Sir with Love* (1967), and *Stand and Deliver* (1988), which also deal with the interface of schooling and the harsh realities of inner-city life, *Dangerous Minds* does more than simply narrate the story of an idealistic teacher who struggles to connect with her rowdy and disinterested students. *Dangerous Minds* functions as a dual chronicle. In the first instance, the film attempts to represent "whiteness" as the archetype of rationality, "tough" authority, and cultural standards in the midst of the changing racial demographics of urban space and the emergence of a resurgent racism in the highly charged politics of the 1990s. In the second instance, the film offers viewers a mix of compassion and consumerism as a pedagogical solution to motivating teenagers who have long given up on schooling as either relevant or meaningful to their lives. In both instances, "whiteness" becomes a referent for rearticulating racially coded notions of teaching and learning and also for redefining how citizenship can be constructed for students of color as a function of choice linked exclusively to the marketplace.

Providing an allegory for representing both the purpose of schooling and the politics of racial difference as they intersect in the contested space of the urban public schools, *Dangerous Minds* skillfully mobilizes race as an organizing principle to promote its narrative structure and ideological message. Black and Latino teenagers provide the major fault line for developing classroom pedagogical relations through which "whiteness," located in the authority of the teacher's privileges against the racially coded images of disorder, chaos, and fear. The opposition between teacher and student, white and nonwhite, is established in the first few scenes of the film.

The opening sequence, shot in grainy monochrome, depicts a rundown urban housing project teeming with poverty, drug dealing, and danger. Against this backdrop, disaffected black and Latino children board a school bus that will take them to Parkmont High School and out of their crime- and drug-infested neighborhoods. This is one of the few shots in the film providing a context for the children's lives: the inner city has become a site of pathology, moral decay, and delinquency synonymous with the culture of working-class black life. Featuring a hip-hop music score that includes artists such as Coolio, Sista, and Aaron Hall, the sound track is present only as a backdrop to the film.

Although the driving beat of hip-hop reinforces the gritty urban realism that provides a tidy summation of these kids' everyday lives, it is completely ignored as a cultural or pedagogical resource for learning about their histories, experiences, or the economic, social, and political limits they face daily. More-over, the musical score's marginality to the plot of *Dangerous Minds* serves to reinforce the right-wing assumption that rap music signifies black culture as a culture of crime and violence. The sound track to this film stayed at the top of the charts for weeks, providing a reminder of how black culture is commodified in the dominant media.

Framed by a racial iconography and a musical score that construct minority students as both the objects of fear and subjects in need of discipline and control, the audience is prepared for someone to take charge. Enter LouAnne Johnson, a good-hearted ingenue thrust into the classroom of "at-risk" kids like a lamb led to slaughter.

A divorced ex-marine, LouAnne Johnson turns up at Parkmont High in order to student-teach and finish her degree. She is immediately hired as an English teacher in the "Academy School," a euphemism for warehousing students who are considered unteachable. Dressed in frowzy tweeds and white lace, LouAnne enters her class triumphant and full of high hopes to meet a room filled with Latino and black kids who have brought the "worst" aspects of their culture into the classroom. As music blares amidst the clatter of students shouting, rapping, and dancing, LouAnne is presented with a classroom in an inner-city school that appears to be disorderly and out of control. Leaving the safety of her white, middle-class culture in order to teach in a cultural war zone filled with chaos and potential danger, LouAnne Johnson is presented to the audience as an innocent border crosser. Against this image of innocence and goodwill, white America is offered the comforting belief that disorder, igno-rance, and chaos are always somewhere else—in that strangely homogenized, racial space known as the urban ghetto.[6]

After LouAnne's attempt to greet them, the students respond with the taunting epithet "white bread." Confused and unable to gain control of the class, LouAnne is accosted by a male student who makes a mockery of her authority by insulting her with a sexual innuendo. Frustrated, she leaves the class and tells Hal, a friend who teaches next door, that she has just met the "rejects from hell." He assures her that she can reach these students if she can figure out how to get their attention. These opening scenes work powerfully in associating black and Latino kids with the culture of criminality and danger. They also make clear that "whiteness" as a racial identity, embodied in Lou-Anne Johnson, is both vulnerable and the only hope these kids have for moving beyond the context and character of their racial identities. In other words, "whiteness" as a racial identity is being constructed through the stereotypical portrayal of black and Latino kids as intellectually inferior, hostile, and childish while coding "whiteness" as a norm for authority, orderliness, rationality, and control.

The structuring principles at work in *Dangerous Minds* perform an ideological function in their attempt to cater to white consumers of popular culture. Pedagogy performs a doubling operation as it is used in this film. As part of the overt curriculum, the film focuses on teaching in an inner-city school and constructs a dominant view of race as embodied in the lives of urban black and Latino children. On the other hand, the film's hidden curriculum works pedagogically to recover and mark the ideological and cultural values that construct "whiteness" as a dominant form of racial identity. Hollywood films about teaching have a long tradition, but rarely do they use the theme of teaching merely as a tool for legitimating a conservative view of "whiteness" as a besieged social formation, and subordinate racial identities as a threat to public order. The conservative and ideological implications of how "whiteness" is constructed in this film can be seen through a series of constructions.

The film tells us nothing about the lives of the students themselves. The audience is given no sense of their histories or experiences outside the school. Decontextualized and dehistoricized, the students' cultural identities appear marginal to the construction of race as an organizing principle of the film. Racial differences in this film are situated in the spatial metaphor of center and margins, with the children of color clearly occupying the margins. At the center of the film is the embellished "true story" of LouAnne Johnson, who not only overcomes her initial failure to motivate these students but also serves as a beacon of light by convincing them that they need to abandon their notions of who they are and what they know if they are to become more civilized and cultured (and more white).

In this context, racial conflict is resolved through a colonial model in which white paternalism and missionary zeal provide the inspiration for kids from deprived backgrounds to improve their character and sense of responsibility by reading poetry. In this movie, the children simply appear as a backdrop for expanding LouAnne's own self-consciousness and self-education, rather than offering an opportunity for understanding their coming of age or how racism works in the schools and larger society. Whenever these kids do face a crisis regarding an unwanted pregnancy, the threat of violence, or dropping out of school, LouAnne invades their homes and private lives, using the occasion to win the kids' allegiance or draw attention to her own divorce, physical abuse, or sense of despair. If any notion of identity occupies center stage, it is not that of the kids but that of a white woman trying to figure out how to live in a public space inhabited by racialized others.

The notion of authority and agency in *Dangerous Minds* is framed in a pedagogy of "tough love" that serves to mask how racial hierarchies and structured inequality operate in the schools and to connect them to the larger society. Authority in *Dangerous Minds* is initially asserted when LouAnne Johnson shows up on the second day of class wearing a leather jacket and jeans. Reinventing herself as a military officer on leave, she further qualifies her new "tough" no-nonsense look by informing her students she is an ex-marine who knows karate. Suggesting that fear and danger are the only emotions they recognize as important, she crosses a racial divide by rooting her sense of authority in a traditionally racist notion of discipline and control. Once she gets the group's attention, she moves onto more lofty ground and begins the arduous task of trying to develop a pedagogy that is both morally uplifting and pedagogically relevant. Choice becomes for LouAnne the theoretical axis that organizes her classroom approach. First, on the side of moral uplift (complete with a 1990s conservative whitewashing of history), she tells her students that there are no victims in her class. Presumably, this is meant as a plea to rouse their sense of agency and responsibility, but it rings hollow, since LouAnne has no understanding of the social and historical limits that shape their sense of agency. Of course, some students immediately recognize the bad faith implicit in her sermonizing call and urge her to test it with a dose of reality by living in their neighborhood for a week.

LouAnne appears to confuse her own range of choices, in part predicated on her class and racial privileges as a white person, with those of her students, even though they lack the power and resources to negotiate their lives politically, geographically, or economically with the same ease or options. She has no sense that choice springs from power and that those who have limited power have fewer choices. The subtext here reinforces the currently popular right-wing assumption that character, merit, and self-help are the basis on which people make their place in society. Of course, in a hierarchical and social structure organized by race, economic power, gender, and other key determinants, "whiteness" emerges as the normative basis for success, responsibility, and legitimate authority. By suggesting that white educators can ignore how larger social considerations affect racial groups, white privilege, experience, and culture are relieved of complicity with, if not responsibility for, racist ideology and structural inequalities.

Choice is not only trivialized in LouAnne's classroom, it provides the basis for a pedagogy that is as indifferent to the lives of poor inner-city kids as it is demeaning. Relying on the logic of the market to motivate the children, LouAnne rewards classroom cooperation with candy bars, a trip to an amusement park, and dinner at a fancy restaurant. Baiting students with gimmicks and bribes casts a moral shadow on the pedagogical value of such an approach or the teacher as a kind of ethical exemplar, and it also makes clear how little LouAnne knows about the realities of her students' lives. Knowing little about the skills they need to survive, LouAnne is indifferent to their experiences, interests, or cultural resources. This becomes clear in three pivotal instances in the movie.

In the first instance, LouAnne attempts to motivate the students by giving them the lyrics to Bob Dylan's "Mr. Tambourine Man." Indifferent to the force of hip-hop culture (though marketing executives appeared to know the draw and impact of hip-hop on the film's audience when designing the sound track), her intervention into popular culture appears as nothing less than an act of cultural ignorance and bad pedagogy. But more revealing is LouAnne's attempt to relate Dylan's lyrics to the most clichéd aspects of the students' culture, namely, violence and drugs. Not only does she ignore the cultural resources and interests of her students, but she also frames her notion of popular culture in a text from the 1960s, almost twenty years before these students were born. Rather than excavating the traditions, themes, and experiences that permeate her students' lives, in order to construct her curriculum, she simply avoids their voices altogether in shaping the content of what she teaches. Beneath this form of pedagogical violence, there is also the presupposition that whites can come into such schools and teach without theory, ignore the histories and narratives that students bring to school, and perform miracles in the children's lives by mere acts of kindness.

LouAnne's romantic version of schooling has no sense of what it means to teach urban youth survival skills. Her ignorance is reflected in another scene when she visits the grandmother of two black students missing from school for several days. Because the boys' grandmother has pulled them out of school, LouAnne decides to reason with her in order to get the students back into her class. The grandmother meets her in the yard and refers to her as a "white bread bitch." The grandmother is indignant over what the boys have brought home for homework and tells LouAnne that "her boys have got bills to pay and that she should find some other poor boys to save." Regardless of the fact that Bob Dylan's lyrics are irrelevant to the kids' lives, the black grandmother is represented as an obstructionist. Yet she is actually closer to the truth in suggesting that what LouAnne has passed off as useful knowledge will not help the boys survive life in the ghetto nor will it change the conditions that create urban squalor.

LouAnne's pedagogy is diversion, refusing to give students skills that will help them address the urgent and disturbing questions of a society and a culture that in many ways ignores their humanity and well-being. She does not teach them to question the intellectual and cultural resources they need to address the conditions they have to deal with every day. How to survive in a society, let alone remake it, is an important question that cannot be separated from the larger issue of what it means to live in a country that is increasingly hostile to the existence of poor white and black kids in the inner cities. But LouAnne ignores these issues and instead offers her students material incentives and, in doing so, turns them into consuming subjects rather than social subjects eager and able to think critically in order to negotiate and transform the worlds in which they live.

In one pivotal exchange, students ask LouAnne what reward they will receive for reading a poem. She surprises both her students and the wider audience by insisting that learning is its own best reward. In doing so she switches her pedagogical strategy, completely unaware of the consequences or limitations of the marketplace strategy that she has used most of the semester.

LouAnne's sense of privilege also becomes evident in her boundless confidence in her authority and moral superiority. She believes that somehow her students are answerable to her in terms of both their classroom performance and their personal lives; her role is to affirm or gently "correct" how they narrate their beliefs, experiences, and values. LouAnne takes for granted that she has a right to "save them" or run their lives without entering into a dialogue in which her own authority and purity of intentions are called into question. Authority here functions as a way of making invisible LouAnne's own privileges as a white woman while simultaneously allowing her to indulge in a type of moralizing commensurate with her colonizing role as a white teacher who extracts from her students love and loyalty in exchange for teaching them to be part of a system that oppresses them.

LouAnne's inability to enter into a dialogue with her students is apparent in two important exchanges with them. In one scene, LouAnne breaks up a fight between Emilio and some other students and then demands from Emilio a full explanation:

> LOUANNE: "Was it worth it? You like to hit people? Why? You feel angry?"
> EMILIO: "You're trying to figure me out. You going to try to psychologize me. I'll help you. I come from a broken home, and we're poor, okay. I see the same fucking movies you do."
> LOUANNE: "I'd like to help you, Emilio."
> EMILIO: "Thank you very much. And how you going to do that? You going to give me some good advice—just say no—you going to get me off the streets? Well forget it. How the fuck are you going to save me from my life?"

Emilio is trying to educate her, but LouAnne is not listening carefully. She assumes a moralizing posture that is totally indifferent to understanding the complex forces shaping Emilio's life. Nor can this great white hope consider that her students' histories and worldviews might be usefully incorporated into her pedagogy in order to teach kids like Emilio the survival skills they need to cope with the conditions of their surroundings.

In another exchange, LouAnne takes Raul, a promising student, to a fancy restaurant because his group won a poetry contest. Not only is Raul uncomfortable in such a place, but he tells LouAnne he had to steal an expensive leather jacket so that he wouldn't humiliate himself and her because he wasn't dressed properly. LouAnne has assumed that Raul can cross with ease the border to the class to which she has access. There is also the suggestion that for working-class kids such as Raul to succeed in life, they need the cultural capital of white upper-middle-class people like herself.

Dangerous Minds functions mythically to rewrite the decline of public schooling and the attack on poor black and Latino students as a part of a broader project for rearticulating "whiteness" as a model of authority, rationality, and civilized behavior. The politics of representation at work in this film reproduces a dominant view of identity and difference that has a long legacy in Hollywood films, specifically Westerns and African adventure movies. As Robin Kelley points out, the popularity of many Hollywood films, especially Western and African adventures, is as much about constructing "whiteness" as it is about demonizing the alleged racialized Other. He notes that in this racialized Hollywood legacy, "American Indians, Africans, and Asians represent a pre-civilized or anti-civilized existence, a threat to the hegemony of Western culture and proof that 'whites' are superior, more noble, more intelligent."[7]

Dangerous Minds is an updated defense of white identity and racial hierarchies. The colonizing element of this narrative is highlighted in the image of Michelle Pfeiffer as a visiting white beauty queen whose success is partly made possible by market incentives and missionary talents.

Against LouAnne Johnson's benevolence and insight is juxtaposed the personality and pedagogy of Mr. Grandy, the black principal of Parkmont High. Grandy is portrayed as an uptight, bloodless bureaucrat; a professional wannabe whose only interest appears to be in enforcing school rules (Hollywood's favorite stereotype for black principals). Grandy rigidly oversees school policy and is constantly berating Johnson for bypassing the standard curriculum, trying nontraditional forms of teaching, and taking the students on unauthorized trips. As a black man in a position of leadership, he is depicted as an obstacle to the success of his charges and ruthlessly insensitive to their needs. When Emilio visits Grandy's office to report another student who is trying to kill him, Grandy orders him to leave because he failed to knock on the office door. Then, after leaving the building, Emilio is shot and killed a few blocks from the school.

This film portrays black professionals as the real threat to learning and civilized behavior, with whites, of course, simply there to lend support. In contrast to Grandy, Johnson's "whiteness" provides the racialized referent for leadership, risk taking, and compassion. This is revealed at the end of the film when the students tell her that they want her to remain their teacher because she represents their "light." In this context, *Dangerous Minds* reinforces the highly racialized, though reassuring, mainstream assumption that chaos reigns in inner-city public schools and that white teachers alone are capable of bringing order, decency, and hope to the those on the margins of society.

SUTURING WHITENESS

Directed by David Siegel and Scott McGehee, *Suture* (1993) explores the location of identity in a dominant racial politics. Central to the film's politics is the way in which it organizes its plot around two narratives. On the one hand, the directors use the discursive narrative, which develops through character dialogue and adopts the conventional form of the crime thriller. Set in the a plot about murder and framed identity, *Suture* presents the story of two half brothers, Vincent Towers and Clay Arlington. Under police investigation for killing his father, the rich and ruthless Vincent sets up a scheme in which he first plants his driver's license and credit cards in his working-class, half brother's billfold. He then convinces Clay to drive his Rolls Royce to the airport. Clay does not realize that Vincent has placed a bomb in the car, which can be triggered by remote control through the car phone. Vincent waits until Clay leaves for the airport, and when Clay is sitting in the front seat, he calls him, setting off the bomb. After the explosion, Vincent leaves town, assuming that the police will mistake Clay for himself. Unfortunately for Vincent, Clay survives the explosion, although he has to undergo massive reconstructive surgery on his face. In fact, the damage to Clay is so extreme that the police and doctors who treat Clay believe that he is Vincent.

Clay survives the ordeal but is amnesiac and also believes that he is Vincent. In fact, everyone who comes in contact with Clay believes he is Vincent. As Clay/Vincent undergoes psychoanalysis and repeated bouts of surgery, he falls in love with Renée Descartes, a beautiful and renowned plastic surgeon. In the meantime, Vincent breaks into his old house to kill him, but Clay shoots him first and disposes of his body. By the time he kills Vincent, Clay has regained his memory but refuses either to slip back into his old identity or to give up his half brother's identity and life.

What is so remarkable about *Suture* is that it is simultaneously mediated by a visual narrative completely at odds with the discursive narrative and unsettles the audience's role as "passive" spectators. Clay does not look anything like Vincent. In fact, Clay is half black but is treated throughout the film as if he were white. In a scene fraught with irony and tension, Renée Descartes takes off Clay's bandages and tells him that he has a Greco-Roman nose, which allegedly proves that he "isn't inclined to deviant behavior, like killing people."

Memory and identity in this film are fluid and hybridized rather than fixed and sutured. Black identity is presented as a social construction that cannot be framed in essentialist terms. Clay assumes all the markings of white experience and culture, and it is only the audience that is able to mediate his newly assumed cultural capital by virtue of his blackness. But there is more at work in this film than a critique of black essentialism; there is also the ironic representation of "whiteness" as both invisible to itself and at the same time the norm by which everything else is measured.

That is, "whiteness" in *Suture* becomes the racial marker of identity, power, and privilege. Playing the visual narrative against the discursive narrative, *Suture* evokes a peculiar form of racial witnessing in which it exposes "whiteness" as an ideology, set of experiences, and location of privilege. It does so not by trading in binaristic oppositions in which bad whites oppress good blacks but by calling into question the racial tension between what the audience sees and hears. The discursive narrative in the film privileges language while denying the defining principle of race, but the visual narrative forces the audience to recognize the phenomenological rather than the political implications of race, identity, and difference. As Roy Grundmann notes, "We initially want to jump out of our seats to scream at the characters who (mis?)take Clay for Vincent, especially upon such comparative 'evidence' as videos, photos, and a police lineup with a witness who knew Vincent."[8]

In this case, racial difference is defined entirely through a representational politics of visual imagery that assails both the liberal appeal to color blindness and a power-evading aesthetic of difference that reduces racial identities to lifestyles, marketing niches, or consumer products. Breaking with the Hollywood cinematic tradition of presenting "whiteness" as an "invisible" though determining discourse, *Suture* forces the audience to recognize "whiteness" as a racial marker, an "index of social standing or rank."[9] But in the end, *Suture* provides no means for framing "whiteness" outside the discursive and visual politics of domination. The film's attempt to develop a representational politics certainly forces the viewer to demystify and debunk "whiteness" as invisible, outside the modalities of power and identity, but it does nothing to develop a power-strategic politics that refuses to accept "whiteness" as a racial category that has only one purpose, which is closely tied to, if not defined by, shifting narratives of domination and oppression. This might explain why *Suture* eventually engages in a reductionistic moralizing by suggesting that Clay should be condemned for wanting to be white, doing so without really engaging "whiteness" in a more dialectical or critical fashion.

A PEDAGOGY OF WHITENESS

Dangerous Minds and *Suture* offer contrasting narratives of race that can be used pedagogically to deconstruct both racial othering and "whiteness" as part of a broader discourse on racial justice. The incongruous juxtaposition of these two films opens up a pedagogical space for reading representations of "whiteness" as an ideology and a site of power and privilege. Similarly, rejecting singular definitions of "whiteness" gives educators an opportunity to construct more complex models for theorizing "whiteness" through a multiplicity of social relations, theoretical positions, and affective identifications.

Rather than simply dismissing *Dangerous Minds* as a racist text, critical educators should read it symptomatically for the ways in which it articulates and reproduces "whiteness" as a form of racial domination in the public space of the inner-city classroom. Offering an unapologetic reading of "whiteness" as a trope of order, rationality, insight, and beauty, *Dangerous Minds* is an important pedagogical text for students to address how "whiteness" and difference are portrayed in the film and how race consciously or unconsciously shapes their everyday experiences, attitudes, and worldviews. The issue is not to force students into viewing *Dangerous Minds* as either a good or a bad film but to engage the broader social conditions through which the film's popularity must be understood. One pedagogical task is to get students to think about how *Dangerous Minds* portrays the ethical and racial dilemmas that animate the larger racial and social landscape and how this film reworks or affirms their own intellectual and affective investments as organized through dominant racial ideologies and meanings at work in this highly racialized text.

Students may offer a number of responses to a film such as *Dangerous Minds*. But given the popularity of the film, and the many favorable reviews it received, it is reasonable to assume that the range of readings available to white students is a mix of dominant and conservative interpretations.[10] Rather than stressing that students are diverse readers of culture, it is important pedagogically to recognize that the issue of ownership and control of the apparatuses of cultural production places enormous limits on both the readings made widely available to students and the popular context from which to understand dominant notions of racism. When racist difference does enter into classroom discussion, it likely will focus on the disruptive behavior of black and Latino students in school, behavior often regarded as characteristic of an entire social group, a form of cultural pathology implying that minorities are largely to blame for their educational problems.

Similarly, when students destabilize or critically address "whiteness," they are likely to do so in a power-evasive discourse in which white racism is often reduced to an act of individual prejudice removed from the messy contexts of history, politics, and systemic oppression.[11] This suggests that it is unlikely that white students will recognize LouAnne's pedagogy and insistence on the value of middle-class cultural capital as a racist attempt to teach black and Latino students that their own narratives, histories, and experiences are uncivilized and crude. And yet, however popular such dominant readings might be, they offer educators a good opportunity to question their codes and ideologies. For instance, the ideological link between the privileging of white cultural capital and the ongoing, degrading representation of the Other in Hollywood films about Africa, television sitcoms, or, more recently, in violent black youth films may not at first be evident to students but certainly can become an object of analysis as various students in the class are given alternative readings.

At best, *Dangerous Minds* offers white students an opportunity to explore a popular text that embodies much of what they generally learn or (mis)learn about race without initially putting their own racial identities on trial. When analyzed in conjunction with the viewing of *Suture,* a different set of claims about "whiteness" emerge that raise other possibilities for examining the relationship among whiteness, race, and racism. *Suture* presents a critical reading of whiteness as a dominant social and cultural construction and attempts through an unsettling visual narrative to reveal how it wages symbolic violence through its refusal to name its defining mechanisms of power and privilege. In doing so, *Suture* forces students, especially white students, to consider problematizing the assumption that issues regarding race and racial politics are largely about blacks as a social group. The dominant defense of whiteness as a universal norm is visibly thrown off balance in this film and makes whiteness a racial category open to critique. In rupturing whiteness as a racially and politically neutral code, *Suture* provides an opportunity for educators to talk about how white people are raced, how white experience is constructed differently in a variety of public spaces, and how it is mediated through the diverse but related lens of class, gender, and sexual orientation.

Played off against each other, the two films engage in a representational politics that illuminates whiteness as a shifting political category whose meaning can be addressed inside rather than outside the interrelationships of class, race, ethnicity, and gender. In other words, these films' structuring principles provide intertextually a theoretical basis for challenging whiteness as an ideological and historical construction. It is precisely the tension generated between these films that invites entrance into a pedagogy that commences with what Gayatri Spivak refers to as "moments of bafflement." Although such pedagogical tensions do not guarantee the possibility of de-centering whiteness in order to render "visible the historical and institutional structures from within which [white teachers and students] speak," they do provide the pedagogical conditions for students and teachers alike to question and unlearn those aspects of whiteness that position them with the space and relations of racism.[12]

Although it is impossible to predict how students will actually react to a pedagogy of bafflement that takes whiteness and race as an object of serious debate and analysis, it is important to recognize that white students usually resist analyzing critically the "normative-residual space [of] white cultural practice."[13] Resistance in this case should be examined for the knowledge it yields, the possibilities for exploring its silences and refusals. Pedagogically, this means allowing students to air their positions on whiteness and race, regardless of how messy or politically incorrect such positions might be.

But there is more at stake here than providing a pedagogical space for students to narrate themselves, to speak without fear in the contexts of their own specific histories and experiences. Rather than arguing that students simply be allowed to voice their racial politics, I am suggesting that they be offered a space marked by dialogue and critique in which they can engage, challenge, and rearticulate their positions by analyzing the material realities and social relations of racism.

Needless to say, the issue of making white students responsive to the politics of racial privilege is fraught with the fear and anger that accompany having to rethink one's identity. Engaging in a pedagogy that prompts white students to examine their social practices and belief systems in racial terms may reinforce the safe assumption that race is a stable category, a biological given, rather than a historical and cultural construction. For instance, AnnLouise Keating observes that when teaching her students to examine whiteness critically, many of them come away believing that all whites were colonialists, despite her attempts to distinguish between whiteness as the dominant racial and political ideology and the diverse, contingent racial positions that white people assume.[14]

Despite the tensions and contradictions that any pedagogy of whiteness might face, teachers should address those histories that have shaped the normative space, practices, and diverse relationships that white students have inherited through a legacy of racial privilege. Analyzing the historical legacy of whiteness as an oppressive racial force means that students must engage in a critical form of memory work while fostering less a sullen silence or paralyzing guilt and more a sense of outrage at historical oppression and a desire for racial justice in the present.

Keating explained the problems she faced when attempting to get white students to question or reverse their assumptions about whiteness and racial privilege:

> These reversals trigger a variety of unwelcome reactions in self-identified "white" students, reactions ranging from guilt to anger to withdrawal and despair. Instructors must be prepared to deal with these responses. The point is not to encourage feelings of personal responsibility for the slavery, decimation of indigenous peoples, land theft, and so on that occurred in the past. It is, rather, to enable students of all colors more fully to comprehend how these oppressive systems that began the historical past continue misshaping contemporary conditions. Guilt-tripping plays no role in this process.[15]

Keating is not entirely clear, however, on how educators can avoid guilt-tripping students or to what degree they should be held responsible (accountable) for their current attitudes. Making whiteness rather than white racism the focus of study is an important pedagogical strategy. Analyzing whiteness opens up theoretical and pedagogical spaces for teachers and students to describe how their own racial identities have been shaped in a broader racist culture and what responsibilities they might assume for living in a time in which whites are accorded privileges and opportunities (though in complex and different ways) largely at the expense of other racial groups. Yet as insightful as this strategy may be, more theoretical work needs to be done to enable students to appropriate the tools necessary for them to politicize whiteness as a racial category without closing down their own sense of identity and political agency.

Although both *Dangerous Minds* and *Suture* offer an opportunity for students to see how dominant assumptions about whiteness can be framed and challenged, neither film addresses what it means to rearticulate whiteness in oppositional terms. The portrayal of whiteness as neither a form of racial privilege nor a practice of domination necessarily establishes the basis for white students to rearticulate their own whiteness in ways that go beyond their overidentification with or desire to be "black" at the expense of their own racial identities.

A critical analysis of whiteness should address its historical legacy and existing complicity with racist exclusion and oppression, but it is equally important that such an examination distinguish between whiteness as a racial practice that is antiracist and those aspects of whiteness that are racist.[16] When whiteness has been treated in pedagogical terms, the emphasis is almost exclusively on revealing whiteness as an ideology of privilege and domination mediated largely through the dynamics of racism.[17] Such interventions are crucial to developing an antiracist pedagogy, but they do not go far enough. I am concerned about what it means for those of us who engage in an antiracist pedagogy and politics to suggest to students that whiteness can be understood only in terms of the common experience of white domination and racism. What subjectivities or points of identification become available to white students who can imagine white experience only as monolithic, self-contained, and deeply racist? What are the pedagogical and political stakes in rearticulating whiteness in antiessentialist terms so that white youth can understand and struggle against the legacy of white racism while using the particularities of "their own culture as a resource for resistance, reflection, and empowerment"?[18]

All students need to feel that they have a personal stake in their racial identities, but one that allows them to assert a view of political agency in which they can join with diverse groups around a notion of democratic public life that affirms racial differences through a "rearticulation of cultural, social, and political citizenship."[19] Linking identity, race, and difference to a broader vision of radical democracy suggests a number of important pedagogical considerations. First, students need to investigate the historical relationship between race and ethnicity. David Roediger is right in warning against critical theorists' conflation of race and ethnicity, especially in light of a history of ethnicity in which white immigrants saw themselves as white and ethnic. According to Roediger, the claim to ethnicity by white immigrants, especially those from Europe, did not prevent them from defining their racial identities through the discourse of white separatism and supremacy.[20] In this case, such immigrants did not ignore white ethnicity; instead, they affirmed it and, in some cases, linked it to the dominant relations of racism.

The issue of racial identity can be joined to what Stuart Hall calls the "new ethnicity."[21] For Hall, racial identities can be understood through the notion of ethnicity, but not the old notion of ethnicity that depends in part on the suppression of cultural difference and a separatist notion of white identity. Hall's attempt to rewrite ethnicity as a progressive and critical concept does not fall into the theoretical trap that Roediger describes. By separating ethnicity from the traditional moorings of nationalism, racism, colonialism, and the state, Hall posits the new ethnicity as a referent for acknowledging "the place of history, language, and culture in the construction of subjectivity and identity, as well as the fact that all discourse is placed, positioned, situated, and all knowledge is contextual."[22]

Extending Hall's insights into ethnicity, I contend that the diverse subject positions, social experiences, and cultural identities that inform whiteness as a political and social construct can be rearticulated in order for students to recognize that "we all speak from a particular place, out of a particular history, out of particular experience, a particular culture without being constrained by [such] positions. . . . We are all, in that sense, ethnically located and our ethnic identities are crucial to our subjective sense of who we are."[23] In Hall's terms, whiteness cannot be addressed as a form of identity fashioned through a claim to purity or some universal essence, but as one that "lives with and through, not despite difference."[24]

Hall provides a theoretical language for racializing whiteness without essentializing it; he also argues correctly that ethnicity must be defined and defended through a set of ethical and political referents that connect diverse democratic struggles while expanding the range and possibilities of democratic relations and practices. Redefined in the theoretical parameters of a new ethnicity, whiteness can be read as a complex marker of identity defined through a politics of difference subject to the shifting currents of history, power, and culture. In this case, the political potential of Hall's new ethnicity thesis is that it rests on a democratic vision that sees racial identity as a principle of citizenship and radical democracy whose aim is the "expansion of egalitarian social relations, and practices."[25]

The new ethnicity defines racial identities as multiple, porous, complex, and shifting and, in doing so, creates a theoretical opening for educators and students to move beyond framing whiteness as either good or bad, racially innocent or intractably racist. In this context, whiteness can be addressed through its complex relationship with other determining factors that usurp any claim to racial purity or singularity. At the same time, whiteness must be addressed in power relations that exploit its subversive potential while not erasing its historical and political role in shaping other racialized identities and social differences. Unlike the old ethnicity that defines difference in essentialist or separatist terms, Hall's notion of the new ethnicity defines identity as an ongoing act of cultural recovery, acknowledging that any particular claim to racial identity offers no guarantees regarding political outcomes. But at the same time, the new ethnicity provides a theoretical service by allowing white students to go beyond the paralysis inspired by guilt or the anxiety/fear of difference that fuels white racism. In this context, whiteness gains its meaning only in conjunction with other identities such as those informed by class, gender, age, nationality, and citizenship.

By positioning whiteness in a notion of cultural citizenship that affirms difference politically, culturally, and socially, students can see how their whiteness functions as a racial identity while still being critical of those forms of whiteness structured in dominance and aligned with exploitative interests and oppressive social relations. By redefining whiteness as more than a form of domination, white students can construct narratives of whiteness that both challenge and form a basis for transforming the dominant relationship between racial identity and citizenship, one informed by an oppositional politics. Such a political practice suggests new subject positions, alliances, commitments, and forms of solidarity between white students and others struggling to expand the possibilities of democratic life, especially as it affirms both a politics of difference and a redistribution of power and material resources.

George Yúdice argues that as part of a broader project for articulating whiteness in oppositional terms, white youth must feel that they have a stake in racial politics that connects them to the struggles being waged by other groups. At the center of such struggles is both the battle over citizenship redefined through the discourse of rights and the problem of resource distribution.

This is where identity politics segues into other issues, such as tax deficits, budget cuts, lack of educational opportunities, lack of jobs, immigration policies, international trade agreements, environmental blight, lack of health care insurance, and so on. These are the areas in which middle- and working-class whites historically have had an advantage over people of color. However, today that advantage has eroded in certain respects.[26]

As part of a wider attempt to address these issues, Yúdice suggests that white youth can form alliances with other social and racial groups who recognize the need for solidarity in considering issues of public life that undermine the quality of democracy for all groups. As white youth struggle to find a cultural and political space from which to speak and act as transformative citizens, educators should think about what it means pedagogically and politically, in order to help students redefine whiteness as part of a democratic cultural politics.

Central to such a task is the need to challenge the conventional leftist analysis of whiteness as a space between guilt and denial, a space that offers limited forms of resistance and engagement. In order for teachers, students, and others to come to terms with whiteness existentially and intellectually, they need to take up the challenge in our classrooms and across a wide variety of public sites of confronting racism in all its complexity and ideological and material formations. But most important, whiteness must provide a diverse but critical space from which to wage a wider struggle against the many forces that undermine what it means to live in a society founded on the principles of freedom, racial justice, and economic equality. Rewriting whiteness in a discourse of resistance and possibility represents more than a challenge to dominant and progressive notions of racial politics; it offers an important pedagogical challenge for educating cultural workers, teachers, and students to live with and through difference as a defining principle of radical democracy.

NOTES

1. I want to thank Bernard Bell, my colleague at Penn State University, for this insight (personal communication).

2. Howard Winant, *Racial Conditions* (Minneapolis: University of Minnesota Press, 1994), p. xiii.

3. I think Houston Baker is instructive on this issue in arguing that race, for all its destructive tendencies and implications, has also been used by blacks and other people of color to gain a sense of personal and historical agency. This is not a matter of a positive image of race canceling out its negative underside. On the contrary, Baker makes a compelling case for the dialectical nature of race and its possibilities for engaging and overcoming its less desirable dimensions while extending it in the interest of a transformative and democratic polis. See Houston Baker, "Caliban's Triple Play," in

Henry Louis Gates Jr., ed., *Loose Canons: Notes on the Culture Wars* (New York: Oxford University Press, 1992), pp. 381–95.

4. James Snead, *White Screens, Black Images* (New York: Routledge, 1994), esp. chap. 10, "Mass Visual Productions," pp. 131–49. For an analysis of the importance of race in the broader area of popular culture, two representative sources are Michael Dyson, *Reflecting Black* (Minneapolis: University of Minnesota Press, 1993); and Henry A. Giroux, *Fugitive Cultures: Race, Violence, and Youth* (New York: Routledge, 1996).

5. Ruth Frankenberg, *The Social Construction of Whiteness* (Minneapolis: University of Minnesota Press, 1993), p. 49.

6. On the localization of crime as a racial text, see David Theo Goldberg, "Polluting the Body Politic: Racist Discourse and the Urban Location," in Malcolm Cross and Michael Keith, eds., *Racism, the City and the State* (New York: Routledge, 1993), pp. 45–60.

7. Robin D. G. Kelley, "Notes on Deconstructing 'the Folk,'" *American Historical Review* 97 (December 1992): 1406.

8. Roy Grundmann, "Identity Politics at Face Value: An Interview with Scott McGehee and David Siegel," *Cineaste* 20 (1994): 24.

9. David Theo Goldberg, *Racist Culture: Philosophy and the Politics of Meaning* (Cambridge: Blackwell, 1993), p. 69.

10. For instance, see Jon Glass, "'Dangerous Minds' Inspires Teachers," *The Virginian-Pilot,* September 2, 1995, p. B1; Catherine Saillant, "School of Soft Knocks," *Los Angeles Times,* October 11, 1995, p. B1; Sue Chastain, "Dangerous Minds No Threat to This Tough Teacher," *Times Union,* August 13, 1995, p. G1.

11. For example, in Ruth Frankenberg's study of white women, radical positions on race were in the minority; and in Gallagher's study of white college students, liberal and conservative positions largely predominated. See Frankenberg, *The Social Construction of Whiteness.*

12. Gayatri Chakravorty Spivak, *Post-Colonial Critic: Interviews, Strategies, Dialogues,* ed. Sarah Harasym (New York: Routledge, 1990), pp. 137, 67.

13. Frankenberg, *The Social Construction of Whiteness,* p. 234.

14. AnnLouise Keating, "Interrogating 'Whiteness,' (De)Constructing 'Race,'" *College English* 57 (December 1995): 907.

15. Ibid., p. 915.

16. This distinction is taken up in Frankenberg, *The Social Construction of Whiteness,* p. 7.

17. For example, see James Joseph Scheurich, "Toward a White Discourse on White Racism," *Educational Researcher,* November 1993, pp. 5–15; Christine Sleeter, "Advancing a White Discourse," *Educational Researcher,* November 1993, pp. 13–15.

18. In this context, Hall is not talking about whites but about blacks. It seems to me that his point is just as relevant to redefining whiteness as it is to debunking the essentialized black subject, though this should not suggest that such an appropriation take place outside the discourse of power, history, inequality, and conflict. See Stuart Hall, "Ethnicity: Identity and Difference," *Radical America* 13 (1991): 57. Fred Pfiel raises a similar set of issues about white masculinity in Fred Pfiel, *White Guys* (London: Verso Press, 1995), pp. 3–4.

19. See George Yúdice, "Neither Impugning nor Disavowing Whiteness Does a

Viable Politics Make: The Limits of Identity Politics," in Christopher Newfield and Ronald Strickland, eds., *After Political Correctness: The Humanities and Society in the 1990s* (Boulder, CO: Westview Press, 1995), pp. 255–85.

20. David Roediger, "White Ethnics in the United States," in his *Towards the Abolition of Whiteness* (London: Verso, 1994), pp. 181–98.

21. Stuart Hall takes up the rewriting of ethnicity in a variety of articles; see especially Stuart Hall, "New Ethnicities," in David Morley and Kuan-Hsing Chen, eds., *Stuart Hall: Critical Dialogues in Cultural Studies* (New York: Routledge, 1996), pp. 441–49; Stuart Hall, "Cultural Identity and Diaspora," in Jonathan Rutherford, ed., *Identity, Community, Culture, Difference* (London: Lawrence and Wishart, 1990), pp. 222–37; Stuart Hall, "Ethnicity: Identity and Difference," *Radical America* 13 (June 1991): 9–20; Stuart Hall, "Old and New Identities, Old and New Ethnicities," in Anthony D. King, ed., *Culture, Globalization and the World System* (Binghamton: State University of New York Press, 1991), pp. 41–68.

22. Hall, "New Ethnicities," p. 29.

23. Ibid.

24. Hall, "Cultural Identity and Diaspora," p. 235.

25. Chantal Mouffe, "Feminism, Citizenship, and Radical Democratic Politics," in Judith Butler and Joan Scott, eds., *Feminists Theorize the Political* (New York: Routledge, 1992), p. 380.

26. Yúdice, "Neither Impugning nor Disavowing Whiteness," p. 276.

19

The "Look" Returned: Knowledge Production and Constructions of "Whiteness" in Humanities Scholarship and Independent Film

E. Ann Kaplan

> "Look, a Negro!" It was an external stimulus that flicked over me as I passed by. I made a tight smile. "Look, a Negro!" It was true. It amused me. "Look, a Negro!" The circle was drawing a bit tighter. I made no secret of my amusement.   Frantz Fanon, *Black Skin, White Masks*

" 'Mama, see the Negro! I'm frightened!' " This familiar quotation from Frantz Fanon's *Black Skin, White Masks* literalizes black self-alienation (in the context of French colonialism) produced dramatically through the "look." The gaze of the white Swiss child at Fanon startled him out of an inner identification that did not include blackness as something horrifying, different, to be objectified.[1]

Diasporan peoples of color in different historical periods, contexts, and locations have described a remarkable commonality in the experience of sudden self-alienation.[2] Also, historically, blacks (in different diasporan contexts) have been writing about blackness and whiteness while, until recently, whites (in various dominant discursive formations) have mainly been writing about blackness. The fact that most of the explicit comments about "the look" are by male people of color is in itself interesting, although to dwell on this would take me too far afield in the short space available.[3]

I believe that "the look" has to do with complicated issues that feminist film scholars have taken up regarding the different ways that males and females function in patriarchal societies, with males much more the bearer of the look and women the receiver of the look. Elite black males (often the ones speaking in these texts), have formed an idea of themselves rather like that of white males. It is the shocking experience of suddenly being the receiver of a white, self-alienating gaze that is traumatic for them. White women, like black women (not to equate the experiences, however), have grown up as objects of a male gaze (white or black) and thus are less startled to be objectified. I find it interesting that as black women, bell hooks and Toni Morrison focus on the terror of whiteness, the terror that many women have of men that is exacerbated for black women confronting white males. In this chapter, I will try to illuminate the complexities of the new research by whites on whiteness by linking it to the earlier scholarly, aesthetic, and activist projects of blacks and women.

All along, blacks have been conscious of their psychic splitting, often described as an inner/outer split, with writers like W. E. B. Du Bois, Fanon, hooks, or Arjun Appadurai recording this psychic splitting. In the context of American slavery, we may recall Du Bois's brilliant insight into black's double consciousness:

> It is a peculiar sensation, this double-consciousness, this sense of always looking at one's self through the eyes of others, of measuring one's soul by the tape of a world that looks on in amused contempt and pity. One ever feels this twoness— an American, a Negro; two souls, two thoughts, two unreconciled strivings, two warring ideals in one dark body, whose dogged strength alone keeps it from being torn asunder.[4]

Here Du Bois recognizes American blacks' conscious psychic splitting—parallel to, or following from, the Fanonian moment of the "look"—and the suffering this brings.

More recently, in her influential "Representations of Whiteness," bell hooks revised some of Du Bois's "doubleness" from a black female perspective: "This contradictory longing to possess the reality of the (white) Other, even though that reality wounds and negates, is expressive of the desire to understand the mystery, to know intimately through imitation, as though such knowing worn like an amulet, as mask, will ward away the evil, the terror." But "black looking," hooks shows, was strictly controlled by whites: "Black slaves, and later manumitted servants, could be brutally punished for looking, for appearing to observe the whites they were serving, as only a subject can observe, or see." Later on, hooks wonders what she saw "in the gazes of those white men who crossed our thresholds that made me afraid, that made black children unable to speak."[5]

Arjun Appadurai (born to a Brahmin family in Bombay but now living in America) describes himself as having experienced the pain of the "look," this time from an enraged white man (whose car was temporarily stopped by Appadurai's) greeting Appadurai with "a stream of invective, in which the punchline, directed to me was: 'Wipe that dot off your head, asshole' or words to that effect." Appadurai comments: "It's not exactly that I thought I was white before, but as an anglophone academic born in India and teaching in the Ivy League, I was certainly hanging out in the field of dreams, and had no cause to think myself black."[6]

White people reading such works may believe they empathize with the situations each explores. But how many whites have experienced a similar discrepancy among inner self-construct, inner identifications, and response from the Other to outer bodily manifestations? Responses that somehow do not correspond to the inner self?

"Look, an old lady! Mama, see the old lady! I'm frightened!" In her 1990 film *Privilege,* Yvonne Rainer explores inner and outer discrepancies for white postmenopausal women. Referring explicitly to Fanon's work and the self-alienation of blacks because of white supremacy, Rainer links the blindness of whites to their privilege for being white with the U.S. culture's negative attitude toward postmenopausal women. She focuses on such women's definition as "dis-eased," pathological, and needing to be "cured" by the medical establishment.

For a 1995 example of the sorts of definitions Rainer alerted us to in 1990, consider the language that doctors were using in relation to new possibilities for storing women's ovaries and then replacing them after menopause. Dr. Bernardine Healey is quoted as worrying about elderly women becoming pregnant: "A crumbling scaffold riddled with osteoporosis probably is not an ideal one to go through nine months of pregnancy." To her credit, Dr. Healey does go on to admit that "if women used ovary transplants to postpone menopause indefinitely, it would equalize men and women in terms of their reproductive life span. It means . . . that the biological clock gets turned back."[7]

But Dr. Arthur Caplan, director of the Center of Bioethics at the University of Pennsylvania, pointed out that when menopause is forestalled indefinitely, it changes people's idea of the life cycle. "It may mean that what we think of as a key sign of aging in women doesn't happen. We see ourselves very differently when fundamental biological cues don't happen. It forces us to rethink who we are and what we are in the life course."[8]

What is interesting here is seeing these doctors struggling with the discursive formation regarding older women. It would change their way of thinking if suddenly older women, as a familiar assumed category, could not be relied on to be that category. It would destabilize their mental framework, and as Healey observed, it would equalize men and women in the life cycle, something that older men are not interested in!

We must not collapse into one another the different contexts for Other gaze–produced self-alienation, so in this chapter I explore parallels among the cases of people of color, aging women, and scholars of whiteness studies. The case of people of color reversing the look (as they have been doing for some time) provides a model for resisting marginalizing and domination; the case of aging white women, inspired by minority perspectives on white culture, is an example of some whites' discovering experiences of self-alienation; finally, the case of white (initially male) scholars studying whiteness represents a third stage, namely, the complex response by liberal white males to the efforts of both blacks and women to challenge white male privilege. I see whiteness studies as emerging directly out of the perspectives of blacks and women exposed to white males and as needing analysis of its purposes and effects.

In order to make my case about whiteness studies and prepare to analyze its impact, I first review how peoples of color, particularly in the last decade or so, have been self-consciously reversing the white gaze that so devastated Frantz Fanon. People of other colors have long recognized white as a color—not at all naturalized. I have already referred to some of the powerful statements about whiteness as difference (often an unpleasant difference) made by people of color after their first contact with white travelers.[9] In accordance with my own areas of expertise, I make my case using film and women's texts.

Examining how women of color represent whiteness in film (as they have in literature)[10] provides a way for white women spectators to adopt the perspectives of women of other colors. In this way, white women can see the qualities of whiteness as seen by black women and think about stereotypes of whiteness that might enable them to sense—by analogy—the pain of the long tradition of stereotypes of blackness, now well documented in many scholarly texts.

A brief look at two short films by women of color—Julie Dash's *Illusions* (United States, 1982) and Tracy Moffatt's *Nice Colored Girls* (Australia, 1986)— reveals the different ways in which ethnic minorities have reversed the white and imperialist gazes and offered alternative identifications.

Dash focuses on both white men and women in her short film *Illusions.* Interestingly, these women share qualities analogous to those of the white man in Moffatt's film. In *Illusions,* the perspective is self-consciously and unambiguously that of the black "passing" heroine, Mignon Duprey. The camera is often positioned in her point of view, and in many scenes, we hear her voice-over. Even the apparently neutral shots use Duprey's perspective. C.J., the white male head of the film studio, is not quite so obviously disgusting as the white man in Moffatt's film, but he is entirely self-centered, arrogant, and pompous. Toward Duprey, he is both lascivious and condescending. But had he known she was black, he would not have hired her to work for him (up through World War II, Hollywood was a completely segregated, whites-only institution).

Meanwhile, the white women are seen negatively as narcissistic and self-involved. Mainly secretaries, the women are imaged with heavy makeup, as sneering and condescending to those below them and as supercilious and ingratiating to those above them, like Mignon. Their bodies are imaged as stiff, tight, and awkward, as against Mignon's relaxed, svelt, and slender body. The white women worry about their looks, primp in front of the mirror, put on lipstick, and stroke their bodies. Their voices have unnatural lilts; they blink their eyelashes in ways intended to be sexy but only look ridiculous.

These traits are epitomized in the white female star, whose performance is given a lot of screen time in order to allow us to see her self-centered and spoiled behavior. Her vapid voice has to be energized and vitalized by the beautiful voice of a young black woman, Esther, being dubbed onto the white vainglorious body.

Illusions, then, offers a dramatic reversal of the usual Hollywood stereotypes of beautiful, slender, and intelligent white women and large, unattractive, and stupid-sounding black women. It shows how whiteness is seen by black women. *Illusions,* furthermore, links this idea of whiteness to America as a nation, with Hollywood as its mouthpiece: The film is set in 1942 wartime America; the studio is called "National Studios"; and the arrogant assimilation to itself of grandiose propaganda war aims is made obvious.

Moffatt's film, *Nice Colored Girls,* offers a different example of reversing the white gaze. An Aboriginal Australian, Moffatt uses archival quotations by white colonial travelers and folklore passed down by women aborigines to reverse the white gaze. The film moves beyond hooks's concept of an "oppositional" gaze to construct a complete reversal of the gaze. It is not just a resisting look but also puts the project of looking in the position of the aboriginal female protagonists. Moffatt reworks past black perspectives when blacks were confronted by white travelers and colonialists, by equating these travelers with white men in the present looking for "exotic" sex, as seen by contemporary aboriginal women.

Moffatt's film does more than remind us of past images of whiteness; it links those quotations of the "girls'" ancestors and their perception of the white man they rob in the bar. The man is "slumming" and looking for exotic sex with the black prostitutes. His qualities of loudness, loutishness, lasciviousness, and insensitivity are equated with those of the early white male travelers and colonialists. In addition, the women's distaste for his body, his entire person, is made clear. The camera forces us to see the man through the black women's eyes; we must adopt the aboriginal women's perspective. Through this strategy, we come to understand how the aboriginal women continue the tradition their ancestors started of defending themselves in their victimized situation by manipulating white men's sexual interest in them as "exotic." In this film, the white man's body and manners are indeed disgusting, so much so that we have no compunctions about enjoying the women's stealing his money and leaving him drunk in the bar.

Partly because of such texts reversing the white gaze, whites have been unable to continue being unaware of their own psychic splitting in the construction of themselves as white. Up to this time, whites' self-definition as having no color and being superior has depended on their difference from blackness as something specific—a color, an entity—and inferior. This now obvious deep psychic repression was exposed in the film scholar Richard Dyer's 1988 paper "White." Dyer notes that "white" had been naturalized as "not a color" and then looks at the way whiteness is constructed in different film genres in Hollywood. White film scholars' shock at these revelations shows the degree to which whiteness has become naturalized as neither a race nor a color.[11]

Yvonne Rainer followed up on Dyer's work in her 1990 film *Privilege*. Her earlier films produced a reversal of the male gaze in many different ways, perhaps culminating in her 1990 *The Man Who Envied Women*. In *Privilege*, Rainer combines the work of white feminists in reversing the male gaze with the realization of white women's privilege vis-à-vis minorities. But she then links the marginalization of aging women to that of minorities in ways that I can discuss only briefly here.[12]

"Look, Mama, an old lady!" Jenny, Yvonne Rainer's heroine, critiques the rejecting gaze of the patriarchal and youthful American culture and remarks (across footage of a 1950s teen movie) that she cannot "get used to our screwed up morality that denies middle-aged women the right to be beautiful, loving, and idealized by men."[13]

The main way in which Rainer complicates and deepens her story about menopause is the strategy of a film-within-a-film. Rainer reverses what happens so often—namely, women of color as the missing term—by having her black heroine control the film's discourse. The heroine, Yvonne Washington (YW), is a black filmmaker making a documentary about menopause, who takes over from the film persona, Yvonne Rainer (YR). This image of a menopausal black woman with agency, authority, and control reverses in one image both a Hollywood stereotype of the passive, invisible, infantilized black woman and that of the witchlike, evil, or "declining" menopausal woman. It is YW's animated, teasing interview with Jenny that provides the film's main focus.

Through her white heroine, Jenny, Rainer explores the ways in which white women are narcissistic and insensitive to issues of race. Her black heroine, Yvonne Washington, and her Latina heroine, Diga, berate Jenny for her "white-ways." They reveal Jenny's privilege and narcissism regarding color, although near the end of the film, after revisiting her 1960s young woman-hood, Jenny begins to get a glimpse of the realities of her whiteness and to articulate her needs and losses: "So what do I do now that the men have stopped looking at me? I'm like a fish thrown back into the sea. . . . It's hard to admit that I still want them to look. . . . My biggest shock in reaching middle age was the realization that men's desire for me was the linchpin of my identity." [14] Jenny becomes aware of the split between her inner and outer body as the film documents her oppression as a postmenopausal, aging woman who, while still feeling young and attractive inside, receives the rejecting "look" of males and the medical establishment.

Relying on a binary such as "inner/outer" is problematic given the theoretical arguments relegating such a distinction to an archaic modernist perspective. Part of my aim in this chapter is, therefore, to argue that we need to move away from a binary model of knowledge production. I need to show not only how pervasive the binary model is but also how reversing the binary has been an important stage in being able to see the need to replace binarism.

Just like blacks, aging people experience things in terms of an inner/outer binary. They do not feel much inner change because time's passing provides an illusory continuity. Even though change is slowly, but daily, taking place in the body, the mirror is an inadequate device for monitoring the subtle changes. Many years seem to go by without visual alterations, but around menopause, sudden, obvious outer bodily changes offer an immediate visual impact to people whom one has not seen for a while or whom one does not know. Both old skin and colored skin are harder to disguise than other kinds of difference, and they thus become objects of the rejecting gaze of the other, creating the self-alienation I noted earlier.

As I reflect on the recent focus on "whiteness" in humanities scholarship, it seems that these scholars, too, are inducing a kind of self-alienation in a binary knowledge structure that was interesting to compare with—and that was surely inspired by—the other cases just studied. The rapidity with which white scholars have become fascinated with the topic of whiteness—not really much of a critical category earlier—requires a closer look in light of what the perspectives of marginalized blacks and women have demonstrated to white males.[15]

One puzzling aspect of the new research is that in the 1990s, most of the books by whites on issues of whiteness have been by male scholars, just as most of the articulations of the shock of the white gaze have been by the black males cited earlier. Roediger's *The Wages of Whiteness* examines how white workers came to identify themselves historically as specifically white in order to fend off attempts by blacks to take their jobs. Eric Lott's history of minstrelsy deals with white males' affirmation of their whiteness by masquerading as black. Fred Pfeil's *White Guys* considers liberal white males' bewildered sense of exclusion from feminist and minority agendas. George Yúdice looks at white working-class men; Michael Rogin writes about whiteness; and in an interesting essay, Peter Erickson explores the white male critic's position from three different perspectives.[16]

In this research, male scholars "discover" whiteness as a racial category. Although we must use categories to understand the many complex phenomena in the world, until now we have had categories for blacks and women but not for males and whites, who have been the unspoken "norm" according to which others were put into categories. For this reason, the new focus on whiteness as a category is interesting, but we need to understand why whites—and mainly white males—are writing about whiteness now. What does this mean? Why is the focus by white male scholars largely on men? What was (and still is) at stake for white men once they become aware of whiteness as a construction depending on blackness for its very definition? Why has there been so little attention by white women to how white femaleness functions?[17]

I do not have answers to these questions. But we can ponder both positive and less positive reasons. For example, the research seems to mark a change in the relationship between American whites and blacks. The focus surely has to do with our historical moment and is multidetermined. As I have argued, one of the forces producing this new focus is the research by scholars of color and white feminists that has finally penetrated white defenses. Because of their work, white males can no longer refuse to see whiteness as a color; they must see it as a strategy, a power play, a vehicle itself for mastery.

Whiteness studies thus arose originally from positive motives: white males began to turn the gaze on themselves so as to interrupt the (perhaps uncon-scious) repetition of their privileged position in the studies by white scholars of "the Other"—a position that once again put white men in the position of control, dominance. White women have also done research on minorities in response to criticism of their lack of attention to groups other than white.[18] However, a danger arises in the new whiteness research that could not have been anticipated, namely, that focusing on whites' re-perception of themselves in the category of white, though a new perspective, may produce a different kind of obsession with whiteness that is nevertheless still an obsession. (Is there a way out of this box?)[19]

A second positive motive is taking responsibility for white male privilege and exposing its basis in the unconscious normalizing of whiteness. Liberal white male scholars are surely responding here to the perspectives that blacks and feminists have voiced over the past thirty or so years.

Less positive reasons have to do with the frustration of white liberal males with the generalizations by both women and people of color about privileged white men. As Fred Pfeil notes, many white men have not felt that privileged and also have been working in activist organizations for the rights of women and minorities. It is hard for them to endure the monolithic and negative labels often attached to all white men. The turn to think about whiteness was therefore partly to problematize the essentializing of the "white male" label that has lumped all the varied positions of white men together in one op-pressing group.

But why is it white men who have begun this research, rather than white women? I offer one possible explanation.

My understanding of why white men rather than white women in America created whiteness studies is based on an unconscious construction of "America," the nation, and the public sphere as closely linked to white male identity in a way that it usually is not for white women. That is, given the gender constructs in white Anglo-American cultures from the seventeenth through the nineteenth centuries, it was white males who engineered colonial-ism, imperialism, and slavery. This is not to deny white women's complicity and involvement: I intend merely to note that the power (complicit with male investment in technologies and instrumental knowledges) to create these historical institutions has been in white male hands.

Thus, the criticism by blacks and women of white male patriarchy may seem to attack something essential even in white male liberal identities. Such male scholars were perhaps inspired to investigate the historical constructions of whiteness in the public sphere in order to explain the destabilization produced by the research by blacks and women. Male-to-male relations are perceived to be central in any account of the nation, so that in order to understand America and its racial dilemmas today, we must, in addition, understand black and white male relationships and histories, and also the transferences and projections in the work of some male scholars who use psychoanalysis.

I turn to psychoanalysis not to explain black–white relations per se but to suggest a process that might be under way in humanities research on whiteness. I have suggested that basing the unconscious construction of the white identity on its difference from the black identity relies on the psychoanalytic understanding of splitting (whites split off the inner hated and violent part of themselves—negation turned inward—and project it onto blacks), in conjunction with economic motives and political expediency. Here I argue for a way in which an analogous process may lead to a better understanding of such differences.

It has been important for white men and women to focus on whiteness as also a color, as it lessens the naturalizing of whiteness as a norm somehow different from other colors. It interrupts the idea that only others are "colored" and therefore "less" or "different" (white persons do not feel "different" or the "Other").

The cinematic strategies used by women of color that I examined earlier offer one way of rousing white viewers from their narcissistic absorption in their own perspectives and unconsciously superior identities. In beginning with the parallel between Fanon's "Mama, see the Negro! I'm frightened!" and an imaginary different self-alienating look ("Mama, look, an old lady!), I have suggested how parallels to other shocking results of "the look of the Other" (such as aging) might help whites with the problem of relating to the other as the subject, without dominance or narcissistic absorption—given the global flows of peoples, capital, information, cultures, and technologies.

In turn, in regard to white male whiteness studies, the insights of feminist psychoanalysis in conjunction with aging women's experiencing of a self-alienating gaze of the white male Other may enable white males to see that their new interest in whiteness studies will be politically useful only to the extent that their research enables the undoing of themselves, of their own white privilege. The danger in the turn to whiteness in humanities scholarship is that it may retain a binary model of knowing that does not actually challenge otherness.

Psychoanalysis may provide a model for a radically relational practice of knowledge production that will challenge the binary model. It is the oppressive structure of the objectifying look—and the reliance on exterior bodily signs—that feeds prejudice and hate. As Jessica Benjamin observes, only by working through the expression of hatred (really a projection of inner hated self-objects)—an expression that the Other survives—can subjects recognize the autonomy of the Other. In her words, "Any act of the subject toward the other that has an impact 'negates' the other, breaks into the other's absolute identity with her- or himself in such a way that the other is no longer exactly what she or he was a moment before."[20]

Perhaps whites researching constructions of whiteness is one way for them to confront—and survive—the negativity of black subjects as part of making possible the real recognition of black subjectivity. In this way, the focus on whiteness would not in fact be a reinscription of whiteness or a different obsession with whiteness. Rather, it would be an essential opening toward recognizing the black autonomous subject. Once such recognition is in place, relational knowing becomes possible, and binary thinking can recede. Indeed, what I have argued here is that much of the knowledge of the past half-century produced by blacks and women has provided the context for moving on to relational, instead of binary, thinking. White males seem to be the last group that needs to learn how to think and know relationally.

In this process, humanities research is both mimicking and helping produce a new racial consciousness, if not racial change, in whites. Like the white man in Moffatt's film who loses his money (his "capital"), the cultural equivalent is happening in humanities scholarship as white male (and female) scholars begin to relinquish their cultural capital.

NOTES

1. Fanon continues, "My body was given back to me sprawled out, distorted, recolored, clad in mourning in that white winter day." The inner self-constructs (Fanon implies that he thought of himself in some sense as "white"—hence he is "recolored" as black) found themselves in conflict with outer manifestations of the body—in this case, a dark skin color—which is a superficial accident of geographical location. And yet the cultural, historical, economic, and political accumulation of connotations by the time the Swiss child sees Fanon have made such a superficial accident deeply determining. Fanon is in mourning—ironically for whiteness on that "white winter day"—in a country that literally exudes whiteness (its snow-capped mountains) and metaphorically (Switzerland as resistant to immigrants). See the film *Journey of Hope*.

2. As will be clear later on, many black women novelists have written about the terror of whiteness and about the disgust that whiteness produces in the black subject. But the focus on the damaging power of the gaze is most often articulated by males.

3. But see two new books by women: Ruth Frankenberg's *White Women: Race Matters* (Minneapolis: University of Minnesota Press, 1993); and Mab Segrest's *Memoirs of a Race Traitor* (Boston: South End Press, 1994).

4. W. E. B. Du Bois, *Souls of Black Folk* (1903) (Greenwich, CT: Fawcett Publications, 1961), pp. 16–17.

5. bell hooks, *Black Looks: Race and Representation* (Boston: South End Press, 1992), pp. 166, 168, 170.

6. Arjun Appadurai, "Heart of Whiteness," *Callaloo* 16 (1993): 802.

7. Gina Kolata, "Surgery Preserves Parts of an Ovary for Replanting," *New York Times,* December 12, 1995, p. A1.

8. Ibid., p. C3.

9. From early slave narratives by men and women to Mary Louise Pratt's *Imperial Eyes* (New York: Routledge, 1993) and Hortense Spillers's "Mama's Baby, Papa's Maybe: An American Grammar Book," *diacritics* 17 (1987): 65–81; to Du Bois's *Souls of Black Folk*; to Frantz Fanon in the 1950s; through 1960s American black writers like Rap Brown, James Baldwin, Ralph Ellison, Eldrige Cleaver, Malcolm X, and Angela Davis; to black women's powerful fiction—such as that by Alice Walker, Toni Morrison, Toni Cade Bambara, Paule Marshall, Mary Helen Washington, Maya Angelou, on to today—we can see that for blacks, the question of whiteness is not new. However, it would be interesting to compare and contrast changes in how whiteness has been described by blacks across the decades. A study of discursive frameworks in which blacks discuss whites and whiteness would surely show parallels with changes in the ways blacks were positioned vis-à-vis white society at any specific historical moment.

10. For example, see Toni Morrison's *Playing in the Dark: Whiteness and the Literary Imagination* (New York: Randon House, 1993). See additional essays by Harryette Mullin, "Optic White: Blackness and the Production of Whiteness," 24 *Diacritics* (Summer–Fall 1994): 71–89. Also see Anna Maria Chupa, *Anne, the White Woman in Contemporary African-American Fiction: Archetypes, Stereotypes, and Characterizations* (New York: Greenwood Press, 1990).

11. Richard Dyer, "White," *Screen* 29 (1988): 445–64. Hazel Carby makes a similar point in her "The Politics of Difference," *MS,* September–October 1990, pp. 84–85, and in her "The Multicultural Wars," *Radical History Review* 54 (Fall 1992): 7–18.

12. See E. Ann Kaplan, "Resisting Pathologies of Race and Aging in Films by Rainer and Tom," in Philippa Rothfield and Paul Komorasky, eds., *Rethinking Menopause* (New York: Routledge, in press).

13. See the script of *Privilege* in Scott Macdonald, ed., *Screen Writings: Scripts and Texts by Independent Filmmakers* (Berkeley and Los Angeles: University of California Press, 1995), p. 300.

14. Ibid., pp. 316–17.

15. To check that the mobilization of the category "white/whiteness" was relatively recent, I looked at the *MLA Bibliography* and the *Reader's Digest.* I found many entries over the past ten years for blackness (by both black and white writers) and a rapid increase in the category of whiteness by white writers in more recent years.

16. David R. Roediger, *The Wages of Whiteness: Race and the Making of the American Working Class* (London: Verso, 1991); Eric Lott, *Love and Theft: Blackface Minstrelsy and the American Working Class* (New York: Oxford University Press, 1993); Fred Pfeil, *White Guys* (London: Verso, 1996). Compare Peter Erickson, "Profiles in Whiteness," *Stanford Humanities Review* 3 (Winter 1993): 98–111.

17. As indicated earlier, black women have long talked (especially in fiction) about

the terror of whiteness and the disgust with white femaleness, culminating in bell hooks's essays referred to earlier.

18. Indeed, part of the reason that women have largely ignored whiteness studies is that they have been taking such criticisms very seriously. For example, see Jane Gaines's 1988 critique of white psychoanalytic feminist film criticism, "White Privilege and Looking Relations: Race and Gender in Feminist Film Theory," *Screen* 29 (1988): 12–27. And as I have argued elsewhere, wrongly attributing to psychoanalytic methods the lack of attention to minoritiy women nevertheless made an important case for white feminist film scholars' extending their research to groups other than white.

19. Surely once again, whites studying nonwhites in film feel more comfortable writing about blackness than about whiteness. Why else was it so easy—once a narrow understanding of a politics of identity (only blacks can work on blacks, whites on whites) had been critiqued—unless because this research again put white scholars in the position of mastery, control? The work indirectly situates people of color as something to be remarked, noted, explained; as something "not normal" needing attention because they are different. Although one may say that this is quibbling—that the critique obscures the sympathetic ideology of white scholars writing about ethnicity, anxious to expose the wrongs done to people of color—nevertheless, the position of mastery in undertaking this research cannot be overlooked. Yet (putting white scholars in a "damned if I do, damned if I don't" situation), I have also said that scholarship on whiteness may also be a problem because it puts whiteness once again at the center where it has always been, if now with consciousness where before was unconsciousness.

20. Benjamin continues: "This process of negation, acting on the other, and being recognized—Winnicott's destruction with survival—is initially the opposite of the turning in on the self." Jessica Benjamin, "Sympathy for the Devil," in her *Love Objects* (New Haven, CT: Yale University Press, 1995), p. 210.

20

Literature in the Country of "Whiteness" From T. S. Eliot to *The Tempest*

Jerry Phillips

> Living in a nation of people who decided that their world-view would combine agendas for individual freedom and mechanisms for devastating racial oppression presents a singular landscape for a writer. When this world-view is taken seriously as agency, the literature produced within and without it offers an unprecedented opportunity to comprehend the resilience and gravity, the inadequacy and the force of the imaginative act.
>
> Toni Morrison, *Playing in the Dark*

In "Tradition and the Individual Talent" (1919), T. S. Eliot contends that "every nation, every race, has not only its own creative, but its own critical turn of mind." [1] For some time now, we have spoken of "national culture" as the ultimate measure for affiliating literary texts. But what then should we make of "race" in Eliot's formulation? How exactly is "race" implicated in the "creative" and "critical turn of mind"? What hold does "race" have on "individual talent"? Can one speak of "race" as a logic of "tradition," a code of national community? Finally, what is the role of "race" in establishing a hierarchy of minds, a hierarchy of literary texts? Eliot's assertion takes in all the major concerns of the contemporary literary critic: the relationship between aesthetic evaluation and cultural hegemony, between fictional works and the "imagined community," between "race" and creativity, and between institutional and textual power. These matters have been key to the ongoing controversy regarding the appropriate literary curricula for the nation's universities and schools.

Consider, for instance, the question asked by Saul Bellow on the subject of multiculturalism: "Who is the Tolstoy of the Zulus? The Proust of the Papuans? I'd be glad to read them."[2] Bellow's rhetorical inquiry suggests that a "Zulu Tolstoy" or a "Papuan Proust" is not forthcoming; indeed, his exasperated tone implies the self-evident absurdity of such an expectation. The Zulus have not produced a Tolstoy, nor have the Papuans generated a Proust; hence we have no compelling reason to entertain their literary works. In Bellow's glib reasoning, the proper names of Tolstoy and Proust become signifiers of universal genius; by extension, the Zulus and the Papuans become signifiers of provincial mediocrity. Bellow claims that if authors of genius existed in either culture, "I'd be glad to read them." That he has not been exposed to such writers says to him that they do not exist.

It is not by chance that Bellow draws his examples of the inferior literary culture from the lengthy list of formerly colonized peoples. The colonized "other"—the "heathen," the "savage," the "brute," and the "nigger"—has long provided the comparative cultural ground for elevating the colonizing subject to "universal genius." Behind Bellow's assertions we can discern the echo of the colonizer's discourse, a discourse tied to a sorry political history of denigrating the creative and critical potential of those deemed racially inferior.

In 1834, Thomas Babington Macaulay declared that "a single shelf of a good European library is worth the whole native literature of India and Arabia."[3] Then again, in the context of plantation slavery, Thomas Jefferson reflected that "never yet could I find that a black had uttered a thought above the level of plain narration; never saw even an elementary trait of painting or sculpture."[4] Macaulay's and Jefferson's remarks are by no means untypical in the discourse regarding colonial/racial oppression, and its influence throughout the field of cultural production has been profound. Its traces are everywhere— in the language of the literary text and in the rhetoric of criticism. T. S. Eliot could meaningfully speak of the "racial" literary imagination, and Saul Bellow could speak of literary excellence in a "racialized economy of value" because literature—as "culture"—has long been part of the project of imagining, constructing, and securing hierarchically organized human differences.

No matter what the historical epoch, the literary text articulates—but is also formed out of—the prevailing complex of social ideologies. In this chapter I maintain that certain literary texts illuminate the pedagogy of whiteness, the way one learns to experience oneself as a member of the "white race." The writer's real dependency on the rhetoric of "race" is not to be thought of as simply a matter of theme and symbol; the ontology of character, the phenomenology of setting, and the epistemology of a narrative point of view all are heavily implicated in the racialization of literary language. Conversely, the rhetoric of the literary text offers some insights into the lived experience of "race" as a political taxonomy of the subject, a logic of economic interests, and an incitement to remarkable fantasies.

The pedagogy of whiteness is also to be found in certain turns of the critical mind. T. S. Eliot warned that tradition "cannot be inherited, and if you want it you must obtain it by great labor" (p. 71). Eliot's message was taken to heart by a cadre of American writers, "the Southern agrarians." In *I'll Take My Stand* (1930), the agrarians outlined their opposition to what they took to be the degradation of "the Southern agrarian tradition" brought on by the relentless advance of industrial capitalism. They contended that "neither the creation nor the understanding of works of art is possible in an industrial age except by some local and unlikely suspension of the industrial drive."[5] The relation between art and society is itself a function of the relationship between a turn of mind and a totality of human activity. In his contribution to the collection "Remarks on the Southern Religion," Allen Tate argues that the antebellum "Southern mind was simple, . . . personal and dramatic, rather than abstract or metaphysical; and it was sensuous because it lived close to a natural scene of great variety and interest."[6] The "mind" imagined here is not identical with all southern peoples but seems to pertain to only certain elite members of "the white race": those whose heightened sensibility enables them to create (and/or appreciate) art.

In this context, consider the claim made by another contributor, John Crowe Ransom, that in contrast to "our vast industrial machine," the old South "practiced the . . . European philosophy of establishment as the foundation of the life of the spirit."[7] According to Ransom, the pathological tendency of capitalistic materialism throws into relief the "lesson of each of the European cultures now extant . . . —that European opinion does not make too much of the intense practical enterprises, but is at pains to define rather narrowly the practical effort which is prerequisite to the reflective and aesthetic life" (pp. 4–5). The myth of the antebellum South offered by the agrarians is notable for its apologetic treatment of racial slavery.

Ransom would have us believe that the old South was "a kindly society. . . . Slavery was monstrous enough in theory, but, more often than not, humane in practice. . . . In the *ante-bellum* South . . . the different social orders . . . were committed to a form of leisure, and . . . their labor itself was leisurely" (p. 14). Note that the idealization of plantocracy is inextricably tied to the "form of leisure" that Ransom deems necessary for "the life of the spirit." That the spirit of the master (the one who lives for aesthetics) is realized at the expense of the slave's body does not trouble Ransom, because the logic of white supremacy assumes that people in the old South "were for the most part in their right places" (p. 14). Indeed, the life of the "white" mind in the old South was absolutely dependent on the enforced social death of the "black" body. The (a)morality of exploitation was thus incorporated into the moral economy of aesthetics.

John Crowe Ransom and Allen Tate were key proponents of the New Critical approach to literature. The turn of mind demonstrated in their writings on southern agrarianism—what might be called the white mythology of "establishment"—makes itself felt in the New Critical model of the literary text. In his essay "Tension in Poetry," Tate maintains that "good poetry is a unity of all the meanings from the furthest extremes of intension and extension."[8] This vision of the poem as a blending of "extremes," an achieved organic unity, finds its ideological corollary in the "feudal society" of the old South, where social hierarchy and social order (allegedly) went hand in hand. In brief, the aestheticization of life writ large in the myth of "the old South" is subtly reproduced in the New Critical emphasis on art as a spiritual transcendence of this world.

To the extent that it elevated the ideality of form over the materiality of content, the New Criticism made it easy to associate literature with the elitist project of spiritual cultivation (i.e., "humanization"). The legacy of the New Criticism has been considerable. As Addison Gayle notes,

> When the English departments accepted the *ars poetica* of the Southern agrarians ... they substantiated the Southern myth and gave authenticity to a society constructed along class lines. Their hypnotic attraction to the Greek ideal [of civility] led them to accept the agrarian formula of a master class for whose personal comfort a literature is created.

Ransom and Tate imagined themselves as working within the neoclassical tradition of the fine arts, but in reality, their criticism championed "the worst of the plantation tradition"—narratives of "mammies" and "belles," "happy darkies" and impossibly honorable masters.[9]

The aesthetics of the plantation romance played an important role in culturally consolidating the political romance of the "white race" as God's chosen people. Theodore W. Allen speaks of the white race as "the truly peculiar institution" of American history.[10] Thus the problem confronting us as we finally break free of the New Criticism's legacy is considering the countless ways in which U.S. literary works aided in the naturalization of whiteness, the ways in which the materiality of content and the ideality of form were dialectically combined with a view to turning an earthly people into a heavenly people.

The involvement of the literary text in the political meaning of whiteness creates a relationship between literature and violence, literature and oppression, literature and evil. There is no escaping the fact that what Toni Morrison calls a "racially inflected language" will bear all the marks—in its very aesthetic texture—of a worldly power that has been employed to denigrate and brutalize, enslave and exterminate.[11] The deep impress of "white power" on the body of the literary work forces us to attend to Walter Benjamin's dictum that "there is no document of civilization which is not at the same time a document of barbarism."[12] Those writers, readers, and critics who claim the aesthetic for the white mythology of "establishment"—that is, the elevation of the "white race" to a chosen status—must turn a blind eye to the barbaric practices informing the political economy of racial oppression. In effect, they make the literary text an accomplice of the overseer and the colonial invader, and the racialization of the "other" an entertaining ("moral") drama.

Ward Churchill observes that in regard to its treatment of "the invasion of America," so much nineteenth-century U.S. literature amounts to "little more than a literary 'Manifest Destiny.'"[13] Writers like James Fenimore Cooper textually duplicated the logic of colonialism by envisaging "the Indian" as a creature of their own fancies—now a "savage," now a "serpent," now a white man's trusty aide. Thus did the doctrine of aesthetic freedom contribute to the ideological imprisonment of real people in dehumanized stereotypes. Thus did the barbarism of colonialism work its way into the "civilized" craft of the novel. The conclusion of a typical "frontier" novel is invariably identical with the imagined triumph of the "white race."

"No poet, no artist of any art, has complete meaning alone," noted T. S. Eliot. "His significance, his appreciation is the appreciation of his relation to the dead poets and artists. You cannot value him alone, you must set him, for contrast and comparison, among the dead" (p. 72). The "appreciation" of the artist in relation to his or her dead predecessors is culturally institutionalized—inside and outside the academy—in the form of "tradition." However, "what we have to see is not just 'a tradition,'" observes Raymond Williams, "but a *selective tradition:* an intentionally selective version of a shaping past and a pre-shaped present, which is then powerfully operative in the process of social and cultural definition and identification."[14]

To what end has the U.S. literary tradition traditionally been selected? "American literature," writes Toni Morrison, has long been regarded as "the preserve of white male views, genius, and power" (p. 5). We must therefore accept that criticism as the work of "appreciation" that brings forth "tradition" has never stood on neutral ground in race matters.[15] This fact alone poses considerable problems of audience and authorship for the individual text and critic. In *What Is Literature?* (1948), Jean-Paul Sartre observes the following about the ethics of the literary text:

> Although literature is one thing and morality quite a different one, at the heart of the aesthetic imperative we discern the moral imperative. For, since the one who writes recognizes, by the very fact that he takes the trouble to write, the freedom of his readers, and since the one who reads, by the mere fact of opening the book, recognizes the freedom of the writer, the work of art, from whichever side you approach it, is an act of confidence in the freedom of men.[16]

In a society that knows racial oppression as an integral aspect of class domination and the subordination of women, the exchange economy of litera-ture outlined by Sartre—the mutual recognition of freedom by the writer and the reader—is made an impossibility. The literary text in the setting of "tradi-tion," in the symbolic field of "whiteness," has always presupposed the "unfree-dom" of certain (potential) readers; indeed, in the "morality" of its style (the community announced by its formal rhetoric), the text often acknowledges that particular subjects—the individual members of an oppressed group—will never form part of its imagined audience. When Cooper wrote in *The Prairie* (1824) that the Louisiana Purchase "gave us the sole command of the great thoroughfare of the interior, and placed the countless tribes of savages, who lay along our borders, entirely within our controul [*sic*],"[17] it becomes abundantly clear that "savages" were not envisaged as the readers of his work.

This, then, is the paradox of literature in the strange country of "whiteness": On the one hand, "the freedom of writing implies the freedom of the citizen"; indeed, "writing is a certain way of wanting freedom."[18] Yet on the other hand, "until very recently, and regardless of the race of the author, the readers of virtually all American fiction have been positioned as white,"[19] a fact that testifies to the literary institutionalization of white supremacy. In regard to its formal properties, how has the literary work coped with this paradox?

If we accept Benjamin's claim that the civilized work of art also is barbaric and Sartre's claim that the authentic literary work presupposes an ideal of human freedom, we must recognize that the effect of whiteness on the literary imagination cannot be incidental or negligible. Indeed, it raises the seminal question of the relationship between culture and power. Culture is not simply reducible to power, and it is not free from power's determining influence. Rather, the investment of literature in whiteness speaks eloquently of the bind of culture in power, and it leads me to consider how literary texts keep alive the sense of utopia—the ideal of human freedom—in a fallen world. Against the "reality-principle" of the ideology of "establishment," that is, the alleged necessity or inevitability of institutionalized political domination, the literary text often poses what Ernst Bloch calls "the utopian function," the cultivation of hope, the critical imagining of universal freedom.

Bloch describes the utopian function in the following terms: "the utopian function . . . keeps the alliance with everything dawning in the world. . . . [The] utopian function is the unimpaired reason of militant optimism." The future-time orientation of ideas born out of a hopeful imagination stands in contrast to "those of recollection, which merely reproduce perceptions of the past and thereby increasingly hide in the past. . . . [The] ideas of the imagination . . . carry on the existing facts toward their future potentiality of otherness, of their better condition in an anticipatory way." [20]

In regard to the discourse of "race," we can see the logic of Bloch's formulations in a passage from W. E. B. Du Bois's *The Souls of Black Folk* (1903):

> I sit with Shakespeare and he winces not. Across the color line I move arm in arm with Balzac and Dumas. . . . I summon Aristotle and Aurelius and what soul I will and they come all graciously with no scorn nor condescension. So wed with Truth, I dwell above the Veil. Is this the life you grudge us, O Knightly America? [21]

Du Bois avows here a utopian literary democracy. The great work of art exists beyond "the color line" and has no commitment to the barbarism of Jim Crow. The great artists make room for all in the province of their works; no reader (whatever his or her social identity) is subject to "scorn nor condescension." The "Truth" of the work lifts Du Bois above "the Veil"; it shows him that the ideal of human freedom lodged in his heart will always have time on its side, because the future is forever our possible redemption. In short, the experience of reading Shakespeare or Balzac or Dumas momentarily negates the real hold of "race" on the subject—the historical institutionalization of "whiteness" and "blackness"—and enables us to imagine an untrammeled community, for which we must fight if we want it to exist in our lifetime.

Du Bois is well aware that white supremacist America regards itself as a "thousand-year reich," and thus it must begrudge African Americans the literary realm, with its imaginative spur to political consciousness.[22] *The Souls of Black Folk* is thus written with a view to claiming the future against the barbaric demands of the past. To the extent that a text (like Du Bois's) encourages the reader to see beyond "the Veil," to recognize the contingent face of power, it relates to what Marx termed "the poetry of the future," the creative imagining of freedom grounded in the practical activity of revolution.[23] The poetry of the future will negate the prose of the past, ideas of "recollection"—"whiteness," "blackness," "establishment," the protocols of "the color line," the culture of "scorn." The poetry of the future will draw from, but also help create, a new economy of language—one born not from domination but from solidarity; one that knows difference not as a basis for social hierarchy but as a splendid, "neutral" feature of the human condition. Clearly, such a language would hold great significance for the rhetoric of "race."[24]

"The view that race is a biological fact, a physical attribute of individuals, is no longer tenable," writes Barbara Fields. "Race ... is a purely ideological notion" whose meaning is always determined by the interplay of culture and power.[25] "Race" as an irreducible category of being exists only as a fiction in our minds. Thus the question that must concern us as we analyze the value of "race" in the aesthetic project is the role of rhetoric and dialectic in making the fiction of race seem real. In other words, how are we persuaded by an art of discourse that race matters? What systems of logic have contributed to the belief in "race," which Ashley Montagu calls "a widespread contemporary myth"?[26]

In our endeavor to answer these questions, we can do no better than follow the lead of Jean-Paul Sartre, who wrote in *Anti-Semite and Jew* (1946) that we must ask of the anti-Semite "not 'What is a Jew?' but what have you made of the Jews?"[27] Thus when we read Kipling, we should demand of him: "What have you made of colonized Indians?" And we should also ask, "What would you have us make of them after the experience of your art?"

THE REVOLT OF THE MASSES

> Labor cannot emancipate itself in the white skin where in the black skin it is branded.   Karl Marx, *The Process of Capitalist Production*

"For the most part," observes Toni Morrison, "the literature of the United States has taken as its concern the architecture of a *new white man*" (pp. 14–15, italics in original). The existential parameters of white racial identity were established at a certain juncture in history, through policies advanced by plantation elites in the so-called settler colonies of the New World. A proto-American text that offers insight into the historicity of whiteness is William Shakespeare's *The Tempest*.

The Tempest has elicited a great deal of commentary as a fanciful dramatization of the paradigmatic colonial encounter. My intention here is more specific, to point out the standing of the play as a remarkable discourse on the politics of racialization. Prospero informs us that next to Caliban, "a savage and deformed slave," "most of men" are "angels" (1.2.481–82).[28] Miranda declares that Caliban is "a thing most brutish," a perfect specimen of a "vile race" (1.2.357–58). Caliban's ontological status seems to be that of the monstrous anomaly—the *lusas naturae* as conceived by ancient and medieval lore.

Shakespeare parodies the rhetoric of teratology (the precolonial imagining of the exotic "other") in the humorous episode in which Trinculo and Stephano mistake the bodily shape of a prostrate (enrobed) Caliban: "What have we here? A man or fish?" inquires Trinculo (2.2.24). Caliban's character is, in part, given substantial meaning by the traditional rhetoric of the wild man as a monstrous race. But as comic irony is brought to bear on this rhetoric, its authority as an imagining of the "other" is considerably lessened, thereby creating more ideological room for the emergent discourse of "savagery" and its particular ethos of "race." The transition from "wildness" to "savagery," from "monstrosity" to "racial inferiority," is produced by the worldly interests of colonial desire: the expropriation of indigenously owned land and the exploitation of enslaved or indentured labor.

Whereas "monstrosity" bespoke the will of God and was not readily amenable to the secular demands of rulers, "savagery" said much more about the devil and explicitly demanded the negative response of the "civilized." In short, the "vile race" as savage race evoked the slave master. Thus Caliban accuses Prospero of expropriating that which does not belong to him, namely, Caliban's person and the island: "Thou most lying slave,/Whom stripes may move, not kindness! I have used thee/(Filth as thou art) with humane care" (1.2.344–46). Note that Prospero's statement contains an anthropological claim (which is also an ethical claim) about Caliban's character: we are asked to believe that Caliban is more responsive to "stripes" (i.e., violence) than he is to "kindness." Indeed, Prospero's discourse is the key element in the dramatic confirmation of Caliban as "a savage and deformed slave." According to Prospero, Caliban is "a born devil" (4.1.189), a "misshapen knave," as "disproportioned in his manners/ As in his shape" (5.1.291–92). The conflation of savagery with fallen nature and the deployment of physiognomical values to advance a charge of barbarism work together to confirm an immutable interiority in Caliban's character, which will become, in a deepening rhetoric of "science," the "biology of race."

In Caliban, the "thing of darkness" that Prospero acknowledges as his own (5.1.275–76) we recognize as the real historical debasement of the colonized or enslaved "other." For example, in his 1902 white supremacist novel *The Leopard's Spots,* Thomas Dixon has one of his characters assert:

> The Ethiopian cannot change his skin, or the leopard his spots. . . . The more you educate, the more impossible you make his position in a democracy. Education! Can you change the color of his skin, the kink of his hair, the bulge of his lips, the spread of his nose, or the beat of his heart with a spelling-book? The Negro is the human donkey. You can train him, but you can't make of him a horse.[29]

This remarkable passage (an explicit rejoinder to the humanitarian pretensions of Reconstruction) echoes Prospero's claim that "Nurture can never stick [on]" Caliban (4.1.190). That *The Tempest* is invested in the denigration of "blackness" seems relatively clear; what, then, about the play as a nascent exploration of "whiteness" as a housing of class issues?

The Tempest demonstrates that the base material for the architecture of whiteness is the substantive meaning informing the category of "servant" vis-à-vis that of "slave." Although at one point he speaks of keeping Caliban "in service" (1.2.287), Prospero habitually refers to him as "my slave," "thou poisonous slave," and "thou most lying slave." In short, the play encourages us to view Caliban as a "slave" rather than a "servant." As opposed to enslavement, the authentic exemplars of servitude are Trinculo the jester and Stephano the butler. These two worthies agree to work with Caliban in order to depose Prospero, the island ruler. But significantly, their revolt against Prospero is not aimed at the principle of hierarchical rule. As Stephano says to Caliban, "Monster, I will kill this man [i.e., Prospero]: his daughter/and I will be king and queen, save our Graces! and/Trinculo and thyself shall be viceroys" (3.2.103–5).

This commitment by servants to social hierarchy and the fact of domination that it entails play a large role in the construction of the racialized slave. Stephano calls an inebriated Caliban "Servant monster," but in no time at all he terms him "My man-monster" (3.2.11). The drunken Caliban sees Stephano as "a new master," a "god" to whom he will swear himself "subject" (2.2.148). The comic element here is the spectacle of a lower-class "knave" masquerading as a "lord." In laughing at the absurdity of the scenario, we laugh at the (revenge) fantasy of the servants, that they will one day be the masters. However, in the comedy of misrule, a devastating point (regarding the project of radical politics) is observed: Stephano's and Trinculo's commitment to the oppressor's model of society limits their capacity to remain in league with Caliban, to regard him as an equal. Indeed, they waste no time in developing a language of hierarchical differentiation between themselves as "servants" and Caliban as a "Servant monster" (i.e., a "slave"). Caliban is given the derisive name of "mooncalf," a move closely paralleling the real work of colonial ideology, which turned indigenous tribal peoples into "negroes" and "Indians" and then later, into "niggers" and "varmits."

As a proto-American text, *The Tempest* presents a situation in which "servants" and "slaves" band together in a revolt against their masters. Prospero's "art," the "high charms" made possible by his books, enables him to suppress the insurrection and thus preserve the "natural" order of hierarchical rule. Note that Prospero does not call for the punishment of the servants but instead leaves this to the discretion of their masters. His response to Caliban, however, is somewhat different. As a person over whom he exercises "sovereignty," Caliban must "look" for his "pardon" (5.1.293–94). Prospero's "art" is an art of politics, of counterrevolution. He understands that given the right circumstances, servants and slaves will make common cause against the masters and that they must therefore be ruled by division.[30] The servants' rebellion is explained by their drunkenness, but that by Caliban, the slave, is explained by his demonic nature, his physiognomical makeup, in brief, his "race." We begin to see in this genealogy of lower-class rebellion the protoarchitecture of the white race. That is, Prospero's "art," his "magical" system of rule, might be viewed as a prophetic commentary on the stabilizing value of white supremacism.

What W. E. B. Du Bois termed "the constant lesion of race thinking" received its start in colonial America.[31] Lerone Bennett describes that origin as follows:

> From 1619 to 1660, a period of primary importance in the history of America, America was not ruled by color. . . . The breaking of the developing bonds of community between Negro and white American began with a conscious decision by the power structures of Colonial America. In the 1660's, men of power in the colonies decided that human slavery, based on skin color, was to be the linchpin of the new society.[32]

From the masters' point of view, the institutionalization of white skin privilege was a necessary step in securing the social stability that would permit lucrative capital accumulation. As Theodore Allen puts it, "Every plantation colony faced the same social control problem; each required a buffer social control stratum to stand between the mass of slaves and the numerically tiny class of slaveholders. In the Americas there was no such historically developed middle stratum, and therefore it had to be invented." He argues that "the white race" was invented "as the solution to the problem of social control." The social promotion of the white race reduced all Africans and African Americans to "one undifferentiated social status, a status beneath that of [any white person]. This is the hallmark of racial oppression in its colonial origins, and as it has persisted in subsequent historical contexts."[33]

In 1649, William Bullock, the author of a book on Virginia, described servants as "idle, lazie, simple people . . . such as have professed idlenesse, and will rather beg than work."[34] In the racialized world of colonial North America, this traditional portrait of the depraved "masterless man" was increasingly applied to slaves rather than servants, thus permitting the latter to escape the worst aspects of ideological debasement. Indeed, the enforced social death of slaves made possible a new social life for servants—a life of opportunity and material prosperity that they hitherto had only dreamed of.

As Edmund Morgan observes about the colony of Virginia:

> Virginia's ruling class, having proclaimed that all white men were superior to black, went on to offer their social (but white) inferiors a number of benefits previously denied them. In 1705 a law was passed requiring masters to provide white servants whose indenture time was up with ten bushels of corn, thirty shillings and a gun, while women servants were to get 15 bushels of corn and forty shillings. Also, the newly freed servants were to get 50 acres of land.[35]

This institutionalization of white skin privilege was translated into a hegemonic social policy of "affirmative action" for the members of the servant class, as opposed to their brother and sister slaves. The newly freed servant was given a place to stand in the (plantation) social hierarchy as a member of the "buffer social control stratum"—the "white race"—whose gun could be counted on in the state of emergency constantly imagined by the masters: the revolt of the masses, the uprising of slaves. The broad ideological lineaments of this counterrevolutionary figure can be detected in *The Tempest* in the character of Ariel.

Ariel appears in the play as the objective correlative of Prospero's genius, his art of safely managing the affairs of the world. Prospero calls Ariel a "servant"; Ariel calls Prospero "my noble master" (1.2.301). Thus we see a properly functioning hierarchical relationship based on an ethic of reciprocity. Prospero uses Ariel to realize his wishes, although he promises to discharge Ariel—that is, free him from his indentures—at a definite time (in fictional time, forty-eight hours from the beginning of the dramatic action). "I prithee,/Remember I have done thee worthy service," says Ariel (1.2.247–48). Through the magical agency of Ariel—who might be regarded as the eyes and ears of the master, the disciplinary apparatuses of the militia and the police—Prospero is able to suppress the insurrection of Caliban and the servants. After the rebellion has been put down, Prospero emancipates Ariel; "Be free, and fare thou well!" says the master to his trusty servant (5.1.318).

In the logic of class conflict underpinning the play's dramatic action, Ariel must be seen as representing a counterrevolutionary position. Ariel is a servant, but instead of demonstrating solidarity with other servants and slaves, he looks on them with the eyes of the master. Indeed, he performs the "service" of the perfect colonial panopticon; all-seeing but not seen, everywhere and nowhere. In the ideological profile of Ariel, we can see the repressive capability histori- cally located in the colonial soldier, the overseer, and the lowly "white" man, who defends the house of the master against the violence of rebellious slaves. Ariel is described as "an airy spirit," but many of the weightiest issues in *The Tempest* are woven into his character: the increasing prestige of servitude in regard to the deepening culture of enslavement; the servant's acceptance of the master's worldview; the admission of the servant into the master's project of social control; and, finally, the readiness of the servant to join the master in keeping down "unruly," "uncivilized" slaves. We cannot make sense of the rhetoric and dialectic of "race" in *The Tempest* without considering these issues.

Barbara Fields writes that "many historians tend to accord race a transhistor- ical, almost metaphysical, status that removes it from all possibility of analysis and understanding."[36] Texts like *The Tempest* enable us to move the category of race from metaphysics to the domain of history, from whence it arose and where (one hopes) it will eventually disappear. *The Tempest* dramatizes evidence that can be used in an analysis of the historical process in which "servants" are proletarianized under the rubric of "whiteness" and "slaves" are chattelized under the rubric of "blackness"—a process significant in the history of capital- ist class struggle.

From even the most cursory survey of this history, we can see that servants (i.e., "white" workers) have time and again shown more interest in keeping slaves as slaves than in allowing them to become fellow servants. Indeed, hierarchically minded servants have been key to the master's consolidation of power over socioeconomic matters. Master-minded servants have not only violently resisted the "uplift" of the slave but have also bitterly resented any attempt to reduce servants to the status of slaves. They recognize that at the bottom of the social hierarchy is social death, the realm of nonpersonhood. The fear of social debasement—which, paradoxically, does not have to extend into a critique of all hierarchy—speaks volumes about the social meaning of lower-class "whiteness."

The historian W. J. Cash notes that plantation slavery made "the common white" a party to the "ego-warming and ego-expanding distinction between the white man and the black."[37] Thus, this same man (as a prototype of the "white" worker) cannot view his potential social degradation (at the hands of the master) as anything other than a "blackening" of his whiteness, a "niggerization" of his being.[38] The "niggerized," master-minded "white" worker is more likely to channel his resentment into a "race war" than into a "class war," and hence he effectively upholds what Du Bois calls a "tottering capitalism, built on racial contempt."[39] This same worker believes that it is his right to be treated as "white," and he will do all he can to further "blacken the blacks," to maintain the social distance between himself and them. This complex of virulent racism, the love of social hierarchy, the fear of social death, and the righteous commitment to violence can be seen in white supremacist literary works, from Thomas Dixon's *The Clansman* (1905) to Andrew Macdonald's *The Turner Diaries* (1978). In elevating the chimera of "race" above the reality of class—in defending domination per se—such a complex is not only anti-black and anti-Semitic but is also antisocialist and anticommunist. In sum, it denies that human liberation is an ongoing struggle in history.

CONCLUSION: THE MORALITY OF CONTINGENCY

This chapter has analyzed the position of the literary text in the country of whiteness. If the language of literature has enlivened what Ralph Ellison terms "the sterile concept of 'race' "[40] by strategically employing the (Aristotelean) measures of "persuasion" and "dialectic," then it has also challenged the concept of race, through its critical revelation of the contingent, historical, and arbitrary nature of all human identities, especially those arising on the slave plantation and the colonial "frontier." Regimes of power usually imagine themselves as permanent social arrangements; however, as James Baldwin points out, "The artist must know, and he must let us know, that there is nothing stable under heaven."[41] The artist is obliged to reveal the relative aspect of power, the fact that a regime is made and therefore can be unmade. In this respect, the literary text holds out the promise of utopia, that the *optima res publica*—the best state—is yet to come, that history is still on our side.

In regard to race matters, we critics should commit ourselves to illuminating issues of contingency, historicity, and arbitrariness; to redeeming literary and critical language; to realizing that things could and should be different; to acknowledging that hope is necessary; and, finally, to recognizing that the poetry of the future is always with us.

NOTES

1. T. S. Eliot, "Tradition and the Individual Talent," in David Lodge, ed., *20th Century Literary Criticism: A Reader* (Chicago: University of Chicago Press), p. 71 (subsequent page references to this book are in parentheses).

2. Cited in Robert Oakeshott, "Is England Dumbing Down?" *The Spectator,* January 20, 1996, p. 32.

3. Cited in Benedict Anderson, *Imagined Communities: Reflections on the Origin and Spread of Nationalism* (London: Verso, 1983), p. 86.

4. Thomas Jefferson, *Notes on the State of Virginia,* in *The Life and Selected Writings of Thomas Jefferson,* ed. Adrienne Koch and William Peden (New York: Random House, 1993), p. 240.

5. Twelve Southerners, *I'll Take My Stand: The South and the Agrarian Tradition* (New York: Harper, 1930), p. xv.

6. Allen Tate, "Remarks on the Southern Religion," in *I'll Take My Stand,* pp. 171–72.

7. John Crowe Ransom, "Reconstructed but Unregenerate," in *I'll Take My Stand,* pp. 8, 15 (subsequent page references to Ransom are in parentheses).

8. Allen Tate, "Tension in Poetry," in Ray B. West, ed., *Essays in Modern Literary Criticism* (New York: Rinehart, 1948), p. 272.

9. Addison Gayle, "Cultural Hegemony: The Southern White Writer and American Letters," in John A. Williams and Charles F. Harris, eds., *Amistad 1* (New York: Vintage Books, 1970), p. 19.

10. Theodore W. Allen, *Racial Oppression and Social Control,* vol. 1 of *The Invention of the White Race* (London: Verso, 1994), p. 24.

11. Toni Morrison, *Playing in the Dark: Whiteness in the Literary Imagination* (New York: Vintage Books, 1992), p. 13 (subsequent page references to this book are in parentheses).

12. Walter Benjamin, "Theses on the Philosophy of History," in Hannah Arendt, ed., and Harry Zohn, trans., *Illuminations: Essays and Reflections* (New York: Schocken Books, 1969), p. 253.

13. Ward Churchill, *Fantasies of the Master Race: Literature, Cinema and the Colonization of American Indians,* ed. M. Annette Jaimes (Monroe, ME: Common Courage, 1992), p. 26.

14. Raymond Williams, *Marxism and Literature* (Oxford: Oxford University Press, 1977), p. 115 (italics in original).

15. For a detailed treatment of racial ideology in literary criticism, see Henry Louis Gates Jr., *Figures in Black: Words, Signs and the "Racial" Self* (New York: Oxford University Press, 1977), pp. 3–58.

16. Jean-Paul Sartre, *What Is Literature? and Other Essays,* trans. Bernard Frechtman (Cambridge, MA: Harvard University Press, 1988), p. 67.

17. James Fenimore Cooper, *The Prairie* (Oxford: Oxford University Press, 1992), p. 92.

18. Sartre, *What Is Literature?* p. 69.

19. Morrison, *Playing in the Dark,* p. xii.

20. Ernst Bloch, *The Utopian Function of Art and Literature,* trans. Jack Zipes and Frank Mecklenberg (Cambridge, MA: MIT Press, 1988), pp. 107, 105.

21. W. E. B. Du Bois, *The Souls of Black Folk* (New York: Bantam Books, 1989), p. 76.

22. For African Americans, the connection between literary culture and political freedom has a long-standing significance. It originated under the regime of plantation slavery, in which human chattel were actively denied the power of literacy. Thus, the slave narrative was always a revolutionary, counterhegemonic production.

23. Karl Marx, *The Eighteenth Brumaire of Louis Bonarparte* (New York: International Publishers, 1984), p. 18.

24. That a language purged of racial referents is still largely unimagined is a mark of how far we have to go to achieve the end of "race."

25. Barbara Fields, "Ideology and Race in American History," in J. Morgan Kousser and James McPherson, eds., *Region, Race, and Reconstruction: Essays in Honor of C. Vann Woodward* (New York: Oxford University Press, 1982), pp. 149, 151.

26. Ashley Montagu, *Race, Science and Humanity* (Princeton, NJ: Van Nostrand, 1963), p. 11.

27. Jean-Paul Sartre, *Anti-Semite and Jew,* trans. George J. Becker (New York: Schocken Books, 1948), p. 69.

28. William Shakespeare, *The Tempest* (Harmondsworth: Penguin Books, 1987). All quotations are from this edition.

29. Thomas Dixon, *The Leopard's Spots: A Romance of the White Man's Burden* (New York: Grosset & Dunlap, 1902), pp. 463–64.

30. In 1676, an uprising of slaves, servants, and frontiersmen in the colony of Virginia—Bacon's rebellion—made the problem of social control a preeminent concern of the masters. As is the case today in the area of global capital, the masters in colonial America sought the optimal "investment climate" for the surplus capital they appropriated from the labors of others. This climate was not defined by a specific social component—say, "participatory democracy"—but by the functionalist (amoral) paradigm of "political stability." In colonial North America, white supremacy was the key to stability, and in time it created a culture of its own.

31. W. E. B. Du Bois, "Prospect of a World Without Race Conflict," in Dan S. Green and Edwin D. Drivek, eds., *W. E. B. Du Bois on Sociology and the Black Community* (Chicago: University of Chicago Press, 1978), p. 297.

32. Lerone Bennet, "The White Problem in America," in *Ebony,* ed., *The White Problem in America* (Chicago: Johnson, 1966), p. 8.

33. Allen, *Racial Oppression and Social Control,* pp. 13, 24, 32.

34. Cited in James Horn, "Servant Emigration to the Chesapeake in the Seventeenth Century," in Thad W. Tate and David L. Ammerman, eds., *The Chesapeake in the Seventeenth Century: Essays on Anglo-American Society* (New York: Norton, 1979), p. 56.

35. Cited in Howard Zinn, *A People's History of the United States* (New York: Harpers, 1980), p. 37.

36. Fields, "Ideology and Race in American History," p. 144.

37. W. J. Cash, *The Mind of the South* (New York: Doubleday, 1940), p. 51.

38. From the moment that "servants" and "slaves" were racially defined, the putative "niggerization" of the "white" worker has been a perennial theme of U.S. history and accounts in no small part for the persistence of white supremacist terrorism.

39. Du Bois, "Prospect of a World Without Race Conflict," p. 294.

40. Ralph Ellison, "*An American Dilemma:* A Review," in Joyce A. Ladner, ed., *The Death of White Sociology* (New York: Random House, 1973), p. 95.

41. James Baldwin, "The Creative Process," in *The Price of the Ticket: Collected Nonfiction 1948–1985* (New York: St. Martin's Press, 1985), p. 316.

21

Toward a New Abolitionism
A *Race Traitor* Manifesto

John Garvey and Noel Ignatiev

Race Traitor calls itself a journal of the New Abolitionism, with the motto "Treason to whiteness is loyalty to humanity." The journal takes its stand on two points: first, that the "white race" is not a natural but a social category and, second, that what was historically constructed can be undone. The first of these points is now widely accepted; scientists have concluded that there are no biological standards for distinguishing one "race" from another, and social scientists have begun to examine how race was constructed and how it is reproduced. The "social construction of race" has become something of a catchphrase in the academy, although few have taken the next step. Indeed, we might say that until now, philosophers have merely interpreted the white race; the point, however, is to abolish it.

The white race is a club that enrolls certain people at birth, without their consent, and brings them up according to its rules. For the most part, its

Adapted from *the minnesota review* 47 (Spring 1997): 111–14.

members go through life accepting the privileges of membership but without reflecting on the costs. When they do question the rules, the officers are quick to remind them of all they owe to the club and warn them of the dangers they will face if they leave it.

The white club does not require that all members be strong advocates of white supremacy, merely that they defer to the prejudices of others. It is based on the assumption that all those who look white are, whatever their reservations, fundamentally loyal to it. This assumption is kept in place by a pervasive system of race privileges, so embedded in the social structure that they are reproduced daily—but without reflection—by most of the actors. Just as the capitalist system is not a capitalist plot, racial oppression is not the work of "racists," but of people who in many cases would be sincerely offended if accused of complicity with white supremacy.

For an example of how the club works, look at the hostility of the police toward the exploited. All over the world, police officers beat up poor people, without regard to color. What is unusual and must be accounted for is not why they beat up black people but why they do not usually beat up poor whites. It works in this way: The cops look at a person and then decide on the basis of his or her color whether that person is loyal to or an enemy of the system they are sworn to serve and protect. The police do not stop to find out whether the black person whom they are beating is an enemy; they assume it. It does not matter whether the victim goes to work every day, pays taxes, and crosses only on the green light. Occasionally, they bust an outstanding and prominent black person, and the poor whites cheer the event, because it confirms their conviction that they are superior to all black people.

On the other hand, the cops do not know for sure whether the white person to whom they give a break is loyal to them; they assume it. The nonbeating of poor whites is time off for good behavior and an assurance of future cooperation. Their color exempts them to some degree from the criminal class. In fact, this is how the entire working class was defined before race was invented and is still treated in those parts of the world where race does not exist as a social category. It is a cheap way of buying some people's loyalty to a social system that exploits them.

Race Traitor aims to abolish this white club, to break it apart, to explode it. The abolitionists recognize that "whites" cannot individually abandon the privileges of whiteness. The white club does not like to lose a single member, so that even those who step out of it in one situation find it virtually impossible not to step back in later, if for no other reason than the assumptions of others. The point is not for individuals to become unwhite (although that is good when it happens, as with John Brown) but to blow apart the social formation known as the white race, so that no one is "white." How can this be done?

What would happen if the police could not discern a loyal person by color alone? What if there were enough people who looked white but were really enemies of the official society, so the cops did not know whom to beat and whom to leave alone? What would they do then? They would begin to "enforce the law impartially," as the liberals say, beating only those who "deserve" it. But as Anatole France points out, the law prohibits rich and poor from sleeping under bridges, begging in the streets, or stealing bread. The standard that governs police behavior all over the world (except where race exists) is wealth and its external manifestations, such as dress and speech. At the present time, the class bias of the law is partially repressed by racial considerations, and the removal of those considerations would give it free rein. Poor whites would find themselves on the receiving end of police justice, just as black people now do.

The effect on poor whites' consciousness and behavior is predictable. With color no longer serving as a handy guide for the distribution of penalties and rewards, European Americans of the downtrodden class would at last be compelled to face their real condition of life and their relations with humankind. It would be the end of the white race and the beginning of a new phase in the struggle for a better world.

The abolitionist project does not depend on winning over to "antiracism" the majority of whites or even the majority of working-class whites. Instead, the abolitionists seek to compel official society to turn millions of so-called whites against it, by casting doubt on the white skin as a badge of loyalty and thereby rendering it useless as a protection from abuse. Theirs is, quite frankly, a strategy of provocation.

How many would it take to rob the white skin of its predictive value? No one can say. How much counterfeit money has to circulate in order to destroy the value of the official currency? The answer is, not much: in the past, 5 to 10 percent fake has been enough to undermine public faith in the genuine stuff. Whiteness is the currency of this society, and so destroying it would take only enough counterfeit whites (race traitors) to undermine the confidence of the police and other representatives of official society in their ability to differentiate between friends and enemies by means of color.

The abolitionist strategy depends on the coming together of a minority determined to break up the white race. What would the members of a determined minority have to do to plant doubt about the reliability of the white skin? They would have to break the laws of whiteness so flagrantly as to make it impossible to maintain the myth of white unanimity. Such actions would jeopardize their own ability to exercise the privileges of whiteness. This is what would define them as race traitors.

What would this mean in practice? It would mean white people's responding to every manifestation of white supremacy as if it were directed against them. On the individual level, it would mean, for instance, responding to an antiblack remark by asking the speaker, "What makes you think I'm white?" On the collective level, it would mean developing programs to oppose the institutions that reproduce race. Abolitionists oppose tracking in the schools, oppose all mechanisms that favor whites in the job market, and oppose the police and courts, which define black people as a criminal class. Besides opposing them, they seek to disrupt their functioning. They reject no means of attaining their goal. Indeed, the willingness to go beyond socially acceptable "antiracism" is the dividing line between "good whites" and traitors to the white race.

The journal *Race Traitor* aims to serve as an intellectual center for the new abolitionism. Its task is to chronicle and analyze the making, remaking, and unmaking of whiteness. It publishes articles on current events, history, popular culture, reviews, fiction, and poetry. The most important of these are personal accounts of individual and collective breaks with white solidarity—termed the "Huck Finn moment" after the turning point in the novel when Huck decides to break with what he calls "sivilization" and to take the steps that will lead to Jim's (and his own) freedom. *RT* is intended to serve as a forum for discussion among those who recognize that whiteness is a social problem. A recent issue carried twenty-nine pages of letters from readers, along with replies from the editors.

The readers of *Race Traitor* are mainly (1) counterculture activists, including young people influenced by anarchist philosophy and by skinheads (!) who designate themselves as "antiracist"; (2) educators interested in issues of multi-culturalism (of which the journal has been critical); and (3) prison inmates (*RT* has published several articles from present and former prisoners and has been banned from one prison as "inflammatory"). A significant minority of readers are Afro-American or Afro-Caribbean (as are eight of the seventeen contributing editors), and some copies are circulated outside the United States. *RT* has definitely escaped from the academy and the traditional Left. (From its standpoint, the terms *Left* and *Right* are practically meaningless.) In only three years, *RT* has managed to introduce a new notion into the debate on race. The next task is to develop that notion into a movement.

Contributors

Matthew P. Brown received his doctorate from the University of Virginia and is currently a visiting assistant professor in the English department at Coe College.

Ross Chambers is the Marvin Felheim Distinguished Professor of French and comparative literature at the University of Michigan. He is the author of many books, including *Room for Maneuver: Reading Oppositional Narrative* (Chicago). He is currently contemplating a book (*Loiterature*) that will address the connection among the tradition of the flaneur, realism, and contemporary cultural studies.

Barbara Ching is an assistant professor of English at the University of Memphis. Besides her many articles on cultural studies, she is the author of *Hard Country, High Culture, and Postmodernism* (Oxford).

Kate Davy is the dean of the School of Fine Arts at the University of Wisconsin at Milwaukee. She is currently working on a book about performance at the WOW cafe.

Grant Farred teaches at the University of Michigan. He edited a collection of critical essays on C. L. R. James (Blackwell) and has written several articles on race and cultural studies.

John Garvey works in the Office of Academic Affairs at the City University of New York. He is the coeditor and cofounder (with Noel Ignatiev) of *Race*

Traitor: Journal of the New Abolitionism and the coeditor (also with Ignatiev) of *Race Traitor* (Routledge).

Henry A. Giroux is the Waterbury Chair Professor of Education at Pennsylvania State University. He is the author of numerous books, including *Border Crossings; Disturbing Pleasures* (Routledge) and, most recently, *Fugitive Cultures: Race, Violence and Youth* (Routledge).

Warren Hedges is an assistant professor of English at Southern Oregon State College. He is currently at work on *Death and Breeding: Gender, Race and Reproduction in American Realism*.

Mike Hill is an assistant professor of English at Marymount Manhattan College and the associate editor of *the minnesota review*. He is working on *After Whiteness* (NYU) and a book on the history of crowds.

Noel Ignatiev is currently a lecturer at Harvard University. He is the author of *How the Irish Became White* (Routledge), the cofounder and coeditor (with John Garvey) of *Race Traitor: Journal of the New Abolitionism,* and the coeditor (also with Garvey) of *Race Traitor* (Routledge).

E. Ann Kaplan is a professor of English at the State University of New York at Stony Brook, where she also directs the Humanities Institute. Her recent books include *Motherhood and Representation: The Mother in Popular Culture and Melodrama* (Routledge) and *Looking for the Other: Feminism and the Imperial Gaze* (Routledge).

Amitava Kumar teaches in the English department at the University of Florida. He is a columnist for *Liberation* (India) and a member of the New York–based photo co-op Impact Visuals. His writings have appeared in several journals, among them *Rethinking Marxism, Critical Quarterly, Modern Fiction Studies,* and *the minnesota review.* He is also the editor of *Class Issues* (NYU).

Eric Lott teaches at the University of Virginia. Besides his many articles on race and whiteness, he is the author of *Love and Theft: Blackface, Minstrelsy and the American Working Class* (Oxford).

Jeffrey Melnick has taught at Simmons College, Harvard University, and Trinity College. He is the author of *A Right to Sing the Blues: African Americans,*

Jews and Cultural Power (Harvard) and is now working on a book provisionally entitled *The Book of Love: Doo Wop Music and Racial Identities.*

Warren Montag is an associate professor of English at Occidental College. He has a book forthcoming on Spinoza (Verso) and is the author of *The Unthinkable Swift* (Verso) and the editor of a book on Spinoza (Minnesota) and a book by Pierre Macherey (Verso).

Annalee Newitz is a doctoral candidate at the University of California at Berkeley. She is the coeditor (with Matthew Wray) of *White Trash* (Routledge). She also serves on the production team of the e-zine *Bad Subjects* and will edit a volume (also with Wray) based on *Bad Subjects* (NYU).

Fred Pfeil teaches in the English department and the American Studies Program at Trinity College. He has had stories, reviews, and articles in *The Nation,* the *Village Voice,* and a variety of literary magazines. His books include *Another Tale to Tell* (Verso) and, most recently, *White Guys: Studies in Postmodern Domination* (Verso).

Jerry Phillips is an assistant professor of English at the University of Connecticut. He is currently completing a book on exoticism in Herman Melville's novels.

David R. Roediger teaches history at the University of Minnesota. He has published widely on the topic of whiteness and class. His recent books include *The Wages of Whiteness* and *Towards the Abolition of Whiteness* (both Verso).

Michael E. Staub teaches English and American Studies at Bowling Green State University. He is the author of *Voices of Persuasion: Politics of Representation in 1930s America* (Cambridge) and various articles on race. He is currently writing a book on masculinity and race in American culture since the 1960s.

Robert H. Vorlicky is an associate professor of drama at the Tisch School of the Arts, New York University. He is the author of *Act Like a Man: Challenging Masculinities in American Drama* (Michigan) and the editor of the collection *Tony Kushner in Conversation* (Michigan). He is currently working on *See Hear: Bodies, Languages and the Politics of U.S. Male Solo Performance.*

Gayle Wald is an assistant professor of English at George Washington University in Washington, D.C., and is working on *Crossing the Line: Racial Passing in Twentieth-Century American Literature and Culture* (Duke).

Matthew Wray is a doctoral student in ethnic studies at the University of California at Berkeley. He is the coeditor, with Annalee Newitz, of *White Trash* (Routledge). He also serves on the production team of the e-zine *Bad Subjects* and will edit (with Newitz) a collection based on *Bad Subjects* (NYU).

Index